Herbert of Bosham

YORK MEDIEVAL PRESS

York Medieval Press is published by the University of York's Centre for Medieval Studies in association with Boydell & Brewer Limited. Our objective is the promotion of innovative scholarship and fresh criticism on medieval culture. We have a special commitment to interdisciplinary study, in line with the Centre's belief that the future of Medieval Studies lies in those areas in which its major constituent disciplines at once inform and challenge each other.

All enquiries of an editorial kind, including suggestions for monographs and essay collections, should be addressed to: The Academic Editor, York Medieval Press, Department of History, University of York, Heslington, York, YO10 5DD (E-mail: pete.biller@york.ac.uk)

Details of other York Medieval Press volumes are available from Boydell & Brewer Ltd.

Herbert of Bosham
A Medieval Polymath

Edited by
Michael Staunton

THE UNIVERSITY *of York*

YORK MEDIEVAL PRESS

First published 2019

A York Medieval Press publication
in association with The Boydell Press
an imprint of Boydell & Brewer Ltd
PO Box 9, Woodbridge, Suffolk IP12 3DF, UK
and of Boydell & Brewer Inc.
668 Mt Hope Avenue, Rochester, NY 14620–2731, USA
website: www.boydellandbrewer.com
and with the
Centre for Medieval Studies, University of York

ISBN 978 1 903153 88 8

A CIP catalogue record for this book is available
from the British Library

The publisher has no responsibility for the continued existence
or accuracy of URLs for external or third-party internet websites
referred to in this book, and does not guarantee that any content
on such websites is, or will remain, accurate or appropriate

This publication is printed on acid-free paper

Printed and bound in Great Britain by TJ International Ltd, Padstow, Cornwall

Contents

Illustrations

Contributors

Julie Barrau is Lecturer in Medieval British History at the Faculty of History, Cambridge, and Fellow of Emmanuel College.

Laura Cleaver is the Ussher Lecturer in Medieval Art at Trinity College Dublin.

Christopher de Hamel is a Fellow of Corpus Christi College, Cambridge, and was Fellow Librarian 2000–2016.

Matthew Doyle teaches at St. Michael's College School, Toronto.

Anne J. Duggan is Emeritus Professor of History at King's College London.

Sabina Flanagan is Visiting Research Fellow in the Department of History at the University of Adelaide.

Michael Staunton is Associate Professor of History at University College Dublin.

Nicholas Vincent is Professor of Medieval History at the University of East Anglia and a Fellow of the British Academy.

Editorial Preface

Herbert of Bosham often complained that he was unappreciated. But how can one properly appreciate someone who advised Thomas Becket and rebuked Henry II to his face, who wrote a Life of Becket that is unlike any contemporary work of hagiography or history, whose theological expertise and ambition led him to produce one of the most visually arresting illuminated Bible books of his age and who also happened to be one of the most skilled Christian Hebraists of the Middle Ages?

Not that Herbert made it easy on himself. His stance on church–crown relations was sometimes so intemperate that Thomas Becket had to rein him in. When the church sought reconciliation with Henry II after Becket's murder, Herbert continued to rail against both king and ecclesiastics. While others who knew Thomas much less well were writing Lives of the saint amid the glow of martyrdom, Herbert was writing a work in honour of Peter Lombard just at the time that Peter's work was being condemned as heretical. When Herbert finally wrote a Life of St Thomas, a decade and a half later, he ignored the miracles that still drew crowds to Thomas's tomb at Canterbury, and focused on the cause for which he had died, thus reopening wounds that others had chosen to soothe. Though a learned and inventive theologian, Herbert never wrote a full-length work of theology. Instead he buried his proofs of the existence of God and his disquisitions on mystic theology in the middle of the *Liber Melorum*, a celebration of the concordances between Christ and St Thomas that has remained largely unread to this day. Herbert's letter collection, apparently put together by his own hand, does not include any correspondence between the mid-1170s and the late 1180s, a period of his life about which we have hardly any information from any source. And we would not have known that Herbert apparently had a better grasp of Hebrew than any known western Christian contemporary, were it not for the discovery in the middle of the twentieth century of a work written in obscure exile at the end of his life.

Herbert presents other problems for those who seek to approach his work today. The scholarly, linguistic and cultural challenges that face anyone who seeks to grapple with the world of a twelfth-century intellectual are compounded by the erudition, originality and range that he displays. If an understanding of any of his works requires application and knowledge, how much more does a rounded appreciation demand? Yet this is something worth striving for. As long ago as 1951, Beryl Smalley urged that Herbert be studied in the round as a twelfth-century man of letters.[1] Since then, it has become all the more apparent that there is overlap

---

[1] Full references to and discussion of the works referred to in the Foreword may be found in Chapter 1.

between the different facets of Herbert of Bosham's life and work. It is this recognition – that while each aspect of his life and work requires individual expertise, the different dimensions of Herbert of Bosham inform each other – that has prompted the contributors here to collaborate in this book.

Herbert has always suffered from criticism, dismissal and neglect, but he has also had his champions. Though he was spoken of as a difficult character, he was employed by Henry II and by Thomas Becket, Pope Alexander III gave him a glowing reference, and his scholarly work was supported first by the archbishop of Sens and later by the bishop of Arras. Though he complained of the English, 'I have no friends in that land of forgetfulness', the monks of Canterbury remembered him in their obituary list as 'our brother'. His works fell into relative obscurity for centuries, and he was only remembered, if at all, for his association with Becket, until John Allen Giles undertook to edit the *Historia*, the *Liber Melorum* and the Letters. Giles's editions gained further currency when they were used by Jean-Paul Migne in his *Patrologia Latina*, and by James Craigie Robertson in his Rolls Series edition. Though Giles and Robertson showed impatience at Herbert's theological digressions, they realised that he was both an outstanding witness to his times and an original talent. The discovery of the commentary on Jerome's Hebrew psalter prompted a new interest in Herbert the theologian, starting in the 1950s with Beryl Smalley and Raphael Loewe, and developed in subsequent decades by Smalley, the single individual most responsible for the modern appreciation of Herbert's work. Most importantly, she drew the connection between Herbert the theologian and Herbert the politician.

Around the turn of the century Herbert's work suddenly became the subject of sustained scholarship. Within the space of two years, three PhD dissertations were completed on the subject of Herbert of Bosham: Deborah Goodwin and Eva De Visscher's studies of the *Psalterium cum commento*, and Jessica Weiss's study of the *Liber Melorum*. Goodwin and De Visscher's quite different and complementary studies have since been published. At the same time, others were at work on different aspects of Herbert's life and work: as a letter-writer, historian and hagiographer; as a pupil of Peter Lombard and a reviser of his work; as the supervisor of a lavish project of illustrations. In 2006 an e-mail group was set up with the aim of putting those scholars working on Herbert of Bosham in contact with each other, and the following year a meeting was held at the International Medieval Congress at Leeds. Then, in 2013, a conference on Herbert of Bosham was held at Cambridge, sponsored by the Association for Manuscripts and Archives in Research Collections and hosted by the Parker Library, Corpus Christi College. This was accompanied by an exhibition of almost all the known manuscripts of Herbert's works. The papers in this volume all derive from this collaboration over the past decade or so. Some were first delivered at the conference in Cambridge and since revised; others are more recent.

The title of the first paper, 'An Introduction to Herbert of Bosham', is self-explanatory. It provides a survey of what is known of Herbert's life, and a brief discussion of each of his works. It is aimed at those coming to Herbert for the first time, but also at those who know about some aspects of his work and would like to know more, and seeks to provide direction to existing scholarship on the subject.

Anne Duggan's paper, 'Master Herbert: Becket's *eruditus*, Envoy, Adviser, and Ghost-Writer?' takes a closer look at the various roles that Herbert undertook in the service of Thomas Becket, surveying his witness to *acta*, his letter-writing and his diplomatic activities. Though an odd-man-out among the archbishop's learned men, Herbert had a significant place in Thomas's life. A loyal and outspoken friend and counsellor, his advice had a direct impact on Thomas's course of action, but he would struggle to find a role after his master's death.

The next two papers look at Herbert's less well-known relationship with his first master – Peter Lombard. Matthew Doyle, in 'Herbert of Bosham and Peter Lombard', notes that studies of Peter's school have often failed to take Herbert into account, while specialist studies of Herbert have tended to downplay his intellectual formation at the school of the Lombard. Yet his first major work, a revision of Peter's commentaries on the Psalms and Pauline Epistles, can, he argues, be seen as part of a wider enterprise in the 1160s and 1170s involving the students of Peter Lombard.

Laura Cleaver's paper, 'Pages Covered with as Many Tears as Notes: Herbert of Bosham and the Glossed Manuscripts for Thomas Becket', looks at Herbert's revision of the Great Gloss from a different angle. These lavishly illustrated volumes are testament to Herbert's awareness of the power of visual appearances and fondness for fine things. Here the evidence for their production is revisited, and the case is made for identifying an image of a semi-naked figure as a representation of Herbert himself, bereft after the departure of the martyr.

One of the more neglected of Herbert's works is his letter collection, the subject of Julie Barrau's paper, 'Scholarship as a Weapon: Herbert of Bosham's Letter Collection'. She provides, for the first time, an analysis of the collection, its production and its contents, and highlights certain themes that run through them. The letters show Herbert engaged in arcane theological controversies, denouncing his enemies and developing elaborate parallels between biblical figures and participants in the Becket dispute.

Michael Staunton's paper, 'Time, Change and History in Herbert of Bosham's *Historia*', looks at Herbert's narrative of Thomas Becket's life, usually referred to as the *Vita S. Thomae* but called by Herbert the *Historia*. It addresses the theme of time and change in Herbert's work and shows how his portrayal of Thomas dwelled on both the archbishop's change of life and how his struggle and martyrdom changed those around him, including his biographer Herbert.

Nicholas Vincent's paper, 'John Allen Giles and Herbert of Bosham: The Criminous Clerk as Editor', looks at the career of Herbert's first editor and the circumstances in which his work was first edited. During his long and tragic life, John Allen Giles published nearly 180 books, among them a two-volume edition of Herbert of Bosham's *Historia*, *Liber Melorum* and letters. Giles, more than anyone, was the person responsible for bringing Herbert's works to wider attention, and his editions remain the main point of access for the *Liber Melorum* and the letters.

Even though Herbert's manuscripts are about ten times more rare than complete Gutenberg Bibles, they have led lives as eventful and troubled as their author. The most notorious incident concerning Herbert's manuscripts is the mutilation and theft of a large number of leaves from Arras MS 649, the fullest copy of his composite work on Thomas Becket, the *Thomus*. Sabina Flanagan's paper tracks down the 'unscrupulous librarian' responsible for the theft of the leaves, and traces the story of how, over a period of two centuries, and involving various collectors, editors and scholars, the leaves were lost, found, lost again and rediscovered.

Christopher de Hamel is in the highly unusual position not only of having handled most of the surviving manuscripts of Herbert, but also of identifying newly discovered ones, and owning a number of them himself. Here he provides a personal recapitulation of his encounters with Herbert's manuscripts, outlining the remarkable series of events that put them in his possession – even though, as he admits, it took him many years to realise what they were.

The final item in this volume is an edition by Nicholas Vincent of a newly discovered letter by Herbert of Bosham, his confirmation of a legal settlement made at Paris by Cardinal Peter of Pavia, sometime between 1174 and 1178. Even in such a technical document, Herbert's personality comes through, designating himself as a former clerk to the glorious martyr and associating himself with St John the Evangelist.

This book is not meant to be the last word on Herbert of Bosham. Contributors were still making discoveries about his life and work as the book was going to press, and it is clear that much remains to be discovered about him. It is hoped that the papers included here will encourage others to explore the career of a fascinating and unusual medieval polymath whose works oscillate between public and private concerns, the rational and mystical, the worldly and the spiritual. Perhaps it will also mark the first step towards new editions of his works, many of which remain unedited.

I am grateful to all the contributors to this volume, and to all those who have otherwise participated in this collaborative enterprise. Special thanks go to Anne Duggan, who supported the collaboration from the outset, to Christopher de Hamel, who generously hosted the conference at the Parker Library, and to Caroline Palmer and Pete Biller for all their help in bringing the book to completion. I would also like to acknowledge the contribution of the late Jennifer O'Reilly, who introduced me to the Lives of Thomas Becket and suggested that I take a closer look at Herbert of Bosham.

Michael Staunton

Abbreviations

CCCC	Cambridge, Corpus Christi College
CCCM	*Corpus Christianorum Continuatio Mediaevalis*
CCSL	*Corpus Christianorum, Series Latina*
CSEL	*Corpus Scriptorum Ecclesiasticorum Latinorum*
CTB	*The Correspondence of Thomas Becket, Archbishop of Canterbury, 1162–1170*, ed. A. Duggan, 2 vols. (Oxford, 2000)
EHR	*The English Historical Review*
Fitzstephen	William Fitzstephen, *Vita Sancti Thomae*
HB	*Epistolae Herberti de Boseham in persona S. Thomae Cantuariensis et aliorum scriptae*, 2 vols., ed. J. A. Giles (London, 1845-46); repr. in *PL* 190
LJS	*The Letters of John of Salisbury*, ed. and tr. W. J. Millor, H. E. Butler and C. N. L. Brooke, 2 vols (Oxford, 1955, 1979)
MTB	*Materials for the History of Thomas Becket, Archbishop of Canterbury*, ed. J. C. Robertson and J. B. Sheppard, 7 vols, RS 67 (London, 1875–85)
ODNB	*Oxford Dictionary of National Biography* (Oxford, 2004)
PL	*Patrologiae Cursus Completus, series Latina*, ed. J.-P. Migne, 221 vols (Paris, 1844–64)
PR	*The Great Roll of the Pipe* (Pipe Roll Society)
RS	*Rerum Britannicarum Medii Aevi Scriptore*s ('Rolls Series'), 251 vols (London, 1858–96)

CHAPTER ONE

An Introduction to Herbert of Bosham

Michael Staunton

H ERBERT of Bosham (c. 1120–c. 1194) was Thomas Becket's closest advisor and confidant, his inseparable companion through his exile and the most enthusiastic champion of his cause. A pupil of Peter Lombard and almost certainly of the school of St Victor, he was a skilled and original biblical scholar. He produced a lavishly ornamented revision of Peter Lombard's *Great Gloss* on the Psalms and Epistles and a commentary on the literal sense of Jerome's *Hebraica* version of the Psalms, a project that reveals him as more learned in Hebrew than any known Christian contemporary. When he wrote about recent events in his letters, and in his two works devoted to Thomas Becket, the *Historia* and the *Liber Melorum*, he brought to them the skills and preoccupations of a theologian. Herbert's own works and the writings of contemporaries give us a wealth of information about his career, but he was also a very self-reflective writer who revealed much about his own feelings and motivations. He was a person who would attract admiration and patronage, but also a difficult character, who complained of being shunned and neglected. His works and reputation have had a similarly chequered path, though the more attention that has been paid to his writings, the more his depth of learning, his versatility and originality have been appreciated. What follows is intended to provide a guide to the uninitiated, and direction to those who would like to know more about Herbert's life and work.[1]

---

[1] For surveys of Herbert of Bosham's life and works, see B. Smalley, 'A Commentary on the *Hebraica* by Herbert of Bosham', *Recherches de théologie ancienne et médiévale* 18 (1951), 29–65; summarised in B. Smalley, *The Study of the Bible in the Middle Ages*, 3rd edn (Oxford, 1983), pp. 186–95; B. Smalley, *The Becket Conflict and the Schools* (Oxford, 1973), pp. 59–86; J. Weiss, 'Herbert of Bosham's *Liber Melorum*: Literature and Sacred Sciences in the Twelfth Century' (Unpublished PhD dissertation, Harvard University, 2003), pp. 5–45; D. L. Goodwin, *'Take Hold of the Robe of a Jew'. Herbert of Bosham's Christian Hebraism* (Leiden and Boston, 2006), pp. 1–50; M. Staunton, *Thomas Becket and his Biographers* (Woodbridge, 2006), pp. 63–74; E. De Visscher, *Reading the Rabbis. Christian Hebraism in the Works of Herbert of Bosham* (Leiden and Boston, 2014), pp. 1–6; F. Barlow, 'Bosham, Herbert of (d. c. 1194)', *ODNB*.

Early life and education

At the end of the *Historia*, Herbert gives a list of Thomas's *eruditi*, his 'learned men'. Last and least of these, he says, is 'the disciple who wrote these things, Herbert by name, English by nation, and from birth and surname "of Bosham"'.[2] This is the name that others give him too, and there is no reason to doubt that he came from that seaside town in West Sussex, two miles west of Chichester. Herbert's birth is conventionally dated to *c.* 1120, which would make him a close contemporary of Thomas Becket, but this is rough estimation.[3] Nothing is known of Herbert's mother, but his father, it seems, had once been a priest. When he and Henry II met at Angers in May 1166, the king angrily dismissed him as the son of a priest, to which Herbert replied, 'I am not the son of a priest, since I was not born to a priest, although later my father became a priest.'[4]

For a man of such impressive learning and of such frequent self-reference, Herbert gives us frustratingly little information on his education. His first teacher in theology was Peter Lombard, master of the cathedral school of Notre Dame in Paris, and author of the *Sentences*, whom Herbert called 'my master of pleasant memory, Peter, bishop of Paris'.[5] Herbert paid tribute to his distinguished teacher in his first major work, a revision of Peter's *Great Gloss* on the Psalms and Epistles, and in the preface to that work he described him as 'that great doctor … the man who first taught me in such things'.[6] Herbert could have studied at Paris as early as the mid-1140s and as late as the mid-1150s.[7] Before that he must have acquired a strong foundation in grammar and rhetoric, but where or in what manner he did so we do not know. In old age he mentioned that he had begun to learn Greek and Hebrew in

---

[2] *Materials for the History of Thomas Becket, Archbishop of Canterbury*, ed. J. C. Robertson and J. B. Sheppard, 7 vols, RS 67 (London, 1875–85) [henceforth *MTB*], iii, 529: 'Inter quos, auctore Domino, quasi abortivus et eruditorum minimus, discipulus qui scripsit haec, Herbertus nomine proprio, natione Anglus, et sicut natione et cognomina de Boseham'. See John 21:24.

[3] Smalley, *Becket Conflict*, p. 59, suggests this date on the grounds that Herbert's friend William le Mire, abbot of St Denis, called him 'senex' in a letter of 1173x1176, and that Herbert says he knew William of the White Hands (1135–1202) when the latter was a little boy. The letter is printed by H. H. Glunz, *History of the Vulgate in England from Alcuin to Roger Bacon* (Cambridge, 1933), pp. 346–7.

[4] Fitzstephen, *MTB*, iii, 101: 'neque filius sum sacerdotis, qui non fuit genitus in sacerdotio, licet postea sacerdos fuerit pater meus'.

[5] *Epistolae Herberti de Boseham in persona S. Thomae Cantuariensis et aliorum scriptae*, ed. J. A. Giles (henceforth *HB*), no. 1, *PL*, 190.1418: 'magistri mei suavis recordationis Petri Pariensis episcopi'.

[6] Preface to the first volume of the glossed Psalter in Glunz, *History*, p. 343: 'Nichil tamen in illustris doctoris illius preiudicium qui horum fuit glosator, et meus in hac doctrina institutor precipuus, asseritur'. See M. Doyle, *Peter Lombard and His Students* (Toronto, 2016), pp. 198–235, and his article below, pp. 55–63.

[7] Smalley, *Becket Conflict*, p. 62, thought likely a date of *c.* 1150, but Doyle, *Peter Lombard and His Pupils*, pp. 199–200, has suggested that Herbert may have been one of his first pupils, enrolling in his school *c.* 1145 and studying with him long enough to gain the title.

his youth.[8] Though his Greek studies do not seem to have got very far, his Hebrew, at least later in life, was more advanced.

This is what Herbert himself says about his education, but it is clear that the school of St Victor in Paris played a very significant role in shaping his thought, even though he does not acknowledge that debt directly or make any reference to study there. Peter Lombard had close connections to St Victor, so it is not surprising that Herbert should have encountered the canons and their teaching. Even if he had not met Hugh of St Victor before his death in 1141, he could have been introduced to his thought by his pupils, Andrew and Richard. Hugh's influence is especially evident in the mysticism of the *Liber Melorum*, but his views on the importance of the literal sense of scripture also underpin Herbert's approach to the *Psalterium cum commento*. The latter work has been seen as connected to, if surpassing, Andrew's engagement with Jewish scholarship, and the language of Herbert's prologue recalls that of Andrew's preface to his commentary on the prophets. Beryl Smalley suggests that Herbert could have attended Andrew's lectures before 1147 or after 1154/5. Deborah Goodwin sees it as especially likely that he knew Richard of St Victor, a supporter of Becket during his exile.[9]

Our first sighting of Herbert in any public capacity occurs at the end of September 1157 at Frederick I's court at Würzburg, where the emperor welcomed embassies from many realms, including England. Frederick's biographer Rahewin recorded the assembly and inserted a flattering letter from Henry II to Barbarossa, which ends with the words, 'Regarding the hand of St James about which you wrote to us, Master Herbert and our clerk William will give our reply to you in person. Witnessed by Thomas the chancellor at Northampton.'[10] It has long been assumed that this refers to Herbert of Bosham. His presence at the German court might explain William Fitzstephen's description of him, about twelve years later at Angers, 'wearing a tunic and cloak of green cloth of Auxerre, hanging from his shoulders in the German style.'[11] The envoys were charged with politely refusing the emperor's request for the return of the hand of St James, which had been at Reading abbey since the return of Henry II's mother, Matilda, to England in 1126 after the death of her husband, the emperor Henry VI. This letter suggests that Herbert had returned to England from Paris as 'master', that by 1157 he was established as a royal servant long enough to be entrusted with delicate and high-level diplomacy, and that he was likely attached to the chancellor's office.

---

[8] Dedicatory letter to *Psalterium cum commento*, ed. Smalley, 'Commentary on the *Hebraica*', pp. 30–1.

[9] See Smalley, *Becket Conflict*, p. 62; Goodwin, *'Take Hold of the Robe'*, pp. 12–14.

[10] *Ottonis episcopi Frisingensis et Rahewini Gesta Frederici*, ed. F.-J. Schmale (Darmstadt, 1965), p. 406: 'De manu beati Iacobi, super qua nobis scripsistis, in ore magistri Heriberti et Wilhelmi clerici nostri verbum posuimus. Teste Thoma cancellario aput Northamt'. See Smalley, *Becket Conflict*, pp. 59–60; K. J. Leyser, 'Frederick Barbarossa, Henry II and the hand of St James', *EHR* 356 (1975), 481–506.

[11] Fitzstephen, *MTB*, iii, 99–100: 'habens de quodam panno viridi Autisiodorensi tunicam et pallium, ab humeris more Alamannorum deprendens'.

Thomas's disciple

The next time we see Herbert is in early summer 1162 in the company of Thomas Becket, recently elected archbishop, on the road from London to Canterbury for consecration. As Herbert reports it, Thomas told him of a dream in which a venerable person stood beside him and offered him ten talents. At the time Herbert hesitated to give an interpretation, but he later understood that the vision signified the man of the gospel parable who received five talents, traded with them, and gained five more.[12] Next Thomas asked Herbert to watch out for him in his new role as archbishop: to tell him in private what others were saying about him, and that if he should be deficient in his work, to point out his failings, frankly but in confidence.[13] Although Herbert says that Thomas enjoined this task on others too, all the signs are that he quickly gained a special position in the archbishop's household. Years later he would refer to himself as 'your servant, who ministered to you in the chains of the gospel',[14] and early on it seems that his role was as a scriptural advisor. William Fitzstephen calls him Thomas's 'master in the holy page',[15] and Herbert describes how, every morning, and sometimes even when travelling, the new archbishop would summon him to guide him in the mysteries of the scriptures.[16] As Anne Duggan shows, Herbert appears as witness to a few archiepiscopal *acta*, but he is usually well down the list.[17]

Herbert accompanied Thomas to the papal council of Tours in May 1163, where the archbishop was received with great honour.[18] He was also present at the public confrontations of 1163 and 1164 that exposed the growing tensions and then the collapse in relations between the archbishop and the king, and he later recorded them in the *Historia*. He attributes to Thomas a lengthy speech in defence of ecclesiastical liberties at the council of Westminster of October 1163, adding, in the words of St John the Evangelist, 'This is the disciple who gave testimony concerning these things and heard and wrote these things.'[19] He gives full details of the Council of Clarendon in January 1164, and says that on the road back to Canterbury, Thomas privately confessed to Herbert his guilt at his insufficient defence of the church's rights. Herbert reassured him, and advised him that, like David, Peter and Paul, he should learn from his misdeeds, and after a fall rise up all the stronger.[20] Herbert was with his master at Northampton in November 1164, and describes himself on the last day of the conference as sitting at the archbishop's feet, holding the cross, as

---

[12] Matt. 25:14–16.

[13] *MTB*, iii, 185–6.

[14] *MTB*, iii, 532: 'Mihi ergo puero tuo, qui tibi in vinculis evangelii ministrare consueveram'. See Philemon 13.

[15] *MTB*, iii, 58: 'ait archiepiscopo suus in divina pagina magister Herbertus'.

[16] *MTB*, iii, 204–6; see also 376, 379; *Liber Melorum, PL*, 190.1362.

[17] Below, pp. 32–5.

[18] *MTB*, iii, 253–5.

[19] *MTB*, iii, 272: 'Hic est discipulus qui testimonium perhibet de his et audivit et scripsit haec'. See John 21:24.

[20] *MTB*, iii, 292.

courtiers glared and pointed at them threateningly. The archbishop said to Herbert, 'I fear for you now, but you should not fear for yourself, for you will yet share in my crown.'[21] Herbert reassured Thomas that, like Constantine, with the cross as their triumphal standard, they were sure to be victorious.[22] When another witness, William Fitzstephen, heard Herbert urging Thomas to excommunicate his enemies should they lay their hands on him, he intervened to advise the archbishop instead to follow the example of the apostles and martyrs, and pray for his persecutors and bear anything they might impose on him.[23] It is an early sign of how Herbert's trenchant advice would sometimes be countered by more moderate voices.

Fitzstephen adds that in the hurried departure from the council, the pressure of the crowds meant that Herbert was unable to get on his horse, so he jumped on Thomas's horse and rode with him to their lodgings.[24] That night, the archbishop looked meaningfully at his disciple when the reading at dinner included the line from the gospel, 'When they shall persecute you in this city, flee into another',[25] and Herbert was one of a handful whom Thomas informed of his plan to flee England. They did not flee together; rather, Herbert was sent to Canterbury to take what he could from the archbishop's revenues and cross the sea and await him at the monastery of St Omer at St Bertin's.[26] There they reunited a couple of weeks later, where Herbert revealed that he had been able to retrieve only 100 marks and a silver vessel to support their exile.[27] By now, the king's envoys had crossed the sea on a mission to Louis VII of France and Pope Alexander III. Herbert and an unnamed companion were charged with following behind them, and they were received well by the French king at Compiègne, and later by the pope at Sens, where they laid the ground for Thomas's own meetings with these men.[28]

The pope directed the exiles to the Cistercian monastery of Pontigny, south-west of Sens, and there they remained for two years. This, wrote Herbert, was the time of rest from action that Thomas had always longed for, when he was able to devote himself to prayer and meditation and the study of scripture, canon law and theology, with Herbert as his teacher. He says that the Psalms and the Epistles were never out of the archbishop's hands, and it was at Pontigny that Thomas encouraged Herbert to revise Peter Lombard's commentary on those books, a work that would be completed after the archbishop's death.[29] Though Herbert could see the value of this retreat from the world, it did not suit him – he describes it as living in solitude between the monks

---

[21] *MTB*, iii, 307: '"Timeo", inquit, "jam tibi: veruntamen tu non timeas; adhuc enim coronae meae particeps eris"'.

[22] *MTB*, iii, 307–8.

[23] *MTB*, iii, 58.

[24] *MTB*, iii, 68.

[25] *MTB*, iii, 312: 'Si vos persecuti fuerint in ista civitate, fugite in aliam'. See Matt. 10:23.

[26] *MTB*, iii, 312–13, 329–30.

[27] *MTB*, iii, 329–30.

[28] *MTB*, iii, 332–5.

[29] *MTB*, iii, 357–9, 379; Glunz, *History*, p. 342.

and the stones.[30] When Henry II forced their expulsion from Pontigny, Herbert enthusiastically proposed that they should take up King Louis's standing offer of hospitality at the Benedictine abbey of St Columbe, just outside Sens, and although Thomas was concerned that his disciple was too eager to return to courtly and urbane delights, he was finally persuaded, and they remained there for the rest of the exile.[31] Herbert goes into exuberant praise of his host country, 'sweet France' (*dulcis Francia*), sweet on account of its clement weather, but more truly for the innate morals of the people, the goodness of the princes and the gentleness of the kings.[32]

Herbert's revenues were confiscated, along with those of the other exiles, when he fled into exile. In May 1166 he, along with two other of the archbishop's clerks, met King Henry at Angers to plead for their restoration. In William Fitzstephen's famous account, John of Salisbury first made his case before the king, graciously but unsuccessfully. Next Herbert was called in, and as he entered the king said to his men, 'See, here comes a proud one'.[33] Herbert proceeded to lecture his host on the necessity to correct an erring king, and the king's astonishing error in putting his royal customs in writing. When the king snapped at him that he would not listen to such words from the son of a priest, Herbert said that one who is not born to a priest is not the son of a priest, just as one who is not born to a king is not a king's son (Henry's father was Geoffrey, count of Anjou).[34] This quip provoked amusement even among Henry's courtiers, but Herbert later complained that it brought repercussions from the king.[35]

In 1165 Pope Alexander wrote to Henry, bishop of Troyes, proposing Herbert for the provostship of that church, but nothing came of it.[36] Instead he spent the exile at Thomas's side, acting in various guises on his behalf.[37] He wrote letters for him, though his drafts often seem to have been rejected in favour of more diplomatic versions, and he continued as his theological guide. Most important, perhaps, was his role as one of Thomas's erudite 'companions in battle' in stiffening the archbishop's resolve. With the exception of his decision to issue censures against his enemies at Vézelay in 1166,[38] Thomas tended to consult his *eruditi* at every turn, and we regularly see Herbert presenting his advice individually or as part of a group.[39] Herbert presents himself at the peace conference at Montmirail pushing his way through the crowd of distinguished persons and whispering in the ear of

---

[30] *MTB*, iii, 366, 379, 381.

[31] *MTB*, iii, 401–2, and for his praise of Sens, 403. Herbert's interview with King Louis: *CTB*, i, no. 108.

[32] *MTB*, iii, 407–8.

[33] *MTB*, iii, 99: 'En videbitis quendam superbum intrare'.

[34] *MTB*, iii, 100–1.

[35] *HB*, no. 1, *PL* 190.1422.

[36] *MTB*, v, no. 132, pp. 241–2. He called him a man 'renowned for his learning and reputation' ('pro litteris et honestate sua celebris').

[37] See below, pp. 29–54.

[38] *MTB*, iii, 390–1.

[39] *MTB*, iii, 400–1.

the archbishop, urging him to tread carefully in giving concessions, and to learn the lesson of how he had given in to the royal customs at Clarendon. The archbishop was immediately swallowed up by the crowds, but remained looking at Herbert, and in the end he took the stance that the disciple had advised.[40]

In July 1170 a peace settlement was made between king and archbishop at Fréteval that also included Herbert and Thomas's other clerks. In August Herbert went with John of Salisbury to King Henry's court near Domfront in Normandy to secure the promised restoration of their possessions, but the king addressed his remarks to John and gave them no satisfaction.[41] Herbert led a mission to organise the restoration of the exiles' English properties in early October 1170, including a visit to the Young King's court,[42] but was soon back in France. Herbert was with Thomas when he was at the port of Wissant, preparing to sail to England, and heard the pilot's warning that they were going to face certain death. While one of their companions, Gunther, advised that they should delay, Herbert said that the choice was either to withdraw in disgrace or proceed manfully.[43] He describes Thomas's triumphant return to his own church of Canterbury as a presage of glorious martyrdom,[44] but this was the last of Thomas's public triumphs that Herbert would witness. On 27 December Thomas told his disciple that he had decided to send him to King Louis, the archbishop of Sens and other princes of France to inform them of the new persecutions the returned exiles were enduring.

Years later, Herbert recalled his last conversation with his master. Unable to control his tears, he said, 'Holy father, why have you decided this, why do you do this? For I know for certain that I will never again see you in the flesh. I offered to stand with you loyally, but as it seems to me, you wish to defraud me of the fruit of your consummation, I who have up to now been with you in your trials. Now I see that I who was a companion in your struggle will not be a companion in your glory.'[45] The archbishop, equally tearfully, agreed that he would never see him again in the flesh but assured him that he would not be deprived of the fruit of his glory. And he added that he wished him to leave because 'the king sees you as more troublesome than others in the cause of the church'.[46] So, on 27 December, the feast of St John the Evangelist, the disciple took leave of his master. At this point in his narrative he writes, 'I pray with all my heart, with all my soul and with all my strength, that I be found worthy to see in heaven him whom I will never see again

---

[40] *MTB*, iii, 421–3.

[41] *MTB*, iii, 468.

[42] *CTB*, ii, no. 311; *MTB*, vii, no. 685, p. 342.

[43] *MTB*, iii, 472–6.

[44] *MTB*, iii, 479–80.

[45] *MTB*, iii, 485–6: '"Pater sancte", inquiens, "cur ita disposuisti, cur facis sic? scio quippe et certus sum me de caetero te in carne ista non visurum. Ego quidem proposui vobiscum fideliter stare; veruntamen, ut mihi videtur, fructu consummationis tuae defraudare me quaeris, qui hucusque tecum in tentationibus tuis permansi; ne ero, sicut nunc video, socius gloriae, qui fui socius poenae"'.

[46] *MTB*, iii, 486: 'rex habeat te in causa ecclesiae caeteris suspectiorem'.

in this world, and share in his crown, I who was a companion in the battle.'[47] Later he would report a vision in which the martyr appeared to him. Herbert said that it was perhaps better that he had not been present at the time of the murder, since as a sinner he would have perished spiritually, but Thomas insisted that he would not have perished – he would have been baptised in the martyr's blood.[48]

Writing alone and mourning alone

Herbert lived on for more than twenty years after Thomas's murder and during this time he would produce the bulk of his writings, but he would never forget the battle and his companionship with his master. One of the earliest surviving responses we have to the murder is written by Herbert to the pope in the name of William, archbishop of Sens. He begins: 'In writing this, or rather before writing, I stopped and hesitated, still unsure what kind of expression I could use to bring before you the horrifying and savage murder of the Lord's anointed.'[49] Herbert also made his own views on the murder clear when he wrote on his own behalf to the pope demanding that the king and his son suffer censure and lose their royal privileges.[50] To Cardinals Albert and Theodwin, commissioned to pass judgment on the king, he complains that the 'Satan of the North' is fleeing to Ireland to escape. He reports an interview with King Louis, who lamented the apparent impunity of the killers, and says that he had heard that the pope had relayed a secret message to King Henry saying the church wanted reconciliation.[51] In another letter he urges the pope to order that a mass for St Thomas be celebrated in every church.[52]

These positions are consistent with Herbert's views before the murder, and many of them are echoed by contemporaries. The king initially appeared unrepentant for his role in the murder and prepared to contest any restrictions imposed on him by the church, and his visit to Ireland was widely regarded as an evasion of his reckoning with the papal commissioners.[53] But such opinions were voiced less freely after the settlement at Avranches in 1172, and especially after the king's penance at Thomas's tomb in 1174. Herbert's principles also determined the course

---

[47] *MTB*, iii, 486: 'id toto corde, tota anima, et totis viribus deprecor, ut quem deinceps non sum visurus in tempore videre merear in aeternitate, et fieri particeps in corona, qui socius fui in pugna'.

[48] *MTB*, iii, 502.

[49] *HB*, no. 33, *PL*, 190.1465=*MTB*, vii, 429 no. 735, 'Inter scribendum haec, immo prius quam scriberem, mox steti et haesi, dubius admodum quo dictionis genere nuper patrati sceleris atrocitatem, et supplicii in christum Domini recenter illati immanitatem, clementiae vestrae oculis praesentarem'.

[50] *HB*, no. 34. This section is not printed in *PL*: see Cambridge Corpus Christi College [henceforth CCCC] MS 123, f. 53v.

[51] *HB*, no. 39, *PL*, 190.1469–70 (1469): 'Aquilonaris ille Satanas'.

[52] *HB*, no. 40, *PL*, 190.1471.

[53] See C. Ó Clabaigh and M. Staunton, 'Thomas Becket and Ireland', in *'Listen, O Isles, unto Me'. Studies in Medieval Word and Image in Honour of Jennifer O'Reilly*, ed. E. Mullins and D. Scully (Cork, 2011), pp. 87–101, 340–3, at 88–92.

of his life after the murder. In his letter to the pope he complains that Thomas's clerks are being forced to swear that they will keep the king's peace, do nothing to his detriment and not leave his lands without his licence or send letters across the sea. Others, he says, including John of Salisbury and Gunther, had been forced to take the oath, but Herbert's refusal has meant his exclusion from England.[54] The pope wrote to Herbert calling him 'a devoted and special friend of the church', acknowledging his current difficulties and expressing the hope that the cardinals' mission would settle the status of Thomas's clerks and their restoration to England.[55] But, as Herbert writes to John, bishop of Poitiers, men were remonstrating with him to return, saying that his was a foolish exile when peace had been offered.[56] John of Salisbury told Herbert that the archdeacon of Canterbury was accusing him of indulging in a voluntary absence, not a true exile. Herbert responds that his exile is just and is justified by the mandate of a higher authority.[57] Throughout all his difficulties, he was comforted by the appearance to him in a vision of the *neomartyr* Thomas, commending to him the verse of the Psalm, 'Redeem me from the calumnies of men, so that I keep your mandates'.[58]

So Herbert stayed in France and, apart from a period in the late 1180s, he would seem to have spent the rest of his life there. When Thomas had sent Herbert away in December 1170 he had directed him to the archbishop of Sens, William of the White Hands, and we find him in the aftermath of the murder writing letters on his behalf. Herbert had known William since he was young, he had previously written letters on behalf of his brother, Henry the Liberal, count of Champagne, and it is likely that William was the lord whose business Herbert said kept him from returning to England.[59] William led the campaign to bring King Henry to heel, threatening an interdict on his lands and writing to the pope in urgent terms, and he also played an important role in the production of Herbert's first major work, his edition of Peter Lombard's *Great Gloss* on the Psalms and Pauline Epistles. Current opinion holds that although the work was begun at Pontigny at Thomas's suggestion, it was completed either at Sens or at Paris between 1172 and 1176. Though the project was coordinated by Herbert, it required the work of others, most likely professional artists from Paris, and was thus an expensive and ambitious undertaking. Herbert dedicated the work to William of Sens and it may be that he, also a pupil of Peter Lombard, provided the necessary support.

Herbert's edition was a fitting memorial to his teacher at a time when his reputation was under attack. It stands as early evidence of Herbert's biblical

---

[54] *HB*, no. 34, *PL*, 190.1466–7 and CCCC MS 123, ff. 52v–53r.

[55] *HB*, no. 41, *PL*, 190.1471.

[56] *HB*, no. 28, CCCC MS 123, ff. 55r–v.

[57] *HB*, no. 35, *PL*, 190.1467.

[58] Glunz, *History*, p. 344; see Ps. 117:134: 'Redime me a calumpniis hominum, ut custodiam mandata tua'. Here the context appears to be criticism of his revision of Peter Lombard's *Great Gloss*; but he also refers to this reading in *HB*, no. 38, to John of Poitiers, CCCC MS 123, f. 55r, and in the *Liber Melorum*, *PL*, 190.1404.

[59] *MTB*, vii, 512 no. 769; Smalley, *Becket Conflict*, p. 71.

scholarship and has been hailed as a landmark in book production. But that Herbert devoted himself to this work in these years tells us much about how different he was to his peers, and how unsuccessful in comparison. His colleagues in Thomas's party had prospered: John of Salisbury became bishop of Chartres, Lombard of Piacenza was made a cardinal, and then archbishop of Benevento. Many of those who had hardly known Thomas – Edward Grim, Guernes de Pont-Ste-Maxence, William of Canterbury – wrote Lives of the saint, claiming to tell the true story of the archbishop and martyr. The monks of Canterbury, who had been so cool towards their archbishop, were now rich in money and status on account of pilgrims to the tomb of St Thomas. Herbert, meanwhile, found it hard to find any position in a church, or any defined role. Some time after April 1174, Pope Alexander wrote to the new archbishop of Canterbury, Richard of Dover, asking him to allot Herbert his revenues for three years because he wished to teach theology.[60] Where this school was to be, or what happened to this venture, we do not know, but it was around this time that Herbert appears in Paris as witness to a judgment pronounced by the papal legate Peter of Pavia in a dispute between the abbot of St Geneviève and some of his tenants. This has been dated to between 1175 and 1178.[61] We also know that he visited St Denis during the abbacy of William le Mire, i.e. after 1172/3.[62]

Then Herbert disappears from the record, and the next we hear of him he is writing his account of the life of St Thomas. On three occasions in the *Historia* he notes the time when he is writing: at one point in the fourteenth year since the murder (1184), then at the time of the death of King Henry's son Geoffrey (19 August 1186), then in the fifteenth year (1185).[63] If the bulk of the work was done between 1184 and 1186, it is likely that some was written before then and that additions were made to it later. The picture he presents of himself at this time is of a man bereft of his master and his companions. 'In writing this I mourn alone', he writes, 'and in mourning I write alone.'[64] His companions in the battle are almost all now dead: 'They have passed away, while I am yet in danger, abandoned in the midst of fires and waves.' And so, he says, the task of writing about what he saw and heard of the great man has been reserved uniquely to him.[65] At the end of the *Liber*

---

[60] Smalley, *Becket Conflict*, p. 71: S. Loewenfeld, *Epistolae pontificum romanorum ineditae* (Graz, 1959), p. 207, no. 347.

[61] Smalley, *Becket Conflict*, p. 71; R. de Lasteyrie, *Cartulaire générale de Paris*, i (Paris, 1887), no. 519, p. 429. See Appendix, below, pp. 184–7.

[62] Smalley, *Becket Conflict*, pp. 71–2.

[63] *MTB*, iii, 192: 'a viri hujus de hoc mundo excessu jam quartus-decimus annus sit quo scribo haec'; p. 461: 'Pariter et in Gaufridi morte, dum adhuc hanc historiam scriberem, archipraesulis vaticinium adimpletum'; p. 497: 'Ecce enim quintus decimus annus hic ex quo gesta sunt quae nunc scribuntur'. See *MTB*, iii, xxii, and below, p. 16.

[64] *MTB*, iii, 496: 'inter scribendum haec solus doleo, et inter dolendum solus scribo'.

[65] *MTB*, iii, 497: 'et jam fratres mei, quondam passionis socii, qui mecum audierunt et viderunt, fere quotquot ab humanis rebus exempti in Christo dormiunt. Ipsi quidem transierunt, me periclitante adhuc et in mediis ignibus et fluctibus derilicto. Unde singulariter mihi, qui adhuc superstes, scribendi de tanto viro, domino meo et alumno, quae vidi vel audivi reservatum opus et opera haec'. See also p. 192: 'Unde et, ni fallor,

Melorum, his sequel to the *Historia*, he again reflects on this period of his life. His lord has been taken away from him and he is left to proceed on his pilgrimage alone, without a companion, without solace or aid. He says that he stayed for a time when writing his *Historia* in the 'British world' (*orbis Brittanicus*), but when he was there the prelates of the land shunned him, perhaps in fear of the king's old anger against him. He marvels that these prelates adore every day the relics of Thomas's dead body but spurn his 'living relics' (*vivae reliquiae*). Now his lord and master ascends his fiery chariot, like Elijah, but the disciple, still suffering in pilgrimage, fulfils in himself whatever is lacking to Thomas's passion.[66]

Despite the bitterness expressed here, we should not assume that the mid-1180s represented an especially low point for Herbert. He had been using this language ever since Thomas was murdered. In a letter to the pope in its immediate aftermath he referred 'the relics of the killed father' and complained that he had been abandoned alone.[67] To his allies in Thomas's cause, John of Salisbury, Gunther, John of Poitiers, and the cardinals Albert and Theodwin, he wrote that he was fulfilling the things lacking to Thomas's passion in his own flesh, that he had been abandoned alone in the midst of fire and waves and that he was left without his allies to fight the battle and suffer the pressure alone.[68] In fact, by the mid-1180s he seems to have been reconciled to the king and to his church of Canterbury, allowing him to return to England. In the *Liber Melorum* he describes an audience with King Henry, the place and date unspecified, during which Herbert accused the king of responsibility for the murder and Henry said it had indeed been carried out for him, but not by him.[69] This meeting seems to have paved the way for a return to England and at least partial restoration of his possessions. The Pipe Roll for Essex in 1187 records a fine of one mark for a forest offence, indicating that he held land, and this fine was recorded every year until 1194.[70] A letter of Master David of London also mentions that the church of Dodington near Faversham was held by Herbert.[71]

When Heraclius, patriarch of Jerusalem, visited England in 1185 to promote the crusade, he met Herbert and told him that Thomas's murder had been miraculously revealed in the Holy Land soon after the event.[72] Herbert seems to have done some work for Baldwin, who was consecrated archbishop of Canterbury in early

---

secreta quadam dispositione Altissimi, caeteris jam fere omnibus de mundo sublatis qui mecum viderunt et comministraverunt pontifici, mihi quasi soli adhuc reservato hoc reservatur, ut juxta exemplar quod prae caeteris multis, pontifici similiter obsequentibus, diligentius et familiarius intueabar, praesentis et post futuri saeculi hominibus caelestem caelestis imaginem explicem'.

[66] *Liber Melorum*, PL, 190.1403–4; 2 Kings 2:11; Coloss. 1:24.

[67] *HB*, no. 34, *PL*, 190.1466: 'reliquias etiam interfecti patris'.

[68] *HB*, no. 35, CCCC MS 123, f. 34r; *HB*, no. 36, CCCC MS 123, f. 35r; *HB*, no. 38, CCCC MS 123, f. 55r; *HB*, no. 39, PL 190.1470.

[69] *Liber Melorum*, PL, 190.1312–15.

[70] PR 34 HII, 1187–8, p. 38; see Smalley, *Becket Conflict*, p. 72.

[71] *Magistri David Londonensis epistolae*, in *Spicilegium Liberianum*, ed. F. Liverani (Florence, 1863), no. 13, pp. 613–15; see *MTB*, iii, xxii.

[72] *MTB*, iii, 513–16.

1185. Despite his words about the English pontiffs, he says he has no complaint against the two successors to Thomas, Richard and Baldwin,[73] and he prefaces his *Historia* with a letter addressed to Baldwin and his canonical successors. Gervase of Canterbury, chronicler of the dispute between Baldwin and his monks over the building of a collegiate church at Hackington outside the city, writes of Herbert's intervention in the dispute. In December 1187 Herbert, 'master and clerk of the glorious archbishop and martyr Thomas, came to Canterbury as if out of special love', and spoke to the convent 'with the elegant eloquence of which he was full'.[74] Herbert urged the monks to throw themselves on Baldwin's mercy, but the prior responded that they were bound to maintain the liberty of the church as it had been handed down by their predecessors. Herbert, marvelling at their constancy, told the monks, 'Then, if this is so, you must either give in disgracefully, or stand manfully.' These are the words that Herbert, by his own account, spoke to Thomas many years earlier, urging him to return from exile to Canterbury, and there are many other allusions in Gervase's work to Herbert's *Historia*, suggesting that the author shared this work with him.[75] Herbert wrote his *Liber Melorum* as a sequel to the *Historia*, and he writes at the end as if he is back in France. Still, it was probably completed not long after the former work and, like its predecessor, probably drew on some writings that he had composed earlier, such is the recurrence of ideas and images also found in the *Historia* and in his letters. It was after this, in the 1190s, that Herbert put together his letter collection. The last two personal letters, dating from 1190 or 1191, are between Herbert and William Longchamp, bishop of Ely, royal chancellor and papal legate.[76] Herbert's friendship with Longchamp is intriguing. A difficult and controversial figure, capable as an administrator but politically wayward, trusted by King Richard but reviled by many contemporaries, he presents an interesting comparison to Thomas Becket.[77]

These last two letters also hold our only external evidence for Herbert's final project. Herbert indicates that he is at the end of the work that he has sweated over for years, a work 'on the Psalms translated from the Hebrew truth by Father Jerome', and Longchamp says that he hopes it is indeed finished so that they will

---

[73] *Liber Melorum*, PL 190.1403–4.

[74] *The Historical Works of Gervase of Canterbury*, ed. W. Stubbs, 2 vols, RS (London, 1879–80), i, p. 393: 'Herebertus etiam de Boseham, gloriosi pontificis et martyris Thomae magister et clericus, quasi ex speciali dilectione Cantuariam accessit, eleganti quo pollebat eloquio venerabilem et decora dignum memoria Gaufridum suppriorem inducere cupiens, ut totam ecclesiae causam humilitate vel satisfactione interposita archiepiscopi committeret arbitrio'.

[75] Gervase, i, p. 394: 'aut cedendum est turpiter, aut standum viriliter'. See 1 Chron. 28:20; Ps 26 (27):14; Goodwin, '*Take Hold of the Robe*', p. 23. On Gervase's debt to Herbert, see M. Staunton, 'Thomas Becket in the Chronicles', in *The Cult of St Thomas Becket in the Plantagenet World, c. 1170–c. 1220*, ed. P. Webster and M.-P. Gelin (Woodbridge, 2016), pp. 95–112, at 104–9.

[76] *HB*, nos. 44, 45, *PL*, 190.1473–4.

[77] See M. Staunton, *The Historians of Angevin England* (Oxford, 2017), pp. 281–307. Gervase of Canterbury was one of those more sympathetic to Longchamp.

be able to meet.[78] This is the *Psalterium cum commento* which Herbert produced at the Cistercian monastery of Ourscamp in the diocese of Arras in Flanders. In the prefatory letter, addressed to Peter, bishop of Arras (1184–1203), he writes that he has recently transferred from the turbulence of the court – suggesting perhaps that he has been working for Longchamp – to the tranquillity of Ourscamp. Peter welcomed him there as long as he chose one of three options: to be a monk, to teach or to write.[79] Herbert chose the latter, and the result was the only known commentary on the literal sense of the Psalms in Jerome's *Hebraica* version. Since its discovery in the middle of the twentieth century, this work has attracted much interest, and it reveals Herbert as perhaps the most important Christian Hebraist of his age. The extent of his Hebrew vocabulary, the range of Jewish sources he draws on and the evidence of at least one Jewish interlocutor suggest a degree of engagement with Hebrew scholarship that surpassed that of others, even at a time of renewed Christian Hebraism.

The example of the *Psalterium* – almost unmentioned in his other works and unknown until the twentieth century – shows us again that Herbert could say a great deal about himself but leave much to be discovered. We do not know for sure how he learned Hebrew, or how he came to this topic. We do not know if he wrote anything else at Ourscamp, or how this last work of his was received. Nor do we know exactly when he died, but the disappearance from the Essex Pipe Roll of his recurring forest fine in 1194 suggests he was dead by then. The likelihood is that, unlike his master, he died quietly, in obscure exile. In the nineteenth century J. C. Robertson reported a local tradition at Bosham that Herbert was buried in the church, though there is no other evidence to back this up.[80] In time, the remarkable body of work that he left behind would excite the interest of scholars and take us back to the singular individual who produced them.

Revision of the Magna Glosatura

Herbert's first major work was a deluxe edition of Peter Lombard's *Great Gloss* on the Psalms and the Epistles, known as the *Magna Glosatura*.[81] The project was begun

---

[78] *HB*, nos. 44–5, *PL*, 190.1474: 'Et quidem opusculo super psalmos ab Hebraica veritate a Patre Hieronymo translatos completo, in quo jam per annos desudavi, spero me volente Domino vos visurum et vel in transitu tam desiderato vestro colloquio frui'.

[79] Printed in Smalley, 'Commentary on the *Hebraica*', pp. 31–2.

[80] *MTB*, iii, xxiii.

[81] Discussed by C. R. Dodwell, *The Canterbury School of Illumination* (Cambridge, 1954), pp. 104–9; C. de Hamel, 'Manuscripts of Herbert of Bosham', in *Manuscripts at Oxford: An Exhibition in Memory of Richard William Hunt (1908–1979)*, ed. A. C. de la Mare and B. C. Barker-Benfield (Oxford, 1980), pp. 39–41; C. de Hamel, *Glossed Books of the Bible and the Origins of the Paris Book Trade* (Cambridge, 1984), pp. 38–54; C. de Hamel, 'A Contemporary Miniature of Thomas Becket', in *Intellectual Life in the Middle Ages: Essays Presented to Margaret Gibson*, ed. L. M. Smith and B. Ward (London, 1992), pp. 179–84; W. Cahn, *Romanesque Manuscripts: The Twelfth Century*, 2 vols. (London, 1996), ii, pp. 107–9; P. Stirnemann, 'En quête de Sens', in *Quand la peinture était dans les livres: Mélanges en l'honneur de François Avril*, ed. M. Hoffmann, E. König, and C. Zöhl

while Herbert was in exile with Thomas, perhaps as early as 1165, then continued after Thomas's murder, involving a number of scribes and illustrators. Herbert's revision of Peter Lombard's work is a testament to his first teacher, and a defence of his reputation, while also honouring Herbert's most famous pupil, Thomas Becket, and their study of the scriptures together. The four huge volumes are renowned for their lavish illustrations, supervised by Herbert but thought to have been executed by professional artists. They are now divided between Cambridge and Oxford: Trinity College Cambridge holds the first part of the Psalms edition (MS B.5.4) and the two volumes of the Epistles (B.5.6 and B.5.7). The second part of the Psalter is in Oxford Bodleian MS Auct.E.inf.5.

Throughout his career, Herbert showed a deep interest in the Psalms and in the works of St Paul, an interest which he imparted to Thomas Becket. He describes how they studied together at Pontigny, 'especially those two holy books the Psalms and the Epistles, like two spiritual eyes, mystic and moral'.[82] In his preface to the revision Herbert writes that Thomas had wished him to make Peter's glosses available, and he refers to the library at Pontigny. He explains that Peter's glosses on the Psalms and Epistles were meant to clarify those of Anselm of Laon, but his work had not been entirely finished when Peter became bishop of Paris in 1159, and he died the following year. Herbert gives a hint of another motivation when he refers to critics barking like dogs, tearing his work to pieces.[83] Peter had been accused of heresy after his death, and the pope enlisted another of the Lombard's former students, William, archbishop of Sens, to refute these supposed errors. But, as Matthew Doyle notes, it would appear that William responded by supporting a project, already begun, that would defend his master's reputation.[84]

The work was almost certainly begun while Thomas was still alive – a cancelled leaf shows an early dedication to Thomas and a portrait of the archbishop.[85] After Thomas's death Herbert lived at Sens and he rededicated the work to William of the White Hands as archbishop of Sens, thereby dating it to 1176 at the latest.[86] Whether

---

(Turnhout, 2007), pp. 303–12; S. Panayotova, 'Tutorial in Images for Thomas Becket', in *The Cambridge Illuminations: The Conference Papers*, ed. S. Panayotova (London, 2007), pp. 77–86; Doyle, *Peter Lombard and his Students*, pp. 198–235; and the papers by Doyle and Cleaver below, pp. 55–63, 64–86. The prefaces are printed in Glunz, *History*, pp. 346–50. For a selection of images from Bodleian MS Auct. Inf. 6 see http://bodley30. bodley.ox.ac.uk:8180/luna.

[82] *MTB*, iii, 379: 'praesertim sacri illi duo libri, Psalterii videlicet et Epistolarum, tanquam duo spirituales oculi, mysticus et moralis'.

[83] The prefaces are printed by Glunz, *History*, pp. 341–50.

[84] See Doyle, *Peter Lombard and His Students*, pp. 201–9, and below, pp. 60–1. See also Goodwin, '*Take Hold of the Robe*', pp. 30–2.

[85] De Hamel, 'Contemporary Miniature of Becket'.

[86] Glunz, *History*, pp. 342–6, 348–50. Herbert prefaced to the commentary on the Epistles a letter from William le Mire in reply to Herbert's request for a translation of some Greek prologues to the epistles. William styles himself abbot of St Denis, which dates the letter to 1172/3 at the earliest: ibid, pp. 346–8.

it was produced at Sens or at Paris is uncertain.[87] It was an expensive undertaking, using good parchment and painted initials, some in gold, and requiring the work of a number of professional artists. Herbert wrote the prefaces, checked and filled in authorial attributions and supervised the work as a whole – his directions to illustrators survive.[88]

The volumes were meant to inform and impress. The Psalms commentary has received most attention: it required more effort, because the Lombard had already revised his commentary on the Epistles, and it is more lavishly illustrated. In the centre of the page is Peter's commentary, incorporating the biblical text, in two columns. The first letter of each Psalm is lavishly decorated, and the first letter of each verse is also marked with an ornamental initial. He corrects authorial attributions by placing in the margin such figures as Augustine, Jerome or Cassiodorus, holding scrolls with the words, '*Non ego*', '*Ego aliter*' or similar, pointing a lance to an incorrect attribution. Peter Lombard had already grouped the Psalms by subject, but Herbert went further by giving each subject its own specific illustration in the margin, and listing the other Psalms that touched on that subject. Herbert's revision also signals an early interest in the Hebrew text and in textual criticism in general. He places to the left of the main text Jerome's *Hebraica* translation, and he notes in the preface that he has collated many variant texts. While the edition of the Pauline Epistles is perhaps less spectacular – no thematic scheme existed for them, so there is no equivalent here to the Psalter's subject illustrations – it includes similar illuminated initials at the start of each letter, and some representations of the authorities in the margins.

As a work inspired by Thomas and completed in the wake of his murder, the revision of the *Great Gloss* also gives us some insight into the relationship between Herbert and his master. The Psalter opens with a large illuminated image of Thomas standing and giving orders to Herbert holding a scroll (see Fig. 4.1). Laura Cleaver suggests that the illustrations accompanying Psalm 109 could also represent Thomas the martyr, and a lamenting semi-naked figure looking up to him Herbert himself, abandoned after his master's departure (see Fig. 4.8).[89] Herbert's four volumes found their way to Christ Church, Canterbury, where they remained, shelved with Thomas's books, until the Dissolution.[90]

Historia

Herbert's narrative of the life and death of Thomas Becket is usually known as the *Vita S. Thomae* and counted among the twelfth-century Lives of the saint, but in

---

[87] Dodwell, *Canterbury School*, pp. 104–9, suggested that Herbert's editions were produced at Pontigny; de Hamel, *Glossed Books*, pp. 38–54, argued that if Herbert began his research there, they were executed in Paris in the 1170s from combined exemplars of Lombard's glosses and Herbert's notes and emendations. Panayotova, 'Tutorial in images', p. 77, considers Sens the more likely location.

[88] Panayotova, 'Tutorial', p. 78, identifies four artists.

[89] Below, pp. 81–6.

[90] Smalley, *Becket Conflict*, p. 82; de Hamel, below, pp. 169, 171–4, 176–7, 180–1.

many ways it stands apart from them. It was begun around 1184, much later than those other Lives, it does not seem to borrow from those earlier works, and it is quite different in character from them. Herbert called this work the *Historia*, and it is a very valuable independent narrative of Thomas's life, but it is more than a history too. As the author himself acknowledges, it often smacks more of theology than history, and it is, furthermore, a very personal and self-reflective work. It might be described as a personal memoir of Thomas's struggle by a devoted disciple and theologian.[91]

As noted,[92] the bulk of the work seems to have been done *c.* 1184–*c.* 1186. But Herbert also draws on letters which he had written decades earlier, and he may have continued to add to it – he refers to Henry II's death in 1189, though he usually discusses the king as still alive.[93] In the *Liber Melorum* he mentions that he spent time in the 'British world' while writing it, but whether the return to England prompted him to write, or vice versa, is unclear. The *Historia* is about 80,000 words long and divided into seven books of unequal length. Herbert passes quickly over Thomas's early life, but dwells in great detail on his life as archbishop, his struggles with the king, the exile and the murder. Especially valuable is the information on the exile, which none of the other biographers witnessed well.

There are many unique features to Herbert's work. The prefatory letter, addressed to Archbishop Baldwin and his canonical successors, reveals different priorities to those advanced by other biographers. Herbert presents his work as a literary monument to Thomas which will serve as a model to Thomas's successors, 'so that as he did, you ought to do the same'.[94] He says he will not include Thomas's miracles (nor does he include his correspondence), and instead urges Baldwin and his successors to follow Thomas's deeds, and especially his zeal for the church.[95] Another innovation is his 'day in the life' of Thomas in his first year as archbishop. There he describes the archbishop's secret ministrations to the poor and his private asceticism, how he celebrated mass, how he judged cases, and his demeanour at the dinner table. This section is addressed directly to pontiffs, and it is possible that it was once planned as a separate work. One of the most discussed passages in Herbert's *Historia* is touched off by his account of how Thomas was accustomed to say mass quickly. Herbert explains that Thomas rushed through the mass so as to avoid wandering thoughts, which leads him into a description of his own doubts. What, he wondered, if the church's belief in the Incarnation were false, and the Jews were right in saying the Lord had not yet been incarnated? Would the Christian faith then be unfounded? Troubled by these matters, he dreamed that he saw the host quivering and spinning around in the chalice as if in perpetual

---

[91] On this work see *MTB*, iii, xvii–xxviii; Smalley, *Becket Conflict*, pp. 59–86; J. O'Reilly, 'The Double Martyrdom of Thomas Becket: Hagiography or History?', *Studies in Medieval and Renaissance History* 7 (1985), 185–247; Weiss, 'Herbert of Bosham's *Liber Melorum*', pp. 46–77; Staunton, *Thomas Becket and His Biographers*, pp. 63–74.

[92] Above, p. 10.

[93] *MTB*, iii, 461.

[94] *MTB*, iii, 156: 'ut, quemadmodum fecit ipse, et vos similiter faciatis'.

[95] *MTB*, iii, 156.

motion. The next day he told Thomas of his vision. He immediately responded that the movement in the chalice indicated Herbert's own fluctuation of mind, and at this Herbert was consoled and his faith in the sacrament of the altar grew firmer.[96]

Herbert regularly pauses to reflect, often at great length, on his literary task. This first occurs when he is about to discuss Thomas's consecration as archbishop. Up to now he has been able to write about the chancellor in a worldly style, but now he is unsure 'how I, a foul and ignorant painter, can adequately trace the heavenly image of Christ's new pontiff as distinct from the worldly image of the secular man'.[97] Moses was allowed to contemplate the exemplar of divine law on the mount, but he has only been able to observe his master in the valley of tears.[98] After he has told of Becket's new life as archbishop he pauses again. In writing about Thomas in this way he might, he says, seem a tedious wordsmith, and 'to smack too much of a theologian and too little of a historian'. But, he insists, this is necessary, since his task is 'not only to explain the archbishop's deeds but the reason for them, not only what was done but the mind of the doer'.[99] When he comes to Thomas's murder he repeatedly interrupts his account, protesting that it is more pleasant for him to continue writing about the living, fighting Thomas than to write about the martyr in heaven. For, while he depicts the archbishop in the struggle, he still seems to be with him, but once he turns to his triumph, Thomas flies away from him, like Elijah, leaving his disciple naked and bereft.[100]

Thomas grouped his *Historia* with the *Liber Melorum*, as well as a *Homily on St Thomas* and a copy of the Constitutions of Clarendon and – he was fond of puns – called this composite work the *Thomus*. A copy of the *Thomus* is recorded in Christ Church, Canterbury, alongside Herbert's four volumes of the *Great Gloss* revision, and this may have been Herbert's own manuscript. Only a fragment now survives.[101] The fullest surviving version of the *Thomus* is Arras, Bibliothèque de la Ville, MS 649, a late twelfth-century manuscript that once belonged to the monastery of St Vedast, Arras and that may have been copied from the version Herbert brought to Ourscamp. In the early nineteenth century a substantial number

---

[96] *MTB*, iii, 213–15; See Smalley, 'Commentary on the *Hebraica*', pp. 61–3; eadem, *Study of the Bible*, p. 192; Smalley, *Becket Conflict*, pp. 75–6; S. Flanagan, *Doubt in an Age of Faith. Uncertainty in the Long Twelfth Century* (Turnhout, 2008), pp. 81–5, 176–7.

[97] *MTB*, iii, 190: 'quomodo, foedus pictor et ignarus, non jam in homine saeculi imaginem terreni, sed in novo et tanto Christi pontifice caelestis digne valeam imaginis lineamenta depingere'.

[98] *MTB*, iii, 191.

[99] *MTB*, iii, 247–8: 'In his, inquam, pontificis exsequendis operibus forte nimis morosus videor, et in ipsorum commendatione operum taediosus inculcator verborum, et potius theologicae aedificationi quam gestorum viri historicae explanationi insistere, et ita nimis theologum, historicum vero parum, sapere. Verum quivis notans nos sic saltem non judicet, sed advertat prius nos non solum pontificis opera, sed et causas operum, quod et supra jam nos dixisse meminimus, explicare: quasi non solum facta, sed et animum facientis, quem ab ipso sic accepi factore'. See also pp. 532–4.

[100] See below, pp. 53, 124–6.

[101] See de Hamel, below, pp. 171–4.

of leaves, at irregular intervals, were cut out by an unscrupulous librarian, and the tale of the search for the missing leaves and their eventual recovery is told below.[102] Oxford, Corpus Christi College MS 146, dating from the late thirteenth or early fourteenth century, contains the *Historia*, but without its first three books, and the *Liber Melorum* without its conclusion.

Although Herbert pleaded with the reader not to abridge his work, it was circulated most widely as part of the composite Life, the *Quadrilogus*. This work was first compiled by E., a monk of Evesham, at the instigation of Henry Longchamp (brother of William Longchamp), and went through various versions, including a translation into English.[103] A thirteenth-century compilation, made by the Cistercian monk Thomas of Froidmont, also uses substantial sections from Herbert's work.[104] In these compilations most of Herbert's reflections were trimmed away, leaving the still substantial historical material. In addition, several abbreviations of Herbert's work survive, apparently made for other Cistercian houses in Flanders and France.[105] And in the fifteenth century a monk of Christ Church, Canterbury used part of Herbert's *Historia* for an epic poem in English.[106]

Liber Melorum

The *Liber Melorum* is a long, difficult, erudite and original work that is hard to categorise. It concerns the consonance between Thomas's battle and reward and that of Christ, but it ranges from historical narrative and personal reminiscence to proofs of God's existence and Christology. It survives as the second part of the *Thomus*, as described above, and was printed by Giles in 1845, and it is in the version of that edition pirated by Migne in the *Patrologia Latina* that it is most readily accessible.[107] Robertson printed some extracts along with the *Historia* in *Materials* III, but said that 'to reproduce such a work at full length would be an utter waste of paper and type; for in it the author's love of irrelevant and unreadable discourse is indulged to a degree which is almost inconceivable'.[108] Others have been more

---

[102] See below, pp. 136, 137, 140, 148n.125, 149, 151, 154, 156–67, 175, 176, 178, 182. T. Craib, 'The Arras MS. of Herbert of Bosham', *EHR* 35 (1920), 218–24, printed a number of the missing leaves from a transcript of Sir Thomas Phillipps.

[103] The text of the original *Quadrilogus* is in *MTB*, iv, 266–424; the English translation in *The Early English South-English Legendary*, ed. C. Horstmann, Early English Text Society original series 87 (London, 1887), pp. 106–77. See A. Duggan, 'The Lyell Version of the *Quadrilogus* Life of St Thomas of Canterbury', *Analecta Bollandiana* 112 (1994), 105–38.

[104] *Thomas von Froidmont: Die Vita des heiligen Thomas Becket: Erzbischof von Canterbury*, ed. and tr. P. G. Schmidt (Stuttgart, 1991).

[105] Brussels, Bibliothèque Royale MS IV 600 fols. 1r–100v; Charleville, Bibliothèque Municipale MS 222, fols. 1v–104v; Brussels, Bibliothèque Royale MS 3329 (20618). See Weiss, 'Herbert of Bosham's *Liber Melorum*', p. 41.

[106] C. Horstmann, ed., 'Thomas Becket, epische Legende von Laurentius Wade', *Englische Studien* 3 (1880), pp. 411–69.

[107] J. A. Giles, *Herberti de Boseham S. Thomae Cantuariensis Clerici a Secretis Opera quae Exstant Omnia* (Oxford, 1845); repr. *PL*, 190.1069–1474.

[108] *MTB*, iii, xxv–xxvi.

appreciative of what it tells us about the aftermath of Thomas's murder, and about Herbert's theology. Smalley took some interest in it, particularly Herbert's proofs of God's existence.[109] More recently, Jessica Weiss provided a thorough analysis of the work in her unpublished PhD dissertation of 2003, to which the following summary is indebted.[110]

Herbert employs a musical allegory to structure and describe the *Liber Melorum*. He is a singer, accompanying himself on the lyre, performing three melodies (*meli*), which make up the three chapters of the work. Each *melus* addresses a consonance (*consonantia, concordia, consimilitudo, harmonia*) between the soldier (*miles*), Thomas, and the commander (*imperator*), Christ. The first consonance is between the visible battle of the soldier and that of the commander: in other words, between the passion of St Thomas and that of Christ. The second is between the visible reward of the soldier and that of the commander, that is, between the signs of Thomas's glory after death and the signs of Christ's glory after death. The third consonance, between the invisible reward of the soldier and that of the commander, represents the unity between Thomas, and indeed all the saints, and God, in the next life.[111] Between the first and second *meli*, and between the second and third, Herbert introduces what he calls *modulationes*, where he describes how the lyre needs to be adjusted to play in different modes according to the material. The first *melus* is played on low strings, corresponding to the human qualities in Thomas and Christ, such as pain and grief, and calls forth compassion; the second is performed using middle strings, and calls forth joy; the third *melus* uses the higher notes, evoking what is divine in Christ and his saint, and prompts jubilation. This is broadly how the *Liber Melorum* works, but within these divisions there is some variation.[112]

The first *melus* concerns the parallels between the life of the soldier and that of the commander, their 'visible battle' (*visibilis pugna*). These are presented in 'notulae', a pun on musical notes and chapters. For example, the soldier was welcomed by a great gathering of the poor on his return to Canterbury, as the commander was at Jerusalem when he approached his passion. The commander was crucified by four soldiers, the soldier similarly killed by four.[113] Such parallels had been drawn by other writers soon after Thomas's death.[114]

The second *melus*, on the 'visible palm' (*visibilis palma*) of the soldier and commander, addresses correspondence between their victorious deaths, as shown in the aftermath. This is the section of most historical interest, as it provides unique information on the penance of the murderers and the king, and on the cult. Herbert discusses how those who shed Thomas's blood were themselves washed clean in the

---

[109] Smalley, *Becket Conflict*, pp. 80–1.

[110] See n.2 above.

[111] Herbert discusses the principles behind these parallels: *Liber Melorum*, PL, 190.1329.

[112] Thomas also uses a musical allegory in the sermon for St Thomas's Day, which follows on from the *Liber Melorum* in the Arras manuscript: PL, 190.1403–13; see P. B. Roberts, *Thomas Becket in the Latin Preaching Tradition* (Turnhout, 1993), p. 25.

[113] *Liber Melorum*, PL, 190.1295, 1298.

[114] E.g. William of Canterbury, *MTB*, iii, 1–2.

blood of the martyr. Thanks to the martyr's intervention, they were saved, making a pilgrimage to Jerusalem and dying there.[115] Herbert describes the pilgrimage of Louis VII to the martyr's tomb, before turning to the penance of Henry II. He reports that the king had spoken to him about the murder, and insisted that it had not been carried out through him, but accepted that it had been done on his behalf and in order to seek his favour. He also discusses pilgrimage to Thomas's tomb, and the use of phials to carry the 'water of St Thomas'. If, up to now, Herbert has been concerned with the parallels between events in the life, death and triumph of Thomas and Christ, in the second part of the second *melus* he dwells on certain symbols associated with Thomas and their biblical parallels, for example, between Thomas's phials and Christ's cross, and between Thomas's garments and those of the ancient Israelites.

The third *melus* occupies almost two-thirds of the whole, and marks a turn away from history, hagiography and personal reminiscence to theology. Here, in exploring the 'invisible reward' (*invisibilis palma*) of the soldier and commander, parallels are replaced by unity. Instead of Thomas responding to the song of the commander, he and the other saints now sing in unity with Him. The music is more highly pitched and more subtle. The stated theme is the unity of Thomas and Christ, or, more generally, of God and his saints, and while Herbert sometimes refers specifically to Thomas, more often he discusses the saints in general. He distinguishes three unities: the unity of nature alone, that is, the unity of three things in God; the unity of grace alone, that is, in God between God and man assumed into the unity of person; and the unity of nature and grace, being the unity between the Lord the bridegroom and the church the bride. One of the most notable aspects of the third *melus* occurs in Herbert's discussion of the first unity where he outlines eight proofs of the existence of God. Weiss sees these proofs as largely platonic, but although their elements are common in tradition, they do not seem to have been copied from any known source.[116] Herbert also includes an extended discussion of contemplation, which look back primarily to Hugh of St Victor. Weiss suggests that the main influence on Herbert's discussion is Hugh of St Victor's *Commentary on the Celestial Hierarchy of Saint Dionysius the Areopagite*,[117] perhaps via the teaching of Richard of St Victor. The second unity concerns the second person of the Trinity, and the combination of human and divine nature in Christ. God, he writes, chose to become man to invite all men to the third unity, the unity of Christ and the church, of God and the saints. Herbert devotes less space to this third unity because of the difficulty of knowing about it, since it concerns their unity in the next world, or momentarily in this world as in the case of theophany. Herbert confesses that, not

---

[115] *Liber Melorum*, PL, 190.1303–5. Herbert's account of the murderers' fate has been shown to be more plausible than previously thought: see N. Vincent, 'The Murderers of Thomas Becket', in *Bischofsmord im Mittelalter: Murder of Bishops*, ed. N. Fryde and D. Reitz (Göttingen, 2003), pp. 211–72.

[116] See Doyle, *Peter Lombard and His Students*, pp. 234–5.

[117] PL, 175.923–1154.

being among the elect few, he does not have the gift of theophany.[118] He is unable to describe the divine essence or approach God through scripture. Rather, he is 'like a hungry man carrying on his journey unbroken bread, the kernel in the shell, the marrow in the bone'.[119] The *Liber Melorum* is nonetheless evidence of the scale of his ambition, beginning as it does with his friend Thomas and developing towards a vision of heaven.

Letter collection

One of the more neglected of Herbert's works is his letter collection. It survives in one manuscript, Cambridge, Corpus Christi College MS 123, fols. 1r–64v, a fourteenth-century copy. The collection was printed by J. A. Giles in 1846, and reprinted by Migne, but many of the letters are abridged, and in some cases most of the letter has been left unprinted.[120] The fullest discussion of the collection to date is Julie Barrau's article below.[121] Barrau sees it as likely that Herbert himself put the collection together towards the end of his life. The rubrics are quite personal, indicating that he is writing 'in exile', or 'against' his enemies, or 'in exile after the martyrdom of St Thomas'.[122] Though the manuscript is missing something at the beginning and end, it includes forty-seven letters, as well as the text of Henry II's settlement with the papacy at Avranches in 1172 and an unidentified final fragment.

The collection reflects quite well the variety of Herbert's interests, though there is an emphasis on his association with Thomas Becket, and the years *c.* 1174–*c.* 1189 go unrepresented. The first letter, written during Herbert's first exile at Sens, is a long disquisition on the identity of the biblical Salome and questions concerning St Anne, the Virgin's mother, addressed to Henry the Liberal, count of Champagne.[123] Herbert's letter to Henry, newly promoted bishop of Bayeux, is written in the style of Bernard of Clairvaux's *De Consideratione*.[124] He includes an exchange of letters with the abbot of St Crispin's, Soissons that indicates his reputation as a writer of

---

[118] *Liber Melorum*, PL 190.1369.

[119] *Liber Melorum*, PL, 190.1365: 'tanquam famelicus portans per viam panem infractum in testa nucleum et in osse medullam'.

[120] *Herberti de Boseham ... opera*, ed. Giles, ii, pp. 207–310. Giles's edition was reprinted in PL 190.1415–74 (henceforth *HB*). The manuscript is accessible via Parker Library on the Web: https://parker.stanford.edu/parker/catalog/fs557zw6332.

[121] See below, pp. 87–103.

[122] E.g. *HB*, no. 19, *PL*, 190.1448: 'Epistola Herberti jam exsulantis ad Gregorium abbatem de Malmesberia'; no. 33, *PL*, 190.1465: 'Epistola Herberti in persona Willelmi Senonensis archiepiscopi ad Alexandrum papam contra interfectores Sancti Thomae Cantuariensis archiepiscopi et martyris'; no. 38, *PL*, 190.1468: 'Epistola Herberti exsulantis post Sancti Thomae martyrium ad Joannem Pictaviensem episcopum'.

[123] *HB*, no. 1, *PL*, 190.1415–22.

[124] *HB*, no. 21, *PL*, 190.1456. Most remains unprinted: see CCCC 123, fols 42r–44r.

sermons.[125] And he writes to the abbot of Vézelay about the treatment of heretics.[126] But a larger proportion of the letters concern either Herbert's struggle, along with Thomas Becket, before 29 December 1170, or his continuation of that struggle just after the murder. Eleven of the letters are written in Thomas's name, some of which appear in the Canterbury collection of Thomas's letters but with variations.[127] It is likely that many of these were not sent, but some of their arguments would find their way into the *Historia*. For example, Herbert includes three responses to the English bishops' appeal against Thomas of 1166.[128] The first that he includes is his own, *Exspectans expectavi*, a long and learned assertion of the right of a prelate to stand up to secular authority. These arguments were later incorporated into the *Historia* as speeches of Thomas and his *eruditi* during the exile in which they worked out the correct response to the tyranny of the royal power.[129]

The letters that post-date the martyrdom are just as interesting. They fill in vital information about Herbert's second exile in France, his difficulties in adjusting to life after Thomas's departure and his rage at those – seculars and ecclesiastics – who stood in the way of Thomas's cause. The tone is often melodramatic and self-pitying, but these letters are self-revelatory in the same ways as his *Historia* is. Here Herbert frequently presents himself as a living relic of the martyr, wandering in pilgrimage amid fire and waves. There is a certain irony in the fact that his laments about being left alone to carry on the struggle are often addressed to those who had been Thomas's allies and continued to venerate his memory: John of Salisbury, Gunther, John of Poitiers. But although we see expressions of affection in Herbert's letters to these men and others, including Hugh du Puiset, bishop of Durham, and William Longchamp, bishop of Ely, there are no sustained communications with ecclesiastics, as there are in the letter collections of John of Salisbury or Peter of Celle. Herbert's letters tend to say more about himself than they do about his correspondents, and for that they are valuable in themselves.

Psalterium cum commento

In the middle of the twentieth century, Neil Ker made a remarkable discovery in the Library of St Paul's Cathedral, London. A manuscript in Case B. 13, listed simply as 'Psalterium. Fourteenth century' in the catalogue,[130] was in fact a copy of a previ-

---

[125] *HB*, nos. 22–3, *PL*, 190.1456–8. The one sermon that survives is found in the *Thomus: Homilia de natalitio martyris dei*, *PL*, 190.1403–13.

[126] *HB*, no. 29, *PL*, 190.1462–3.

[127] *HB*, nos. 2–3, 8–11, 15, 20, 26–8.

[128] *HB*, no. 15, *PL*, 190.1439–40=*MTB*, v, 459–78 no. 221; *HB*, no. 16, *PL*, 190.1439–47=*MTB*, v, 478–90 no. 222; *HB*, no. 17, *PL*, 190.1447=*CTB*, 388–425 no. 95. See Barrau, below, pp. 91–2.

[129] See Staunton, *Thomas Becket and His Biographers*, pp. 124–7.

[130] W. S. Simpson, *St Paul's Cathedral Library. A Catalogue* (London, 1893), p. 68; St Paul's MS 2, catalogued by N. R. Ker, *Medieval MSS in British Libraries I: London* (Oxford, 1969), p. 241. Weiss, 'Herbert of Bosham's *Liber Melorum*', p. 45, notes that around the same time Artur Landgraf noticed this manuscript without remark and identified the

ously unknown work by Herbert of Bosham. Not only that, but it turned out to be a highly unusual work that revealed a final act to Herbert's life, and an entirely new facet to his talents. Herbert had produced a commentary on the Psalms in the *Hebraica* version – that is, the version which Jerome translated from the Hebrew, rather than the Gallican version usually used. And instead of commenting on the spiritual sense of this most mystical and prophetic of biblical books, Herbert chose to set forth its literal meaning. The full significance of this discovery was soon recognised by Beryl Smalley and Raphael Loewe. Smalley, calling it 'perhaps the most exciting specimen of biblical scholarship produced by a Latin writer of the later twelfth century',[131] showed that it revealed Herbert's hitherto underappreciated connections to Victorine scholars of the literal sense, and an entirely unknown familiarity with the Hebrew language and Jewish scholarship. Loewe published excerpts and investigated Herbert's linguistic range and source material, and his conclusion was a striking one: that Herbert was the most competent Christian Hebraist between Jerome in the fifth century and Johann Reuchlin in the fifteenth.[132] Though the last to be discovered, the *Psalterium cum commento* has since become the best studied of Herbert's works. In 2006 Deborah Goodwin published a book-length study of the work, and this was followed by Eva De Visscher's monograph of 2014.[133] Though Goodwin and De Visscher each take Herbert's *Psalterium* as their topic, their approaches are very different: Goodwin pays more attention to Herbert's approach to the literal sense and how his study of Hebrew led him to a deeper understanding of Jewish thought; De Visscher's main concern is an analysis of Herbert's grasp of Hebrew vocabulary, grammar and idiom, and thus his sources, and how he fits into a web of interconnected Hebraist texts during the period. For an understanding of the *Psalterium cum commento* and its place within medieval Christian Hebraism, it is essential to read both.

The *Psalterium* is prefaced by a dedicatory letter to Peter, bishop of Arras (1184–1203), in which Herbert outlines the circumstances in which it was written and his

---

author as 'Herbert of Boscham': *Einführung in die Geschichte Der Theologischen Literatur Der Fruühscholastik* (Regensburg, 1948), p. 55.

[131] Smalley, 'Commentary on the *Hebraica*', p. 29.

[132] R. Loewe, 'Herbert of Bosham's Commentary on Jerome's Hebrew Psalter', *Biblica* 34 (1953), pp. 44–77, 159–92, 275–98, at 54; see also R. Loewe, 'The Mediaeval Christian Hebraists of England: Herbert of Bosham and Earlier Scholars', *Transactions of the Jewish Historical Society of England* 17 (1953), 225–49.

[133] Goodwin, '*Take Hold of the Robe*'; De Visscher, *Reading the Rabbis*. See also D. Goodwin, 'Herbert of Bosham and the Horizons of Twelfth-Century Exegesis', *Traditio* 58 (2003), 133–73; eadem, 'Nothing in Our Histories: A Postcolonial Perspective on Twelfth-Century Christian Hebraism', *Medieval Encounters* 15 (2009), 35–65; E. De Visscher, 'Putting Theory into Practice? Hugh of Saint Victor's Influence on Herbert of Bosham's *Psalterium cum commento*', in *Bibel und Exegese in der Abtei Saint-Victor zu Paris: Form und Funktion eines Grundtextes im europäischen Rahmen*, ed. R. Berndt (Münster, 2009), pp. 491–502; E. De Visscher, '"Closer to the Hebrew": Herbert of Bosham's Interpretation of Literal Exegesis', in *The Multiple Meaning of Scripture: The Role of Exegesis in Early-Christian and Medieval Culture*, ed. I. van't Spijker (Leiden, 2009), pp. 249–72.

purpose in producing such a commentary.[134] He says that during the previous year he had transferred from the turbulence of the court (possibly a reference to service to William Longchamp) to the tranquillity of the monastery of Ourscamp in the diocese of Arras. Peter had given him the choice of becoming a monk, of teaching or of writing, and he had chosen the latter. The result is 'a new edition of the Psalter translated by father Jerome into the Latin language from the Hebrew truth, untouched up to these days by the doctors'.[135] He does not, he says, strive to attain to the heights of the spiritual sense, but instead, like a crawling animal, he cleaves to the ground, following only the lowest sense. Here, then, Herbert sets out quite clearly what his work amounts to: a unique commentary on the literal sense of the Psalter in Jerome's *Hebraica* version.

Herbert was correct in his claim: no Christian commentator is known to have expounded the literal sense of the Psalter. Herbert had already shown some interest in exegesis of the literal sense in his letter of 1166/7 in which he refuted the legend of the triple marriage of St Anne and sought to establish accurately the identity of Salome.[136] No doubt a strong influence in this regard was the school of St Victor. Hugh of St Victor recommended that the letter of the text, its sense and its contextual meaning be studied before advancing to the spiritual senses.[137] There is also a direct connection to Hugh's pupil, Andrew of St Victor, in Herbert's preface to the *Psalterium cum commento*, which shows strong similarities to Andrew's general prologue to his exposition on the twelve prophets.[138] Herbert had already shown an interest in textual criticism and Hebraism in his revision of Peter Lombard's *Magna Glosatura*. In the preface to that work he said that he had edited the Psalms text from a number of manuscripts and had compared the *Hebraica* version to the text used by Peter Lombard. He notes that they differ in many respects and that these differences have given rise to disputes with Jews.[139] There he also includes the *Hebraica* text, and some marginal notes relate to Hebrew and to rabbinical sources. In the *Historia*, too, his digression on the doubts regarding the Incarnation veer into a discussion of Old Testament sacrifices and Jewish views of the Messiah.[140] But none of his earlier works give any sign of the scale of Herbert's knowledge of Hebrew or engagement with Jewish scholarship that is revealed in the *Psalterium cum commento*.

No Hebrew characters appear in Herbert's work, but the *Psalterium* includes more than 100 Hebrew words in Latin transliteration – a common practice among

---

[134] Printed in Smalley, 'Commentary on the *Hebraica*', pp. 31–2.

[135] Smalley, 'Commentary on the *Hebraica*', p. 32: 'psalterii editionem novam a patre Ieronimo sermone latino ab hebraica veritate translatam, et usque ad hos dies a doctoribus intactam'.

[136] *HB*, no. 1, *PL*, 190.1369; Smalley, 'Commentary on the *Hebraica*', pp. 35–40.

[137] Goodwin, *'Take Hold of the Robe'*, p. 55.

[138] *Andreae de Sancto Victore opera. 8. Expositionem super duodecim prophetas*, ed. F. A. Van Liere and M. A. Zier (Turnhout, 2007), *CCCM*, 53G; Smalley, 'Commentary on the *Hebraica*', p. 43.

[139] Glunz, *History*, p. 344.

[140] See above, p. 16–17, and below, pp. 156–7.

Christian Hebraists and a precaution against scribal error. The Hebrew vocabulary that is displayed far surpasses that of contemporary Christian Hebraists such as Andrew of St Victor. It raises questions about how much Hebrew Herbert knew and how he learned it. He mentions in the preface that he learned Greek and Hebrew in the first years of his youth, and De Visscher has suggested that his first encounter with Hebrew may have been with the Jewish community in Chichester, near Bosham.[141] As for other Christian Hebraists, an important starting point was Jerome, whom he calls 'the modern alumnus of the synagogue, the foundation of all learning'.[142] Jerome provided Herbert with his base text, the Psalms *iuxta Hebraeos*, i.e. translated directly from the Hebrew Bible, and his tracts on vocabulary and translation from Hebrew (*On Hebrew Names*, *On Hebrew Places* and *Questions in Genesis*) provided a linguistic and methodological basis for Herbert's work. Some of these texts are recorded in Pontigny's library by 1175, so Herbert may have accessed them well before his time in Ourscamp.

De Visscher has established close parallels between Herbert's work and a number of Hebrew–Latin psalters that circulated in England in the twelfth and thirteenth centuries. These include Scaliger 8, a Hebrew psalter with Latin glosses produced in England and pre-dating Herbert's *Psalterium*. Herbert may have used the *Eadwine Psalter*, produced at Christ Church, Canterbury *c.* 1155–60, and including the *Hebraica* version among five translations of the Psalms. Such multilingual psalters might have helped Herbert to develop his knowledge of the Hebrew language, and at the same time influenced his textual criticism and understanding of Jewish exegesis. He may also have had access to other aids known to have circulated in the thirteenth century, such as a dictionary or Hebrew–French glossaries. What is certain is that he directly consulted the commentary on the Psalms by Rashi (Rabbi Solomon ben Isaac of Troyes, *c.* 1040–1105), the main Jewish authority of the period on literal exegesis, whom he sometimes acknowledges as '*litterator*'. Rashi's influence is present on every page. As Smalley puts it, Herbert uses Rashi as another commentator might use a Christian exegete as his one basic source, from which he occasionally diverges.[143] Rashi provides him with essential information on the meaning of Hebrew words, and also gives him access to a wider rabbinical tradition. Herbert draws on some of Rashi's other works too, and on other rabbinical sources – the Midrash Tehillim, Talmud, Targums and Mahberet Manahem – but it seems that this knowledge came to him indirectly. This degree of engagement with rabbinical sources is extraordinary for the time.

Most intriguing of all is Herbert's reference to another source of information. On Psalm 88 (89) he writes that the words 'were translated faithfully into Latin by my *loquax*'.[144] Who is this 'talkative one', and is it the same person he refers to

---

[141] De Visscher, *Reading the Rabbis*, p. 5.

[142] Smalley, 'Commentary on the *Hebraica*', p. 34.

[143] Smalley, 'Commentary on the *Hebraica*', p. 50.

[144] *Psalterium*, fol. 109r: et ipsa eciam explanationis verba secundum quod ab Hebreo in Latinum per loquacem meum fide, ni fallor, translata sunt. See De Visscher, *Reading the Rabbis*, pp. 79–80.

elsewhere as *litterator meus*? Scholars have agreed that such references, combined with the remarkable display of knowledge of Hebrew and rabbinical thought, suggest that Herbert was assisted in his task by a Jewish teacher or teachers. Such assistance would have allowed Herbert, even with limited proficiency in Hebrew, to access translations from the Masoretic text and Rashi, and perhaps also the other rabbinical sources that he draws on. Personal interaction with his '*loquax*' and textual interaction with Rashi deepened his familiarity with the Hebrew text but also opened up new exegetical horizons – Goodwin sees him as a 'cultural Hebraist' whose contact with Jewish thought changed his perspective on certain questions.[145] He sometimes criticises Jewish interpretations of the Psalms, and in particular their avoidance of messianic readings, but he was unusually well informed about Jewish messianic thinking, and could see discrepancies between the Messiah awaited by Christians and that awaited by Jews. His approach is far from polemical, and his attitude to Jews lacks any evident hostility.

Herbert probably wrote his commentary in the 1190s, but the St Paul's manuscript is a thirteenth-century copy. The donor, Master Henry of Cornhill, became chancellor of St Paul's in 1217 and dean in 1243, and died in 1254. Current opinion points to a date of *c*. 1220–*c*.1240, with the earlier range more likely, and a French or possibly English origin. Written in parchment, the Psalter text is in large characters, followed by the commentary in smaller hand, and occasional interlinear glosses.[146] There is no evidence of its being used in the Middle Ages. The dedicatory letter is printed by Smalley, and Loewe transcribed some passages of the text,[147] but the rest remains unedited.

Afterlife

Although Herbert, in exile after Thomas's murder, wrote of England that he had no friend in that land of forgetfulness,[148] he was never entirely forgotten there. Gervase of Canterbury, a prominent representative of the next generation at Christ Church, wrote fondly of him, and directed readers of his *Chronica* to Herbert's *Historia*.[149] A thirteenth-century obituary list at Christ Church remembered him on 20 November and called him 'our brother'.[150] Though his works were seldom copied, the *Psalterium cum commento* survives in a manuscript from the thirteenth century, and the letters in a fourteenth-century copy. As mentioned, substantial sections of the *Historia* were included in composite Lives of Becket, and in the fifteenth century his *Historia* was used as the basis of an epic poem by a monk of Canterbury.

---

[145] Goodwin, '*Take Hold of the Robe*', pp. 4–6, 208–25.

[146] Smalley, 'Commentary on the *Hebraica*', pp. 29–30. Goodwin, '*Take Hold of the Robe*', pp. 64–6.

[147] Smalley, 'Commentary on the *Hebraica*', pp. 31–2; Loewe, 'Herbert of Bosham's Commentary'.

[148] *HB*, no. 30, *PL*, 190.1464: 'in terra illa oblivionis amicum non habere'.

[149] Gervase, i, pp. 175, 393–4.

[150] See Cleaver below, p. 86.

Herbert's position as an advisor of Thomas Becket established him forever as a minor player at least in twelfth-century English history.

It was in the Victorian era that Herbert's work was first properly recognised and brought to wider attention. As Nicholas Vincent outlines below,[151] the most important figure in bringing Herbert to a wider audience was John Allen Giles, an accident-prone clergyman and prolific author who published Herbert's *Historia*, *Liber Melorum* and letters in two volumes of his *Lives and Letters of Thomas Becket* (1845–46). These editions, pirated by J.-P. Migne in his *Patrologia Latina* vol. 190, remain the main point of access for the *Liber Melorum* and the letters. The standard edition of the *Historia* remains that edited by James Craigie Robertson in vol. III of his *Materials for the History of Thomas Becket, Archbishop of Canterbury* published by the Rolls Series in 1877. Although both Giles and Robertson appreciated the historical value of these works, they were scathing about Herbert's tendency to veer into lengthy theological or self-referential digressions. Giles knew of Herbert's revision of Peter Lombard's *Great Gloss*, but suggested it would be best to let it slumber in the Bodleian.

The discovery of the *Psalterium cum commento* in the middle of the next century prompted a reassessment of Herbert's work as a whole.[152] Beryl Smalley and Raphael Loewe established without doubt that Herbert was a biblical exegete of some importance and originality. Smalley also took the crucial step of connecting Herbert the Paris-trained theologian to Herbert the politician and ally of Thomas Becket. In *The Becket Conflict and the Schools* (1973), she demonstrated how Herbert and other intellectuals shaped Thomas's struggle and cast it in theological terms. It is hard to improve on her description there of Herbert as 'a colourful character who enjoyed a scrap … a gifted writer, an original thinker, an artist and the best Hebraist of his century'.[153] Smalley's scholarship has remained fundamental to our understanding of Herbert's life and work, but in recent decades others have increasingly taken up her challenge to study Herbert 'thoroughly and "in the round" as a twelfth-century man of letters'.[154] Manuscript scholars and art historians have taken much interest in his edition of Peter Lombard's *Great Gloss*. Scholars of the Becket dispute and the materials produced by it have found further depths to Herbert's *Historia* and letters. The *Liber Melorum* has, finally, received some focused attention. And the *Psalterium cum commento* has been the subject of two monographs,[155] making it the best studied of Herbert's works.

At this point the most pressing need is for new editions, especially of the letter

---

[151] See below, pp. 127–55.

[152] One group of works has remained undiscovered: Herbert's sermons. His friend, the abbot of St Crispin's, Soissons, wrote to ask Herbert to send him some of his sermons. See *HB*, no, 23, *PL*, 190.1457; Smalley, *Becket Conflict*, pp. 65–6. The one that survives is found in the *Thomus: Homilia de natalitio martyris dei*, *PL*, 190.1403–13. Smalley, *Becket Conflict*, p. 62, rejected a tentative attribution of a group of theological works to Herbert by P. Glorieux, 'Essai sur les "Quaestiones in epistolas Pauli"', *RTAM* 19 (1952), 48–59.

[153] Smalley, *Becket Conflict*, p. 59.

[154] Smalley, 'Commentary on the *Hebraica*', p. 65.

[155] Goodwin, '*Take Hold of the Robe*'; De Visscher, *Reading the Rabbis*. See n.1 above.

collection, the *Psalterium* and the *Great Gloss*, which have been only partially edited, and also of the *Historia* and the *Liber Melorum*, for which we still rely on the work of Giles and Robertson. It is to be hoped too that specialists will continue the effort to place Herbert in his twelfth-century intellectual context, to investigate further the influences on his thought and to establish where his work echoes that of contemporaries and the degree to which he stands apart from them. Something that all students of Herbert's work will acknowledge is the sense that there remains much more to find out.

What is it that makes Herbert, in all his admitted long-windedness, self-indulgence and obscurity, worth reading? I would point to two characteristics that make him an intriguing and compelling writer. One is the way that he combines the spiritual and the worldly, the transcendent and the mundane. Herbert grappled with great themes: the relationship between secular and spiritual power, the union of God and the saints, the coming of the Messiah. He could set out proofs for God's existence and reflect at length on the nature of divine contemplation. But he could also make hard-headed arguments against Henry II's policies, or consider the financial practicalities of the archbishop's exile. He paid as much attention to establishing the meaning of biblical names and places, carefully sifting the linguistic and historical evidence, as he did to the spiritual meaning of the Psalms. Another striking characteristic of Herbert is the way that he moves between the public and the private, the abstract and the personal. It is there not only in his witness to the life of Thomas Becket, or the debt to his teacher that he paid in the revision of the Great Gloss, or the laments at his isolation that punctuate his later letters. When he discussed the eucharist, he began from the point of view of his own doubts on the subject; when he discussed theophany he acknowledged that he did not have access to it. Even when explaining the meaning of Hebrew terms, he shows himself working out those meanings with the assistance of an interlocutor. In his writings we see huge ambition, erudition and originality. At the same time, and to a degree seldom found among contemporaries, we are able to observe the writer as he goes about his work, and glimpse, as he would put it himself, not only what he did but the mind of the doer.[156]

---

[156] *MTB*, iii, 248: 'non solum facta, sed et animum facientis'.

CHAPTER TWO

Master Herbert:
Becket's *eruditus*, Envoy, Adviser, and Ghost-Writer?

Anne J. Duggan

The eruditus

Herbert of Bosham is a first-hand witness of the whole of Becket's career from the chancellorship to his canonisation, excepting only the martyrdom itself. Yet this awkward, courageous, challenging theologian, formed in the Parisian schools and enquiring enough to learn and use Hebrew to considerable effect, is hard to fit into the *eruditi* about whom he left those tantalising thumbnail sketches in his *catalogus*.[1] Herbert saw the *eruditi* in biblical terms. The *catalogus eruditorum* was modelled on the list of King David's mighty warriors (*nomina fortium*) at the end of the second Book of Kings (2 Sam.), who were described in the First Book of Chronicles as 'the leaders of King David's powerful men, who helped him maintain his rule over all of Israel in accordance with the Lord's word that was spoken to Israel'.[2] David's warriors had been strong in arms, but Becket's *eruditi* were powerful in writing (*scripturis*),[3] their mission to defend the God-given authority of their 'David'.[4] Herbert's view of the

---

[1] Herbert's *catalogus eruditorum* is in Book vii of his *Vita sancti Thome*: *MTB*, iii, 155–534, at 523–31.

[2] 2 Kings (2 Sam.) 23:8–39; cf. 1 Chron. 11:10–46, at 10: 'Hi principes virorum fortium David, qui adjuverunt eum ut rex fieret super omnem Israel, juxta verbum Domini quod locutus est ad Israel.' Ralph Niger was later (c. 1190) to apply the analogy of Elijah and Ahab to St Thomas and Henry II in his commentary on the Book of Kings in Lincoln, Dean and Chapter MS 26, fol. 100vb, at 3 Kings 19:4. This discovery is Professor Vincent's, whom I thank warmly. Note that Herbert also compared Thomas to Elijah, below, at n.142.

[3] *Vita, MTB*, iii, 207.

[4] First introduced in connection with Becket's appointment as archdeacon (*archileuita*) of Canterbury (*Vita, MTB*, iii, 169; cf. 171, 'iuuenis noster rex David', it reappeared in *Vita*, Book vi, as Herbert approached the account of the final 'single combat of our David' (ibid., 495: 'nostri Dauid monomachia'), although the alternative portrayal as champion of the Most High had already been introduced in Book iv.26 (ibid., 427), and 'Christ's champion' became a *leitmotif*: 'fortis Christi athleta' (ibid., 466); 'fortis ille athleta Domini arietem Dominici gregis se recognoscens, non cogitabat de fuga sed de pugna, iam intelligens se non ad homines, sed ad bestias pugnaturum ouibus suis sic conuersis in lupos' (ibid., 483–4). The 'champion' image ran through the whole Life, from the letter of dedication to Archbishop Baldwin, 'Vobis enim presertim exemplum dedit exemplaris

role of the archbishop's *familia* was thus informed by stirring images from the heroic history of Israel. Like David's fearless warriors, the *eruditi* stood valiantly beside Christ's champion (*Domini/Christi/athleta*) in the fight for God's law.

Not all the warriors were equal, however. Herbert's conviction that theology, and especially the study of sacred scripture, was the superior science led him to express a distinct coolness towards the 'the crowd (*turba*) of men learned in public law (*in iure forensi*)', which the archbishop always had about him for secular disputes (*ad seculi jurgia*). These employed 'not theological, but a kind of civic eloquence', or, to put it more directly, 'not Godly eloquence, but the language of the town'. 'There is nothing between them and me', wrote Herbert, possibly echoing Tertullian's famous words,[5] 'nor, indeed, do they share this fellowship (*mensa*). Different is their profession; different their fellowship'.[6] There was thus a certain ambivalence in his attitude to the *eruditi*, of whom at least six were legal specialists,[7] and there was a seventh, William Fitzstephen, the later biographer of Becket, whom Herbert ignored completely. One suspects that Herbert was not entirely at home with his new colleagues, whose expertise was so different from his own.

The chosen twenty included one future pope, one cardinal archbishop to be, one later archbishop-elect, five later bishops and three prospective deans of cathedral chapters,[8] in addition to himself, the *discipulus qui scripsit hec, quasi abortiuus et eruditorum minimus*, and Thomas, of course, archbishop, metropolitan, primate,

---

iste uir, ut, quemadmodum fecit ipse, et uos similiter faciatis [...] Et uobis presertim a Deo uocatis et, si ausis, ni fallor tamen uerentibus tanti athlete inire pugnam, subire curam, implere cathedram' (ibid., 156), to Northampton (ibid., 298, 301, 302), to Sens, 'Nam sicut uulgo dicitur, arma pacem ferunt: et iustitia quidem armata, pax uero laureata et inermis describitur utpote que per athletam iustitiam uincit' (ibid., 350), and reached a crescendo in the account of Becket's murder in Book vi, where the Lord's champion fought his final battle: 'nec ergo ultra est quod uerbis protrahere ualeam, breuem sed fortem pugnam, citam sed gloriosam palmam et coronam triumphantis athlete immarcescibilem' (ibid., 497); 'in hac hora tenebrarum, hunc Petri gladium athleta hic noster prompte et fiducialiter exerit, et hoc sicut sacerdotem decuit suos defendit' (ibid., 499); cf. ibid., 359, 490, 491, 493, 496, 498, 501, 504, 505, 508, 513.

[5] Quintus Septimus Florens Tertulliani (*c.* 160–*c.* 225), *De praescriptioe haereticorum*, c. 7 (*PL*, 2.20): 'Quid ergo Athenis et Hierosolymis? quid Academiae et Ecclesiae? Quid haereticis et Christianis?'

[6] *Vita*, *MTB*, iii, 207: 'Inter istos vero sacre legis apocrisiarios taceo inpresentiarum illam quam ad seculi jurgia secum semper habebat in forensi jure peritorum turbam, non quidem theologam, sed potius ciuicam quandam facundiam exercentes. Nihil modo mihi et illis; nec enim ipsi mense istius commensales. Alia potius horum professio, et communio alia.'

[7] Gerard Pucelle, Gilbert Glanvill, Humbert Crivelli, Lombard of Piacenza, Philip of Calne, Ralph of Sarre and perhaps Ariald and Roland of Lombardy, whom he described as *praepotentes in litteris*: A. J. Duggan, 'The Price of Loyalty: The Fate of Thomas Becket's Learned Household', in *Thomas Becket: Friends, Networks, Texts, and Cult* (Aldershot, 2007), no. III, pp. 1–18; A. J. Duggan, 'Clerks of Thomas Becket (act. 1162–70)', *ODNB*, online (Group), but note that Philip of Calne had a very satisfactory career at Reims.

[8] Duggan, 'The Price of Loyalty'. Master Philip of Calne should properly be placed among the 'loyal'.

legate and martyr. Despite his own ritual expression of humility, Herbert could hold his head high among that learned company. In 1165 Alexander III described him as a man 'renowned for his learning and reputation (*pro litteris et honestate sua celebris*)', who deserved promotion 'in consideration of his erudition and probity (*pro obtentu litterature et probitatis*)',[9] but he could not quite equal John of Salisbury, his 'dear colleague',[10] for John had many advantages over the chancery clerk. He had been the equivalent of legal secretary to the former archbishop Theobald for about fourteen years from late 1147[11] and was poised, perhaps, to retain that position in Becket's *familia*. To Becket's service he brought not only the fruits of one of the best educations of the century and superb literary skills but experience of the papal Curia[12] and a wide circle of friends and contacts in continental Europe. Unlike Herbert, whose

---

[9] *MTB*, v, 241–2 no. 132, at 241.

[10] *PL*, 190.1416, 'dilectus socius noster'.

[11] To whom he had been recommended by none other than Bernard of Clairvaux (*PL*, 182.562 no. 361), who described him as 'amicum meum et amicum meorum'. The letter speaks of an earlier verbal recommendation ('Presens uobis commendaueram eum; sed nunc absens multo magis commendo'), possibly late spring 1147, when Theobald and Bernard were both in Paris at the court of Eugenius III: J. P. Haseldine, 'Monastic Patronage and the Beginning of John of Salisbury's Career, with a Revised Chronology for 1147–1148', *Monastic Research Bulletin* 18 (2012), 30–5, at 33. He was not Theobald's *cancellarius*: that office was held by Philip, archdeacon of Norwich, throughout Theobald's archiepiscopate: A. Saltman, *Theobald Archbishop of Canterbury* (London, 1956), **255, 262, 263, 273, 278, 307, 308,** 322 (where *Thom' Lund'* precedes him), 346 (where *Thoma de london'* precedes him, **347,** 368, 378 (where, unsurprisingly, *Thoma Cant' archidiacono* precedes him), **399,** 403, 404 (where *Thoma Lond'* precedes him), 464, **465,** 474 (where *Thoma Lond'* precedes him), **536.** Bold type indicates where Philip precedes John of Salisbury. For John's position in the absence of Master Philip, see ibid., 242 (John precedes Vacarius), 246, 283 (*Thoma London'* precedes him), 317, 370 (*Thoma de London'* precedes him), 405 (*Thoma Londoniensi* precedes him), 482 (*Thomas clericus de Lond'* precedes him), 496 (Vacarius precedes him in the list of *magistri*).

[12] See the summary in D. Luscombe, 'Salisbury, John of (late 1110s–1180)', *ODNB*; cf. F. Barlow, 'John of Salisbury and His Brothers', *Journal of Ecclesiastical History* 16 (1995), 95–109, at 100–8. For his legal learning, see especially M. Kerner, 'Johannes von Salisbury und das gelehrte Rechte', *Proceedings of the Ninth International Congress of Medieval Canon Law, Munich, 13–18 July 1992*, ed. P. Landau and J. Mueller, Monumenta Iuris Canonici. Series C: Subsidia vol. 10 (Vatican, 1997), pp. 503–21, and G. Miezka, 'Zur Benutzung der *Summa Codicis Trecensis* bei Johannes von Salisbury', in *The World of John of Salisbury*, ed. M. Wilks, Studies in Church History, Subsidia 3 (Oxford, 1984), pp. 381–99. For the later influence of the *Policraticus*, see W. Ullmann, 'The Influence of John of Salisbury on Italian Jurists', *EHR* 59 (1944), 384–93; repr. with the same pagination in W. Ullmann, *The Church and the Law in the Earlier Middle Ages. Selected Essays* (London, 1975), no XV. Whether one should go as far as Christopher Brooke in his excellent overview of John of Salisbury, and call John 'a professional lawyer' (C. N. L. Brooke, 'John of Salisbury and his World', in *The World of John of Salisbury*, pp. 1–20, at 7), is doubtful. He could and did draft *apostoli* for Archbishop Theobald, and represented him at the papal Curia, and he could accurately cite the Justinianic corpus (as he did in *Policraticus*) and the *Decretum Gratiani*, but his own intellectual tastes lay elsewhere. See now the splendid collection of studies edited by C. Grellard and F. Lachaud, *A Companion to John of Salisbury*, Brill's Companions to the Christian Tradition, 57 (Leiden, 2015).

scholarly works were all produced during and after the exile, John had already
dedicated his *Policraticus, Metalogicon* and *Entheticus* to Thomas the Chancellor
in 1159;[13] his first letter collection, based on his work for Theobald, was sent to his
old friend and patron, Peter, abbot of Montier-la-Celle *c.* 1161/2;[14] and he was one
of the delegation sent to receive the new archbishop's pallium from Alexander III
at Montpellier in July 1162.[15] His exile, in the course of 1163, and certainly before
Clarendon (January 1164), could be considered providential for Herbert, although
his absence from the critical events of 1164 (Clarendon and Northampton) might
be judged unfortunate for the archbishop.

Herbert's position in the household can be glimpsed from the slim evidence
of witnessed archiepiscopal *acta*. In a confirmation for St Radegund's priory in
Cambridge at the very beginning of Becket's pontificate (1162x1163), he was third, after
Robert (Foliot) archdeacon of Oxford and Master Philip of Calne;[16] in that for Leeds
priory in Kent (1162x1164) he was also third, after Master Arnold of Otford and Master
John of Tilbury.[17] None of the four who preceded him in these charters remained in
Becket's service after 1164/5, however. Robert Foliot withdrew after Clarendon;[18] Philip
of Calne, described as *aegrotatus*,[19] found a place in Reims (for which Thomas recommended him in early 1165,[20] and he received the king's pardon and peace in 1166);[21]
Arnold of Otford is known only from the Leeds charter, and Master John of Tilbury,
who had made an earlier appearance in a notification for Ramsey Abbey on 6 April
1163, described by Herbert as 'an excellent scribe', was 'not summoned'.[22]

---

[13]   *LJS*, i, x. *Policraticus* and *Metalogicon* were among the *Libri Sancti Thome* given to
       Christ Church Canterbury: M. R. James, *The Ancient Libraries of Canterbury and Dover*
       (Cambridge, 1903), p. 85.

[14]   Christopher Brooke (*LJS*, i, ix–x) allowed that there was a possibility that Peter of Celle's
       letter (no. 70, *More sitientis*) acknowleding receipt of a *vasculum litterarum tuarum*
       referred to the *Policraticus*, but my own reading confirms Professor Brooke's, which he
       reaffirmed in a note appended to *The Letters of Peter of Celle*, ed. and trans. J. Haseldine,
       OMT (Oxford, 2001), pp. 716–18. Peter was abbot of Montier-la-Celle (1145–62), abbot of
       St-Rémi of Reims (1162–81), and John's successor as bishop of Chartres (1181–83): *Letters
       of Peter of Celle*, pp. xxxi–xxxii. For suggested redating of some of John's letters, see A. J.
       Duggan, 'Henry II, the English Church and the Papacy', in *Henry II. New Interpretations*,
       ed. C. Harper-Bill and N. Vincent (Woodbridge, 2007), pp. 154–83, at 161.

[15]   *Radulfi de Diceto Decani Lundoniensis Opera Historica: The Historical Works of Master
       Ralph de Diceto, Dean of London*, ed. W. Stubbs, 2 vols, RS 68 (London, 1876), i, p. 307.

[16]   *English Episcopal Acta II. Canterbury 1162–1190*, ed. C. R. Cheney and B. E. A. Jones (Oxford,
       1986), ii, pp. 2–3 no. 3, and Plate I. The terminal date is determined by Robert Foliot's
       withdrawal from Becket's service after the council at Clarendon in January 1164. Herbert is
       followed by 'Roberto capellano, et Willemmo capellano, et Willelmo de Leigrecest'.

[17]   *Canterbury Acta*, p. 11 no. 18.

[18]   Fitzstephen, *MTB*, iii, 46; *Vita, MTB*, iii, book vii (*Catalogus*), 524, 526.

[19]   Fitzstephen, *MTB*, iii, 101.

[20]   *CTB*, i, nos. 56 and 56a; below, n.30.

[21]   Fitzstephen, *MTB*, iii, 101.

[22]   *Canterbury Acta*, ii, pp. 20–1 no. 34; F. Barlow, *Thomas Becket* (London, 1986), Plate 10
       (without the magisterial title).

In one charter for the abbey of St-Bertin at the very beginning of the exile (5x10 November 1164),[23] Herbert appeared fifth, after Archdeacons Baldwin of Norwich and Silvester of Lisieux, Theold, canon of St Martin's and Robert, canon of Merton, Becket's confessor; in the other, of the same date, he was fourth, after Silvester, Theold and Robert,[24] followed in both by Masters Lombard of Piacenza, Ernulf, Gunther of Winchester, Richard of Salisbury, Alexander Walensis *et pluribus aliis.* Of these, Baldwin, Silvester and Theold were fleeting visitors, not members of the *familia,* and Ernulf, who had been keeper of the royal seal when Thomas was chancellor, withdrew from the company in the expectation of a benefice from Rotrou of Rouen.[25] None appears among the *eruditi.* Three years later, in the report of the colloquy at Planches (between Gisors and Trie) in 1167,[26] Herbert was placed second, after John of Salisbury and before Master Lombard of Piacenza, Alexander Galensis and many others.[27] That Herbert ranked before the Bologna-trained lawyer may have given him some satisfaction, in the light of his apparent coolness towards lawyers, even though he placed him second in the *catalogus,* claimed him as a special friend (*comes individuus*) and took advantage of his instruction on the *canones* at Pontigny.[28] Thomas had recruited Lombard to take the place of the civilian Vacarius, who had transferred from Canterbury to York with Roger of Pont l'Évêque in 1154.[29]

---

[23] *Canterbury Acta,* ii, p. 24 no. 39.

[24] *Canterbury Acta,* ii, pp. 24–5 no. 40.

[25] See his plaintive letters to Becket in 1165: *CTB,* i, nos. 64 (1165/66) and 160 (1166x1168), although he transmitted information: i, no 46 (after 2 April 1165), and possibly ii, no. 296 (before 14 June 1170); cf. ibid., ii, 1367–8.

[26] 18 November 1167. Fitzstephen (*MTB,* iii, 95) identifies the location as 'Planches'.

[27] *CTB,* i, 664–75 no. 144, at 664–5: 'archiepiscopus quoque Cantuariensis sedis apostolice tunc nunciatus legatus et cum eo exules eius, Ioannes de Salesberiensi cum Hereberto de Boseham [*corr.*], Lumbardus de Placentia, Alexander Galensis, Gaufridus prior de Penteneia et Garinus canonicus, Robertus [canon of Merton] et Gilebertus [canon from Chicksands Priory] canonici, capellani Cantuariensis: Iohannes Cant' [Planeta], Alanus [unidentified: an 'Alanus' had witnessed a grant for the nuns of SS. Mary and Sexburga of Minster in Sheppey in *Canterbury Acta,* ii, 15 no. 26 (1163x1167): possibly the later Alan of Tewkesbury? (Gervase calls him English)], Ricardus [Peccator, John of Salisbury's brother], Henricus [of Houghton] et multi alii'. M. A. Harris, 'Alan of Tewkesbury and His Letters, I–II', *Studia Monastica* 18 (1976), 77–108 and 299–351.

[28] *Vita, MTB,* iii, 423–4. In the light of Herbert's seeming hostility to lawyers, one should note that he appeared as an assessor with Gerard Pucelle and others, in a case heard by Cardinal Peter (of Pavia) of S. Crisogono in Paris in 1174: below, n.136, and Appendix, pp. 184–7.

[29] Lombard was cardinal deacon of the Roman Church 1170, cardinal priest of S. Cyriaco 1171–79 and archbishop of Benevento 1171–79: *MTB,* iii, 523–4; *Canterbury Acta,* ii, nos. 26, 39–40; K. Ganzer, *Die Entwicklung des auswärtigen Kardinalats im hohen Mittelalter,* Bibliothek des deutschen historischen Instituts in Rom, 26 (Tübingen, 1963), pp. 121–3, correcting Brixius, *Die Mitglieder,* pp. 64, 122; A. J. Duggan, 'Thomas Becket's Italian Network', in *Pope, Church and City: Essays in Honour of Brenda M. Bolton,* ed. F. Andrews et al. (Leiden, 2004), pp. 177–201, at 190–2; *CTB,* ii, 1390–1; J. Taliadoros, *Law and Theology in Twelfth-century England: the works of Master Vacarius (c. 1115/1120–c. 1200)* (Turnhout, 2006).

Although that record may have been drafted by John of Salisbury, it is probably an accurate statement of the relative precedence in the *familia* as it was then constituted. Herbert came second to John, and both may have benefited from the departure of three legal luminaries, Philip of Calne, Ralph of Sarre and Gerard Pucelle. Philip and Ralph found profitable careers in Reims: Philip had a canonry and prebend and taught canon law;[30] Ralph, exiled some time in 1163,[31] had a distinguished career as canon, Master of the schools, archdeacon of Soissons and, for the last thirty years of his life, dean of the cathedral church (1176–96),[32] during which he oversaw the compilation of a large decretal collection (*Brugensis*, post 1189/91).[33] His loyalty to his old master remained constant, however. He was very probably the

---

[30] Peter the Chanter later recalled (in his *Questiones*) that Master Philip of Caune (= Calne), exiled partisan of St Thomas then teaching in Reims, had concluded that the sale of offices was simoniacal, and that Pope Alexander III had said the same: J. W. Baldwin, *Masters, Princes and Merchants: The Social Views of Peter the Chanter and his Circle*, 2 vols (Princeton, 1970), i, p. 176; ii, p. 117 n.4; cf. S. Kuttner and E. Rathbone, 'Anglo-Norman Canonists of the Twelfth Century', *Traditio* 7 (1949/51), 279–339, at 289. Becket's later letter, congratulating Master Fulk on his appointment as dean of Reims in 1167, referred to his earlier patronage of Masters Philip (of Calne), Ralph (of Sarre) and others: *CTB*, i, no. 163, at n.5. I am grateful to Dr Ludwig Falkenstein for confirming (6 March 2013) his conviction that Philip had a canonry and a benefice at either St-Symphorien or SS. Timothé-et-Apollinaire, a dependency of the abbey of Saint-Rémi; cf. P. Demouy, 'Des Anglais à Reims au XIIe siècle, in *La Champagne, terre d'acceuil de l'Antiquité à nos jours*, ed. S. Guilbert (Nancy, 1994), pp. 175–86, at 180. Herbert of Bosham's note in the *catalogus* mistakenly says that he returned to England ('repatriauit').

[31] *Vita*, *MTB*, iii, 526. On Ralph, cf. Smalley, *Becket Conflict*, pp. 210–12.

[32] *CTB*, ii, 1384–5; L. Falkenstein, 'Zu Entstehungsort und Redaktor der Collectio Brugensis', in *Proceedings of the Eighth International Congress of Medieval Canon Law, San Diego*, ed. S. Chodorow (Città del Vaticano, 1992), pp. 117–62, at 140–4 and n.108 (which supersedes W. M. Newman, *Les Seigneurs de Nesle en Picardie, XIIe–XIIIe siècle*, 2 vols [Paris/Philadelphia, 1971], i, pp. 116–17); further refinements in Falkenstein, 'Radulf von Reims als papstlicher Delegat und seine Mitdelegaten', in *Grundlagen des Rechts. Festschrift für Peter Landau zum 65. Geburtstag*, ed. R. Helmholz, P. Mikat, et al. (Paderborn/Munich, etc., 2000), pp. 301–32. Thomas and John of Salisbury unsuccessfully supported his promotion as dean in 1167 (*LJS*, ii, 438–9, at the end of a letter to Walter, cardinal bishop of Albano).

[33] This combined decretals received in Reims with materials from the Wigorniensis-Appendix–Bamberg tradition, which had its roots in England: C. Duggan, *Twelfth-Century Decretal Collections and their Importance in English History* (London, 1963), pp. 54–5, 145–6, 189–91; C. Duggan, 'Decretal Collections from Gratian's *Decretum* to the *Compilationes antiquae*: The Making of the New Case Law', in *The History of Medieval Canon Law in the Classical Period, 1140–1234. From Gratian to the Decretals of Pope Gregory IX*, ed. W. Hartmann and K. Pennington (Washington, DC, 2008), pp. 246–92, at 285–6; Falkenstein, 'Zu Entstehungsort … der Collectio Brugensis', pp. 120, 144; another associate was Garnerus, the scribe who copied *Brugensis* and Burchard of Worms's *Decretum* (Reims, bibl. Mun. MS 674) and was in 1192 appointed as master of the Reims schools by Archbishop William of the White Hands: see P. Landau, with L. Falkenstein, 'Die Dekretsumme "Tractaturus magister" und die Kanonistik in Reims in der zweiten Hälfte des 12. Jahrhunderts', *Zeitschrift der Savigny-Stiftung für Rechtsgeschichte. Kanonistische Abteilung* 131/100 (2014), 132–52, at 145–7.

unnamed *nuntius* who reported to Becket on the doings in the Curia in July 1164;[34] he remained a member of the 'Reims Group', which included Peter of Celle, by then abbot of St-Rémi, John of Salisbury, Philip of Calne and Master Fulk, then canon, later dean of Reims,[35] and he made a splendid donation of thirty-eight volumes to Canterbury after Becket's death, probably in homage to the martyr.[36] Gerard Pucelle's career was equally successful, oscillating between teaching canon law in the schools in Paris and Cologne and serving Becket's successor, Richard of Dover, before election as bishop of Coventry-Lichfield in 1183.[37]

In the light of their subsequent careers, any one of them them might have taken pride of place in Becket's *familia*, had he stayed. Herbert also benefited from John of Salisbury's semi-detached status, living in Reims as the guest of his old friend, Abbot Peter.[38] Apart from Robert of Merton, Becket's confessor, whom Herbert did not include among the *eruditi* and whose influence on the archbishop is nowhere recorded,[39] no one was in more continuous attendance than Master Herbert, his guide in biblical theology. He was present at all the critical moments, had privileged access and, according to his own record, exercised a decisive influence on two or three occasions.

---

[34] *CTB*, i, 120 no. 33.

[35] Fulk, nephew of Dean Leo, was dean of Reims from 1167/8 to 1175.

[36] Between 1170 and 1175, for the donor is named simply 'Ralph of Reims' in one of the surviving volumes (Cambridge, Pembroke College, MS 210) and in Prior Henry of Eastry's catalogue of Christ Church books: James, *Ancient Libraries of Canterbury and Dover*, pp. 86–8; C. F. R. de Hamel, *Glossed Books of the Bible and the Origins of the Paris Book Trade* (Cambridge, 1984), pp. 39–44 and plates 14c and 14e.

[37] Master Gerard was a man of established reputation as a teacher of theology and Roman and Canon Law in Paris (1155–62). He received his first benefice from Thomas and followed him into exile, but there is no mention of his whereabouts until, with papal approval, he went on a mysterious mission to Cologne in late 1165/66. There he established a school of canon law (1166–68), made his peace with Henry II (1168), returned to teach in France (1170–4) and then became a leading light in Archbishop Richard's household (1174–80). He returned to Cologne for a couple of years (1180–82), returned to Canterbury and was elected bishop of Coventry-Lichfield (Sept. 1183–Jan. 1184). For relations with the exiles, see *LJS*, ii, nos. 158, 184–6, 226, 277, 297; *CTB*, i, nos. 107, 168 a–b, 175 at n.3, 176 n.3. For his legal career, see P. Landau, 'Gérard Pucelle und die Dekretsumme *Reverentia sacrorum canonum*: zur Kölner Kanonistik im 12. Jahrhundert', in *Mélanges en l'honneur d'Anne Lefebvre-Teillard*, ed. B. d'Alteroche et al. (Paris, 2009), pp. 623–38, at 627–30; P. Landau, *Die Kölner Kanonistik des 12. Jahrhunderts. Ein Höhepunkt der europäischen Rechtswissenschaft*, Auftrag des Rheinischen Vereins für Rechtsgeschichte e.V. in Köln, part 1, ed. D. Strauch (Badenweiler, 2008), pp. 8–11; A. J. Duggan, 'Making Law or Not? The Function of Papal Decretals in the Twelfth Century', in *Proceedings of the Thirteenth International Congress of Medieval Canon Law, Esztergom 2008* (Plenary Lecture), ed. P. Erdő and S. A. Szuromi (Città del Vaticano, 2010), pp. 41–70, at 44 and 55.

[38] J. Barrau, 'Jean de Salisbury, intermédiaire entre Thomas Becket et la cour capétienne', in *Plantagenêts et Capétiens. Confrontation et héritages*, ed. M. Aurell and N.-Y. Tonnerre (Turnhout, 2006), pp. 505–16, at 516, 'Son rôle fut, au bout du compte, davantage dans la construction de la doxa sur l'archevêque et les autres participants au conflit, que dans une réelle activité diplomatique.'

[39] Barlow (*Thomas Becket*, p. 79) thought that the omission was due to jealousy!

One would be inclined to doubt Herbert's self-regarding claims were it not for Fitzstephen's corroboration of his position as Becket's *magister in divina pagina* and the familiarity that led Becket to share his horse with Herbert at Northampton.[40] And from Fitzstephen's pen comes the physical description:

> Tall, elegant, and finely attired, with a tunic of green cloth of Auxerre and a cloak, hanging from his shoulders to his ankles in the German fashion, becomingly decorated with borders.[41]

This was the man who had the nerve to give Henry II as good as he got at Angers in 1166, when the king called him 'this son of a priest'. 'I am not the son of a priest', he retorted, 'since I was not born in the priesthood, although my father later became a priest, just as he is not the son of a king unless his father was king when he was conceived'.[42] That smart remark probably cost Herbert any hope he had of preferment in England.[43]

One suspects that Thomas saw something of his former self in the fashionable and outspoken cleric, whom he had known in the very different world of the chancery. It is not surprising, then, to learn from Herbert that immediately after his elevation Thomas had asked not only for scriptural tuition but also for guidance on his own demeanour and information on the tittle-tattle among the people.

> 'This I wish, this I enjoin on you, that you should privately and confidentially tell me what men are saying about me [...] For many things may be said about me which are not said to me, in the same way that much may be said about others, and especially the rich: many things may be said about them among the people, but little or nothing to them. Equally, point out any aberration if you yourself should see and judge that it oversteps the limits.' Adding at the end of his speech, 'For four eyes see more carefully and clearly than two'.[44]

Spoken in the first person and addressing Herbert in the colloquial second person, this instruction suggests a close relationship, even friendship, between the two men. Disparate they may have been in status and in learning, but they were about the

---

[40] Fitzstephen, *MTB*, iii, 68.

[41] Fitzstephen, *MTB*, iii, 99–100: 'Ipse, quidem, statura ut erat procerus et forma uenustus, etiam satis splendide erat indutus, habens de quodam panno uiridi Autisiodorensi tunicam et pallium, ab humeris more Alemannorum dependens, ad talos demissum, ornatum decenter contingentibus suis.'

[42] Fitzstephen, *MTB*, iii, 101. Although Henry was the grandson of Henry I, his father was only count of Anjou.

[43] He later (1167) warned an unknown eminent recipient against courtiers who might slander him because he had in the previous year spoken insolently to their lord the king of England: *PL*, 190.1422.

[44] *Vita, MTB*, iii, 186: 'hoc volo, hoc tibi injungo, de cetero quem homines me esse dixerint onfidentius mihi et secreto edicito [...] Multa quippe amodo de me, que non mihi, dicentur, quemadmodum et de aliis, et presertim diuitibus; plurima passim in uulgo de ipsis, et pauca uel nulla ipsis. Pariter et excessum indica, si quo tu ipse uideris et iudicaueris excedentem.' Et in calce sermonis adjiciens, 'Circumspectius quippe [...] et clarius quatuor quam duo oculi uident'.

same age and similar in taste and character. Herbert admired the impressive figure of the chancellor and archbishop, and it is probable that Thomas warmed to the fashionable cleric who spoke his mind.

Envoy

Herbert seems also to have impressed men of power. He had been sent by Henry II as the senior of two emissaries to Frederick I in 1157, with the delicate mission of refusing the emperor's request for the return of the relic of St James which Empress Matilda had brought with her to England, following the death of her husband, Henry V;[45] and Becket sent him to shadow Henry II's envoys to Louis VII and the papal Curia in Sens in 1164. Together with another *cautius … eruditus*, Herbert had a very encouraging interview with King Louis at Compiègne;[46] and although they arrived a day after the king's envoys, they managed to have a quick conversation with Pope Alexander on the evening of their arrival in advance of the formal reception of the royal embassy, which they witnessed.[47] It may be significant that Herbert described his companion as 'more guarded and learned', perhaps in contrast with his own somewhat robust approach. He gives no clue to the man's identity, but Master Henry of Houghton, who had earlier been warmly received by King Louis in late October 1163, is a possibility.[48]

Herbert approached Louis again, two years later in 1166, when the exiles were forced to leave Pontigny;[49] in 1170, after the Peace of Fréteval, accompanied by John of Salisbury, he sought restoration of important lordships from Henry II;[50] and he headed the small party sent to organise the restoration of the exiles' English properties in early October 1170, which involved a mission to the Young King's court.[51] His last mission, after Becket's murder, was again to King Louis and to his brother-in-law William, then archbishop of Sens.[52] The missions to the French court

---

[45] K. J. Leyser, 'Frederick Barbarossa, Henry II and the Hand of St James', *EHR* 90 (1975), 481–506.

[46] *Vita, MTB,* iii, 332–3. It was there that King Louis revealed Henry II's denunciation of 'Thomas, the former archbishop of Canterbury […] publicly condemned in my court as a lawless and perjured traitor' (*MTB,* v, 134 no. 71, *Sciatis quod Thomas,* 'Thomas, qui fuit Cantuariensis archiepiscopus, in curia mea a plenario baronum regni mei concilio ut iniquus et proditor meus et perjurus publice judicatus est') and his own reply (lost).

[47] *Vita, MTB,* iii, 332–5.

[48] When he was on his way to the papal Curia in Sens: see his report, *CTB,* i, no. 20, datable to *c.* 9 Nov. 1163. Fitzstephen recorded Henry as riding immediately in front of the archbishop as they rode away from Montmirail in Jan. 1169: *MTB,* iii, 96–7; cf. *CTB,* i, nos. 12–16, 19 at n.2, 20; Duggan, *Thomas Becket,* pp. 87–9. He was not listed among the *eruditi,* however, and his later career is unknown: *CTB,* ii, 1374–5.

[49] *CTB,* i, no. 108.

[50] The barony of William de Ros, Saltwood Castle, and custody of Rochester Castle.

[51] Their report is *CTB,* ii, no. 311, written before 15 October 1170. Herbert is named as one of the emissaries in *MTB,* vii, 342.

[52] For William of the White Hands, Louis VII's brother-in-law, see L. Falkenstein, 'Wilhelm von Champagne, Elekt von Chartres (1164–1168), Erzbischof von Sens (1168/69–1176),

achieved their objective; those to the English courts failed, but they had little hope of success in the circumstances. In the interview with Henry II, for example, John of Salisbury was rebuffed with the words, 'Oh John, I shall never give you (meaning the archbishop) a castle, unless I first see that you behave differently towards me than you have done hitherto.'[53]

It is noteworthy, however, that, apart from the immediate aftermath of Northampton, Herbert seems not to have represented Thomas at the papal court. That task was given to a succession of other *magistri*: Henry of Houghton (October 1163),[54] Hervey of London (mid-1164–65),[55] Hervey of London and Gunther of Winchester (1165–67),[56] Gilbert Glanvill (mid-1165?),[57] John Planeta (? after 12 June 1166–mid-1167),[58] Alexander Llewellyn and John Planeta (late 1167–70),[59] Master Lombard (mid-1168–late 1168),[60] unnamed messengers (after 2 February 1167;[61]

Erzbischof von Reims (1176–1202), Legat des apostolischen Stuhles, im Spiegel päpstlicher Schreiben und privilegien', *Zeitschrift der Savigny-Stiftung für Rechtsgeschichte. Kanonistische Abteilung* 89 (2003), 107–284; L. Falkenstein, 'Guillaume aux blanches mains archevêque de Reims et légat du siège apostolique (1176–1202)', *Revue d'Histoire de l'Église de France* 91 (2005), 5–25.

[53] *Vita, MTB*, iii, 468.

[54] Above, n.48.

[55] *CTB*, i, nos. 36, 62.

[56] When Alexander III began his journey back to Italy in April 1165 (Alan of Tewkesbury, *MTB*, ii, 347), Thomas followed him as far as Bourges, where he took his leave of the pope, while Hervey and Gunther remained with the Curia. Alexander and John replaced them at the Curia in December 1167: *CTB*, i, no. 62 and n.1.

[57] *CTB*, i, no. 62.

[58] Bearer of the notification of the Vézelay sentences to the Curia (*CTB*, i, nos. 79–80). He was still there in February 1167, when Thomas reported on the consternation caused by the triumphant return of John of Oxford and other royal envoys (*CTB*, i, no. 123), but was back in time for the Gisors-Trie colloquy on 18 November 1167. The use of the form 'Iohannes Cantor' in the account of Gisors-Trie, found in the seventeenth-century edition (R. de Beauchamp, *Historiae Franco-Merovingicae Synopsis* [Douai, 1633], pp. 936–40, at 936), is almost certainly a mistake for 'Iohannes Cant(uariensis)', the name by which he is addressed in Becket's letter (*CTB*, i, no. 123). The correct version 'Iohannes Cant.' occurs in *Vita et processus sancti Thome Cantuariensis martyris super ecclesiastica libertate* (Johannes Philippi: Paris, 1495), sigg. kiirb–kiiiva, at kiirb (*CTB*, i, no. 144, n. *j*).

[59] *CTB*, i, nos. 157, 161; ii, nos. 230, 244, 267 n.4.

[60] He carried *CTB*, i, no. 168 (June 1168) and perhaps also *CTB*, i, no. 172 (after 2 July 1168). When John of Salisbury sent *LJS*, ii, no. 179 (July 1168), Lombard was *en route* to Benevento, where he was appointed *subdiacomus curie*, a position often conferred on legal specialists: A. Ambrosioni, 'Alessandro III e la chiesa Ambrosiana', in *Miscellanea Rolando Bandinelli. Papa Alessandro III*, ed. F. Liotta (Siena, 1986), pp. 1–41. He returned to France in late 1168, for he had received an oral report on the conference at Montmirail (6–7 Jan. 1169) from Bernard de Corilon (*MTB*, vi, no. 451). He probably joined the entourage of William of Sens (*LJS*, ii, no. 286, pp. 630–1), and returned finally to Benevento in autumn 1169, in the company of Archbishop William and the papal envoy Gratian.

[61] Carrying *CTB*, i, nos. 123–6.

mid-1170[62]) and even, on one occasion (*c.* November, 1169), Thomas took advantage of the embassy of two envoys from Archbishop Øystein of Nidaros to transmit a batch of letters to curial recipients.[63] Even after Becket's murder, it was Alexander and Gunther who went again to the Curia in early 1171, carrying letters of protest from France, including one drafted by Herbert, *in persona Willelmi archiepiscopi Senonis*.[64] Either Herbert was too flamboyant to represent the exiled archbishop at the papal Curia, or too highly valued as a reliable confidant, as well as Becket's guide to the deeper mysteries of scripture.[65]

Herbert as counsellor

More controversial is the question of Herbert's role as adviser. Apart from William Fitzstephen's record of his own exchange with Master Herbert at Northampton, intended for Becket's ears, where Fitzstephen, quoting a canon from Gratian, prevailed over Herbert's more robust advice to excommunicate forthwith anyone who laid impious hands on the archbishop,[66] all evidence of Herbert's advisory role comes from his own pen. His interventions range from confidential encouragements to multi-page disquisitions, and twice or possibly three times, on his telling, they had significant effect on the archbishop's course of action.[67]

The first occurred when Thomas poured out his regret for his failings as they rode away from Clarendon. Herbert reassured him: if he had fallen, the Lord would support him so that he could rise up stronger; if, like Peter, he had offended by word, like Peter he should avoid offending in deed (*Si uerbo offendisti ut Petrus, Petri instar opere ne offendas*). And he offered some support to the archbishop's refusal to seal the schedule of constitutions: 'It is good and just to observe good royal customs,

---

[62] *CTB*, ii, no. 273.

[63] *CTB*, ii, no. 233; cf. Øystein/Eystein, archbishop of Nidaros/Trondheim, *CTB*, ii, Appendix 1, *s.v.*

[64] *MTB*, vii, no. 735, *Inter scribendum hec* (the envoys are named, ibid., 433); *CTB*, ii, 1363–4.

[65] *Vita, MTB*, iii, 204–6.

[66] Fitzstephen, *MTB*, iii, 58–9, FitzStephen's response to Herbert, spoken so that Becket should hear it: 'Si sententiam in eos proferret, uideretur omnibus, quod ex ira et impatientia, hoc quod posset, in ultionem sui fecisset. Et procul dubio contra decreta ageret; ut scribit beatus Gregorius Ianuario archiepiscopo (Gratian's *Decretum*, C.23 q.4 c.27), "Nil te ostendis de coelestibus cogitare, sed terrenam te habere conuersationem significas, dum pro uindicta proprie iniurie, quod sacris regulis prohibetur, maledictionem anathematis inuexisti. Unde de cetero omnino esto circumspectus atque sollicitus, et talia cuiquam pro defensione tuae iniuriae inferre denuo non presumas. Nam si tale aliquid feceris, in te scias postea esse uindicandum.'" Being denied direct access to the archbishop, Fitzstephen motioned to Thomas to follow the example of Christ on the cross, rather than act on Herbert's advice to excommunicate anyone who laid impious hands (*manus impias*) upon him (*Vita, MTB*, iii, 58): 'Domine, si forte miserint manus impias in uos, in promptu habeatis excommunicationis in eos ferre sententiam; ut tamen spiritus saluus fiat in die Domini'.

[67] The flight from Northampton, insistence *on salvo honore Dei* at Montmirail and the return to England in early December 1170, despite the bad omens and the advice of Master Gunther: below, at nn.70, 77, 82.

but if, as you say, there are others, newly invented by your enemies to the detriment (*detrimentum*) of the Church, it is well known what should be done …'[68] On the last day of the court/council at Northampton, when Becket expressed concern for the welfare of his household, Herbert insisted that he should not be fearful for himself or for the *discipulus*, 'for you have raised that noble triumphal cross, holy and terrible against every power, in which many have won many battles (*erexisti enim nobile illud et triumphale uexillum, omni potestati sanctum et terribile, in quo multi multa bella uicerunt*)', reminding him of Constantine's victory against earthly and heavenly powers.[69] Later, at supper, as Thomas and the *eruditi* were listening to the account of the persecution of 'Bishop Liberius', there occurred a significant moment. When the Gospel passage, 'If they persecute you in this city, flee to another' was read, the archbishop looked at the *discipulus qui scripsit haec*. It was then, wrote Herbert, 'as I now think', that 'he conceived the plan of evangelical flight'.[70] Although Thomas did in fact flee before cock-crow, sending the *discipulus* to Canterbury to collect what money he could to take to the monastery of St-Bertin,[71] one suspects that Herbert was gilding the lily here, since Thomas had attempted flight twice in the interval between Clarendon and Northampton.

Once installed at Pontigny, it was Herbert who reproved him for his severe fasting;[72] and when Thomas asked his companions, 'What then shall we do, brave brothers (*Quid ergo faciemus, uiri fratres*)?', after King Henry threatened the Cistercians with dire consequences if they continued to support his enemies,[73] it was the *discipulus … qui scripsit hec* who spoke first (*ante ceteros mox erupit in uocem*). Herbert reminded him that the French king had offered refuge in any city or town he chose, an offer he had deferred until it should be necessary.[74] It is unlikely that Thomas needed reminding about the warm welcome he had received from King Louis, but his reply reveals much about their relationship: 'But now it seems to me, brother, that you are again seeking the trappings of the court and the delights of the town'. This was an exchange between friends. Thomas knew his Herbert, and the *discipulus* was duly sent to arrange the transfer to the Benedictine monastery of Ste-Colombe, just outside Sens.[75]

Possibly more significant was the Montmirail incident (7 January 1169). When

---

[68] *Vita, MTB*, iii, 289–92, at 290–2.

[69] *Vita, MTB*, iii, 307–8.

[70] *Vita, MTB*, iii, 312; cf. Matt. 10:23. Robertson, n.1, correctly pointed out that Herbert's identification of the bishop was mistaken, for it was the Arian bishop Demophilus who quoted the words reported in the *Historia Tripartita*.

[71] *Vita, MTB*, iii, 313.

[72] *Vita, MTB*, iii, 377–9.

[73] *CTB*, i, no. 115, at pp. 556–7.

[74] Louis had made an offer in mid-1164, perhaps in the *litteras sua dilectione magna et consolatione plenas*, which Becket's *nuntius*, possibly Ralph of Sarre, did not risk sending (*CTB*, i, no. 33, at n.6), which Thomas declined in *CTB*, i, no. 35 (mid-July 1164), but there may have been another at Soissons after Becket's flight.

[75] *Vita, MTB*, iii, 399–403, at 400, 'Sed uideor mihi nunc, frater, inquit, quod aulicos iterum apparatus et urbanas delicias queras.'

it seemed that Thomas might omit *salvo honore Dei* from his submission to the king, following immense pressure from the mediators and the indecision of the *eruditi*, whose counsel failed in the crucial moment, it was the *discipulus qui scripsit hec* who whispered in his ear, 'My lord, take care that you walk warily (*Domine, inquiens, uideto quomodo caute ambules*)'.[76] There followed a moment of high drama. Solemnly, in the presence of the two kings, Thomas sought the king's mercy, blaming himself for the disturbance and affliction of the church, before concluding:

> And so, my lord, in the presence of our lord the king of the French, and the bishops and princes and others here present, I now submit myself to your mercy and judgment over the whole case that today lies between you and me,

and then added, *salvo honore Dei* (*et salvo ordine meo*),[77] to the indignation of Henry II and the astonishment of all, including King Louis, who blamed him for undermining the peace.[78] Herbert may indeed have uttered the whispered words, but whether they were decisive is open to doubt. The *discipulus*, however, duly praised his steadfast bearing, promising that the Most High would honour him in the sight of the world.[79] King Louis, indeed, soon came round to Becket's way of thinking, when he learned that Henry had broken solemn engagements entered into at Montmirail. Thomas had been wise not to make the peace urged on him by so many, he said, and the (others) would have been wise to follow the counsel of someone who knew the mind and habits of that king.[80]

Finally, on the beach at Wissant, when Master Gunther advised against returning to England, it was Herbert who made a long address to the contrary. They really had no option, he argued, for if they stayed in Flanders or returned to Sens, they would become burdens rather than honoured guests to their protectors. 'We must either turn back in shame, or go forward boldly and act courageously (*Igitur aut regrediendum turpiter aut procedendum audacter et agendum uiriliter*)', he declared, setting before Thomas the prospect of glorious martyrdom. 'How fortunate, my lord, would the exile be, if after exile it were granted from above that you should become not only a martyr, but the first of the last martyrs (*Quam felix, domine,*

---

[76] *Vita, MTB,* iii, 421; below, n.112.

[77] *Vita, MTB,* iii, 418–21, at 421: 'Ego igitur, inquit, domine mi, super tota que inter uos et me uertitur hodie causa, uestre clementie et arbitrio in presentia domini nostri regis Francorum et pontificum et principum et aliorum qui hic astant me nunc subiicio.' When Henry refused to allow the phrase *salvo honore Dei,* Thomas tried to revert to the standard *salvo ordine meo* formula, normally attached to ecclesiastical oaths, but Henry would have none of it. The papal commissioners' report from Simon of Mont-Dieu and Engelbert of Val-St-Pierre (*MTB,* vi, no. 451) and Becket's report to Cardinal William of Pavia (*CTB,* ii, no. 184) reported *salvo ordine meo* as the sticking point.

[78] *Vita, MTB,* iii, 422–3, at 423: 'rex mox uehementer scandalizatus in archipresulem excanduit'. But Barlow, *Thomas Becket,* p. 180, saw Becket as a 'sombre, ravaged, and bitter failure' of forty-eight.

[79] *Vita, MTB,* iii, 430.

[80] *Vita, MTB,* iii, 438; cf. Robert of Torigny, *Chronica,* in *Chronicles of the Reigns of Stephen, Henry II, and Richard I,* ed. R. Howlett, 4 vols, RS 51 (London, 1868–71), iv, 235–6, 240; *LJS,* ii, 603 n.3; *CTB,* ii, no. 244 at n.28.

exsilium, si post exsilium daretur desuper ut non solum martyr, sed et nouissimorum martyrum primitie fieres)? 'Your word (*sermo*) is true', Thomas replied to Herbert, 'but hard, and who will fulfil it?'; then, turning to Gunther, he said, 'Indeed, Gunther, I see the land [echoing Moses, who saw the Promised Land, although he was not permitted to enter it[81]] and, with God's help I shall enter it, knowing most certainly that there my passion awaits.'[82] Herbert's assessment of the situation was surely accurate, but whether Thomas spoke the words attributed to him or imbued them with the meaning given by Herbert may be questioned. The fact of Becket's martyrdom may have coloured Herbert's report of the conversation, and much else beside, just as it inspired his account of a vision in which Becket saw himself thrust into a church by four *milites* who scraped off the crown of his head.[83] Nevertheless, there is much substance in the image of Herbert as the utterly loyal, constant and reliable companion who was prepared to stand by Becket, literally, no matter what, and whose mere presence was reassuring.

Writing in the golden glow of the posthumous cult, and seeing at close hand the transformation of the courtier into the suffering exile, it was natural for Herbert to imbue critical moments with prophetic import, but in the cruel light of circumstance Thomas could not have been so confident of a glorious outcome. His last letter to King Henry (late October 1170)[84] laid out the stark prospect and his willingness to face it:

> I had intended, my lord, to return to you, but fate is drawing me, unhappy wretch that I am, to that afflicted Church; by your licence and grace, I shall return to her, perhaps to die, to prevent her destruction, unless your piety deigns swiftly to offer us some other comfort. But, whether we live or die, we are and will always be yours in the Lord; and whatever happens to us and ours, may God bless you and your children.[85]

There is no reason to challenge Herbert's account of Gunther's attempt to dissuade him. He was not alone, for the envoys' report from England, to which one must suppose Herbert had subscribed, since he was one of their number, had concluded:

> Again and again, my lord, we impress on your memory, that you should not hurry into England unless you are able to secure the unadulterated grace of

---

[81] Num. 27:12, etc.

[82] *Vita, MTB*, iii, 473–6, esp. 474 and 476, '"Fidelis", inquit, "ut videtur sermo tuus, sed durus, et quis implebit illum?"'

[83] *Vita, MTB*, iii, 405–6.

[84] Written after receipt of the envoys' letter (*CTB*, ii, no. 311), which reported their failure to secure the substance of the peace of Fréteval.

[85] *CTB*, ii, no. 320, at pp. 1334–5: 'Ad uos, domine, redire proposueram, sed me miserum ad miseram ecclesiam necessitas trahit; ad illam, uestra licentia et gratia, rediturus, et fortasse, ne illa pereat, periturus, nisi uestra pietas aliam nobis consolationem celerius prestare dignetur. Sed siue uiuimus siue morimur, uestri sumus et erimus semper in Domino; et quicquid nobis contingat et nostris, benefaciat uobis Deus et liberis uestris.'

the lord king. For there is no man in England, even among those you trust, who does not despair entirely of the peace.[86]

In any case, the archbishop's resolution was probably fixed before the exchanges with Herbert and Gunther.

Becket's regard for Herbert was demonstrated in their last exchange, on 27 December 1170. When the weeping *discipulus* protested at being sent on a final mission to King Louis and the archbishop of Sens, Thomas insisted, explaining, 'I wish you to go, especially because the king holds you more suspect than the others in the Church's cause.'[87]

The advice of the eruditi

It is Herbert's pen that produced the compelling record of discussions with the 'mighty warriors' who followed Thomas into exile. In early 1165, not long after their arrival at Pontigny, after hearing not only that the king had forbidden prayers to be said for the archbishop, but that their properties had been sequestrated and their families expelled from England,[88] Herbert describes the *eruditi* encouraging their master in an allocution that covers almost five pages of the Rolls Series edition:[89]

'Lord,' they said, 'why did your face fall and your countenace change when you heard the latest news from England? Allow us, please to speak to you. Your cause and that of those who have followed you is the same: the same penalty, the same fight, and, please God, the same triumph and the same crown.'[90]

This was reinforced by a long string of quotations from the Psalms, Jeremiah and Hosea, describing the terrors that would befall those who had acted against them, leading to the stirring conclusion:

'If we have faith, we must never hesitate, for even if we must struggle with difficulty, inasmuch as the quarrels/disputes are wearisome, especially against one so powerful and unyielding, the outcome of our cause will be all the happier.'[91]

The opening passage in Becket's even longer reply (seven pages) reads:

---

[86] *CTB*, ii, no. 311: 'Hoc sepe et sepius, domine, uobis memorie committimus, ne in Angliam uenire festinetis, nisi puriorem gratiam domini regis adipisci possitis. Non est enim in Anglia, nec etiam, solus inter omnes de quibus confidebatis, quin omnino de pace desperet.'

[87] *Vita, MTB*, iii, 485–6.

[88] See *Precipio tibi, MTB*, v, no. 78.

[89] *Vita, MTB*, iii, 362–6.

[90] *Vita, MTB*, iii, 362: '"Domine", inquiunt, "quare in auditu noui nuntii huius ab Anglia, facies tua sic concidit et uultus sic est in diuersa mutatus? Nos nunc alloquentes te si placet uel modicum sustine. Tibi quippe et nobis, qui secuti sumus te, communis est causa, communis poena, communis pugna, fauente Domino et communis erit uictoria et communis corona."'

[91] *Vita, MTB*, iii, 366: 'si fidem habemus, nequaquam hesitandum, quod etsi laboriose

'Blessed be the Lord who through your learning prepares my hands for battle and has set my arms as a bow of bronze, giving me such learned and vigorous companions for my struggle. Already I see that you are much stronger in the contest than I, whom you call your lord and leader. Therefore I devoutly thank Him by whose bounty I have so many assistants, whom it is safer that I should follow than that they should follow me. [...] Summoned by your example and strengthened by your word, I shall, as I said, follow you, and with the Lord's favour thus directing my steps beneath me to the end, my limbs shall not fail in following you.'[92]

In all, the whole exchange occupies twelve pages of direct speech.

On the face of it, it is difficult to believe that Master Herbert should have been able to recall so much after nearly twenty years, or that the *eruditi* spoke in unison. More probably it represents something of the general consensus, the collective advice (*communis consilium*) of the group, retrospectively reconstructed, based on snippets of memory and coloured by Herbert's own outlook. Nevertheless, the broader image, of an embattled archbishop taking advice at every turn, which runs throughout the *Thomus*, is persuasive. At Westminster (1163), when the king sprang the idea of *traditio curie*, Becket's response was made *cum prefatis eruditis suis librato consilio*; at Clarendon (January 1164), he acted *prehabito cum eruditis suis consilio, sicut in aliis*.[93] Counsel was taken and acted upon, but Herbert gives no details; nor, apart from some whispered admonitions from Herbert himself, is there any mention of collective counsel from the *eruditi* in the detailed account of the trial at Northampton.[94]

Thereafter, with the exception of the issue of the Vézelay sentences (12 June 1166),[95] when, according to Herbert, Thomas did not discuss his intentions in advance, in order to protect his household from the unremitting anger of the king,[96]

certemus, siquidem lites laboriose sunt, presertim contra aduersarium tam potentem, tam durum, cause nostre exitus exinde multo erit felicior'.

[92] *Vita*, *MTB*, iii, 366–73, at 366, 367: 'Benedictus Dominus, qui uestra eruditione manus meas docet ad prelium, et posuit ut arcum ereum brachia mea, tam infatigabiles, tam eruditos et tam strenuos certaminis mei mihi socios dans. Iam quippe uos uideo me, quem dominum et ducem uestrum nominatis, multo magis in agone fortiores. Unde et illum deuota prosequor actione gratiarum, cuius muneris est quod tales et tantos habeo coadiutores, quos ut ego sequar tutius est quam quod me ipsi. [...] Et ego uestro prouocatus exemplo et roboratus uerbo, uos, ut dixi, iam sequar, et fauente Domino et dilatante sic gressus meos subter me usque in finem, tali mei non deficient uos sequendo'.

[93] *Vita*, *MTB*, iii, 368, 384.

[94] *Vita*, *MTB*, iii, 296–312. Herbert's account should be compared with Fitzstephen, *MTB*, iii, 49–70.

[95] Thomas excommunicated the occupiers of Canterbury estates, the drafters and implementers of the Constitutions of Clarendon, the royal clerks (Richard of Ilchester, John of Oxford) who had attended the imperial council of Würzburg (1165) and, according to Frederick I's encyclical, had sworn to accept the authority of the new anti-pope, 'Paschal III', and he suspended the Bishops Gilbert Foliot of London and Jocelin de Bohun of Salisbury: *CTB*, i, nos. 76–81; cf. Duggan, *Thomas Becket*, pp. 110–16.

[96] *Vita*, *MTB*, iii, 387: 'suis parcens in hoc, ne uidelicet qui eum sequendo magnam jam ob

the *eruditi* were consulted at nearly every turn. The three letters to King Henry[97] were approved by them: *verbo hoc ab archipraesule proposito, nobis sic placuit verbum;*[98] and when the king's rebuff pushed Thomas to contemplate resignation, they strongly counselled against it ('now is not the time to flee, but to fight'), and the archbishop was duly persuaded by the advice of his *eruditi* so that '[he] thought no more of deserting his pastoral obligation, but rather of exercising it more forcefully and manfully in the future than he had in the past'.[99]

The bishops' appeal against the Vézelay sentences[100] provoked a lively debate:

Therefore the diverse opinions of his *eruditi* were assembled before the archbishop, he intervening in his usual way, repeatedly inquiring and raising questions about the law,[101]

after which Thomas sent an 'elegant response' to the appeal letter (*libellum appel-latorium*), 'expressing his own view and written in his own style (*sensa suo proprio conceptam et proprio stylo exaratam*)'.[102] One would love to know the substance of that debate, but here, as elsewhere, Herbert's prejudice against the law led him to pass over details which a modern historian would like to know. Even on the drafting of this important response, his description hides more than it reveals. Herbert's own letter collection shows that the 'elegant response' (*Fraternitatis uestre scriptum*) was one of three proposed rejoinders to the appeal: one by Herbert himself, one by Master Lombard and a third, corresponding with the version finally sent to the bishops. Precisely how much was composed by St Thomas remains in doubt. John of Salisbury later commended the 'great wisdom and propriety' of the finished product,[103] but that does not exclude the possibility of some collaboration. Indeed, John's own hand may be glimpsed, perhaps indirectly, in an echo of a line from Terence's *Eunuchus*.[104]

Herbert's anti-legal bias is demonstrated in the otherwise full account of the negotiations at Planches (18 November 1167), when Cardinals William of Pavia and Otto of Brescia, *uiri et in diuino et in humano iure periti*, tried to persuade Becket to accept peace terms which did not explicitly mention the Constitutions of Clarendon. They understood, they said, that the king would consider them abolished, and cited both laws (Roman and canon) to show that consent was sometimes tacit and

id regis iram incurrerant, in majus et perpetuum forte inducerentur odium'.

[97] *CTB*, i, nos. 68, 74, 82; discussed in Duggan, *Thomas Becket*, pp. 106–10, 116–17.

[98] *Vita, MTB*, iii, 381–3, at 383.

[99] *Vita, MTB*, iii, 387: 'Archipresul uero ex eruditorum suorum uiua et salubri exhortatione persuasus, iam nihil cogitabat de cura pastorali deserenda, sed potius deinceps fortius quam prius et uirilius exercenda.'

[100] *MTB*, v, no. 204.

[101] *Vita, MTB*, iii, 395: 'Itaque coram archipresule ab eruditis suis diuersa sentientibus super appellatione collatum, ipso, ut moris sui erat, partes suas interponente, et nunc hos, nunc illos de iure crebro sciscitante et opponent.'

[102] *Vita, MTB*, iii, 395. The letter is *Fraternitatis uestre scriptum*, *CTB*, i, no. 95.

[103] *CTB*, i, 456–68 no. 100, at 462–3 n.26, 'prudentissime et elegantissime'.

[104] 'Certe cudetur in uos faba ista': *CTB*, i, 400; cf. Terence, *Eunuchus*, 2.3.89: 'Istaec in me cudetur faba'; *LJS*, ii, 714–15, 'ut ueteri prouerbio dici solet faba cudatur'.

sometimes expressed. The *eruditi* were not persuaded. 'We (*nos*) replied, that [we] could not agree to the formula without specific rejection of the customs, citing the rule of the civil law, that ratification has retrospective force and confirms something already done (*Ratihabitio retro trahitur, et que sunt gesta confirmunt*)'.[105] Silence would not abolish the evil customs but further bind the archbishop to their observance: '"He who does not resist when he can is shown to consent", said one; and "Not only they who do wrong, but also they who agree to it, are judged to be participants [in the wrong doing]"'.[106] The argument was further supported by many canons, which Herbert refrained from citing, 'especially since these are very well known to those who have even a slight knowledge of the law (*presertim cum hec modicum etiam habentibus iuris experientiam notissima sunt*)'.[107] When the cardinals departed empty handed, the English bishops renewed their appeal, and the *eruditi* rigorously examined the law relating to appeals. Again, Herbert omitted the details in the interests of brevity (*causa brevitatis*), *presertim cum talia uiris peritis sint notissima*. The sum of their counsel was that the lesser judge should not defer to an appeal made to avoid justice and harass the oppressed, although 'we begged, warned, and advised that the king's person should not be harmed (*supplicauimus, monuimus, consuluimus ut sola regis persona adhuc remaneret intacta*)'.[108]

At the Montmirail interview (6 January 1169),[109] which took place at the end of a peace conference between Kings Henry and Louis,[110] Henry intimated to those he knew to be favourable to Thomas that he would take the cross to go to Jerusalem if peace were made between him and the archbishop, *ad honorem suum*.[111] Thomas wanted to add *salvo honore Dei*, but was pressed to accept peace without qualification, suppressing any saving clause and placing everything in the king's mercy. Between the proffered peace and the absence of any kind of security clause, the *eruditi* wavered.

---

[105] *Vita*, *MTB*, iii, 410–11; for the Roman law on ratihabitio, see *Digest*, 46.3.12.4 (Ulpian), 'Rati enim habitio mandato comparatur'; *Digest*, 46.8.17 (Marcellus), 'insecuta ratihabitione recte actum videri'. On the ambiguity of silence, *Digest*, 50.17.142 (Paulus), 'Qui tacet, non utique fatetur: sed tamen verum est eum non negare.'

[106] *Vita*, *MTB*, iii, 412, 'Qui non obuiat, inquit, cum potest, consentire probatur: et nec caret scrupulo consensionis occulte, qui manifesto facinori desinit obuiare.' For 'nec caret [...] obuiare', see Gratian's *Decretum*, D.83 c.3. Gratian ascribed the text to 'Innocentius', but it derives from Felix III's letter *Postquam sanctae* to Acacius of Constantinople 483 (JL 592; *PL*, 58.897, 898, *ep*. i). For similar arguments addressed to Henry II in 1166, see *Expectans expectaui* (*CTB*, i, no. 82), at n.4.

[107] *Vita*, *MTB*, iii, 411–12.

[108] *Vita*, *MTB*, iii, 413.

[109] The papal commissioners were Simon of Mont-Dieu (Carthusian) and Bernard de Corilon (Grandmontine), supported by Engelbert, prior of Val-Saint-Pierre in Picardy (Carthusian).

[110] J. Gillingham, 'The Meetings of the Kings of England and France, 1066–1204', in *Normandy and its Neighbours, 900–1250. Essays for David Bates*, ed. D. Crouch and K. Thompson (Turnhout, 2011), pp. 17–42, at 27, 31, 41–2.

[111] *Vita*, *MTB*, iii, 419.

And therefore all our learned men were hesitating, afraid to give advice lest they impeded the peace or caused the Church's case to be lost. In this predicament, then ... all the counsel from our learned came to nothing and their wisdom was useless ... except that some of them muttered that it was not safe to suppress God's honour or ecclesiastical freedom in this way to gain earthly grace ... In this crisis, then, wisdom and counsel failed.[112]

And it was Herbert's whispered advice to 'walk warily' that strengthened his resolve.[113]

Circumstances virtually excluded the exiled household from the business of the third attempt to find a way to peace, for the king agreed to meet the latest papal envoys (Masters Vivian and Gratian), trained lawyers both, at locations in Normandy, which the exiles could not safely enter before they had the king's peace.[114] Only after that peace initiative had finally foundered at Montmartre (18 November 1169),[115] when Thomas rejected the unsecured *pax* proffered by the king, did Herbert record their collective advice. In another set-piece allocution, only slightly shorter (six pages) than the one that had encouraged him at the beginning of the exile, the *eruditi* advised him to take the king at his word and return to his church. Recognising that only the king's denial of the kiss of peace stood in the way of peace, and commenting on the bad effects for the English church of the six-year exile, they argued that Becket's personal cause was over but that the church's remained to be fought in England:[116]

---

[112] *Vita, MTB*, iii, 418–21, at 421: 'Et ideo eruditi nostri quotquot hesitabant, et consilium dare uerebantur, ne uel per ipsos impediretur pax uel ne forte per ipsos Ecclesie causa quam agebant periclitaretur. In hoc igitur casu ... ab eruditis nostris omne consilium periit, et ipsorum sapientia inutilis facta est ... nisi quod quidam submurmurauerunt minime tutum in tali casu Dei honorem, seu libertatem ecclesiasticam, pro gratia terrena acquirenda ita supprimer ... In arcto itaque hoc periit sapientia et consilium.'

[113] Above, at n.76.

[114] Argentan (15–16 August), Domfront (23–24 August), Bayeux (31 August), and Bur-le-Roi (1–2 September).

[115] Gillingham, 'The Meetings of the Kings of England and France', p. 38.

[116] *Vita, MTB*, iii, 451–6, esp. 454–5: 'Cessat igitur nunc ea que precessit persecutio personalis, cui ut iam ostendimus generalis successit, in qua bonus pastor tenetur non se absentare, non fugere, sed ex aduerso ascendere, se opponere et inter gladios etiam nudos et exertos se ingerere, et ita si necesse fuerit, animam suam pro ouibus suis ponere. Tu ergo, Domine, si illorum queris imitari zelum, quorum sortitus es ministerium, illorum uirtutem quorum creditam habes dispensationem, uade et fac similiter. Non ad terreni puluris uno flatu facile dispergendi anheles osculum, nec metuas gladium. Ecclesiam tuam potius, non sub osculo sed sub gladio, si necesse sic etsi nudatam, et spoliatam, etsi conuulsam et euulsam, non recuses, sed maritali zelo cum debita affectione et deuotione suscipias. [...] Regredere igitur et nos tecum [...] Verum quod supra tetigimus de causa metus et periculis si forte terram ingrederemur, nequaquam ideo dicimus quod de tanto rege nostro et tam illustri suspicemur sinistri quidpiam. [...] unde et credibile minime quod moliatur quidquam, presertim aduersum te sacerdotem priorem suum in Deo, et propter Deum, seu etiam aduersum nos, inerme hominum genus, presertim ab ipsomet publice pace et securitate donata. [...] sed in forma pacis oblata mature confidenter et absque omni conscientie scrupulo reuertamur, illum summa gratiarum actione et laude prosequentes in cuius fortitudine reuertemur.' See Ezek. 13:5; 1 John 3:16.

The personal persecution which went before is over, succeeded as we showed by a general one, in which the good pastor is obliged, not to absent himself, not to flee, but to rise up on the other side, station himself, and throw himself in among the naked thrusting swords, and thus, if necessary, lay down his life for his sheep. Therefore, my lord, if you wish to imitate the zeal of those whose ministry you have received, the virtue of those whose stewardship you have, go and do likewise. Do not hanker for the kiss of earthly dust easily dispersed in a single breath nor should you fear the sword. You should not reject your Church, rather embrace her with marital zeal and due affection, if necessary even naked and despoiled, even if torn down and shattered, not under a kiss but under the sword. [...] Return, therefore, and we with you [...] Nevertheless, concerning the reason for fear and the dangers if we were to enter that land, which we touched on above, we are not in any way saying that we suspect anything sinister about our great and illustrious king [...] it is not in the least degree credible that he would attempt anything against you, his first priest in God, and because of God, or even against us, a defenceless race of men, and especially because of the peace and security publicly conferred by himself. [...] let us therefore return quickly, confidently, and without any conscientious scruple on the basis of the proffered peace formula (*forma pacis*), tendering thanks and praise to Him in whose strength we shall return.

This adds up to 'go back and die' – chilling advice indeed – and Herbert did not express dissent from it. Whether it was ever said quite so starkly must remain doubtful, especially since, despite its disclaimer of any suspicions against the king, it seems to presage the later events.

Becket responded that he agreed with all they said, and explained that he would not have rejected the peace if he had not been following the pope's advice to insist on the kiss as a guarantee of whatever peace was offered. They duly agreed with him, that the pope should be consulted on the matter.[117] Herbert does not express any dissent from this view; nor does he record the emotionally charged advice of King Louis that he would not recommend acceptance of such terms for all his weight in gold, which Thomas reported soon afterwards in a letter to Archbishop William of Sens.[118]

---

[117] *Vita, MTB*, iii, 456–7; 458, 'et ipsius sermonem et de mittendo ad dominum papam consilium commendauimus'. On such symbolic acts, see T. Reuter, 'Symbolic Acts in the Becket Dispute', in *Medieval Polities and Modern Mentalities*, ed. J. L. Nelson (Cambridge, 2006), pp. 167–90; H. Vollrath, 'The Kiss of Peace', in *Peace Treaties and International Law in European History*, ed. R. Lesaffer (Cambridge, 2004), pp. 162–83. The papal mandate does not survive, but a later letter to Henry II (1170) mentioned the kiss five times: *MTB*, vii, no. 626, at 205–6; cf. the instructions to Archbishop Rotrou of Rouen and Bishop Bernard of Nevers, *MTB*, vii, no. 623, at pp. 198–201: eight mentions. The requirement may have been deduced from the earliest letters advising Thomas to 'defer to the king in all things as far as you can, *saving the honour of your ecclesiastical status*' and 'recover the grace and goodwill of the illustrious English king by all possible means, as far as you can, while preserving the Church's freedom and the honour of your office': *CTB*, i, 80–5 no. 26 (Sens, 5 March 1164), at 82–3; *CTB*, ii, 224–5 no. 54 (Melgueil, *c*. 22 Aug. 1165).

[118] *CTB*, ii, 1044–55 no. 243, at 1050–1.

Ghost-writer?

Herbert's sadly mutilated letter collection contains eleven pieces drafted by him in *persona b. Thome*,[119] but there is some doubt about their status. Two, certainly, seem to have been adopted, for they occur, with verbal alterations, in the Becket collections;[120] one was certainly superseded, since a parallel letter exists in the Becket dossiers,[121] and a further six, addressed to Alexander III (2), Bishop Roger of Worcester, Robert, provost of Aire, Louis VII and Valdemar I of Denmark, may have been sent, although there is no corroborative evidence.[122] Considerable doubt surrounds the remaining two.[123] There is no doubt that Herbert was one of the *dicta-*

---

[119] Cambridge, Corpus Christi College, MS 123; cf. *PL*, 190.1415–88, reprinted from *Herberti de Boseham Opera Omnia*, ed. J. A. Giles, 2 vols., Patres Ecclesiae Anglicanae (Oxford, 1845), nos. 2–3, 8–11, 15, 20 and 26–8 were written 'in persona b. Thome'; cf. *MTB*, v–vii, nos. 530, 537, 636, 536, 670, 171, 221, 156, and 251, 242, 365. Note my exclusion of no. 177, to Prior of Canterbury, since Herbert wrote it in his own name and in the first person, calling himself 'socius' of the exiled archbishop.

[120] *HB*, nos. 8 and 9 = *CTB*, ii, nos. 260 and 271. To his authorship should also be attributed *Inter scribendum haec*, Archbishop William of Sens's fierce denunciation of Becket's murder, carried to the Curia by Masters Alexander Walensis and Gunther of Winchester. The copy in Herbert's letters (no. 33) has the heading: 'Epistola hec in persona Willelmi Senonensis archiepiscopi ad Alexandrum papam contra interfectores Thome Cantuariensis archiepiscopi et martyris', and it was received into Alan of Tewkesbury's collection, at v. 84 (*MTB*, vii, 429–33 no. 735).

[121] *HB*, no. 15 was set aside in favour of *CTB*, i, no. 95, which Herbert included later as *HB*, no. 17, but he did not claim authorship. For his reference to its presence in Alan of Tewkesbury's collection, see below, n.124.

[122] *HB*, nos. 2 (= *MTB*, vi, no. 530) and 20 (= *MTB*, v, no. 156: Barlow, *Thomas Becket*, p. 138, thought, probably correctly, that it was a reaction to Gilbert Foliot's *MTB*, v, no. 108); 10 (= *MTB*, vii, no. 670), 11 (= *MTB*, v, no. 171: cf. *CTB*, ii, no. 288, which seeks a prebend in St Martin of Tours for 'his dear beloved friend [*dilecto et dilectori amico*], the provost of St-Omer, *c.* May 1170), 27 (= *MTB*, vi, no. 242), and 28 (= *MTB*, vi, no. 365).

[123] No. 3 (= *MTB*, vii, no. 537), to Alexander III. Its structure, in numbered points, looks more like a memorandum for oral presentation or notes for a letter; 26 (= *MTB*, vi, no. 251), to Raymond, cardinal deacon of S. Maria in Via Lata; 27 (*MTB*, vi, no. 242) to Louis VII. My uncertainty about the letter to the cardinal deacon of S. Maria in Via Lata is based on the belief that Master Raymond did not return to Italy with the Curia in mid-1165, and so could not have intervened on Becket's behalf when the exiles feared that legates favourable to Henry II would be appointed (1166–67). Raymond's own position as one of the anti-pope's electors (*Ottonis et Rahewini Gesta Friderici I. imperatoris*, ed. G. Waitz and B. von Simson, *MGH* SrG., 46 [Hanover and Leipzig, 1912], pp. 303–4) might also have undermined his influence, although he had joined Alexander's cardinals to issue their encyclical: *PL*, 200.61–6. On his identity, see A. Gouron, 'Le cardinal Raymond des Arènes: *Cardinalis?*', in *Revue de droit canonique*, 28 = *Mélanges Jean Gaudemet* (Strasbourg, 1978), pp. 180–92 (unknown to B. Zenker, *Die Mitglieder des Kardinalkollegiums von 1130 bis 1159* [Würzburg, 1964], pp. 179–80); R. Weigand, 'Die Glossen des Cardinalis – Raimundus de (Harenis) – zu C.16', in *Recht im Dienste des Menschen: Eine Festgabe für Hugo Schwendenwein zum 60 Geburtstag*, ed. K. Lüdicke, H. Paarhammer, and D. Binder (Graz-Vienna-Cologne 1986), pp. 267–83.

tores upon whom the exiled Becket relied,[124] with Lombard and John Planeta, but there was an even more experienced *dictator* among the *eruditi*.

Although John of Salisbury did not live with the exiles either at Pontigny or at Sens, his residence at St-Rémi in Reims placed him at the centre of what we may call an active Canterbury outpost, although he held back from committing himself too far until his famous interview with King Henry at Angers in 1166 dashed all hope of an honourable peace. From then, however, he took a more explicit role in helping the exiles to decide strategy.[125] Becket sent him a copy of the bishops' appeal with the agreed response and consulted him about a dossier of four letters from various correspondents and the possibility of an interview with Empress Matilda, all in mid/ late July 1166. Becket's letters are lost, but John's long and measured replies survive,[126] the last of which reveals that the matters were discussed with the other members of the Reims circle: Master Philip (of Calne), Abbot Peter of St-Rémi and Masters Fulk (of Reims) and Ralph (of Sarre).[127] From then on, John played a full part in keeping Becket's struggle in the forefront of the minds of his many correspondents across Europe.[128] Even more importantly, as I have argued, his hand can be seen in the drafting of many letters that passed under Becket's name. In addition to the three letters for which there is reasonable evidence that he was the author,[129] I suggested in 2001 that he had drafted another ten letters, partly on consideration of the general style, but more particularly on their use of classical quotations and allusions which distinguished them from the general run of educated clerics who relied on *florilegia*, like Heiric of Auxerre's ninth-century *Collectanea* and the twelfth-century

---

[124] In describing *Fraternitatis uestre scriptum*, Becket's reply to the bishops' appeal against the Vézelay sentences (*CTB*, i, no. 95) as written in Becket's own style, Herbert referred to its presence in Alan of Tewkesbury's collection, 'among other letters which he wrote himself and those written at his command by some of his *eruditi* in his name': *Vita*, *MTB*, iii, 396, 'Exstat enim epistola illa inter ceteras epistolas suas, quas uel ipsemet scripsit, uel aliqui de eruditis suis de ipsius mandato sub eius nomine.'

[125] A. J. Duggan, 'John of Salisbury and Thomas Becket', in *The World of John of Salisbury*, pp. 427–38; reprinted in Duggan, *Thomas Becket: Friends, Networks*, no. II. This concluded, p. 438, 'No matter how strong his wish for the king's pardon, he was not prepared to sell his soul to purchase it.' For the latest studies on John, see *A Companion to John of Salisbury*, especially K. Bollermann and C. J. Nederman, 'John of Salisbury and Thomas Becket', pp. 63–104.

[126] *CTB*, i, nos. 100–2 (*LJS*, ii, nos. 175, 176, 179).

[127] *CTB*, i, no. 102, at 482–5 (*LJS*, ii, no. 179, at 188–91).

[128] Barrau, 'Jean de Salisbury, intermédiaire', p. 516, 'Son rôle fut, au bout du compte, davantage dans la construction de la doxa sur l'archevêque et les autres participants au conflit, que dans une réelle activité diplomatique.'

[129] *CTB*, i, no. 83, to Nicholas of Mont-Rouen, has the heading *Nicholao de Monte pro Cantuariensi* in John of Salisbury's collection (Paris, BnF lat. ms 8562, fol. 1v); *CTB*, ii, no. 280, to Cardinal Albert, was headed *Johannes [. . .] coexulantium nomine* in BL MS Royal 13 A.xiii, *R*, fol. 87r; and the anonymous draft report of Becket's discussions with Cardinals William of Pavia and Otto of Brescia at Planches in November 1167, ibid., i, no. 144 was probably his composition, for it parallels the account sent 'from a friend to a friend' (*Amicus amico*), which Millor and Brooke believed (rightly, as I think) had been sent by John to Bishop John of Poitiers: *LJS*, ii, nos. 230–1.

Florilegium Gallicum.[130] Then, in 2005, I went further. Arguing from similarities in style and content, I suggested that John was responsible for a further twenty-eight letters, mostly sent to the Curia at the same time as those whose classical markers suggest his input.[131] To these I would now add a further three letters sent to the Curia after 5 April 1170, which are connected with two parallel letters, one sent to Cardinal Albert *coexulantium nomine*, and the other addressed by the *coexules* to Master Gratian, then acting head of the papal chancery.[132] These bring the number to forty-four. Furthermore, a letter to the pope in February 1167, expressing the hope that Alexander would not be a 'staff of reeds' (*baculum arundineum*), used the same striking image from Isaiah which John had applied to Louis VII in his first despatch from France in early 1164;[133] and if he wrote that letter, he may have written the other three 'curial letters' issued at the same time.[134]

This evidence suggests that John of Salisbury had the lion's share of the verbal formulation of the important letters sent to the Curia from mid-1166. That puts Herbert's undoubted contribution to the epistolary output of the exiles into a different perspective. Herbert could construct an effective argument, but he tended to over-elaboration, and John's elegant and finely balanced classicised prose may have been deemed more appropriate for the educated élite of the Curia. Herbert was not ignorant of the basic classical learning of the time, however, based probably on *florilegia*. His characterisation of *lectio* (sacred reading) as a kind of whetstone (*uice cotis*) against which prayer was refined came from a line in Horace, for example,[135] but sacred scripture came to his pen much more readily.

---

[130] A. J. Duggan, 'Classical Quotations and Allusions in the Correspondence of Thomas Becket: an investigation of their sources', *Viator* 32 (2001), 1–22, at 8–10 (for the *florilegia*), 12–13 and 16–22 (for John's contribution); reprinted with the same pagination in Duggan, *Thomas Becket: Friends, Networks*, no. IV. For the letters, see *CTB*, i, nos. 117–18, 153, 170; ii, nos. 178, 235, 244, 277, 281, 301.

[131] A. J. Duggan, 'Authorship and Authenticity in the Becket Correspondence', in *Vom Nutzen des Edierens. Akten des internationalen Kongresses zum 150-jährigen Bestehen des Instituts für Österreichische Geschichtsforschung Wien, 3.–5. Juni 2004*, ed. B. Merta, A. Sommerlechner and H. Weigl (Vienna/Munich, 2005), pp. 25–44, at 39–40, and 44 (Appendix 3); reprinted with the same pagination in eadem, *Thomas Becket: friends, networks*, no. V. The letters are: *CTB*, i, nos. 115–16 (linked to nos. 117–18), 157–9 (linked with no. 153), 169, 171–4; ii, 177 (linked with nos. 170 and 178), 233–4, 236, 240, 243, 245–51 (linked with nos. 235 and 244), 300, 302–5 (linked with no. 301). Only two of these letters were sent to non-curial recipients: nos. 158 and 159 to Stephen, chancellor of the king of Sicily and Richard, elect of Syracuse, respectively, and no. 243 was sent to Archbishop William of Sens, who was then *en route* to the Curia. The same holds true for the 'classical marker' group. All, except one, were addressed to curial recipients, and the exception, no. 244, was sent to Masters Alexander Walensis and John Planeta, Becket's representatives at the Curia.

[132] *CTB*, ii, nos. 277–9, linked with nos. 280 and 281, written on behalf of the 'coexules'.

[133] *CTB*, i, no. 124 (*Mittimus sanctitati*, after 2 February 1167), at pp. 592–5, echoing *LJS*, ii, no. 136, at p. 14; cf. Isa. 36:6, 'Ecce confidis in super baculum arundineum, confractum istum, super Aegyptum'.

[134] *CTB*, i, nos. 123, 125–6.

[135] *Vita, MTB*, iii, 205–6; cf. Horace, *Ars Poetica*, 304–5, 'ergo fungar vice cotis acutum | reddere quae ferrum valet, exsors ipsa secandi'.

The *discipulus* remained an odd-man-out among Becket's 'mighty warriors'. Something in his character and demeanour denied him secure employment after Becket's death. Pope Alexander had recommended him for the provostship of Troyes in late 1165, without success.[136] Not only did Herbert not get the preferment, but Bishop Henry suppressed the office. Herbert dedicated his works on Peter Lombard's great gloss on the Psalms and the Pauline epistles to William of Sens (1169–76) before 1176 and the *Thomus* to Baldwin of Canterbury (?1189), but he achieved no known dignity or office. Even his friendship with William de Longchamp bore no tangible fruit,[137] and he ended his days in the diocese of Arras, supported by the Cistercian monks of Ourscamp and Peter, the diocesan bishop (1184–1203), to whom he dedicated his work on the Hebrew Psalter. Yet Herbert's

[136] *Commisse tibi*, *MTB*, v, 241–2 no. 132; Bishop Henry suppressed the office. Alexander III also mandated the papal legates Albert and Theodinus, who negotiated the Avranches settlement in 1172, to secure King Henry's peace for Herbert and the other clerical and lay exiles and their repatriation to England, failing which he promised to do what he would to make suitable provision for him: *PL*, 190.1471–2 no. 41, *Devotionis tuae*; later (1178–81), Alexander mandated Archbishop Richard of Canterbury to allow him to enjoy his Canterbury revenues for three years, while he taught theology 'for his own benefit and that of others (*de suo et aliorum profectu*)': S. Loewenfeld, *Epistolae pontificum romanorum ineditae* (Leipzig, 1885), p. 207 no. 347 (JL 14328), *Cum dilectus filius*. This letter survives only in Cambridge, Trinity College MS R 9.17, fols. 108–129v (the so-called Register fragment), fol. 129r, no. 69: W. Holtzmann, 'Die Register Papst Alexander III in den Händen der Kanonisten', *Quellen und Forschungen aus italienischen Archiven und Bibliotheken* 30 (1940), 13–87, at 69–80, 'Das sogenannte Registerfragment Alexanders III.'; K. Pennington, 'Epistolae Alexandrinae: A Collection of Pope Alexander III's Letters', in *Popes, Canonists and Texts, 1150–1550* (Aldershot, 1993), no. VII. Some connection with the Paris schools may be suggested by Herbert's appearance as an assessor in a case relating to the jurisdiction of the monastery of Sainte-Geneviève decided by the papal legate, Cardinal Peter of S. Crisogono at Saint-Martin-des-Champs in Paris: *Papsturkunden in Frankreich*, viii/1: *Urkunden und Briefsammlungen der Abteien Sainte-Geneviève und Saint-Victor*, ed. D. Lohrmann, Abhandlungen … Göttingen, Phil.-Hist. Klasse, 3rd Ser. 174 (Göttingen, 1989), p. 337 no. 144, dated by Lohrmann 'before 10 July 1178', where 'magister Herbertus de Boseham' appears last in a list which includes 'magister Girardus Puella'. Herbert's own authentification of the cardinal's written judgment, in the form of a *vidimus*, has recently been discovered by Nicholas Vincent in Bibl. Sainte-Geneviève ms 356, p. 224: see Appendix, pp. 184–7. Given the presence of Gerard Pucelle, one might suggest that the cardinal's judgment should be dated 1174, before Gerard joined the household of Archbishop Richard of Canterbury. This would agree with W. Janssen, *Die päpstlichen Legaten in Frankreich vom Schisma Anaklets II. bis zum Tode Coelestins III. (1130–1198)* (Cologne/Graz, 1961), p. 95, who dates it '1174/75'. Peter's presence in Paris in 1174 can also be inferred from Alexander III's rebuke about his handling of the question of charges for the *licentia docendi* in Paris, dated Ferentino, 29 October (1174): *PL*, 190.998–9 no. 1147; JL 12397.

[137] William de Longchamp, then bishop of Ely (1189–97), papal legate (1190–94) and royal chancellor, considered him a dear friend (*dilectissimus suus*) and encouraged him to complete his work on the Hebrew Psalter: *PL*, 190.1474 no. 45 (?1191), 'Et preterea noueritis quod desiderio intimo desincrauimus ut opusculum super psalmos ab Hebraica ueritate a Patre Hieronymo translatos uestra discretio compleuisset, ut impedimento non esset quidquam ulterius, quin uestra presentia et optatis colloquiis uteremur'; *English Episcopal Acta*, xxxi, *Ely 1109–1197*, ed. N. Karn (Oxford, 2005), p. lxxxiii and n.

own description of himself as the 'follower who wrote these things (*discipulus qui scripsit hec*)'[138] presumes a privileged relationship with his master, modelled on St John's self-identification as the *discipulus qui testimonium perhibet de his et scripsit hec*.[139] Even more, in a letter from early 1172, asking Cardinals Albert and Theodwin to keep him in mind, Herbert described his own sufferings as fulfilling 'whatever is missing from the sufferings of my lord, Christ's martyr',[140] a phrase adapted from St Paul's boast to the Colossians that in his sufferings for them he was fulfilling 'whatever is missing from the sufferings of Christ'.[141] This moving self-portrayal adds considerable weight to Laura Cleaver's identification of the two figures on fol. 83r of the Psalms' commentary in Oxford Bodleian Library MS Auct E Infra 6 as the suffering figures of master and disciple. The upper figure shows a much diminished Thomas, denuded of all marks of his archiepiscopal status, except for the barely visible cross-staff in his right hand, pointing with his left to the words *sanctis martyribus* above his head, while the lower figure shows the still-exiled Herbert, pointing down to the words *Dixit Dominus domino meo, sede a dextris meis*. That poignant image is reflected also in the prayer to his martyred lord which Herbert appended to the *catalogus*, in which he begs not to be abandoned, lest he, naked, should 'perish in these frozen wastes (*inter deserti hujus frigora*)', after Thomas, like Elijah, had ascended in his fiery chariot.[142]

Just as St John's was the last of the four Gospels, so Herbert's *Thomus*, begun in 1184, some fourteen years after Becket's murder (29 December 1170)[143] and finally finished after Henry II's death in 1189,[144] was the last of the major biographies by a considerable margin. How much of the detail depended on the memory of a man then in his mid/late sixties and how much on notes taken at the time is impossible to determine. Herbert was the archbishop's confidant, the keeper of his public conscience and leader of the phalanx of the exiled *eruditi*, and it is possible that, like William Fitzstephen at Northampton, he had kept short-hand notes.[145] An ex-Chancery clerk

---

[138] *Vita, MTB*, iii, 161–2, etc.

[139] John 21:24.

[140] *PL*, 190.1469–70 no. 39, at 1470: 'Ego vero in obscuris sicut mortuus saeculi collocatus et ea quae desunt passionum domini mei Christi martyris in me ipso adimplens, in calce sermonis oro et opto vos spiritu consilii et scientie abundare in omnibus, et cum acceperitis tempus pressure mee memores fore.'

[141] Coloss. 1:24: 'in passionibus pro vobis, adimpleo ea quae desunt passionum Christi, in carne mea, pro corpore ejus, quod est ecclesia.'

[142] *Vita, MTB*, iii, 531–2.

[143] *Vita, MTB*, iii, 192, 'praesertim cum a viri hujus de hoc mundo excessu jam quartus-decimus annus sit quo scribo haec'; The death of Henry II's son Geoffrey (1186) occurred 'dum adhuc hanc historiam scriberem': *Vita, MTB*, iii, 461.

[144] *Vita, MTB*, iii, 460–1, reports Becket's dream at Sens, in which a verse ('Mors tulit una duos, tulit altera, sed male, patrem') foretold the deaths of Young King Henry (1183), Geoffrey (1186) and King Henry II himself (6 July 1189). It is possible that 'Mors tulit [...] altera' echoed a verse in *Aurora*, the ingenious verse summary of the Old and New Testaments by Peter Riga (*c.* 1140–1209), a canon of Reims (*PL*, 212.24), referring to the deaths of Mahalon and Chilion, the two sons of Naomi (Ruth 1:5).

[145] A. J. Duggan, 'Roman, Canon, and Common Law in Twelfth-Century England: The

would certainly have had the necessary competence. Even so, some of the longer exchanges, like that between the exiles and Thomas in early 1165[146] and the six-page encouragement to martyrdom in late 1169,[147] raise questions. So, also, does the record of Becket's long address to the cardinals on the day after his formal reception by the pope at Sens, which runs to just over twelve pages.[148] In essence, it is an extended disquisition on St Paul's advice to the Ephesians (Eph. 5: 16) to 'redeem the time because the days are evil (*redimentes tempus quoniam dies mali sunt*)' and the related Gospel admonitions to turn the other cheek, etc. It is almost certainly a true reflection of Becket's own opinion, but in the form presented by Herbert it may be a retrospective construct in the light of the recurrence of echoes of the Ephesians passage in the Becket correspondence.[149] Similarly, the account of Becket's dream, allegedly revealed to the abbot of Pontigny and later to the abbot of Val-Luisant. As he was defending the church's cause against the king in the pope's presence, four knights (*milites*) suddenly appeared and dragged him from the audience chamber into the church, where they scraped off the crown of his head.[150] The close correlation of this account with the murder in the cathedral is certainly suspicious. Nevertheless, with all its weaknesses, of omission, of dramatic construction, of occasional slips in detail, to say nothing of its inordinate length,[151] Herbert's *Thomus* remains one of the best biographies of Thomas the archbishop and martyr. More importantly, it is eloquent testimony to the loyalty of a gifted theologian whose outspoken loyalty condemned him to something approaching lonely oblivion.

Council of Northampton (1164) Re-examined', *Historical Research* 83 (2010), 379–408, at 385.

[146] *Vita*, *MTB*, iii, 362–73: above, at nn.89–92.

[147] *Vita*, *MTB*, iii, 451–6: above at n.116.

[148] *Vita*, *MTB*, iii, 344–56.

[149] *CTB*, i, nos. 54 n.2, 125 n.26, 144, before n.5 (*malitia temporis*); ii, 203 n.21, 204 n.4; cf. ibid., i, 26 n.5, 51 n.7, 93 n.3, 166 n.3; ii, 270 n.1. Peter Lombard's Great Gloss on the Pauline Epistles interpreted 'redeeming the time' as using the time to serve God and pray, not engaging in legal disputes: '*Redimentes tempus*, id est praeparantes vobis opportunitatem serviendi Deo et vacandi divinis … Redimit ille tempus qui perdit, id est dat de suo ut vacet Deo non litibus … Sic perdes de tuo, ut emas tibi quietem; hoc est tempus redimere … ut habeas quietum cor, ne perdas tempus vacandi Deo tuo, a quo vult te avocare damno et litibus' (*PL*, 192.211–12). As reported by Herbert, Thomas argued that St Paul did not teach that 'time should be redeemed' to the destruction of ecclesiastical liberty (*Vita*, *MTB*, iii, 352–4).

[150] *Vita*, *MTB*, iii, 405–6. There are various versions of a vision at Pontigny, in which the Lord told Thomas, 'My Church will be glorified in your blood', but none detailed the nature of the murder or the number of assailants. See, for example, Edward Grim, *Vita sancti Thome* (1173): *MTB*, ii, 353–450, at 418–19, and the account in Alan of Tewkesbury's collecton of Becket correspondence: London, BL MS Cotton Claudius B.ii, fol. 141ra.

[151] Even as he recognised its importance as a record, Professor Barlow called the *Thomus* 'rambling and verbose'; and his judgement on Herbert's commentary on the Hebrew psalter and edition of Peter Lombard's 'great gloss' on the Psalms and St Paul's epistles was equally damning: 'scholasticism pure and simple, [they] have had their day': F. Barlow, 'Bosham, Herbert of (d. *c.* 1194)', *ODNB*.

CHAPTER THREE

Herbert of Bosham and Peter Lombard

Matthew Doyle

ERBERT of Bosham studied theology with Peter Lombard in the 1140s and 1150s.[1] This training was crucial for his later employment. It also had a significant impact on his work, both as editor and author. Despite this, studies of Peter Lombard's school (or immediate sphere of influence) have often failed to take account of Herbert. The broad range of his activity and literary output has meant that those examining the theological tradition of Peter's *Sententiae* have looked elsewhere. At the same time, Herbert's own specialists have sometimes downplayed his intellectual formation in the school of the Lombard. Certainly the work that has received most attention recently, the commentary on the *Hebraica*, owes little to Peter Lombard. But other works are more informed by his training. It was not unusual for Peter's students to work in different areas, and none matched his complete commitment to the theological enterprise. Still, for Herbert, Peter remained 'my master of pleasant memory',[2] and the editions he prepared of Peter's commentaries are a testament to this.

Peter Lombard taught theology in Paris in the 1140s and 1150s.[3] He was under the authority of the chancellor of the cathedral school of Notre Dame, where he was a canon himself.[4] Neither he nor his students, however, lived in the cathedral cloisters. The growing numbers of masters and students in Paris had made that impractical.[5]

---

[1] This article summarises some of the research completed for my book *Peter Lombard and His Students* (Toronto, 2016). For Herbert and his edition of Peter Lombard's commentaries, see especially ch. 8, pp. 198–235.

[2] Herbert of Bosham, *Epistolae*, in *PL*, 190.1418: '[m]agistri mei suavis recordationis'.

[3] For Peter Lombard's career, see *Sententiae in IV libris distinctae: Prolegomena*, ed. I. C. Brady, 2 vols. (Rome, 1971–81), i, pp. 8–39; P. Rosemann, *Peter Lombard* (Oxford, 2004), pp. 34–42.

[4] I. C. Brady, 'Peter Lombard. Canon of Notre Dame', *Recherches de théologie ancienne et médiévale* 32 (1965), 277–95. For the role of the chancellor of Notre Dame, who granted masters their teaching licence, see S. C. Ferruolo, *The Origins of the University: The Schools of Paris and their Critics, 1100–1215* (Stanford, 1985), pp. 189–92, and G. Post, 'Alexander III, the *licentia docendi* and the Rise of the Universities', in *Anniversary Essays in Mediaeval History by Students of Charles Homer Haskins*, ed. C. H. Taylor and J. L. LaMonte (Boston, 1929), pp. 235–78.

[5] The change had happened in 1127. See A. L. Gabriel, 'The Cathedral Schools of

Peter held various positions in the church of Paris in this period, and ultimately retired from teaching in 1159 when he was appointed bishop.[6] The subject he taught, theology, was considered to be advanced study. Students who had completed their training in the liberal arts could choose to progress to theology, medicine or the law.[7] In the arts it was normal to study with different masters, often in large lecture halls. Theology was different. The numbers were smaller, and students chose to study with one master at a time.[8] By the time of the thirteenth-century university, anyone wishing to teach theology should have studied it for at least five years.[9] In the twelfth-century schools, the period of study seems to have been longer. William of Tyre spent 'six years uninterrupted' studying with Peter Lombard, but still did not consider his theological training complete when his master left the schools to become bishop of Paris.[10] He embarked on a further year of study with Maurice of Sully.[11] In this sort of educational environment, a student would be substantially influenced by their master. Students in these theology schools would also be expected to explain their master's positions correctly. In one set of *quaestiones* a master's students are described as 'safe ears'.[12]

Herbert was born around 1120.[13] He entered the schools therefore in the late 1130s, where he would initially have studied the arts. Peter Lombard began to teach theology in the early 1140s,[14] and Herbert's training had certainly finished by the mid-1150s. By 1157 he was already employed by Henry II and took part in diplomatic missions where his position as a *magister* was important.[15] So he would have

Notre-Dame and the Beginning of the University of Paris', in *Garlandia: Studies in the History of the Medieval University*, ed. A. L. Gabriel (Notre-Dame, 1969), pp. 39–64, at 41–2. For the growing numbers of masters and students, see R. W. Southern, *Scholastic Humanism and the Unification of Europe: Foundations* (Oxford, 1995), pp. 198–231; R. W. Southern, 'The Schools of Paris and the School of Chartres', in *Renaissance and Renewal in the Twelfth Century*, ed. R. L. Benson and G. Constable (Cambridge, MA, 1982), pp. 119–132, at 119–121; Ferruolo, *The Origins of the University*, pp. 11–27.

[6] Brady, 'Peter Lombard. Canon of Notre Dame', pp. 277–95.

[7] Southern, *Scholastic Humanism: Foundations*, pp. 212–20, at 230–1; Smalley, *Becket Conflict*, pp. 18–21.

[8] Southern, *Scholastic Humanism: Foundations*, pp. 213–14.

[9] Ferruolo, *The Origins of the University*, p. 306.

[10] William of Tyre, *Chronicon*, ed. R. B. C. Huygens, *CCCM*, 63 (Turnhout, 1986), xix.12, p. 880: '[a]nnis sex continuis diligenter audivimus'.

[11] Ibid. On William's study years, see also Southern, *Scholastic Humanism: Foundations*, pp. 212–14.

[12] '[t]utis auribus loquebatur, id est illis quod instruxerat'. This text, attributed to Peter Comestor, can be found in I. C. Brady, 'Peter Manducator and the Oral Teachings of Peter Lombard', *Antonianum* 41 (1966), 454–90 at 473.

[13] Smalley, *Becket Conflict*, p. 59.

[14] Brady, *Prolegomena*, i, p. 17.

[15] *Ottonis et Rahewini Gesta Frederici I Imperatoris*, ed. G. Waitz and B. von Simson, *MGH SrG*, 46 (Hanover and Leipzig, 1912), pp. 171–2. The mission is discussed in detail in K. Leyser, 'Frederick Barbarossa, Henry II and the Hand of St James', *EHR* 90 (1975), 481–506.

spent several years in the theology school sometime between 1140 and 1155. When Herbert, in the 1170s, completed an edition of Peter's commentary on the Psalms, he included a lengthy preface which recalled his years in the schools and showed his regard for his master.[16] He explained that the commentary had been left unfinished and he had to complete some of the references to authorities:

> Nothing however should be asserted against the judgement of that illustrious teacher, who was the commentator of these works, and my principal instructor in this doctrine ... He however, if by chance he left something that was not quite polished in his works, he is not to be blamed for it, but completely excused. For when he was writing these works, just as I learned from talking to him, it never came into his mind that they would be read publicly in the schools; they were only done in order to bring into clearer light the obscure brevity of the earlier commentator, Anselm of Laon ... When later, at the instance of many, the aforesaid works, not yet fully pruned by the hoe of correction, were read publicly by the master, he was promoted to the see of Paris and in a short time was removed from human affairs. The intention of my weakness therefore is not to attach any note of ignorance or negligence to such a great teacher, who instructed me pre-eminently in this doctrine, or to darken the splendour of such a light of the church.[17]

This excerpt gives a flavour of the close relationship that could exist between a theology master and his students. Peter Lombard confided in Herbert about the origins of his commentary. It is also clear that, even after he left the schools, Herbert had remained up to date on what was happening in Peter Lombard's school. Peter taught the commentary just before becoming bishop in 1159, by which time Herbert had already left the schools.[18]

What was Peter teaching when Herbert studied with him in the 1140s and 1150s? As a theology master, much of his time was spent on scriptural interpretation. When he died, his house and books were donated to the chapter of Notre Dame. These included glossed copies of most of the books of the Bible.[19] These would not

---

[16] The preface can be found in H. H. Glunz, *History of the Vulgate in England* (Cambridge, 1933), pp. 342–6.

[17] Ibid., p. 343: 'Nichil tamen in illustris doctoris illius preiudicium qui horum fuit glosator, et meus in hac doctrina institutor precipuus, asseritur ... Qui tamen, si quid forte non ita ad unguem resecatum in suis operibus reliquerit, non arguendus ob id, sed excusandus omnino. Nam cum hec opera scriberet, nequaquam, sicut ipsomet referente didici, ipsi venit in mentem, quod in scolis publicis legerentur; solum ob id facta, ut antiquioris glosatoris, magistri videlicet anselmi laudunensis, brevitatem elucidarent obscuram ... Cum vero postea ad multorum instanciam a magistro preter spem iam dicta opera publice legerentur, necdum plene correctionis sarculo putatis omnibus, in parisiorum antistitem promotus est et post in brevi humanis rebus exemptus. Nec igitur parvitatis mee intentio est tanto doctori, et qui me precipue in hac doctrina instituit, ullam ignorancie vel negligencie inurere notam seu tanti luminis ecclesie vel in modico obscurare splendorem.'

[18] The letter is further discussed in this context in Brady, *Prolegomena*, i, pp. 126–9.

[19] Brady, *Prolegomena*, i, pp. 19–20. Rosemann, *Peter Lombard*, pp. 39–40. M. J. Clark, 'The

have been commentaries intended for publication but personal copies used for teaching. Peter's positions on biblical texts besides his published commentaries are cited by other authors.[20] He also published a collection of sermons which show that he was adept at handling scriptural passages.[21] In these sermons Peter does not just gloss the opening *incipit*, but also subsidiary passages which allow him to tie in the feast day or season being celebrated.[22]

As well as the Bible, it would be surprising if Peter had not taught the sacraments in his school, since he had studied with Hugh of St Victor.[23] Hugh had taught earlier versions of his work *De Sacramentis* in his school.[24] Also, many theology students went on to have careers in the church and would require such a training. Two of Peter Lombard's students, Adam of Wales and William of Tyre, became bishops,[25] while Herbert was of course a bishop's adviser. Another student, Peter Comestor, held a number of positions in the cathedrals of both Paris and Troyes.[26] By the early 1150s, Peter Lombard was recognising the need for theological material arranged by topic, and this culminated in the first version of the *Sententiae*.[27] He taught this in the 1156–57 and 1157–58 academic years.[28] The students who attended these classes reported that he sometimes went into more detail on certain subjects, and also that he made marginal notes as he was teaching.[29]

This training was important for Herbert's later career. While few of Peter Lombard's students became theology masters themselves, they used the material and skills they had learned in his school in different ways. They also took pride in their training. Peter Comestor and an unnamed student refer to medicine and the law as 'the shallower arts' when compared to theology.[30] Herbert deplored the fact that

Biblical Gloss, the Search for the Lombard's Glossed Bible and the Schools of Paris', *Mediaeval Studies* 76 (2014), 57–113.

[20] M. Colish, *Peter Lombard* (Leiden, 1994), pp. 28–9. Brady, *Prolegomena*, ii, pp. 19–52.

[21] For the sermons, see for example F. Protois, *Pierre Lombard: Evêque de Paris dit le maître des sentences – son époque, sa vie, ses écrits, son influence* (Paris, 1881), pp. 123–48; Brady, *Prolegomena*, i, pp. 95–112; Rosemann, *Peter Lombard*, p. 49; Colish, *Peter Lombard*, pp. 26–7.

[22] I have discussed the sermons extensively in chapter 6 of *Peter Lombard and His Students*, pp. 23–164.

[23] Brady, *Prolegomena*, i, pp. 16–17; Colish, *Peter Lombard*, pp. 18–19.

[24] See the report of his teaching in A. M. Piazzoni, 'Ugo di San Vittore, "auctor" delle *Sententiae de Divinitate*', *Studi Medievale* 23 (1981), 861–955. The chronology of Hugh's *De Sacramentis* is discussed in P. Sicard, *Diagrammes médiévaux et exégèse visuelle. Le Libellus de formatione arche de Hugues de Saint-Victor* (Turnhout, 1993), pp. 119–38.

[25] For William, see n.10 above. See also P. Edbury and G. J. Rowe, *William of Tyre. Historian of the Latin East* (Cambridge, 1988). For Adam of Wales, see J. E. Lloyd, 'Adam, Bishop of St Asaph', in *Dictionary of Welsh Biography down to 1940*, ed. J. E. Lloyd and R. T. Jenkins (London, 1959).

[26] Brady, 'Peter Manducator and the Oral Teachings of Peter Lombard', pp. 483–4.

[27] For the development of the *Sententiae*, see Rosemann, *Peter Lombard*, pp. 54–70.

[28] Brady, *Prolegomena*, i, pp. 122–9.

[29] Brady, 'Peter Manducator and the Oral Teachings of Peter Lombard', pp. 454–90. Rosemann, *Peter Lombard*, pp. 40–1.

[30] Peter Comestor, in his prologue to a commentary on the *Sentences*, calls them the

some were promoted in the church despite being 'ignorant of the sacred scriptures'.[31] Initially, Herbert was in the service of Henry II, but it was his role under Archbishop Thomas Becket that really shows the value of his theological education. According to William Fitzstephen, Herbert's position in the archbishop's household was as *'magister in divina pagina'*, a 'master in the holy page'.[32] This reference is important because it shows that Herbert had completed the theology course with Peter Lombard and was now entitled to call himself a master. It was necessary for an archbishop to have a theology master on hand, particularly one like Herbert who was acquainted with the most recent developments in the Paris schools.[33] Herbert could have assisted the bishop in any number of areas such as the sacraments, or the interpretation of scriptural texts, or the responsibility for the doctrinal knowledge of clerics. He could also have had a role in sermon preparation. Herbert would have experienced Peter Lombard's sermons in Paris, which show a systematic treatment of theme and scriptural text.[34] We know that Herbert did work as a freelance sermon writer later in life.[35] Herbert himself, in the *Vita Sancti Thomae*, emphasised how he and Becket studied the scriptures together, particularly during their exile at Pontigny.[36]

After Becket's death, Herbert's employment situation was more sporadic, but he continued to put his theological training to use. Sometime between 1174 and the end of the decade he attempted to start a school of theology.[37] He received the backing of Pope Alexander III for this, who wrote to the archbishop of Canterbury requesting that Herbert be allocated funds from his property in England.[38] The letter does not say where Herbert intended to teach, but Smalley has pointed to a number of documents which show that he was resident in Paris at the time.[39] If he did try to teach in Paris, he would have required a licence from the chancellor of Notre Dame. Peter Comestor, another Lombard pupil, held that position at the time.[40] The choice of Paris might also explain why nothing more is known of Herbert's proposed

'breviores artes'. The text of this prologue is in R. M. Martin, 'Notes sur l'œuvre littéraire de Pierre le Mangeur', *Recherches de théologie ancienne et médiévale* 3 (1931), 54–66, at 61. Another prologue, edited in ibid., p. 64, makes a similar point: They 'despair of their own abilities after noticing the sheer number of books involved in the study of the holy page'.

[31] *MTB*, iii, 207: '[a]nimarum constituantur pastores, scripturarum ignari'.

[32] Fitzstephen, *Vita*, *MTB*, iii, 58.

[33] For the position see also C. de Hamel, *Glossed Books of the Bible and the Origins of the Paris Book Trade* (Cambridge, 1984), p. 42, who describes Herbert as a 'theological consultant'; Smalley, *Becket Conflict*, p. 63.

[34] See nn.21 and 22 above on the sermons.

[35] Smalley, *Becket Conflict*, pp. 65–6.

[36] *MTB*, iii, 358. Herbert also mentions their studies at Pontigny in the preface to his edition of Peter Lombard's commentaries: Glunz, *History*, p. 342.

[37] Smalley, *Becket Conflict*, p. 71.

[38] *Epistolae Pontificum Romanorum Ineditae*, ed. S. Lowenfeld (Leipzig, 1885), p. 207.

[39] Smalley, *Becket Conflict*, p. 71.

[40] For Comestor's chancellorship, see S. Daly, 'Peter Comestor: Master of Histories', *Speculum* 32 (1957), 62–73, at 66–7, and Post, 'Alexander III, the *licentia docendi* and the Rise of the Universities', p. 273.

school of theology. It was a competitive scholarly environment and he had been away from the schools for twenty years at this point. Peter of Poitiers seems to have been the pre-eminent figure for those who wished to study theology in the tradition of the *Sententiae* in the 1170s.[41] Peter Lombard did not formally teach the *Sententiae* until 1156–58, by which time Herbert seems to have graduated from his school.[42]

Herbert continued to put his theological training to use in his works. The influence of the study of theology on his *Vita Sancti Thomae* has been discussed admirably by Michael Staunton and Jessica Weiss.[43] It is also evident in another work in praise of Becket, the *Liber Melorum*, which contains sections on proving the existence of God and on the Incarnation of Christ. For the latter, Herbert recounts the three main theories of the hypostatic union, and while his treatment is not as extensive as that of his master in the *Sententiae* it has relevance nonetheless.[44] In the 1160s and 1170s Peter Lombard's views on christological questions had become controversial.[45] The *Liber Melorum*, written in the 1180s, is not a key part of that debate, but it should not be ignored. Herbert's contribution to this subject has not been discussed in any of the studies of the controversy. This theological digression in the *Liber Melorum* may also reflect Herbert's recent experience of teaching theology.

Herbert's editions of Peter Lombard's commentaries on the Psalms and the Pauline Epistles date from the 1170s, when the christological controversy was at its height.[46] This remarkable set of four volumes has attracted much attention for its innovative page layout and inventive illustrations.[47] As mentioned earlier, Herbert

---

[41] According to Alberic of Trois Fontaines, Peter of Poitiers taught theology from 1167 to 1205: Alberic of Trois Fontaines, *Chronicon*, ed. P. Scheffer-Boichorst, *MGH SS* 23 (Hanover, 1874), p. 886. For his work, see Philip Moore, *The Works of Peter of Poitiers. Master in Theology and Chancellor of Paris (1193–1205)* (Indiana, 1936).

[42] See n.15 above. This would also explain why Herbert focused more on Peter Lombard's commentaries in his editorial work.

[43] See M. Staunton, *The Lives of Thomas Becket* (Manchester, 2001), p. 10; M. Staunton, *Thomas Becket and His Biographers* (Woodbridge, 2006), pp. 63–75; J. L. Weiss, 'Herbert of Bosham's *Liber Melorum*: Literature and Sacred Sciences in the Twelfth Century' (Unpublished PhD dissertation, Harvard University, 2003), ch. 2, 'Theological and Biblical Rhetoric in the *Historia Thomae*', pp. 46–78.

[44] Herbert of Bosham, *Liber Melorum* (*PL*, 190.1378–81). See also: Weiss, 'Herbert of Bosham's *Liber Melorum*', pp. 195–6; Smalley, *Becket Conflict*, pp. 79–81.

[45] See for example: J. Châtillon, 'Latran III et l'enseignement christologique de Pierre Lombard', in *Le Troisième Concile de Latran (1179): sa place dans histoire*, ed. J. Longère (Paris, 1982), pp. 75–90; L. Nielsen, *Theology and Philosophy in the Twelfth Century: A Study of Gilbert Porreta's Thinking and the Theological Expositions of the Doctrine of the Incarnation During the Period 1130–1180* (Leiden, 1982), pp. 243–362; Colish, *Peter Lombard*, pp. 398–438; P. Rossi, '*Contra Lombardum*: Reazioni alla Cristologia di Pietro Lombardo', *Pietro Lombardo: Atti del XLIII Convegno Storico Internazionale* (Spoleto, 2007), pp. 123–91; C. Monagle, *Orthodoxy and Controversy in Twelfth-Century Religious Discourse: Peter Lombard's Sentences and the Development of Theology* (Turnhout, 2013), pp. 73–137.

[46] I have discussed the editions extensively in this context in chapter 8 of *Peter Lombard and His Students*, pp. 198–235.

[47] See for example: W. Cahn, *Romanesque Manuscripts: The Twelfth Century*, 2 vols. (London, 1996), ii, pp. 107–9; de Hamel, *Glossed Books*, p. 42; L. Smith, *Masters of the*

was careful to explain that the commentary on the Psalms had been left unfinished. Peter Lombard himself had completed two editions of the commentary on the Pauline Epistles.[48] The initial work on these commentaries seems to have taken place during Becket's exile at the abbey of Pontigny in 1164–66, where Herbert was able to check references in the library.[49] But the work was not completed until sometime between 1171 and 1176, and this is thought to have been done by a team of professional illuminators working in the archdiocese of Sens. While Christopher de Hamel considered those illuminators to have been based in Paris,[50] Patricia Stirnemann has more recently suggested that the work took place in Sens itself.[51]

Herbert supervised the work of the scribes and illuminators,[52] and he also wrote prefaces explaining his editorial method. He aimed to make his master's text as accessible as possible, and this was reflected in a number of areas, particularly the noting of authorities, and illustration. In the Psalms commentary, Peter Lombard had grouped the Psalms together by subject. In Herbert's edition, each subject is given a specific marginal illustration and a list of Psalms on the same topic appears beside it.[53] Herbert's own writing can occasionally be seen at the side of the page, providing instruction on what the illustration should be.[54] For Psalms dealing with the passion and resurrection of Christ, the direction *'imago crucis'* – 'a picture of the cross' – can be seen on one folio.[55] For Psalms dealing with the two natures of

Sacred Page: Manuscripts of Theology in the Latin West to 1274 (Notre Dame, 2001), pp. 45–8; C. de Hamel, 'Manuscripts of Herbert of Bosham', in *Manuscripts at Oxford*, ed. A. C. de la Mare and B. C. Barker Benfield (Oxford, 1980), pp. 38–40; *The Cambridge Illuminations: Ten Centuries of Book Production in the Medieval* West, ed. P. Binski and S. Panayotova (London, 2005), pp. 92–4; S. Panayotova, 'Tutorial in Images for Thomas Becket', in *The Cambridge Illuminations: The Conference Papers*, ed. S. Panayotova (London, 2007), pp. 77–86; *Illuminated Manuscripts in Cambridge: A Catalogue of Western Book Illumination in the Fitzwilliam Museum and the Cambridge Colleges*, pt. iii, vol I, ed. N. Morgan and S. Panayatova (London, 2015), pp. 103–17.

[48] Brady, *Prolegomena,* i, pp. 62–89; Colish, *Peter Lombard,* pp. 192–225; Rosemann, *Peter Lombard,* pp. 44–8.

[49] For what was done at Pontigny, see: M. Peyrafort-Huin, *La bibliothèque médiévale de l'abbaye de Pontigny (XIIe–XIXe siècles). Histoire, inventaires anciens, manuscrits* (Paris, 2001), pp. 108–10; E. De Visscher, *Reading the Rabbis: Christian Hebraism in the Works of Herbert of Bosham* (Leiden, 2014), pp. 18–19.

[50] De Hamel, *Glossed Books,* pp. 45–54.

[51] P. Stirnemann, 'En quête de Sens', in *Quand la peinture était dans les livres: Mélanges en l'honneur de François Avril*, ed. M. Hoffmann, E. König and C. Zöhl (Turnhout, 2007), pp. 303–12. For the role of William of the White Hands, archbishop of Sens in these works, see also Doyle, *Peter Lombard and His Students,* pp. 211–12.

[52] Panayotova has explained that although Herbert was 'neither the scribe, nor one of the four main artists involved in the project', his 'intervention is visible in the meticulous planning, rigorous supervision and obsessive editing'. Panayotova, 'Tutorial in Images for Thomas Becket', p. 78.

[53] A thorough discussion of the subject illustrations can be found in ibid., pp. 79–83.

[54] Herbert's handwritten instructions are discussed in ibid., p. 79.

[55] Cambridge, Trinity College, MS B.5.4, fol. 165v.

Christ, Herbert has asked for '*imago hominis igniti*' – 'a picture of a man in flames'.[56] The subjects are also included in the overall table of contents.[57]

The edition of the commentary on the Pauline Epistles is not quite as notable for illumination, and so has not received as much scholarly attention.[58] Although there are fewer marginal figures, every letter except that to the Hebrews begins with the word 'paulus' and so there are a variety of large initial 'P's, often containing a picture of Paul.[59] There are always two: one for the preface and another for the beginning of each letter. One of the most distinctive pages is the opening of the Second Letter to the Thessalonians. As well as the standard features of a list of chapters and preface, one of the 'P's shows a figure engaged in blessing within the rounded top part, which is being held up by a listening disciple forming the stem. The identity of the figure engaged in blessing is clear from the word 'paulus' at the edge of the page.[60] It is not clear why M. R. James considered this volume of the edition to be inferior to the others in terms of decoration.[61]

Herbert is also careful to separate Peter's preface to each letter from the commentary proper, usually by adding *praefatio epistolae* in blue and red ink.[62] It is also clear that Herbert, as a graduate of Peter's school, is thoroughly acquainted with the text. Assistance is provided for navigating the more complex parts of the commentary. A feature of the manuscripts of Peter Lombard's *Sentences* is the use of rubrics: marginal notes which divide the text into headings, and which indicate the theological questions under discussion.[63] We can see the same procedure in Herbert's edition of the commentary on Paul's letter to the Romans. Peter discusses the Incarnation in some detail when dealing with verse 1.3, 'factus est' – 'he was made'. Rubrics have been added in Herbert's edition to show that questions like 'why the Apostle says "made" and not "born"', and 'whether Christ can be described as a creature', are being discussed.[64]

Another striking feature of the edition is the regular inclusion of substantial extracts from earlier commentators. While shorter quotations from the fathers

---

[56] Oxford, Bodleian Library, MS Auct. E. Inf. 6, fol 21v.

[57] The tables of contents can be seen at: B.5.4, fol. 7v; Auct. E. Inf. 6, fol. 1r and fol. 54v.

[58] Cambridge, Trinity College, MS B.5.6 and B.5.7. They are described in M. R. James, *The Western Manuscripts in the Library of Trinity College Cambridge: A Descriptive Catalogue*, 3 vols. (Cambridge, 1900), i, pp. 188–201. The prefaces can be found in Glunz, *History*, pp. 346–50. See also, de Hamel, *Glossed Books*, pp. 22–7, 42–4. These manuscripts, along with volume 2 of the Psalm commentary, are now available in full at the Wren Digital Library: https://www.trin.cam.ac.uk/library/wren-digital-library.

[59] An example is B.5.6, fol. 8v which is reproduced in de Hamel, *Glossed Books*, pl. 18a.

[60] B.5.7, fol. 92v.

[61] 'The ornament is not, I think, so good as in the other volumes.' James, *The Western Manuscripts in the Library of Trinity College Cambridge*, i, pp. 200–1.

[62] See for example B.5.6, fols. 95r–95v (1 Cor.).

[63] I. C. Brady, 'The Rubrics of Peter Lombard's Sentences', *Pier Lombardo* 6 (1962), 5–26. See also Rosemann, *Peter Lombard*, p. 65.

[64] 'Quare factum non natum dicat Apostolus', and 'an Christus sit dicendus creatura'. B.5.6, fol. 10v.

are placed in the margins, longer extracts appear in a smaller font within the columns of the main text. The Pauline commentaries of Jerome and Haimo of Auxerre occur regularly in this format, suggesting that Herbert wished to add their additional authority to his master's treatment of the biblical text. This was particularly important in verses relevant to christology.[65] But the technique is also very prominent in glosses where Peter Lombard's treatment of the text is somewhat brief. An example is the letter to Philemon, which includes sections of the prefaces of Jerome and Haimo, and of Jerome's commentary on verses 13 and 22.[66] Interestingly, however, these extracts are often slightly abridged, presumably for reasons of space.[67]

Herbert's work on the commentaries can be seen as part of a wider enterprise in the 1160s and 1170s involving the students of Peter Lombard. A number of them worked on increasing awareness of his works, through teaching, commentary and preparing editions. Some, like Herbert, are fairly well known. Peter Comestor seems to have begun the tradition of lecturing on the *Sentences* in the Paris schools, while he also wrote an abridgement of book four for wider use.[68] Others – largely anonymous – are known for their work of producing the earliest commentaries and summaries of the *Sentences*.[69] William of Tyre referred to how Peter Lombard's works were 'embraced with veneration, and cultivated with reverence by a group of prudent followers'.[70] It was a group that included Herbert of Bosham.

---

[65] A notable example is Philippians 2:7, on B.5.6, fols. 60–60v. See Doyle, *Peter Lombard and His Students*, pp. 229–231.

[66] B.5.7, fols. 129, 130–130v.

[67] The same is true of the marginal quotations from Jerome's commentary. For his gloss (which was compared with the manuscript text of B.5.7) see Jerome, *Commentaria in Epistolam ad Philemonem*, PL 26, 599–619. Haimo's commentary is incorrectly attributed to Haymo of Halberstadt in PL 117, 361–936. See also, I. C. Levy, 'Commentaries on the Pauline Epistles in the Carolingian Era', in *A Companion to St. Paul in the Middle Ages*, ed. S. R. Cartwright (Leiden, 2003), pp. 159–68.

[68] See Martin, 'Notes sur l'œuvre littéraire de Pierre le Mangeur', pp. 61–2; Luscombe, 'Peter Comestor', pp. 116–18; N. Spatz, 'Approaches and Attitudes to a New Theology Textbook. The "Sentences" of Peter Lombard', in *The Intellectual Climate of the Early University*, ed. N. van Deusen (Kalamazoo, 1997), pp. 27–52, at 35.

[69] For their work, see for example: H. Weisweiler, 'Eine Neue zum Vierten Buch der Sentenzen des Petrus Lombardus', in *Aus der Geisteswelt des Mittelalters: Studien und Texte*, ed. A. Lang (Münster, 1935), pp. 360–86; P. Rosemann, *The Story of a Great Medieval Book: Peter Lombard's Sentences* (Peterborough, ON, 2007), pp. 28–33; M. Colish, 'The Pseudo-Peter of Poitiers Gloss', in *Mediaeval Commentaries on the Sentences of Peter Lombard*, ed. G. Evans and P. Rosemann (Leiden, 2005–10), ii, pp. 1–33.

[70] William of Tyre, *Chronicon*, xix.12, CCCM, 63, p. 880: 'In theologia autem virum in ea scientia singularem, cuius opera que exstant prudentum chorus cum veneratione amplectitur et colit cum reverentia, virum sana doctrina per omnia commendabilem, magistrum videlicet Petrum Lonbardum, qui postea fuit Parisiensis episcopus, annis sex continuis diligenter audivimus.'

CHAPTER FOUR

Pages Covered with as Many Tears as Notes: Herbert of Bosham and the Glossed Manuscripts for Thomas Becket[*]

Laura Cleaver

ACCORDING to Herbert of Bosham, when Henry II asked his chancellor Thomas Becket to become archbishop of Canterbury, Becket, drawing attention to his clothes, declared with irony, 'How religious, how saintly a man you wish to appoint to such a holy see and above such a renowned and holy community of monks! I know most certainly that if by God's arrangement it happened thus, very quickly you would turn your heart and favour away from me, which is now great between us, and replace it with the most savage hatred.'[1] Writing with the benefit of hindsight, Herbert thus has Becket prophesy the dispute that would see him flee the country, returning only to be murdered in Canterbury cathedral in 1170, and speak well of the monks who would promote his cult. Yet Herbert also demonstrates, and attributes to Becket, an awareness of the power of visual appearances and a fondness for fine things.[2] Herbert's interest in extravagantly decorated objects is also attested by the impressive glossed copies of the Psalter and the Pauline

---

[*] This essay would not exist without Michael Staunton, who persuaded me to speak at the Herbert of Bosham conference in 2013, for which I am very grateful. I am also hugely indebted to Christopher de Hamel, who co-organised the conference, and to the conference participants, from whom I learned an enormous amount. Thanks are due both to those who encouraged me that there might be something in the paper I presented, and to those whose scepticism has helped to guide me in revising this work for publication. In particular I would like to thank Anne Duggan, Nigel Morgan, Patricia Stirnemann and Tessa Webber for their generosity in sharing their knowledge with me.

[1] *Vita*, in *MTB*, iii, 181: 'Cui cancellarius schemata quaedam risibilia quibus tunc indutus subridendo ostendens et quasi oculis ingerens, "Quam religiosum," inquit, "virum, quam sanctum in tam sancta sede et super tam celebrem et tam sanctum monachorum conventum constitui desideras: sciturus certissime quod si Domino disponente acciderit sic, citissime a me avertes animum et gratiam, quae nunc inter nos tanta est, in atrocissimum odium convertendam"'; translated in M. Staunton, *The Lives of Thomas Becket* (Manchester and New York, 2001), p. 60.

[2] See also U. Nilgen, 'Intellectuality and Splendour: Thomas Becket as a Patron of the Arts', in *Art and Patronage in the English Romanesque*, ed. S. Macready and F. H. Thompson (London, 1986), pp. 145–58.

Epistles, which he designed and seems to have intended to dedicate to Becket.[3] These volumes survive in four parts: the two sections of the Psalter are now Trinity College Cambridge MS B.5.4 and Oxford, Bodleian Library MS Auct. E Infra 6, and the two volumes of the Epistles are Trinity College Cambridge MSS B.5.6 and B.5.7. The four impressive manuscripts were probably once all the same size, measuring a little more than 470 x 325 mm (the size of the largest surviving volume, that in Oxford), but all have been trimmed and rebound. The manuscripts were lavishly decorated, though the Psalter volumes have had parts of the decoration excised. In addition, four quires have been lost from the second volume of the Psalter, and the bifolio that contained Psalm 1 is missing from the first volume. Both parts of the Psalter and the first volume of the Epistles contain prefaces commenting on the circumstances in which the manuscripts were produced, making them remarkably well-documented manuscripts for the second half of the twelfth century. Moreover, the wealth of material about Becket, including Herbert's own account of the saint's life, completed in the 1180s, provides further evidence for the context in which these volumes were executed. However, scholars have drawn very different conclusions from this evidence, suggesting that the books should be understood as products of Canterbury, Pontigny, Paris or Sens.[4] The aim of this essay is to revisit the evidence for the production of these manuscripts found in Herbert's writings and in the manuscripts themselves. In particular, in retelling this story, I want to suggest that Herbert's accounts of his relationship with Becket may shed light on some of the contents of the historiated initials in these volumes.

---

[3] C. de Hamel, 'A Contemporary Miniature of Thomas Becket', in *Intellectual Life in the Middle Ages: Essays Presented to Margaret Gibson*, ed. L. Smith and B. Ward (London, 1992), pp. 179–84.

[4] H. H. Glunz, *History of the Vulgate in England: From Alcuin to Roger Bacon* (Cambridge, 1933), pp. 218, 341; C. R. Dodwell, *The Canterbury School of Illumination 1066–1200* (Cambridge, 1954), pp. 107–9; B. Smalley, *The Becket Conflict and the Schools* (Oxford, 1973), p. 82; C. de Hamel, 'Manuscripts of Herbert of Bosham', in *Manuscripts at Oxford: An Exhibition in Memory of Richard William Hunt (1908–1979)*, ed. A. C. de la Mare and B. C. Barker-Benfield (Oxford, 1980), pp. 39–41; C. de Hamel, *Glossed Books of the Bible and the Origins of the Paris Booktrade* (Cambridge, 1984), p. 53; A. G. Watson, *Catalogue of Dated and Datable Manuscripts c. 435–1600 in Oxford Libraries* (Oxford, 1984), p. 9; P. Stirnemann, 'Compte rendu: C. de Hamel, *Glossed Books of the Bible and the Origins of the Paris Booktrade* (Cambridge, 1984)', *Bulletin Monumental* 143 (1985), 363–7; P. R. Robinson, *Catalogue of Dated and Datable Manuscripts c. 737–1600 in Cambridge Libraries* (Cambridge, 1988), pp. 92–3; W. Cahn, *Romanesque Manuscripts: The Twelfth Century*, 2 vols. (London, 1996), ii, p. 107; T. A. Heslop, 'Late Twelfth-Century Writing about Art and Aesthetic Relativity', in *Medieval Art: Recent Perspectives*, ed. G. R. Owen-Crocker and T. Graham (Manchester, 1998), pp. 129–41, at 139 n.10; S. Panayotova, 'Tutorial in Images for Thomas Becket', in *The Cambridge Illuminations: the Conference Papers*, ed. S. Panayotova (London, 2007), pp. 77–83, at 77; P. Stirnemann, 'En quête de Sens', in *Quand la peinture était dans les livres*, ed. M. Hoffmann and C. Zöhl (Turnhout, 2007), pp. 303–11.

Books and Becket's exile (1164–70)

Herbert of Bosham claimed that Thomas Becket left England in early November 1164, taking with him nothing except the pallium and his seal, as his signs of office, and a rough cloak, echoing Christ's command to the disciples to travel with nothing.[5] However, Herbert also recorded that he had managed to raise a hundred marks and obtain some silver vessels from Canterbury, on Becket's instructions, suggesting that Becket was not entirely unconcerned with practicalities.[6] Whilst Herbert's account of Becket's flight presents him as Christ-like to a point that stretches credulity, at one point placing him on a borrowed beast of burden, in an echo of Christ's entry into Jerusalem, it seems unlikely that Becket would have taken books with him.[7] Books were, after all, readily available in France. In a note added to the preface to the glossed Psalter, Herbert described the Cistercian monastery at Pontigny (28 miles south-east of Sens), at which Becket established himself on the advice of the pope in late November or early December 1164, as being rich in chests of writings, likening these to the verdant pastures of Psalm 23 (22).[8] Becket was based at Pontigny until 1166. Herbert stressed the generosity and kindness of the monks, but after recent events Pontigny must have seemed extremely quiet. Indeed Herbert famously described this period as one of 'solitude among the stones and the monks'.[9] However, Pontigny was a good place in which to study, and with few distractions Becket was inspired to continue the studies he had begun after being appointed archbishop.[10] According to Herbert, Becket's studies at Pontigny paid particular attention to the Psalms and Epistles, which Herbert described as being like two spiritual eyes: mystical and moral.[11] In the prologue to the glossed

---

[5] *Vita*, *MTB*, iii, 318–19: 'Fugit itaque deposito orario, nihil secum praeterquam insigne illud metropolitanorum, quod pallium dicitur, et sigillum suum, in via portans; non peram, non panem, non in zona aes; sed solum cilicio amictus super nudo secutus est Jesum.' See Mark 6:8–9; Dodwell, *Canterbury School*, p. 108.

[6] *Vita*, *MTB*, iii, 330: 'Et priorum oblitus penitus, confortatus est, ut videbatur, nihil de crastino cogitans, cum tantum dictae solum centum marcae et vasa quaedam pauca argentea solum et totum fuerit nostrae peregrinationis longioris plus annis sex duraturae viaticum.' See Matt. 6:34.

[7] *Vita*, *MTB*, iii, 325–6; Staunton, *Lives*, pp. 120–8. See Matt. 21, Mark 11, Luke 19, John 12.

[8] Glunz, *History*, p. 342: 'In loco pascue (Pontiniaci scilicet, ubi locuples scripturarum armarium) collocavit me dominus' (the text in brackets has been added to the preface between the lines); *Vita*, *MTB*, iii, 357–8; see also M. Peyrafort-Huin, *La bibliothèque médiévale de l'abbaye de Pontigny (XIIe–XIXe siècles): histoire, inventaires anciens, manuscrits* (Paris, 2001); *CTB*, i, 497 n.1.

[9] *Vita*, *MTB*, iii, 379: 'Pontiniaci in solitudine inter petras et monachos solitarii nos delitescentes a saeculo jam remoti'; see also 357–8; Smalley, *Becket Conflict*, p. 63; Staunton, *Lives*, p. 137; F. Barlow, 'Bosham, Herbert of (d. *c.* 1194)', *ODNB*.

[10] *Vita*, *MTB*, iii, 204–6; de Hamel, 'Contemporary Miniature', p. 179.

[11] *Vita*, *MTB*, iii, 379: 'Unde et tantus erat scripturarum amator, quod post horas regulares quotidie sacri codices per totum diem vix de manu ejus discederent; praesertim sacri illi duo libri, Psalterii videlicet et Epistolarum, tanquam duo spirituales oculi, mysticus et moralis'; see also Fitzstephen, *MTB*, iii, 77; H. de Lubac, *Medieval Exegesis: Four Senses of Scripture*, trans. M. Sebanc, 2 vols. (Grand Rapids, 1998), i, 342, n.15; Peter Lombard,

Psalter, Herbert justified the compilation of the Gallican and Hebrew versions of the Psalms with the commentary of the controversial scholar Peter Lombard, under whom Herbert had earlier studied in Paris, on the grounds that Becket had wanted it done.[12] Thus the studies undertaken in this period laid the foundations for the creation of Herbert's great manuscripts.

In addition to the Pontigny library, during the exile Becket seems to have acquired books to equip his studies, perhaps with a view to enriching the resources available at Canterbury on his return.[13] William of Canterbury claimed that Becket returned to England in 1170 with a *bibliotheca*, probably meaning a library.[14] Some of Becket's followers also seem to have managed to maintain substantial libraries during their time in France. In 1165 John of Salisbury, who had followed Becket into exile, wrote to the bishop of Exeter in an attempt to find a way to return to England, noting that 'the exile has undoubtedly been profitable to the archbishop of Canterbury both for his learning and his character'.[15] In addition, John asked if it was advisable to return 'with my books and all my baggage. If so', he added, 'I shall need more horses'.[16]

Further evidence for Becket's library and for books associated with his followers is found in a fourteenth-century catalogue of the monastic library at Christ Church Canterbury compiled by Henry Eastry, now British Library, Cotton MS Galba E IV, and manuscripts associated with this list have often been considered in connection with Herbert's books. The evidence of Eastry's list, however, is far from straightforward.[17] The catalogue lists the '*libri sancti Thome*' as occupying the first part of a '*demonstratio*', or section, of the library.[18] As Christopher de Hamel observed, however, some of these titles may include books acquired before the exile, and the list may also contain books that came to be associated with Becket in the thirteenth century.[19] The catalogue was clearly designed to be used in conjunction with the

Petri Lombardi Parisiensis quondam episcopi Sententiarum Magistri in Totum Psalterium Commentarii, in *PL*, 191.1085; Glunz, *History*, pp. 218–27.

[12] Glunz, *History*, p. 344: 'Quod si hydra multorum capitum necdum sibilare cessaverit, preter ea que iam diximus, contra ipsius venenatos aculeos duplex mihi consolationis antidotum est, quod christus domini, summus sacerdos christi, neomartyr noster sanctus thomas, ita fieri voluit …'; de Hamel, 'Contemporary Miniature', p. 180.

[13] Dodwell, *Canterbury School*, p. 108; de Hamel, *Glossed Books*, p. 45; F. Barlow, *Thomas Becket and His Clerks* (Oxford, 1987), p. 24.

[14] William of Canterbury, *Vita et Passio S. Thomae, Auctore Willelmo, Monacho Cantuariensi*, in *MTB*, i, 87: 'Bibliothecam vero, quam cismarinis interim partibus deponere decreveram, una mecum transferre pro rei vario et incerto compellor eventu, ut quem retro merita non commendant, gratantius excipiatur ad tumulandum possessor ex possessione'.

[15] *LJS*, ii, 48–9.

[16] *LJS*, ii, 48–9; see also P. Stirnemann, 'Les bibliothèques princières et privées aux XIIIe siècles', in *Histoire des bibliothèques françaises*, ed. A. Vernet (Paris, 1989), pp. 173–92, at 173.

[17] M. R. James, *The Ancient Libraries of Canterbury and Dover* (Cambridge, 1903), pp. xxxv–xliv, 7–142; de Hamel, *Glossed Books*, p. 38.

[18] James, *Ancient Libraries*, pp. xxxviii, xliii–xliv; see also T. Tatton-Brown, 'The Medieval Library at Canterbury Cathedral', *Canterbury Cathedral Chronicle* 82 (1988), 35–42.

[19] De Hamel, *Glossed Books*, p. 44.

library, as, frustratingly, the contents of the volumes are not always obvious.[20] Under some titles the description '*hoc volumine continentur*' has been entered in red; however, it is often unclear where the contents of one volume end and those of the next begin. Becket's books are followed by five volumes attributed to Herbert of Bosham ('*libri .m. Herberti de Bosham*'), whose name is underlined in red. These are the first and second parts of the Psalter and the first and second parts of the Epistles; the manuscripts now in Oxford and Cambridge.[21] In addition, the fifth book, '*Thomus*', must be Herbert's life of Becket, and this completes the entries in this part of the list, as the next line declares the start of '*Distinctio Tercia*'. Beneath the marker for the third section is entered '*liber Radulfi Remenensis*', which was taken by M. R. James to indicate a new donor, Ralph of Reims (or Sarre), another of Becket's supporters who, according to Herbert, was also exiled.[22] However, unlike references to other owners, including Herbert and Becket, this entry is not underlined in red, raising the possibility that it instead referred to a book by Ralph. On balance this seems unlikely, as the confusion of *liber* and *libri* in their abbreviated forms occurs elsewhere in the catalogue, and usually an indication of the subject of a book is given as well as the author's name. Moreover, the books that follow Ralph's name are arranged in a similar order to those attributed to Becket, beginning with a glossed copy of Genesis, suggesting that they were understood as a different group. From the titles recorded in the fourteenth century, Ralph's books have much in common with Becket's: both men seem to have had large numbers of glossed books, as well as copies of Peter Lombard's *Sentences*, reflecting the contemporary teaching of the French schools.[23] The result, however, is that it is now difficult to establish which surviving manuscripts were Becket's and which were Ralph's, let alone which volumes might have been acquired during Becket's exile.[24]

The potential for confusion about the original owners of books at Canterbury in the period between Becket's death and Eastry's list, as well as following the dispersal of the library, is further indicated by the list that follows Ralph's name. These include references to '*dupplices*' glosses on Genesis and Matthew, which, given the presence of glossed copies of both texts earlier in the list, was probably intended to underline the presence of second copies.[25] Becket's books also seem to contain multiple glossed copies of some texts, including two volumes on Jeremiah.[26] Whilst it is possible that both Ralph and Becket had duplicate books, perhaps containing the compilations and views of different scholars, just as Becket also had copies of both Anselm and Peter Lombard's works on the Psalter, it is also possible that otherwise unidentified

---

[20] James, *Ancient Libraries*, pp. xxxvii.

[21] James, *Ancient Libraries*, p. 85: 'Prima pars psalterii secundum longobardum / Secunda pars psalterii secundum longobardum / Prima pars epistolarum Pauli secundum longobardum / Secundum pars epistolarum secundum longobardum / Thomus.'

[22] James, *Ancient Libraries*, p. 86; *CTB*, ii, 1384.

[23] De Hamel, *Glossed Books*, p. 12.

[24] See de Hamel, *Glossed Books*, pp. 38–41.

[25] James, *Ancient Libraries*, pp. 86–8.

[26] James, *Ancient Libraries*, p. 82: 'Jeremias glo / Item Jeremias glo.'

glossed volumes had become attached to these collections. Certainly Canterbury boasted a very large number of glossed volumes, which should prompt caution in associating surviving twelfth-century manuscripts with a Canterbury provenance with Becket's exile.[27] A means of checking manuscripts against Eastry's list is provided by the inscription of a library mark in the form 'D ... G ...' for *distinctio* and *gradus*, which appears in some surviving manuscripts including two of Herbert of Bosham's manuscripts: Oxford, Bodleian Library MS Auct. E. Infra 6 ('D.ii.G.xi') and Trinity College Cambridge MS B.5.6 ('D.ii.G.xii').[28] However, the position of these marks at the top of the page has led to some being lost through trimming, and others have doubtless been erased by later owners. Moreover, these marks only confirm a volume's inclusion in the thirteenth- or early fourteenth-century library, not their original owner. Similarly, at least two manuscripts (Cambridge, Corpus Christi College MS 46 and Oxford, Bodleian Library MS Auct. E. Infra 7) have inscriptions identifying them with Becket, but these are also later additions. Thus Herbert's manuscripts are rare surviving volumes that can confidently be associated with Becket's exile.

The creation of Herbert of Bosham's manuscripts

Herbert of Bosham ensured that the reader of his volumes on the Psalms and Epistles was left in no doubt as to their association with Becket. However, the preface to the Psalter begins by describing how, when Herbert was in exile with Becket 'the glorious martyr', they were sustained by God, indicating that the manuscripts were completed after Becket's death.[29] In addition, at the start of both the Psalter and the Epistles, rubrics for the dedications have been added or altered to link Herbert and Becket, with the Psalter version proclaiming (in its fullest form): 'the preface of Herbert of Bosham, inseparable companion of the glorious martyr blessed Thomas in prosperity and in adversity'.[30] In the preface to the Epistles Herbert stresses how difficult he has found it to finish the work whilst mourning for Becket, and suggests that as many tears as notes are to be found on the pages.[31] The first volume of the Psalter (Trinity College Cambridge MS B.5.4) shows signs of water damage at the top of some pages, but there are no obvious signs of tears having been shed on the work. Nevertheless, Becket is prominently identified with the project and work on

---

[27] See Stirnemann, 'Compte rendu', p. 366 n.1.

[28] N. R. Ker, *Medieval Libraries of Great Britain: A List of Surviving Books* (London, 1964), p. 29.

[29] Glunz, *History*, p. 342: 'Dum ego cum dimicante domini prelia prius exule, nunc vero glorioso christi martyre, sancto videlicet thoma cantuariorum antistite, dura exilii aspera in exemplum iusti iudicii dei sustinerem, eiectum et proscriptum in loco pascue collocavit me dominus, eo ipso in ira sua miserationes suas non continens.'

[30] 'Prefatio Herberti de Boseham gloriosi martiris beati Thome sicut in prosperis et in adversis comitis individui.'

[31] Glunz, *History*, p. 348: 'Quod pridem super epistolas opus intenderam et presulatui tuo necdum factum dedicaram, inter eiulatus et lacrimarum sordes vix tandem consummare iam potui. [...] ut pagina subiecta lacrimis non minus quam notis interdum appareret suffuse.'

the manuscripts probably began in his lifetime, even though the prefaces must have been completed after his death in 1170.[32]

The prefaces of both the Psalter and Epistles are addressed not to Becket, but to William of the White Hands, archbishop of Sens. Herbert was sent to William shortly before Becket's murder and seems subsequently to have been employed by the archbishop.[33] This identification allows the date of the composition of the prefaces to be defined as between 1171 (following Becket's murder at the end of 1170) and William's promotion to the archbishopric of Reims in 1176.[34] Moreover, the inclusion at the start of the Epistles of a letter to William le Mire, abbot of Saint-Denis, who took on that office in 1172/3, suggests that the Epistles were still in production at that date.[35] Yet, as de Hamel has demonstrated, in the Psalter the preface seems to be a replacement for a previous dedication, complete with an image of Becket, on four leaves that have been excised. If these leaves contained a dedication to Becket that had been completed with an image, this would suggest that this volume at least was fairly well advanced by 1170. In this arrangement the preface would have followed the three prologues and St Jerome's letter to Sophronius. The new preface was added on a leaf and bifolio inserted at the front of the manuscript.[36] Despite the dedication to William of the White Hands, the new preface to the Psalter is also accompanied by an image of Herbert and Becket, the latter of whom is labelled, and both figures point to a rectangle, presumably representing the book, with a damaged inscription, which seems to begin '*doce illu[m]* ...' or 'teach this ...' (Fig. 4.1).[37] The Psalter thus remained a monument to Becket and Herbert's studies, despite the new dedication.

The creation of the surviving manuscripts was the final stage of a long process of organising text. In the preface to the Psalter Herbert stressed the painstaking labour that had gone into compiling and checking references.[38] The preface to the Epistles claims that the work was begun before William's appointment as archbishop of Sens in 1168 and, given the added reference to Pontigny in the Psalter dedication, the textual work was probably initiated there.[39] Once the text was decided upon, work could begin on the manuscripts, though it is unclear exactly when this was started. In addition, the speed of the work on the manuscripts may have been hindered by

---

[32] De Hamel, *Glossed Books*, p. 42; Panayotova, 'Tutorial', p. 77.

[33] Dodwell, *Canterbury School*, p. 109; Panayotova, 'Tutorial', p. 77.

[34] W. M. Newman, *Les Seigneurs de Nesle en Picardie*, 2 vols. (Paris, 1971), ii, p. 17; *The Letters of Peter of Celle*, ed. J. Haseldine (Oxford, 2001), p. 11 n.4.

[35] *Histoire Littéraire de la France* Vol. XIV (Paris, 1869), p. 374; Panayotova, 'Tutorial', p. 78.

[36] De Hamel, 'Contemporary Miniature', p. 183.

[37] Glunz, *History*, p. 225 n.2; T. Borenius, 'Some Further Aspects of the Iconography of St Thomas of Canterbury', *Archaeologia* 83 (1933), 172–3; de Hamel, 'Contemporary Miniature', p. 181.

[38] Glunz, *History*, pp. 342–3: 'Nec ob id dico quod novum aliquid cuderim, sed preter morem elaboravi in veteri. Concordantias enim psalmorum intero se et ad epistolas, et rursus epistolarum inter se et ad psalmos hinc inde sedulo et laboriose conquisitas, foris in librorum marginibus studui annotare.'

[39] Glunz, *History*, p. 348; Dodwell, *Canterbury School,* p. 109; Panayotova, 'Tutorial', p. 77; Stirnemann, 'En quête de Sens', p. 304; see also n. 8, above.

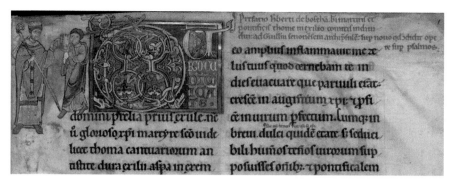

Fig. 4.1 Cambridge, Trinity College MS B.5.4, fol. 1. Commentary on the Psalms, Preface. Herbert of Bosham presents his work to Thomas Becket.

the expense of the project. The volumes are created from very large sheets of good parchment, with few holes, and in the Psalter each verse of each Psalm opens with three painted initials, many of which include gold. The Epistles are similarly lavishly treated, with decorated initials for the preface, commentary and text at the start of each book, and smaller initials at the start of each verse.

Letters from the period of exile at Pontigny express concern about Becket's expenses.[40] In 1165 Arnulf of Lisieux warned that the generosity of Becket's supporters might tail off during a long exile and suggested that it would be prudent 'to consider these matters more frequently, and often go through your expenses with the records of account, and in this way see everything from a single point of view, so that by comparing one thing with another you will be able to estimate the importance everything has'.[41] Shortly afterwards Bishop John of Poitiers counselled Becket to:

> unburden yourself of those you can afford to be without, in consideration of the evil of the times, which promise neither an easy nor a swift return to your see. Your prudence should know that no one will consider it to your dishonour if you choose to be content with a modest and essential number of horses and attendants, in accordance with your present situation and out of consideration for the religious house which is supporting you.[42]

---

[40] See also A. Duggan, 'The Price of Loyalty: The Fate of Thomas Becket's Learned Household', in A. Duggan, *Thomas Becket: Friends, Networks, Texts and Cult* (Aldershot, 2007), ch. 3, pp. 1–18.

[41] *CTB*, i, 196–7 no. 45: 'Hec sunt que bonum est uestram crebrius tractare prudentiam, et rationis instrumentis sepius expensa reuoluere, et sic omnia quasi sub unum conferatis aspectum, ut quid singula ponderis habeant plenius de ipsa possit collatione perpendi.'

[42] *CTB*, i, 216–17 no. 51: 'ut his quibus carere poteritis uos exoneretis, ad temporis maliciam respicientes, que uobis ad propria facilem uel citum reditum minime repromittit. Scire autem uestra debet prudencia quod nemo est qui uobis ad ignominiam reputet, si, presenti statui uos conformantes, sed et domui religiose que uos exhibet

Becket seems thus to have been living in some style at Pontigny, but it does not necessarily follow that the monks supplied the materials and labour needed to copy books for him and his entourage.[43] Certainly, the final appearance of Herbert's books was a long way from the Cistercian ideal of simple, monochrome decoration. Presumably Herbert obtained the resources to fund the lavish manuscripts from Becket's supporters, though again the exact timescale for this remains a matter of conjecture.

In addition to helping to establish the chronology for the production of Herbert's manuscripts, the dedication to the archbishop of Sens, William of the White Hands, may also shed light on the context in which they were produced.[44] Becket and his entourage had gone to Sens in 1164, before settling at Pontigny, because the exiled Pope Alexander III was to be found there. In 1166, under pressure from Henry II, the Cistercian order asked Becket to reconsider his residence with them.[45] As a result, Becket decided to move to the Benedictine abbey of Sainte-Colombe, nearer to Sens, under the patronage of the king of France.[46] The abbey was to serve as his base for the next four years. Sainte-Colombe boasted a new church, which had been dedicated by Pope Alexander III in 1164.[47] For Herbert this move was welcome, and he wrote in praise of Sens and its inhabitants, declaring that among the clergy and townspeople were men of bountiful generosity.[48] William Fitzstephen's account of Becket's life agrees, emphasising the generosity of the French king and singing the praises of the archbishop of Sens, William of the White Hands. Although he did not become archbishop of Sens until 1168, William of the White Hands was a well-connected ally. William Fitzstephen listed some of his family connections, noting that he was 'son of Count Theobald [of Blois], nephew of King Henry I of England, brother to the queen of France and to three counts of France', but he was careful to note that the archbishop earned his promotions on merit.[49]

As archbishop of Sens and later of Reims, William of the White Hands was an attractive potential patron for writers.[50] Peter Comestor dedicated his *Historia Scholastica* to William as archbishop of Sens, and Peter of Poitiers similarly

---

condescendentes, moderato et necessario tam equitaturarum quam personarum numero contenti esse uelitis.'

[43] See also Barlow, *Thomas Becket*, pp. 22–3; Stirnemann, 'Compte rendu', pp. 363–7; P. Stirnemann, 'Le témoignage des manuscrits: scribes et enluminures (1140–1220)', in *La bibliothèque médiévale de l'abbaye de Pontigny (XIIe–XIXe siècles): histoire, inventaires anciens, manuscrits*, ed. M. Peyrafort-Huin (Paris, 2001), pp. 55–78.

[44] Stirnemann, 'En quête de Sens', p. 310.

[45] *Vita, MTB*, iii, 397–8; *Vita, MTB*, v, 365–6.

[46] *Vita, MTB*, iii, 402–4; *CTB*, i, 496–9; see also Barlow, *Thomas Becket*, pp. 19–20.

[47] R.-H. Bautier and M. Gilles, *Chronique de Saint-Pierre-le-Vif de Sens* (Paris, 1979), pp. 206–7.

[48] *Vita, MTB*, iii, 407.

[49] Fitzstephen, *MTB*, iii, 84.

[50] J. R. Williams, 'William of the White Hands and Men of Letters', in *Haskins Anniversary Essays in Mediaeval History*, ed. C. H. Taylor and J. L. La Monte (Boston and New York, 1929), pp. 365–88.

dedicated his *Sentences* to him, showering the archbishop with praise. Both men were influential teachers and held the office of chancellor of Notre Dame in turn, placing them at the centre of the proto-university in Paris. William of the White Hands was responsible for controlling teaching in the diocese of Sens, which included Paris, and in 1170 Pope Alexander III wrote ordering him to insist that a doctrine about Christ's humanity, associated with Peter Lombard, was not to be taught or studied in the schools of Paris. Herbert must have been hoping that William's patronage would help his career, and perhaps even that he would help to meet the final costs of completing the manuscripts after Becket's death. It is plausible that at Sens from 1166 Herbert had access to the financial resources to support the creation of his great manuscripts, as well as to books and those skilled in book production (perhaps carrying material to and from Paris).[51] Given Herbert's movements in Becket's service in the later 1160s, including his return to Canterbury with Becket in 1170, it is conceivable that he left the project with scribes and artists in Sens, which might also help to explain the extensive notes made by Herbert for correction, presumably undertaken in his absence.

The large number of corrections in Herbert's manuscripts, with sections of text thoroughly erased and replaced both before and after the decoration was added, suggests that this was the scribes' first attempt to transfer Herbert's work into a neat copy, but the manuscripts were executed by highly trained scribes. In the Psalter the translation from the Hebrew caused particular problems, and has a fairly high rate of correction. As Stella Panayotova has demonstrated, in both the Psalter and Epistles, notes, probably in Herbert's own hand, require the addition of or alterations to both text and decoration, not all of which have been completed, suggesting that he was closely involved in the project.[52] For the most part, these notes served to correct errors, rather than requiring major changes of plan, though Herbert may have been responsible for the decision to divide the volumes into two parts, which necessitated significant revisions.

Once the text of Herbert's manuscripts had been copied, the bifolios were ready to be decorated. The painting of the initials and marginal figures in large and elaborate volumes such as Herbert's usually represents the final stage of a complex process of compilation and organisation. Indeed, in Herbert's manuscripts notes were made at the extreme edges of the pages by the scribes, indicating the letters and words to be painted. The work was completed by several artists, probably working with assistants, and on the whole was allocated by quire.[53] The first volume of the Psalter seems to have been completed by a group of artists deliberately working in a consistent style. In the second volume another artist added the initials to the preface and the start of Psalm 74, but the group of artists responsible for the decoration of the first volume seems to have completed the rest of the manuscript. These artists were also responsible for the decoration of a glossed book of Numbers that found

---

[51] See also Stirnemann, 'En quête de Sens', and M. Doyle, above, pp. 60–1.

[52] Panayotova, 'Tutorial', pp. 78–9.

[53] Panayotova, 'Tutorial', p. 78; Stirnemann, 'En quête de Sens', p. 309.

its way to the Bibliothèque Municipale in Chartres (MS 182).[54] The involvement of multiple people in the glossed Psalter volumes is suggested by the variations in the execution of the creatures that inhabit many of the initials, though on the whole an attempt seems to have been made to work in a standard style (Fig. 4.2). Also notable are the sketches for the initials that appear in quires xxxi–xxxiv of the Psalter. In other quires similar sketches seem to have been more or less carefully erased by the artist, and where the sketches are visible, the painted initials are often simpler in form than the sketch. For example, on fol. 66 of the Oxford volume the initial P has a simple pattern, painted over a design including a human figure (Fig. 4.3). This may again suggest a division of labour, as well as a desire to accelerate the pace of the project as it neared completion, replacing complex designs with simpler ones and not pausing to erase the sketches.

The Pauline Epistles were decorated by groups of artists with more diverse styles.[55] The artists responsible for the Psalter completed the first seven quires of the first volume of the Epistles, as well as quires ix–xi, xiii and xviii–xix, although the decoration of quire xiii is crudely executed. The remainder were done by an artist using similar motifs, but with finer detailing, more human faces and without using gold, whom Patricia Stirnemann identified as working in an English style (as opposed to the French style of the rest of the illumination).[56] Finally, the artist responsible for the initials in the preface to the second volume of the Psalter seems to have directed the decoration of the second volume of the Epistles, with the exception of quire xxviii, which was executed by the artist who completed most of the Psalter. Herbert must therefore have had access to a substantial number of artists.

The introduction of a new artist for the last volume of the Epistles and the preface to the second volume of the Psalter may provide an insight into the sequence of execution. The preface to the second volume suggests that the entire Psalter was originally to be one volume, and the quire numbers in both the Psalms and Epistles continue through both parts.[57] Herbert justifies the decision to separate the sections, pointing out that this makes them easier to use.[58] As single volumes these manuscripts would have been hefty tomes, with around 350 and 375 folios for the Psalms and Epistles, respectively. The start of the second volume of the Psalter provides further evidence to suggest that the change was made relatively late in the process. The first two folios appear now to be single leaves, as is folio 8, from which the original first folio was cut. This is not quite the midpoint of the Psalter, but the division at this point allowed for the least disruption to the existing quires. The

---

[54] Y. Delaporte, *Les Manuscrits Enluminés de la Bibliothèque de Chartres* (Chartres, 1929), p. 43; de Hamel, *Glossed Books*, p. 45.

[55] Stirnemann, 'En quête de Sens', p. 309.

[56] Stirnemann, 'En quête de Sens', p. 309.

[57] Glunz, *History*, p. 346: 'Cum liber psalmorum unus sit et non plures, ipsum tamen preter morem quidem, set non preter causam, in duos secavimus thomos.'

[58] Glunz, *History*, p. 346: 'Ad continendum quippe et contrectandum habiliora et apciora fiunt singula, quam si simul omnia uno sint pressa volumine; et etiam quia simul et sepe plus plurium poterit lectioni prodesse, huiuscemodi in libris parcialis divisio.'

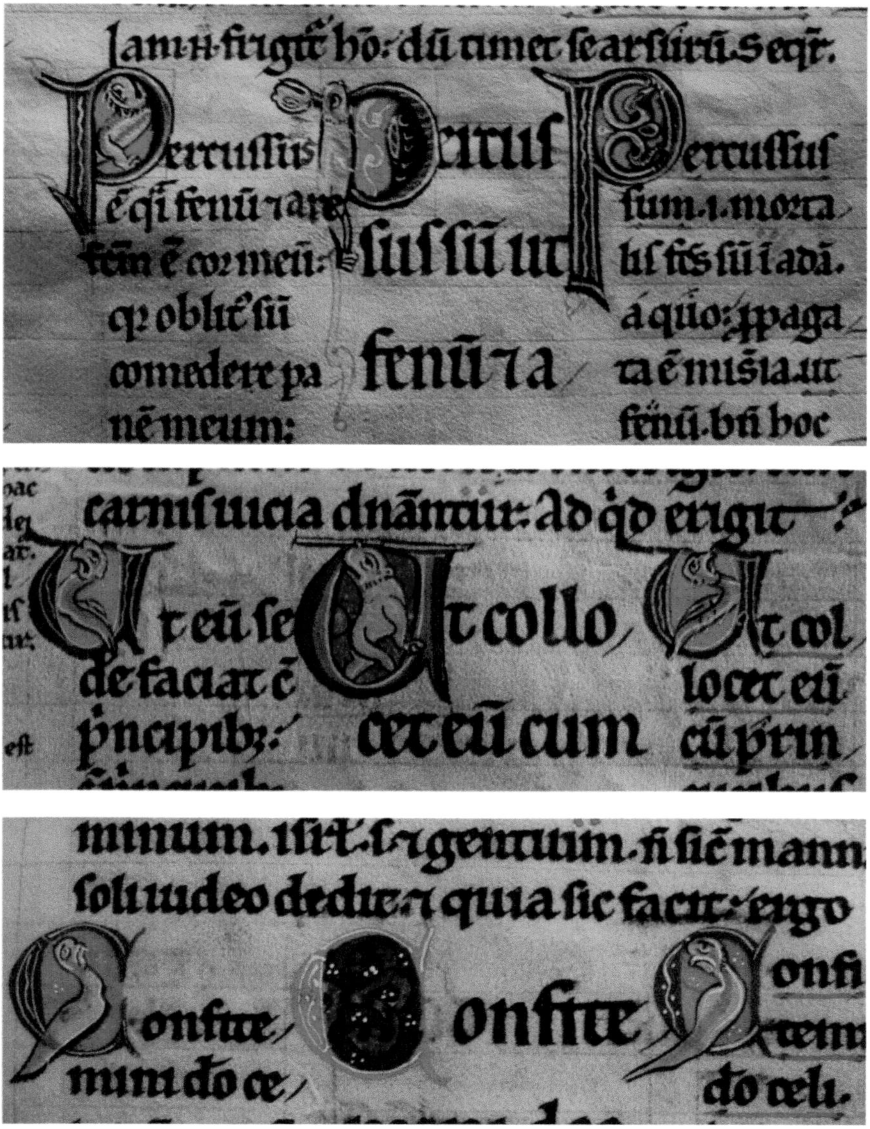

Fig. 4.2 Oxford, Bodleian Library MS Auct E Infra 6 details from fols. 56, 88, 124. Commentary on the Psalms. Initials inhabited by creatures.

Fig. 4.3   Oxford, Bodleian Library MS Auct E Infra 6 fol. 66. Commentary on the
Psalms. Initials painted over sketches. A human figure is visible in the sketch on
the left.

current folio 1 was then completed with the capitula list for Psalms 74–100 and the
start of Psalm 74, before the preface was added on the preceding leaf and the top
of folio 1.[59] The leaf cut away from the first quire of the second volume is now to be
found at the end of the first volume (folio 183), where it was preserved because it
contained the end of Psalm 73. At the end of the Psalm a rubric has been inserted
stating that this is the end of the first part of the Psalter, though the start of Psalm 74
has been left and thus appears twice.

As part of the process of division other changes were made to the Psalter's
capitula lists. The capitula for all the Psalms were listed at the start of the first volume
(fols. 7v–9v), but the list for Psalms 51–100 has also been inserted as a single leaf at
folio 133. Similarly, the final section of the capitula list has been added as a separate
sheet at folio 55 of the second volume. This has again resulted in duplication, as the
end of Psalm 50 appears both before and after the added list. The Epistles have a
similarly awkward division, with the start of the material for Galatians marked for
removal on the last folio of the first volume, after which several leaves have been
cut out. The start of the letter then begins the second volume, with a gathering of
just two bifolios, presumably replacing those excised from the previous volume.
The divisions of the manuscripts might indicate that the artists responsible for the
preface to the second volume of the Psalter and the bulk of the second volume of
the Epistles came late to the project. In this case the decoration of the Psalter would

---

[59] Stirnemann, 'En quête de Sens', p. 309.

have been substantially completed before that of the second volume of the Epistles, although work could have progressed on both texts simultaneously.

The division of labour may also explain the distribution of figurative imagery through the manuscripts' initials. As already noted, in the second volume of the Psalter some sketches for initials containing human figures have been completed with abstract designs or with the birds or beasts that occupy the majority of the initials. Amongst these creatures are naked figures in a range of colours, sometimes in contorted poses. These are particularly concentrated in the second volume of the Psalter. Some of the figures may have been inspired by the Psalm text. For example, at Psalm 118:9, 'By what doth a young man correct his way? By observing thy words', a naked man appears to be contemplating the letter above his head, literally observing the words (Fig. 4.4). However, the presence of two naked figures, one with a bow and arrow and the other upside down, grasping the tail of a creature, in the same Psalm at verse 57, 'O Lord, I have said, I would keep the law', is much less easily explained. In addition to the naked men, a few more specific characters are included in initials. For example, on fol. 102 at Psalm 118:41 (in the Hebraicum version), 'And let thy mercy come to me Lord, your safety according to your word', a mermaid suckles another. The significance of this imagery is again unclear, and it may simply indicate the artists' freedom to decorate some initials as they wished. This certainly seems to have been the case in the minor initials, as the two versions of Psalm 74:2 have been treated differently, with the commentary text in the version in the first volume boasting a bird, whilst in the replacement leaf at the start of volume two a face has been included.

Fig. 4.4   Oxford, Bodleian Library MS Auct E Infra 6 fol. 97v. Commentary on the Psalms. A naked man contemplates the words to Psalm 118:9, 'By what doth a young man correct his way? By observing thy words.'

Fig. 4.5   Oxford, Bodleian Library MS Auct E Infra 6 fol. 21v. Commentary on the Psalms. A man on fire labelled '_homo in igne, deus in homine_'. The instruction to the artist is visible on the left.

Yet Herbert of Bosham took great interest in other aspects of the decoration. As Panayotova has shown, Herbert devised a set of images to be placed in the margins next to the start of some Psalms, serving as a form of visual gloss, paralleling the inscriptions in the margin beside each new Psalm.[60] For example, Psalms that are deemed to refer to the two natures of Christ as God and man are marked with an image of a man on fire labelled '_homo in igne, deus in homine_' (Fig. 4.5).[61] Similarly, in both the Psalter and the Epistles Herbert used images of the authorities who were cited in the commentary to offer corrections to the attributions. The figures hold scrolls with inscriptions such as '_cave_', '_non ego_' or '_ego aliter_'. Herbert has again made notes specifying the inclusion of and corrections to these figures (Fig. 4.6).[62] These images were completed by more than one artist, further underlining that these were Herbert's idea.

The large historiated initials

Most of the marginal authors, including the figure of Augustine in the second part of the Psalter, were completed by the artist responsible for the image of Becket and Herbert at the start of the Psalter, and this artist also seems to have painted four

---

[60] Panayotova, 'Tutorial', pp. 80–2.
[61] Panayotova, 'Tutorial', p. 81.
[62] Panayotova, 'Tutorial', p. 79.

large initials in the Psalter containing clothed human figures. These figures have distinctive faces, usually featuring a large area between the eyebrows, emphasised by dark lines, often with the suggestion of an indentation over the nose, downward-turning lips and upward-looking eyes. The first two initials are in the prefatory material to the Psalter on folios 6v and 10. The first appears at the start of Jerome's preface and shows Jerome wearing a blue cloak over a pink tunic and with a long white beard, seated at a writing desk with quill and knife, in the act of producing his translation. The second initial begins the start of Peter Lombard's introduction, and is placed at the end of the first capitula list. The four male busts inside the initial presumably represent the prophets referred to in the text, which begins by singling out David from amongst 'all the prophets through whom the revelation of the Holy

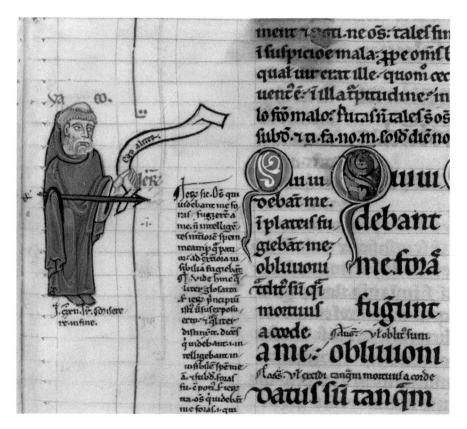

Fig. 4.6   Cambridge, Trinity College MS B.5.4 fol. 82. Commentary on the Psalms. Jerome corrects Peter Lombard's attribution, holding a scroll with the inscription '*ego aliter*'.

Fig. 4.7 Oxford, Bodleian Library MS Auct E Infra 6 fol. 84. Commentary on the Psalms. A bird flies upwards towards Christ, as part of the opening words of Psalm 110, 'I will praise thee, O Lord, with my whole heart: for thou hast heard the words of my mouth. I will sing praise to thee in the sight of his angels.'

Spirit has been made known'.[63] The four figures are markedly different, presumably to emphasise the diversity of the prophets. This artist seems also to have painted the figures in the opening initials to Psalms 109 and 110. At Psalm 110 the upper roundel in the initial C contains a tiny bust of Christ, with a cruciform halo. In the lower roundel is a bird, with its wings represented twice to suggest motion, flying upwards towards Christ (Fig. 4.7). Again it seems appropriate to read this imagery as a response to the opening words of the Psalm 'I will praise thee, O Lord, with my whole heart: for thou hast heard the words of my mouth. I will sing praise to thee in the sight of his angels.'

The other Psalm that opens with an initial containing clothed human figures is much less straightforwardly associated with the text. Psalm 109 begins 'The Lord said to my Lord, sit at my right hand until I make your enemies your footstool'. This

---

[63] 'Cum omnes prophetas spiritus sancti revelatione constet esse locutos, David prophetarum eximius quodam digniori atque excellentiori modo velut tuba spiritus sancti, quam alii prophetavit.'

Psalm was identified in Herbert's capitula list as the seventh of the Psalms about the two natures of Christ, and a figure of a man on fire was once included in the inner margin at the start of the Psalm, but this has been excised (Fig. 4.8). Where the Psalm was given a historiated initial in other manuscripts from the second half of the twelfth century, the artists often chose to show God enthroned. Sometimes these images included God the Father and Christ seated together, giving the Psalm a Christological interpretation (for example, Oxford, Bodleian Library MS Douce 293 fol. 100v; Amiens Bibliothèque Municipale MS 19 fol. 133). In other versions the artist chose to represent David, in accordance with the *titulus* included in Herbert's manuscript, which identifies the Psalm as a Psalm of David (for example, Oxford, Bodleian Library MS Gough Lit. 2 fol. 120; Vendôme Bibliothèque Municipale MS 20 fol. 166). The largest of the three initials (for the Hebrew, Gallican and commentary texts) in Herbert's manuscript, that for the Gallican text, is filled with swirling vines populated by birds, beasts and fighting red and blue men. On the upper left are the remains of a red man skewering a lion with his sword. Whilst this imagery resonates with the reference to enemies in the Psalm, it is not, however, an explicit illustration of the text.

Yet a relationship between text and image is explicitly suggested by the figures in the other two initials, both of whom point to the text. In the initial at the start of the Hebrew version is a figure with twisted limbs, naked except for his cloak, resting his head on one hand whilst pointing at the text, perhaps at the word '*meis*' (my), which has been stretched to fill the available space. This figure looks up at the figure in the initial to the start of the commentary, who, following the layout for the text and initials adopted throughout the book, is above him on the right. This figure wears a pink tunic with a blue cloak and a round red hat. He carries a white staff with a cross-head, and both points and looks at the text above him. Walter Cahn identified the nearly-naked figure as a lamenting prophet, and the position of the figure is similar to that of a marginal figure labelled '*propheta lamentans*' in the first volume of the Psalter, which according to the capitula list was originally one of three figures marking Psalms of lamentation. However, the sole surviving marginal prophet wears a tunic beneath his cloak (Fig. 4.9). This figure resembles other images of Jeremiah lamenting over Jerusalem. Cahn did not comment on the other figure at Psalm 109, but the inclusion of specific attributes suggests that he was supposed to be identifiable. The presence of the cross-headed staff suggests a connection with the church, whilst the fact that this figure looks and points to the word '*martyribus*' from the end of the previous section of commentary raises the possibility that this could be a representation of the martyr uppermost in Herbert's mind: Thomas Becket. In this context the rounded hat could be read as a mitre, and rounded mitres appear frequently in images of the period, including images of Peter Lombard in Walters Art Museum MS W.809 fol. 1 and Valenciennes Bibliothèque Municipale MS 186 fol. 2v.[64] Moreover, the choice of a red hat resonates with the

---

[64] J. P. Turcheck, 'A Neglected Manuscript of Peter Lombard's *Liber Sententiarum* and Parisian Illumination of the Late Twelfth Century', *The Journal of the Walters Art Gallery* 44 (1986), 48–69; L. Cleaver 'The Many Faces of Peter Lombard: Changing Perceptions

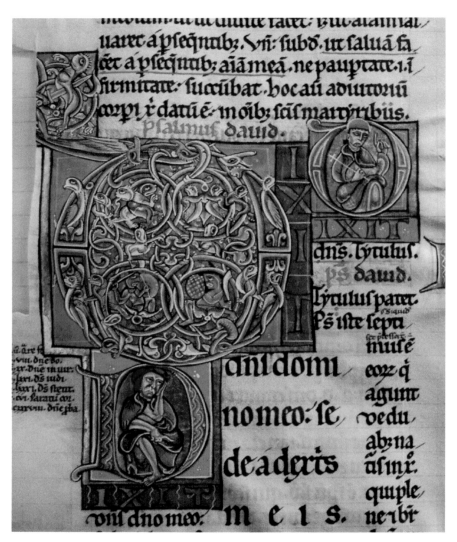

Fig. 4.8　Oxford, Bodleian Library MS Auct E Infra 6 fol. 83. Commentary on the Psalms. Two figures at the beginning of Psalm 109, 'The Lord said to my Lord, sit at my right hand until I make your enemies your footstool.'

Fig. 4.9 Cambridge, Trinity College MS B.5.4 fol. 180. Commentary on the Psalms. '*Propheta lamentans*'.

means of Becket's martyrdom, in which the top of his head was cut off, exposing blood and brains. Such an identification also potentially resonates with the reading of the Psalm, with Becket called to sit amongst the saints at the right hand of God to await the punishment of his enemies. Suggestively, Psalm 109 was the first Psalm sung at Vespers on Sunday, the service (if not the day) during which the martyrdom had taken place.[65] That Herbert was used to identifying with the Psalms in this way is underlined by the preface to the Psalter in which Herbert records having a vision of Becket in which the saint had commended to him the Psalm verse, 'Redeem me from the calumnies of men: that I may keep thy commandments'.[66] In this context, the verse, 'The Lord said to my Lord', may also be significant, as Herbert used the same Latin term (*dominus*) in referring to his relationship with Becket.

A more straightforward image of an archbishop appears in the second volume of the Epistles, executed by the artist who decorated the preface to the second volume of the Psalter and most of the second volume of the Epistles (Fig. 4.10). At the start of the letter to the Colossians, in the initial for the gloss on Paul's name, is an archbishop

of a Master in Images made between 1150 and 1215', in *Spiritual Temporalities in Late-Medieval Europe*, ed. M. Foster (Newcastle, 2010), pp. 33–56.

[65] William of Canterbury, *Vita et Passio*, MTB, i, 131.

[66] Glunz, *History*, p. 344: 'Quod si adhuc scillei in me sevierint canes et latrare non cessaverint, quod solum superest contra ignitos ipsorum morsus: crebra me illius armabo recordatione versiculi, *Redime me a calumpniis hominum, ut custodiam mandata tua*. Hunc quippe versiculum dominus meus neomartyr noster, sanctus thomas, post gloriosum transitum suum in visione mihi apparens pre ceteris psalmorum versiculis commendavit, et quasi in testamento relinquens iniunxit memoriam iugem.'

with a pointed mitre, crosier and pallium. This figure is unlikely to represent Paul, who is depicted at the start of the second letter to the Thessalonians with a red halo, wearing tunic and toga, and with a long beard. The bishop could be another image of Becket, or perhaps of the new dedicatee William of Sens, both of whom could be understood to be following in Paul's footsteps in preaching the gospel and building up the church. Whilst not all the figures in these volumes need necessarily be read in the context of Becket's story, however, the particular identification of the figure at Psalm 109 with the term 'martyrs' suggests that it might be read as Becket.

If the upper figure at the start of Psalm 109 is Becket, who, then, is the figure below? Given the investment of Herbert of Bosham in these volumes I suggest that this lamenting figure might be read as Herbert himself. Herbert's laments appear not only in his account of the production of the Epistles, but also in his account of Becket's *Life*. For example, he describes his tears upon parting from Becket shortly before the murder. Having followed Becket into exile in 1164, Herbert found himself in exile again after 1170, and the preface to the Epistles records his laments.[67] In his life of Becket, written in the 1180s, Herbert again described himself as lamenting, and used a description of a disciple abandoned naked without the cloak of his master, suggesting that he thought of himself in this way, which once again resonates with the image at Psalm 109 in which the figure appears to be naked except for his cloak.[68] Moreover, the nearly-naked figure appears again lower down the page at the start of the commentary on the first verse, where he faces the text with a hand raised, as if speaking. The repetition of the figure below, apparently expounding the text, seems to lend support to the idea that this is the directing mind behind this project.

If the initials to Psalm 109 may be read as an image of Herbert and Becket, they present a contrasting image to that at the preface. Some of the variations may be the result of the limited space available for the initial, with the initial with Becket measuring just 24 mm, compared to the 80 mm used in the preface. This may help to explain why the artist has not included the pallium in the initial. Yet the differences may also be explained by the different contexts. The presentation image celebrates the production of the books for Becket as archbishop in exile. In contrast, the initial to Psalm 109 seems to draw on Herbert's lamentations in the aftermath of the loss of his friend and lord.

The year 1170 was a turning point in Herbert's life. Without his patron and in exile once again he turned to Becket's powerful continental supporters for help. William of the White Hands seems to have given him employment. In the later 1170s Herbert had the support of Pope Alexander III, who ordered the new archbishop of Canterbury to supply Herbert's revenues to enable him to try to follow Peter Lombard's example and teach in Paris.[69] In the 1180s Herbert did spend time in

---

[67] See *Vita*, *MTB*, iii, 485–6; Glunz, *History*, p. 348 (n.31 above).

[68] See *Vita*, *MTB*, iii, 496–7. I am very grateful to Michael Staunton for drawing my attention to this passage.

[69] *Epistolae pontificum romanorum ineditae*, ed. S. Loewenfeld (Leipzig, 1885), p. 207

dem ꝛ onıſ ſımul ꝛ ſeparatım ſecͫ ſeꝛ
ꝛ etates ꝛ condıtıones: moꝛalꞇꝛ ınſtru
ır·Jn fine archıpum̄ monet ſollıcıtū
foꝛe ſuſcepti mınıſterıı ·premıttens
autem ſalutatıonem: a ı ꞇ.

PAVLVS APOS TOL.

rpi ıhu
puolun
tatem dı
et thimo
theuſ fꝛ:
biſ q̈ ſūt
coloſis

AVLVS

cognıto omnı
bꝫ nomıne· aplͤ
ıhu ꝛ· nota om
nıbꝫ dıgnıtate·
recte hıc aptͫ
nomınat· quıa
ꝛ biſ aplͤ erat:
quıbꝫ p dıſcıpu

Fig. 4.10 Cambridge, Trinity College MS B. 5. 7 fol. 70. Commentary on the Psalms. An archbishop at the start of Paul's letter to the Colossians.

England, but ultimately he returned to France, settling in the Cistercian house at Ourscamp. Yet Herbert's books, originally designed for Becket, found their way to Canterbury, where they were recorded under Herbert's name next to Becket's books in the fourteenth-century list and rebound in 1508.[70] At some point while they were still together the Psalter volumes were vandalised, with the removal of many of the disapproving authors and thematic images. This may have been inspired by the earlier correction process, as some of the surviving figures in the first volume have been labelled '*vaco*' (void) in a twelfth-century hand (see Fig. 4.6). Nevertheless, until the Reformation these books were preserved at Canterbury as a memorial to Becket and Herbert's scholarship. Moreover, the Canterbury community remembered Herbert by including him in a thirteenth-century obituary list (British Library Cotton MS Nero C IX), where his obit was recorded on 20 November and he was described as *frater noster* – our brother.[71]

The glossed volumes of the Psalms and Epistles masterminded by Herbert for his lord Thomas Becket provide a remarkable insight into the production of lavish copies of current theological texts in the second half of the twelfth century. These books must have been designed as status symbols as well as theological tools. Initiated in the pastures of Pontigny, but probably produced at Sens, in the intellectual orbit of Paris, the manuscripts represent an enormous commitment of time, materials and money, in addition to Herbert's efforts in compiling and checking material. Herbert seems to have paid close attention to all phases of the work. The death of Thomas Becket in 1170 marked a change of dedicatee, as Herbert sought to rebuild his career. Yet, although work continued, the volumes were never completely finished in accordance with Herbert's instructions, which can still be found in the margins. Instead, through the choice of imagery and the presentation of the works to Christ Church Canterbury, the volumes became a memorial to Herbert's relationship with Becket through good times and bad. Although no tears are visible on the pages, therefore, it seems possible that they are recorded in the remarkable initial to Psalm 109.

---

no. 347; Smalley, *Becket Conflict*, p. 71.

[70] James, *Ancient Libraries*, p. 154, nos. 45, 46, 56 and 57.

[71] R. Fleming, 'Christchurch's Sisters and Brothers: An Edition and Discussion of Canterbury Obituary Lists', in *The Culture of Christendom: Essays in Medieval History in Commemoration of Denis L. T. Bethell*, ed. M. A. Meyer (London & Rio Grande, 1993), pp. 115–54.

CHAPTER FIVE

Scholarship as a Weapon: Herbert's Letter Collection

Julie Barrau

Herbert of Bosham's letter collection would be totally lost if it were not for a single fourteenth-century copy, today in Cambridge, Corpus Christi College MS 123, fols. 1r–64v.[1] It consists of forty-eight letters and letter fragments. Only partially edited by J. A. Giles in the mid-nineteenth century, the letters, which are written in complex and flowery Latin, have been largely neglected, although some of them were included by Robertson in the *Materials for the History of Archbishop Thomas Becket*.[2] Anne Duggan has established with great clarity the (limited) contribution that the collection makes to the much greater body of the Becket correspondence.[3] Eleven letters are presented as drafted by Herbert 'in persona Thomae', but for most of them it is difficult to say that they were ever actually sent.[4] Only two appear in the main Becket collections, with textual differences from the text extant in the Herbert collection.[5] Two letters drafted by Herbert seem to have been rejected by the archbishop and a parallel version actually sent.[6] Another three may have been actually sent, although Anne Duggan did not include them in her edition.[7]

However, the letters written on behalf of Becket constitute only a small part of the collection as we have it. There are also twenty letters written in Herbert's own

---

[1] For a description of CCCC MS 123 (henceforth CCCC 123), see M. R. James, *A Descriptive Catalogue of the Manuscripts in the Library of Corpus Christi College*, 2 vols. (Cambridge, 1912), i, 293–4.

[2] *Herberti de Boseham S. Thomae Cantuariensis clerici a secretis opera quae extant omnia*, ed. J. A. Giles, 2 vols. (London, 1846), ii, pp. 207–310. Giles's edition was reprinted in *PL* 190.1415–74 (henceforth *HB*). Giles numbers 46 items, because he ignored two elements, about which more will be said later in this chapter. However, for ease of reference the Giles letter numbers will be used here.

[3] *CTB*, i, xxiii.

[4] *HB*, nos. 2–3, 8–11, 15, 20, 26–28. See *CTB*, i, xxiii n.5.

[5] *HB*, nos. 8, 9 = *CTB* nos. 260, 271. See also *CTB*, p. xxiii n.6.

[6] *HB*, nos. 3, 15, superseded by *CTB*, nos. 270, 95.

[7] *HB*, nos. 2 to Pope Alexander III, 10 to Roger of Worcester, and 28 to King Waldemar of Denmark.

name, as well as three letters sent to him.[8] There is an intriguing addition: *Ne in dubium*, the text of the settlement established at Avranches in 1172 between Henry II and the papacy.[9] The last extant element in the collection is a fragment completely ignored by Giles, probably because it bears no rubric or other obvious identifiable feature.[10]

Herbert's letters have been overlooked for centuries, and the few people who have taken notice were not always won over.[11] The Latin in which the letters are composed is difficult and convoluted, and they are long winded. They were also edited by a man who had, both literally and metaphorically, little time for them. As Nicholas Vincent shows in another chapter, Giles had to go fast when he edited the letters, and he had other concerns on his mind. This accounts for the frequent transcription mistakes, but not necessarily for Giles's decision to discard about a quarter of the collection. Few letters are actually fully missing: this radical truncation is mainly achieved by shortening some of the letters.[12] Some gaps are extensive, and they get longer and more frequent towards the end of the collection.[13] The boldest cut leaves out twelve consecutive pages in the manuscript.[14] Almost all five pages of a letter modelled on Bernard of Clairvaux's *De consideratione* and written to Henry de Beaumont on the occasion of his elevation to the see of Bayeux in 1165 are also missing.[15] Finally, Giles ignored the four final pages of the collection as it is preserved in the manuscript; the last item in his edition is a fragment of a letter from Arnulf of Lisieux to Becket.[16]

Giles clearly thought that Herbert's florid and reference-laden prose was of limited interest. This would be consistent with the attitude of other nineteenth-century editors: James Robertson thought that identifying the numerous biblical

[8] *HB*, nos. 1, 5, 6, 7, 12, 13, 18, 19, 21, 23, 29, 30, 31, 34, 35, 36, 38, 39, 40, 42. The letters to Herbert are *HB*, nos. 22 (from the abbot of St Crispin, Soissons), 41 (from Alexander III) and 45 (from William Longchamp, already bishop of Ely, after Herbert had left William's household and joined, for the last few years of his life, Ourscamp, so probably between 1192 and 1194).

[9] *HB*, no. 43. On this text and its background, see A. Duggan, '*Ne in dubium*: The Official Record of Henry II's Reconciliation at Avranches, 21 May 1172', *EHR* 115 (2000), 643–58. Another apparently stray element is the last identifiable item (*HB*, no. 46), a fragment of a letter by Arnulf of Lisieux to Becket, now *CTB*, no. 45.

[10] CCCC 123 fols. 63r–64v. Inc. 'fieri in seculo. cur te subtrahis ab hominibus seculi; expl. nam absque fortitudine omnes de quibus propheta dicit Dederunt preciosa queque pro cibo' (with catchword 'ad refocillandam').

[11] Nicholas Vincent dismissed them once as 'long-winded lies'.

[12] Robertson does not describe the Corpus manuscript in his introduction of the three epistolary volumes of his *MTB*. However, the manuscript is listed as 'P' in the list of manuscripts, *MTB*, v, xviii.

[13] From *HB*, no. 32 (CCCC 123 fol. 50r) almost all letters are truncated.

[14] *HB*, no. 15 (*PL*, 190.1439), but in CCCC 123 fols. 18ra–24vb. This is studied in detail *infra*.

[15] *HB*, no. 21 (*PL*, 190.1456CD), in CCCC 123, fols. 42r–44r.

[16] The letter is *Magnam mihi*, written in 1166. It was published most recently as *CTB*, no. 45. In CCCC 123 leaves are clearly missing after 'inuicem ratione' at the bottom of fol. 62v – the text stops mid-sentence and mid-letter.

quotations and allusions in the Becket correspondence would be a waste of time.[17] Giles is equally damning when he vindicates his omissions. The end of a letter written shortly after Becket's death consists of 'a few things about the miraculous power' of the new martyr, 'useless' (*inutilia*) and therefore discarded.[18] Extracts of a 'prolix [...] rhetorical pamphlet' suffice; here Giles refers to Herbert, in an affectionate yet patronising manner, as 'our good Herbert'.[19] Giles justified giving only five lines of the already mentioned letter of congratulation to Henry de Beaumont by saying that they added nothing to the history of Becket, or to any other purpose.[20] However, modern readers might disagree: by knitting together phrases from both *De consideratione* and the sermons on the Song of Songs, Herbert composed a subtle homage to Bernard of Clairvaux; it also shows that he was putting the library of Pontigny, where the exiles were in 1165, to good use.

Giles also decided not to print letters which he thought were already edited elsewhere, often by himself. This sensible decision obscures, however, some differences between the better-known versions of some letters and those that were preserved in Herbert's collection. One such discrepancy can be found in a letter sent in Becket's name to the English episcopate. It was sent after sanctions were pronounced in March 1170 – at long last, Herbert would have certainly exclaimed – against Gilbert Foliot. Anne Duggan attributes its drafting to Herbert, which is confirmed by its presence in the Corpus collection.[21] However, the version preserved by Herbert is slightly different.[22] The Becket collection account described Foliot as 'that most miserable Judas' through whom scandal came, without naming him; the same sentence in the Corpus manuscript spelled out Judas's name ('episcopo Londoniense Gilberto').[23] Letter collections were gathered as a testimony for the future; it is conceivable that such was the intensity of Herbert's lingering feelings of

---

[17] *MTB*, ii, xlix–l.

[18] *HB*, no. 34 (*PL*, 190.1467): 'Sequuntur pauca de virtute miraculosa S. Thomae, inutilia'. In the body of the letter there are three further cuts, ranging in the manuscript from seven lines to half a column. See CCCC 123, fols. 52v–53v. Even less of this letter was printed as *MTB*, vii, no. 798, pp. 576–8.

[19] *HB*, no. 15 (PL, 190.1440): 'Haec ex epistola prolixa excerpta sufficiant: nam nihil est nisi rhetoricus libellus a bono Herberto nostro concinnatus.'

[20] *HB*, no. 21 (PL, 190.1456D): 'Hortatoria, quae sequuntur usque ad finem epistolae, nec ad sancti Thomae historiam spectantia, nec aliter unius assis aestimanda, omitto'. In the manuscript the letter covers fols. 42ra–44rb. On Henry and his long tenure at Bayeux (1165–1205), see E. Crosby, *The King's Bishops: The Politics of Patronage in England and Normandy, 1066–1216* (London, 2013), pp. 255–70. Crosby did not use Herbert's letter. See also J. Peltzer, 'Henry II and the Norman Bishops', *EHR* 119 (2004), 1202–29, at 1215–16.

[21] *CTB*, no. 271, pp. 1154–9, inc. 'Gratias ago Deo meo'. Anne Duggan used the Corpus manuscript only for 'heading and protocol'.

[22] *HB*, no. 9 (PL, 190.1434BC): *Vide inter epp. S. Thomae*. CCCC 123, fols. 12vb–13va.

[23] *CTB*, no. 271, p. 1156: 'Hec est nunc gloria mea quod nunc habitamus in unum, rejecto illo infelicissimo Iuda, uelut putridissimo membro amputato, per quem in nostro corpore tantum scandalum uenit ...'; CCCC 123 fols. 13rb–va: 'Hec est enim gloria mea quod nunc habitamus in unum episcopo Londoniense Gilberto reiecto illo infelicissimo Iuda per quem ...'

outrage and injustice that it made him adamant that readers yet to be born, and less familiar with the minutiae of Becket's struggle, should still be able to identify, and loathe, the martyr's nemesis.

The way letter collections were made in the twelfth century makes it likely that Herbert gathered the collection himself.[24] Collections usually originated with either the writer himself or a devoted friend. Could Herbert's collection possibly be someone else's labour of love? This cannot be fully ruled out, but there are signs that it is unlikely. The collection came together at the end of Herbert's life,[25] and the Corpus witness is a much later, mutilated copy, as well as the only copy. There is no evidence of a wider circulation of Herbert's letters; he was, after all, an obscure figure. The collection is made up of quires of sixteen pages/eight folios, each quire ending with a neat catchword. Its incomplete nature is obvious from its start *in medias res* at fol. 1r.[26] One quire is incomplete: it occupies fols. 57r–59v.[27] There is a new disruption at the end of fol. 62v, in the middle of Arnulf of Lisieux's letter. That was the end of a quire, signalled by a catchword; therefore pages are missing between folios 62 and 63. There is another catchword at the end of fol. 64v, indicating that at least six folios are missing before the pages that Giles fully omitted in his edition (fols. 63r–64v). The presence of a catchword at the end of fol. 64v reveals that there is at least one quire missing at the end of the collection as we have it. It is therefore necessary to be aware that what has survived in the Corpus manuscript is only a partial reflection of the initial intentions of whoever – most likely Herbert – selected and gathered some of his letters into a collection.

Nevertheless, as with any letter collection, this is the result of thoughtful selection. Unsurprisingly, the collection is dominated by Herbert's devotion to Thomas Becket and his loathing of the archbishop's enemies. The letters that were included are predominantly related to the conflict, both during the exile of the 1160s and during the aftermath of the murder (the latter account for twenty out of forty-seven letters); the rest are letters written on behalf of other grandees, such as the two brothers-in-law of King Louis VII, the archbishop of Sens William of the White Hands and his brother Henry the Liberal, count of Champagne.[28]

Herbert was one of the secretaries who wrote on behalf of the exiled archbishop, and his pride in his past as a ghost-writer for his hero shines throughout the

---

[24] See G. Constable, *Letters and Letter Collections*, Typologie des sources du Moyen Âge occidental 17 (Turnhout, 1976), and *The Letters of Peter the Venerable*, ed. G. Constable, 2 vols. (Cambridge, MA, 1967), ii, pp. 6–12.

[25] The latest datable item is *HB*, no. 45, a letter from William Longchamp styled as bishop of Ely; this places the letter after December 1189.

[26] Fol. 1ra: '[dis]cretio tua, serenissime consul'.

[27] *HB*, no. 43 (*Ne in dubium*) finishes incomplete, short of about four lines, at the bottom of fol. 59v. What follow at the beginning of fol. 60r are the last few lines of a letter sent to Herbert, which was not noticed by Giles. This short fragment should really be '*HB*, no. 44'. Giles' *HB*, no. 44 is the answer to this letter, as the rubric makes clear ('Epistola responsalis ad eumdem').

[28] For William, *HB*, nos. 33 and 37; for Henry, *HB*, no. 24. There belong here as well, *HB* no. 4, *in persona* Stephen, bishop of Meaux; no. 25 for Matthew, *praecentor* of Sens.

collection.[29] However, most of the Becket letters that are included in the collection are probably unsent drafts.[30] This is a compelling sign that Herbert composed the collection himself, and wanted to transmit to posterity not just the letters already gathered by Alan of Tewkesbury and John of Salisbury, but also drafts that were eventually rejected.[31] He also preserved for posterity precious evidence of the team-work that went on in the entourage of the exiled archbishop, even when his own contribution was eventually rejected. We know from other sources that what it was judicious or otherwise to include in Becket's letters was a hotly discussed topic in his entourage. John of Salisbury scolded his master for harsh words sent to Cardinal William of Pavia, whose support of Henry II earned him the exiles' loathing.[32] It is remarkable that Herbert preserved in his collection three drafts of the same letter, including his own, unsent one. In the summer of 1166 a whirlwind of events reshaped the situation of Becket and his companions.[33] On Whitsunday, at Vézelay, the archbishop went on the attack for the first time with a series of excommunications and suspensions, targeting especially some of his fellow English prelates.[34] The bishops appealed the sentences with a long and meticulous attack on Becket's character, past and motivations.[35] The three drafts preserved in the collection are versions of Becket's reaction to the appeal, of which one, *Fraternitatis uestre*, was sent and can be found in the earliest Becket letter collections.[36] As well as his own draft, Herbert included another reject, and names his author: Master Lombard, a canonist and steadfast member of the Becket *familia*. Lombard's effort, *Uestre fraternitatis*, is shorter than the other two. It is more restrained in his attacks on the king and does not name Gilbert Foliot as the initiator of the bishops' appeal; it also does not respond to the appeal letter's personal attacks on Becket. That does not make it tepid: it is fiercely critical of a situation described as scandalous and abhorrent to God. John of Oxford, one of the excommunicates, is pilloried, and the appeal is discarded as unlawful.[37] But Becket favoured a fuller answer – and that was *Fraternitatis uestre*, one of the longest letters in a correspondence hardly known for its sense of *breuitas*. It provides a blow-by-blow response, in a heavily biblical, prophetic prose. Herbert's own draft (in the rubric: 'Epistola Herberti … edita in

---

[29] On Becket's secretarial team, see *CTB*, i, xxiii–xxvii.

[30] *HB*, nos. 2–3, 8–11, 15, 20, 26–28.

[31] On the composition of the Becket letter collections, see A. Duggan, *Thomas Becket: A Textual History of His Letters* (Oxford, 1980), pp. 24–160, and *CTB*, i, lxviii–cx.

[32] *LJS*, ii, 396 no. 227: 'Inspectis literis quas domino Willelmo Papiensi mittere decreuistis, etsi mentem scribentis judicare non audeam, stili tamen formam probare non possum.'

[33] The overview of the events of 1162–1174 is Michael Staunton's in his introduction to *The Lives of Thomas Becket* (Manchester, 2001), pp. 15–34.

[34] See A. Duggan, *Thomas Becket* (London, 2004), pp. 104–23.

[35] *CTB*, 372–83 no. 93.

[36] *CTB*, 388–425 no. 95; for its presence in the earliest formal collection see Duggan, *Textual History*, p. 228. It is *HB*, no. 17, in CCCC 123 fols. 29rb–36va, unprinted by Giles.

[37] *HB*, no. 16 (*PL*, 190.1439–47). The rubric reads: 'Epistola Lumbardi in persona Cantuariensis archiepiscopi responsalis ad appellationem episcoporum Angliae scripto factam.' Also printed in *MTB*, v, 478–90 no. 222.

persona Thomae Cantuariensis ... continens responsionem ad libellum eorumdem episcoporum appellatorium') is the *libellus* derided by Giles, as was noted earlier. It is indeed long, but not more so than the chosen draft, so the choice must have been made on other grounds.[38] Herbert's letter is even harsher on Henry II than the other drafts, especially when it compares the king at length with Julian the Apostate and his rejection of Christ;[39] its structure is also less clearly responding to the bishops' letter. In any case, the inclusion of all three drafts sheds some precious light on secretarial practices around Becket, and Herbert's attitude to them. His desire to be remembered for his enduring loyalty to his master, and for the price he had paid for it, shines brightly through the collection, when many others had, as he would have put it, sold their soul for the gold of Egyptians. The remainder of this chapter will explore other leading principles of the gathering. On intentional display are some long-lasting hatreds. Herbert also wanted to pass down to posterity his erudition and talent for scholarly debate, as in the letter on the *trinubium*.[40] The presence of *Ne in dubium*, already noted, also enriches the picture.[41] As Anne Duggan has shown, the version preserved in Herbert's collection is a most important witness of the settlement made in Avranches between Henry II and papal envoys to make peace after Becket's murder[42] – even though it is mutilated.[43] The addition of this not widely circulated text, the only item in the collection that is not strictly epistolary, suggests that it bore great meaning for Herbert, possibly because it outlined the concessions made by Henry to atone for the murder. The selection offered by the collection adds up to a political and intellectual portrait of Herbert, which is likely to be a self-portrait.

The letters were carefully rubricated, and provided readers with some insights into their contents beyond the names of the sender and recipient. They are very favourable to Herbert, and certainly partisan. They make clear, for instance, if a letter was sent while Herbert was 'exsulans',[44] a status that was used by Becket's people as a badge of honour and quasi-martyrdom; interestingly, Herbert continued as a self-styled *exsulans* even after his master's death. They also point out when letters were written *against* certain people, mainly Gilbert Foliot;[45] the adversarial

---

[38] *HB*, no. 15 (*PL*, 190.1439–40). Ignored by Giles, it was however printed by Robertson and runs in print to almost twenty pages (*MTB*, v, 459–78 no. 221).

[39] *MTB*, v, 461–2 no. 221.

[40] *HB*, no. 1 (*PL*, 190.1415–22).

[41] *HB*, no. 43 (*PL*, 190.1472–3). Giles did not print the *carta* much beyond the rubric and the address, but pointed out that it is mutilated.

[42] See Duggan, '*Ne in dubium*', pp. 643–58, particularly at 641–2.

[43] See CCCC 123 end of fol. 59v; about four lines are missing after the last extant words, 'Alexandro et cath ...'

[44] *HB*, nos. 2, 5, 6, 7, 18, 19, 21, 23, 34, 35, 38, 39, 40 and 42.

[45] *HB*, no. 2 (*PL*, 190.1422): 'Epistola Herberti in persona Thomae Cantuariensis archiepiscopi exsulantis ad Alexandrum papam contra Gilbertum Londoniensem episcopum jam excommunicatum'; *HB*, no. 6, to William archbishop of Sens: 'Epistola Herberti exsulantis ad eumdem contra Londoniensem episcopum Romam jam proficiscentem.'

tone and contents that are so typical of Herbert's writing are thus clearly signposted. The phrasing of the rubrics, so consistent with his style and favourite themes, strongly suggests that Herbert wrote them himself. If that was so, it is interesting that the letter to Henri de Beaumont, the bishop of Bayeux, is explicitly presented as modelled on the *De consideratione*: 'In this letter are gathered elements from the treatise of Bernard of Clairvaux, who wrote it at the request of Pope Eugenius.'[46] The borrowing from Bernard is explicit in a manner that is rather foreign to the textual mores of Herbert's times. This may therefore be a nod to the Cistercian brothers of Ourscamp, with whom he lived at the end of his life.

Herbert and his enemies

Herbert was a hot-headed man, as is attested by his famous encounter with Henry II in Angers; he loved Becket in life and death, and equally he loathed his master's foes. As we have seen already, among those Gilbert Foliot held a special place. Other members of the exile's *familia*, most notably John of Salisbury, shared the sentiment and heaped erudite abuse on the man they came to call the *archisinagogus*, the Gospel's 'head of the synagogue'.[47] Gilbert was for the Becket *eruditi* a reincarnation of a series of evil Old Testament figures. Herbert participated in the general detestation of Foliot, and his own letters prove that his feelings boiled high and lasted for decades; it is likely that the most virulent of the letters sent in the archbishop's name were his work. His collection is a short one, compared with the whole host of the Becket correspondence; the selected letters nevertheless offer a plentiful array of comparisons between the bishop of London (and other villains) and foul biblical characters. This allowed him to depict the ongoing conflict as an enactment of the eternal battle between good and evil, God and Satan.

The most common angle to attack them was for mendacity.[48] In exegetical terms that amounted to making them akin to the false prophets inspired by the devil to lead the people into perdition. Jeremiah accused the false prophets of taking the *iter mendacii*, a phrase applied by Herbert explicitly to Foliot: 'This is the bishop of London, who has already walked the road of mendacity.'[49] Cunning liars are worse than open enemies, as Herbert explained to Alexander III in a draft written on behalf of Becket, probably in 1165. Foliot was the pagan (*allophylus*) Goliath championing the Philistines against an implicit David-Becket (or possibly David-Alexander). He was also – making him much more dangerous (*potius periculosior*) – Achitophel, the malicious counsellor who led Absalom into rebellion against his

---

[46] *HB*, no. 21 (*PL*, 190.1456): 'In qua epistola nonnulla sumpta sunt ex tractatu Bernardi Claraevallensis quem fecit ad preces papae Eugenii.'

[47] See for instance *LJS*, ii, nos. 174 and 187; Mark 5:35–8.

[48] *Mendacium/mendax* appear five times, *falsus* and words based on it (*falsitas, falsiloquus,* etc) eight times.

[49] *HB*, no. 7 (*PL*, 190.1433), to William of the White Hands. See Jer. 23:14: 'et in prophetis Hierusalem vidi similitudinem adulterium et iter mendacii et confortaverunt manus pessimorum.'

father, David.[50] The rest of the letter is a systematic justification (*prima objectio, secunda*, etc. to *septima*) of Becket's attitude in Northampton and a condemnation of the king's delegation, led by Foliot, to the *curia* of Alexander III in Sens.[51] The idea that Achitophel was more dangerous to David than Goliath runs throughout the letter. With the help of acolytes such as the *archidiabolus* Geoffrey Ridel, Foliot 'truly was Goliath on the battleground, and Achitophel in conclave'.[52] There are two further references to Achitophel in the letter, which is laced with much more biblical imagery. For instance, Foliot is accused of having 'shredded to pieces' his absent father, and therefore of deserving 'the same curse' as Noah's son Ham, who 'had tried to bare his father's genitals'.[53] The curse of Ham was, of course, to be cast out of the people of God: this ominous comparison is an early claim that Gilbert Foliot would deserve excommunication.

Becket and Herbert's foes were also equated with non-human monsters, for which Revelation was a copious source. In two letters sent in 1170 to William of the White Hands, archbishop of Sens, papal legate and longtime supporter of the exiles, Herbert fumes against a world dominated by evil and treacherous men, especially the mendacious envoys of Henry II, who lied at the papal curia and lied after they left it, spreading venomous falsehoods across Europe.[54] Those two letters are full of scriptural monsters and exegetical evil. In one sentence, Herbert likens the exiles' enemy to the devil, in an elaborate and striking scriptural flourish. Elements from the two verses from Revelation about how the 'great dragon, the old enemy' (Satan) is cast down from Heaven (Rev. 12:9–10) are reworked and woven together.[55] Added

---

[50] *HB*, no. 3 (*PL*, 190.1425): 'Sed quid Goliam significo? Utinam vel solum se Goliam exhibuisset, quin potius periculosior est. Nam sicut clamat mundus, testantur opera, filium adversus patrem quibus potest consiliis instruit, ut idem sit nobis Achitophel in abscondito et Golias in aperto.'

[51] *HB*, no. 3 (*PL*, 190.1425): 'Primo in Anglia apud Northamptune … Praeterea Senonis …' There are various but concording narratives of the incident: see Alan of Tewkesbury, *Vita et Passio S. Thomae martyris*, *MTB*, ii, 338–9; Herbert of Bosham himself, *Vita*, *MTB*, iii, 336; Gerald of Wales, *Gemma ecclesiastica*, in *Giraldi Cambrensis Opera*, 8 vols., ed. J. S. Brewer, J. F. Dimock, and G. F. Warner (London, 1861–91), ii, p. 347.

[52] *HB*, no. 3 (*PL*, 190.1426): 'In omnibus enim his coram populo processit in campum armatus ut Philistis bella dimicare. Verum Golias in campo, in conclavi Achitophel erat, adeo etiam ut nuntiis domini regis proxime a sanctitate vestra revertentibus, Ricardo videlicet Barre et Radulfo archidiacono, verbum pacis, quod tunc sedulo quidem et officiose tractabatur, una cum archidiabolo illo Galfrido Ridel concilii sui nisibus ruperit.'

[53] *HB*, no. 3 (*PL*, 190.1425–6): 'quantis probris et contumeliis lacerasset ipsum patrum suum exsulantem et absentem … Unde et eo solo maledici meruit quod patris sui pudenda revelare attentavit.' See Gen. 9:20–7.

[54] *HB*, no. 5 (*PL*, 190.1433): 'Unum autem est, quod celare non possum, falsiloquos quosdam regis Anglorum nuntios, revertentes a curia, ventosis verbis totam terram implevisse, qui causam vestrae profectionis et negotii intima cuicunque disseminabant et auditoribus etiam sibilabant invitis. Ricardus autem Barre erat princeps prophetiae.'

[55] *HB*, no. 6 (*PL*, 190.1432): 'Ecce enim *draco ille magnus, serpens antiquus*, gladio verbi Dei vulneratus, vel demum nunc de fovea lubrici erroris exire cogitur. Scimus vero quod de malo ad malum egreditur, ut qui prius fraudulenter incessit, amodo fiat manifestus *fratrum suorum accusator*, et induet arma calumniae multo plus graviora quam pugnae.'

scriptural colour is brought to this complex sentence by a quote from Jeremiah about evil being piled up over evil.[56] Exegetical depth is layered in with phrases borrowed from Ambrose of Milan about the Lord's sword and the 'trap of the impudent error' (*fovea lubrici erroris*).[57] This contributes to the image, carefully built by Becket supporters, of their hero fighting God's fight alone against a hostile world. In Psalm 100:8, the passage explained by Ambrose, God announces that he shall 'slay all sinners'. In his comment Ambrose asks, 'but how can one can kill all?' The phrases quoted by Herbert are part of the answer to the question, and the meaning is clear: with God's help, and following His example, Becket will slay his enemies, against all apparent odds. Similarly, one of Satan's monikers in Revelation is 'accuser of his own brothers', which also appears in Herbert's sentence. That borrowing was particularly appropriate, since brotherly betrayal was a reproach thrown time and time again by Becket at fellow clerics, most particularly the English bishops, and among them Gilbert Foliot. What might look to a modern reader as overwrought grandiloquence is, arguably, carefully crafted political argumentation.

Gilbert Foliot was not the only target of Herbert's fiery wrath. Other names have already come up here: Richard Barre, Geoffrey Ridel, and other deceitful advisers of Henry II, for instance John of Oxford who was accused of having sworn on behalf of Henry II to acknowledge the antipope Paschal III at the Diet of Würzburg (1165).[58] However, only one man could compete with the bishop of London in Herbert's bad books: Arnulf, the wily and loquacious bishop of Lisieux.[59] Herbert's pen drips contempt when he describes Arnulf's effort to defend Gilbert Foliot. Herbert wonders whether Arnulf is cut out to be a bishop. More bitingly, he doubts that Arnulf should be called a Christian, since neither Arnulf's words nor his deeds are deserving of that name: the 'iron-hearted' bishop used his 'golden tongue'

The biblical background is provided by Rev. 12:9–10: 'et proiectus est draco ille magnus serpens antiquus qui vocatur Diabolus et Satanas qui seducit universum orbem proiectus est in terram et angeli eius cum illo missi sunt et audivi vocem magnam in caelo dicentem nunc facta est salus et virtus et regnum Dei nostri et potestas Christi eius quia proiectus est *accusator fratrum nostrorum* qui accusabat illos ante conspectum Dei nostri die ac nocte'.

[56] Jer. 9:3: 'et extenderunt linguam suam quasi arcum mendacii et non veritatis confortati sunt in terra quia de malo ad malum egressi sunt et me non cognoverunt dicit Dominus'.

[57] Ambrose of Milan, *Expositio psalmi 118*, ed. M. Petschenig, *CSEL*, 62 (Vienna, 1913), p. 349: 'utinam mihi adspiret haec gratia, ut gladio spiritali, *qui est uerbum dei*, ab ecclesia domini incentiua uniuersa possim abolere uitiorum et terrena auferre delicta, quibus in *foueam* quandam *lubrici* praecipitamur *erroris*, ut de ciuitate dei expellatur iniquitatis operator'.

[58] *HB*, no. 25 (*PL*, 190.1460): 'Auget etiam malorum scandalum quod vulgatissimus ille schismaticus Joannes de Oxenforde vestra quae omni praeest auctoritate absolutus Saresberiensis decanatus tam facile restitutionem meruerit, quasi sit ei in justitiam reputatum publicum illud perjurium schismatis quod, sicut mundus novit clamat, tam enormiter in Alemannia perpetravit, cujus occasione insignem illum schismaticum qui singularem quaerit in mundo principatum'. Cf. C. Harper-Bill, 'Oxford, John of (d. 1200)', *ODNB*. See also *CTB*, i, 560 no. 115.

[59] On Arnulf, see C. Schriber, *The dilemma of Arnulf of Lisieux: New Ideas versus Old Ideals* (Bloomington, 1990).

to lure men into perdition and to attack the rightful.[60] Expelling enemies out of *Christianitas* is a forceful move, even just in words; such words clearly circulated in the Becket circles, since John of Salisbury quipped twice along similar lines.[61] Arnulf was known for his prolixity, and Herbert knew better than anyone the power of words. He put all his hopes for success in them, but he was aware that the opposing side would also display skilful rhetoric and erudition; they had to be discredited before damage was done.[62] This may be why *Magnam michi*, an especially shifty letter from Arnulf, was included in the collection.[63]

Herbert and the Bible

There is no need to elaborate on Herbert's reputation as an outstanding biblical scholar, which has been studied in this volume and elsewhere. Here it is only his use of scripture in his letters that will be scrutinised, and the purposes that that use may have served. The working hypothesis will be that the radical and relentless biblical argumentation that runs through the exile letters of Thomas Becket is largely Herbert's work.[64]

Joseph and Becket: an exercise in typology

The typological structure was central to the Christian meaning of the Old Testament. Indeed, for medieval exegetes, everything spoke of Jesus in the Bible, and typology was one of the modes of this presence. Not relevant solely to Christ, typology establishes that the characters of the Old Testament are *praefigurationes*, or 'types',

---

[60] *HB*, no. 5 (*PL*, 190.1431–2): 'Audivimus proxime aliquos in nostri suggillationem pro persona Londoniensi scriptis suis testimonia in curia perhibituros, quorum unus cismarinus in Normannia, ut dicitur, episcopus est, qui tamen an episcopus sit, licet in episcopis jam senuerit, ignoratur, imo quod verius est, si quis Christum bene recogitet, non dico episcopum sed nec etiam Christianum vere profitebimur, nisi forte verba non opera faciant Christianum, cujus profecto omnis virtus in ore est, lingua aurea, et ferreum cor, cujus epistolare eloquium quod proxime vidimus, contra nos. operose sed viperee nimis conceptum, nimio candore deforme mentitur idolum, quin potius verum idolum est, quia falsum est quod conflavit, et spiritus non est in eo. Is est qui *in ore suo pacem nobiscum loquebatur et nunc occulte ponit insidias*, unde periculosior est de quibuslibet propheta dicit *Sagitta vulnerans lingua eorum: dolum locutus est*.' The last biblical reference is to Jer. 9:8.

[61] *LJS*, ii, no. 219, p. 376 : 'Unum scio, quod salua professione et citra divinae legis injuriam eas non modo episcopus, sed nec Christianus poterit conservare'; *LJS*, ii, no. 225, p. 390: 'Quod autem dico debita, non ad alicujus Henrici tempora referatur, sed ad verbi Dei legitimas sanctiones, quia ex professione non Henricianus esse debet, sed Christianus.'

[62] On disputes over the legitimate use of scripture, see J. Barrau, *Bible, lettres et politique. L'Ecriture au service des hommes à l'époque de Thomas Becket* (Paris, 2013), pp. 299–340.

[63] *HB*, no. 46. See *supra* n.16.

[64] In *CTB* the biblical index comprises about 1,200 references over 329 letters. The 193 letters sent by the archbishop (58 per cent of the whole correspondence) account for 80 per cent of the biblical references: they relied more on the Bible than the letters he received.

of posterior characters of the New.[65] In turn, the characters of the New Testament foreshadow those of later times: that is a foundational frame of hagiography, and is relevant for Herbert's use of typology.

The protagonists of the Becket conflict made liberal use of what Gilbert Dahan called 'historical allegory': 'Old and New Testament figures foreshadow historical figures who were contemporaries of the writers who engaged in such frequently polemical exegesis.'[66] Crucially, it allowed Becket supporters to enfold their struggle in the vast narrative of sacred history, from the Old Testament patriarchs to Henry II. The importance of various protagonists can be measured by the number of biblical figures that are presented as their 'type': Becket himself, first, then Henry II, Gilbert Foliot and some clerical groups, first and foremost the English episcopate. The vast majority of the letters using typological tropes came from the archbishop and his *familia*. Herbert, who was Becket's master in scripture, and whose own letters are, as has already been shown, woven in with a deeply scriptural prose, is almost certainly the main wordsmith responsible for the very specific flavour of his master's letters.[67]

The most basic form of typological pattern is undoubtedly the list. John of Salisbury was particularly fond of it, for instance when, in order to convince Becket that not all English bishops had necessarily forsaken his cause even though they had stayed in England, he composed a list of all the good counsellors who remained in a bad court, or more generally of the just who remained in a place of perdition: Joseph with Pharaoh, Lot in Sodom, Hushai the Archite with Absalom, Daniel in Babylon, Obadiah with Ahab and Jezebel.[68] Herbert used a similar trope in a letter to Wibert, prior of Christ Church, Canterbury, in which he gives a series of names of rightful men who suffered unjustly: Abel, Noah, Job, Daniel.[69] However, the use of lists was just the most rudimentary typological level. More elaborate comparisons, using words such as *praefiguro*, or in the case of historical allegory using adjectives such as *alter* or *noster*, signal a proper engagement with typology. Herbert of Bosham used typology profusely in his *Vita*, mostly to liken Becket to

---

[65] On typology see É. Amann, 'Type', *Dictionnaire de Théologie Catholique*, vol. 15/2 (Paris, 1950), cols. 1935–45; G. Dahan, *L'exégèse chrétienne de la Bible en Occident médiéval. xiie-xive siècles* (Paris, 1999), pp. 344–7.

[66] Dahan, *L'exégèse chrétienne*, p. 345.

[67] John of Salisbury also turned to the Bible and a combative brand of exegesis to defend Becket's cause, but he did not usually live with the exiled archbishop, and therefore cannot have drafted many of his master's letters. On John's possible role as Becket's occasional secretary, see *CTB*, i, xxiv, where Anne Duggan suggests some contribution from John in about eighteen letters, without ascribing any fully to his penmanship. See also J. Barrau, 'La *conversio* de Jean de Salisbury: la Bible au service de Thomas Becket', *Cahiers de civilisation médiévale*, 50 (2007), 229–44, and above, pp. 50–1.

[68] *LJS*, ii, no. 175, p. 162, used again with slight variations in *LJS*, ii, no. 181, p. 204, and no. 184, p. 216.

[69] *HB*, no. 13 (*PL*, 190.1437): 'Nunc autem contra luctum consolationis arma sumenda sunt, ut spes vestra possit habere victoriam. Igitur inter nascentis mundi exordia videamus Abel in campo, Noe in diluvio, Job in sterquilinio, Danielem in lacu, et quia longum esset singulas justorum generationes percurrere, quorum profecto tot sunt flagellati quot justi …'

Christ in his lifetime. The letter to Wibert that has been mentioned demonstrates that sophisticated typology could be turned into a political weapon. The relations between Becket and his chapter had got off to a bad start.[70] Once exiled, Becket lost the only quality that could redeem him in the eyes of the monks, his friendship with the king; between the exiles and the monks of Christ Church the relations were strained, and the resentment was evident on both sides of the Channel. The monastic chapter felt abandoned and caught between two equally frightening perils: on one side, the ever more aggressive encroachments of the king and his agents on their property; on the other side, the risk of ruining their reputation for having abandoned the archbishop in his struggle for *libertas ecclesiae*, a risk doubled by the threat of eternal punishment inflicted by God.[71] As for Becket and his followers, they accused Christ Church of failing to support their fight, especially financially.

In his letter to Wibert, probably sent early in 1165, Herbert presented a typological narrative intended to fill the community of Christ Church with the fighting spirit they lacked. He began by expressing his sympathy for the 'desolation' of the monks: 'you grieve that Jonah was devoured and Joseph sold, and you can not calmly accept the misfortunes of your father and the violence done to your mother'.[72] This sentence establishes the thread that will be followed throughout the letter: the typological connection between Becket, on the one hand, and Jonah and Joseph, on the other. As a consolation, Herbert weaves in a lesson in historical allegory:

> Jonah, when he had already been devoured, was removed from the bowels of the whale, and Joseph, who had been sold by his brothers, actually lived and reigned. Yet [the brothers] had shown their father his bloodied multi-coloured tunic, and said that a ferocious beast had devoured him. Indeed, those who were sent tried to charge our Joseph with various crimes, and denounced him as a dissolute man and a disruptor of the peace of the kingdom and the Church; but everyone saw through their cunning, and no one believed them.[73]

---

[70] As Richard Southern put it, 'they had had to consent to his election, but he was the last man they would have chosen. They had known him as archdeacon of Canterbury, but that was no recommendation … The monks saw little of him, and the little they saw they did not like.' R. W. Southern, *The Monks of Canterbury and the Murder of Archbishop Becket* (Canterbury, 1985), p. 11.

[71] Odo, Wibert's successor as prior, eloquently expressed their dilemma in a letter to Richard of Ilchester; see *MTB*, vii, 52–6 no. 552. Becket's frustration with the brethren is perceptible in his letters; see for instance *CTB*, ii, 910–21 no. 209. John of Salisbury was more explicitly, and increasingly, scathing; see *LJS*, ii, 304–7 no. 205 to Wibert and Odo, and *LJS*, ii, nos. 244, 292, 295 and 300 to the monks.

[72] *HB*, no. 13 (*PL*, 190.1437): 'lugetis Jonam devoratum et Joseph venditum, nec potestis aequo animo patris vestri miserias et matris vestrae injurias tolerare'. The father here is Becket, the mother the church of Canterbury. For the biblical references see for Joseph, Gen. 37, especially 27–8, and for Jonah, see Jon. 1–2.

[73] *HB*, no. 13 (*PL*, 190.1437): 'Verumtamen tunicam polymitam cruentam patri suo ostenderunt, dicentes quia fera pessima devoraverit eum. Nam qui fuerant missi nostro Joseph varia crimina objicere attentarunt, vocantes eum hominem flagitiosum, pacis

Jonah, and Joseph even more, were well-established figures of Christ.[74] Jesus himself made the three days spent by Jonah in the belly of the whale the foreshadowing of his death and resurrection. To regard these two Old Testament figures as *praefigurationes* of Thomas was therefore to liken him implicitly to Jesus. The sentence that follows reveals that the mendacious false brothers are the members of the delegation sent by Henry II to the Curia immediately after the departure of Becket into exile. Herbert tells, without giving names (*ego neminem nominabo*), the well-known episode where two learned members of this embassy, Gilbert bishop of London and Hilary bishop of Chichester, suddenly lost the ability to speak Latin properly and made childish mistakes (*sic loquens, ut qui pueriles litteras and primas dictionum juncturas ignoraret*).[75] The game of typological correspondence makes the pope (*summo patrum patre*) a new Jacob, and the bishops the criminal brothers and liars. Herbert could then draw the lessons from his exercise in historical typology, at which Becket, having been 'our' Joseph, became 'your' Joseph:

> So find comfort, find solace in these words, do not hesitate, but know with certainty that this great God of the Hebrews, who released your Joseph from his prison, and will make great on earth him who today is in a lowly standing.[76]

One of the effects of typology is to contract or even cancel diachrony. Herbert reinforced this by naming the God who 'released' Thomas 'that great God of the Hebrews', a phrase used in Exodus that is rarely found in twelfth-century texts.[77] Whatever the actual effect of the letter on Wibert, there is little doubt that Herbert had hopes that his artful typological retelling of the humiliation of Gilbert and Hilary in front of the pope, as well as his narrative of downtrodden scriptural heroes who later rose to glory, narratives presented as types for the archbishop, would compel the prior and his brethren to muster some courage and rise to the challenge. The Bible, brandished as a world-reflecting mirror, was his weapon of choice, in his own letters as in the epistles he drafted for his master.

Ælfheah, Thomas and 'the family of the lamb'

Another letter, written in 1166 to Gregory, abbot of Malmesbury, is a further example of the care Herbert put into composing his exile correspondence. The

---

regni et Ecclesiae turbatorem: sed omnes in astutia sua comprehensi sunt, nec est creditum verbis eorum …'

[74] See for instance Ailred of Rievaulx, *Opera Omnia II: Sermones I–XLVI*, ed. G. Raciti, CCCM 2A (Turnhout, 1989), no. 15, p. 124: 'Paene omnes Christiani sciunt quod sanctus Ioseph significabat Dominum nostrum, et angustiae quas passus est a fratribus suis significabant passiones quas pertulit Dominus noster a Iudaeis.'

[75] *HB*, no. 13 (*PL*, 190.1437). The letter to Wibert was seemingly the first account of the episode ever to circulate.

[76] *HB*, no. 13 (*PL*, 190.1438): 'Consolamini itaque, consolamini in verbis istis, in nullo haesitantes, sed scientes pro certo quia magnus ille Deus Hebraeorum, qui Joseph vestrum eduxit de carcere, adhuc modicum, et magnum faciet eum in terra.'

[77] See Exod. 3:18, 5:3, 7:16, 9:1;13, 10:3.

letter's main argument was a comparison between Becket and his holy predecessors at Canterbury, Dunstan, Ælfheah and Anselm.[78] Particular emphasis was laid on Ælfheah, the archbishop who was killed by Danish invaders in 1012 and was canonised in 1078. Herbert prefaces his parallel between dead and living archbishops with remarks on the sufferings of the exiles:

> I know that a widespread rumour has already reached your ears about what is happening to them [Becket's supporters] at the moment, and about how much opprobrium has been heaped, allegedly justly, on our archbishop, whom I accompany in his sufferings (*passionum*); and it is true that the sufferings of Christ abound in us just as much as we are abundantly comforted by Jesus Christ.[79]

What Becket and Ælfheah have in common, it is announced here, is *imitatio Christi*, to the point where the saint is identified with Jesus. Further on, Herbert explains in detail how the martyred prelate's example can sustain and comfort the exiles in their tribulations. He explains to the abbot how the exiles had a vision of 'three lights' (the three former archbishops), of whom the middle one had a distinctive wound. That was the ever rosy and glowing martyr, with his torn body, whose wounds, Herbert told the abbot, bore witness to his (Gregory's) words. This evocation of Ælfheah, laden with rhyming or alliterative words ('vultus vulnus', 'roseus et super dilectos rubicundus', 'tripudians et triumphans') is vivid and firmly anchored in the present; its relevance to contemporary events hardly needed spelling out. Herbert then turns to the future, in a grandiose description of the *dies Domini*, when those who fought along with Christ (*commilitones Christi*), 'the family of the Lamb who has been sacrificed since the beginning of times' (*illam Agni familiam occisi ab origine mundi*) will be as one body with Christ (*una cum Christo tali corporis schemate apparebunt*).[80] The brave piety in the face of torture

---

[78] *HB*, no. 19 (*PL*, 190.1448–51). On Gregory, abbot of Malmesbury (probably 1159–68), see D. Knowles, C. N. L. Brooke and V. London, *The Heads of Religious Houses: England and Wales, I: 940–1216*, 2nd edn (Cambridge, 2001), p. 55.

[79] *HB*, no. 24 (*PL*, 190.1459): 'Scio etenim fama celebri divulgante jam ad aures vestras pervenisse, de his quae his diebus facta sunt, quot et quanta videlicet propter justitiam sustinuerit opprobria Cantuariensis noster, cujus passionum ego socius sum, verum sicut abundant passiones Christi in nobis, ita et per Jesum Christum abundat consolatio nostra.'

[80] *HB*, no. 19 (*PL*, 190.1449): 'Jungamus ergo et tolerantiam earumdem passionum ac miseriarum, in quibus nos. adhuc pro tempore versamur, et in quibus et ipsi dum adhuc in carne essent versati sunt, nec est ambiguum inter quot et quanta pericula hanc quam domus Salvatoris ecclesiam rexerint pro qua etiam usque ad sanguinem restiterunt: levemus oculos et respiciamus praenominatos tres vigiles, medium si non vultus vulnus tamen discernit. Medius enim eorum stat quem nos. scimus roseus et super dilectos rubicundus, stat enim martyr tripudians et triumphans toto lacero corpore. Ni fallor, Elphegus est iste cujus vulnera vestra testantur verba, adeo ut et in ipsius corpore vulnerum adhuc exstent cicatrices crudi, aspersio sanguinis et verberum livor, imperatoris sui characterem gerens et pro civitate sibi credita quae sustinuerit summo omnium Patri repraesentans, eo ipso Salvatoris sui imago et Crucifixi sequela; et puto veniente die Domini hujuscemodi commilitones Christi una cum Christo tali corporis

of Ælfheah, Becket and, most crucially for the purpose of the letter, the *familia*, all those who joined them, is compellingly displayed in those two tableaux: in the present the colourful and lurid vision of the martyr, in the future the incommensurate reward of the union with Christ. The tone is especially suited to a monastic reader, and not just by referring to the *familia Christi*; the quoted verse in Revelation (13:8) speaks of the *liber vitae* of the Lamb, which was often commented on by the exegesis of the cloisters to draw the contrast between those who adored 'the Beast' and those who rejected it.[81] Immediately afterwards – this paragraph fills not more than half a *Patrologia* column – Herbert compared Becket to Stephen, the proto-martyr (*alterum Stephanum*), and explained his superiority over Adam, since he resisted temptation.[82] Such a rhetorical masterpiece, *pace* Giles, is anything but empty words; its carefully crafted composition was obviously meant to pull the abbot of Malmesbury over to the side of Becket.

It must have been obvious to Gregory that Herbert, as early as 1166, was depicting his master already as a saint and a potential martyr. This is one of the most striking features of the Becket letters in general, and the relentless scriptural imagery contributed to it. In contrast with other polemical epistolary collections of the time, the letters emanating from the exile's household clearly relied on the Word to fight the good fight.[83] However far from modern literary aesthetics, and from modern ideas about what constitutes a persuasive argument, that was their political weapon of choice, whether to flatter or to threaten. It is clear that Herbert was a key influence in choosing that path.

An arcane exegetical controversy at the service of Thomas Becket

The best example of the unique way Herbert put his exegetical expertise at the service of his master is, paradoxically, one where the biblical matter has no direct relevance, typological or otherwise, to the tribulations of the exiles. It can be found in the first letter of the collection, the beginning of which is missing; that

schemate apparebunt et videbunt tunc in quem pupugerunt, roseum illum martyrum chorum saucium caput cum membris, Imperatorem cum suis, illam Agni familiam occisi ab origine mundi.'

[81] See, for instance, the repeated instances where *liber vitae* and *agnus* are associated or equated in Rupert of Deutz's commentary on Revelation. *Commentarium in Apocalypsim Iohannis apostoli* (*PL*, 169.1075–6, 1205–6).

[82] HB, no. 19 (*PL*, 190.1449): 'Sed transeamus nunc sociam illam ovium occisionis multitudinem; Elphegus in ore est qui fortior stetit inter ictus lapidum in exsilio, quam Adam inter ligna deliciarum in paradiso, fortior fuit inter lapides quam Adam inter poma. Adam odore pomi olfacto mox cecidit et vincitur. At inter lapides stetit Elphegus immobilis.'

[83] Over 500 letters were written in the contest of another heated and protracted conflict opposing clerics – the bitter resistance of the monks of Christ Church Canterbury to their archbishops' plans for a new church. Their use of scripture is limited and uninventive: *Epistolae Cantuarienses: The Letters of the Prior and Convent of Christ Church, Canterbury, from AD 1187 to AD 1199*, in *Chronicles and Memorials of the Reign of Richard I*, ed. W. Stubbs, 2 vols., RS (London, 1865), ii.

letter fills seven columns in the *Patrologia*, eight folios in the manuscript.[84] It was addressed to Henry the Liberal, count of Champagne and brother-in-law of the French king, whose Burgundian court was renowned for its sophistication. His keen interest in the Bible is well documented, since around the same period he asked John of Salisbury for a detailed account of the canon of the Bible and its origins.[85] Herbert's letter broaches an even more arcane topic, the issue of whether Saint Anne, the Virgin's Mother, had been married three times (rather than just once to Joachim), and whether the Mary Salome of the Gospel was the offspring of the third of those marriages to a certain Salome. This complex narrative originated in Haimo of Auxerre's assumption that the three Marys of the Gospels were all Anne's daughters; the *trinubium Annae* gathered some momentum from the end of the twelfth century.[86] In the general context of the development of Marian worship, it contributed, like many other apocryphal yet accepted stories, to filling the many gaps in the history of Christ's mother.[87] Even though the *trinubium* was eventually received into mainstream belief, as is proved by its presence in the thirteenth-century *Legenda Aurea*, it was met with energic resistance in some (limited) quarters, particularly in northern England.

In his contribution to that fight, Herbert opposed the notion of the *trinubium* with typical passion. The letter to the count of Champagne exposed his objections in great detail, and vindicated them with the support of many *auctoritates*, the use of logic and references to Hebrew; nothing, he hammered through his exposé, stood scrutiny to sustain such inanity.[88] Here we see him debating the issue with John of Salisbury, who usefully brought to the debate the commentary on Matthew by the Carolingian exegete Claude of Turin that had been given to him by a master William, a monk of Saint-Denis,[89] and with another *magister* William, also a monk

---

[84] *HB*, no. 1 (*PL*, 190.1415–22), CCCC 123 fols. 1r–4v. Giles left out the last few lines, which read: 'Sciatis quod liber quod Agelii noctium atticarum inscribitur quem a me multotiens requisistis non meus sed Sancte Columbe est.' This suggests that the letter was written after November 1166, when Becket and his entourage settled in the monastery of Sainte-Colombe near Sens.

[85] *LJS*, ii, no. 209, pp. 314–39. On Henry's cultivated court, see J. Benton, 'The Court of Champagne as a Literary Center', *Speculum* 36 (1961), 551–91.

[86] On the controversy, and the attack on the 'Salomites', see M. R. James, 'The *Salomites*', *Journal of Theological Studies* 35 (1934), 287–97, and M. Naydenova-Slade and D. Park, 'The Earliest Holy Kinship Image, the Salomite Controversy, and a Little-Known Centre of Learning in Northern England in the Twelfth Century', *Journal of the Warburg and Courtauld Institutes* 71 (2008), 95–119.

[87] On the growth of Marian worship in the twelfth century, see M. Rubin, *Mother of God: A History of the Virgin Mary* (New Haven, 2009), pp. 119–87.

[88] On Herbert's argumentation, see also D. Goodwin, *'Take Hold of the Robe of a Jew': Herbert of Bosham's Christian Hebraism* (Leiden and Boston, 2006), pp. 29–30.

[89] *HB*, no. 1 (*PL*, 190.1417): 'Et praeterea veniens ad nos. dilectus socius noster magister Joannes Saresberiensis, notus tibi ut arbitror, quamdam schedulam ex parte cujusdam fratris magistri Willelmi Londoniensis viri, ut scitis, litterati et, ut creditur, religiosi, qui apud Sanctum Dionysium monachus est, detulit, quae Claudii super Matthaeum praetitulabatur …'

from Saint-Denis.[90] After pages and pages of scriptural, patristic and linguistic arguments, which would deserve detailed study, Herbert turned to Henry, and covered him with flattering comparisons with, among others, Pythagoras and Constantine. Finally, he exhorted him to ignore the slanders of Henry II's emissaries of the exiles, especially about the infamous altercation between Herbert and the king at Angers the year before.

Herbert's letter is an odd literary beast. Its form recalls theological treatises that affected the epistolary form, such as the almost contemporary treatise by Robert Pullen, published under the title *Sermo de Omnibus humane Uite Necessariis* or *De Contemptu Mundi,* and presented as a letter of consolation addressed to a fictional, powerful and wealthy cleric. However, here the recipient is anything but fictitious. The complex argument and the references heaped up were intended to flatter and captivate the attention of a lay magnate with an unusual taste for intricate theology. Was all that spirited erudition mustered only to retain Henry's friendship and gain his support to the exiles' cause, in the manner of an elaborate letter whose real gist was conveyed by the messenger carrying it? That would be too crude a conclusion. Herbert's letter is an 'epistolary gift', a letter whose very sophistication, proof of the time devoted to it and of the high opinion professed for the recipient, is in itself the message.[91] The long pages about Anne and her ghost husbands are as much a plea for Henry's support as were the few explicit lines that follow them. Herbert, the cleric with a martial bearing, offered the count his learned rhetoric as others would give him their military support or their diplomatic counsel.

Herbert's letters are erudite, prolix, passionate and at times vindictive. They provide a fuller portrait of a man who was a scholar in politics, as intense in his scholarship as he was in his radical activism on behalf of Becket.[92] Scholarship was his weapon, in his Bible-infused prose, his use of typology that created a continuity with prophets and Christ, his sophisticated 'scriptural presents'. His letters' tone and subject matter is all over his master's, which strongly suggests that he played indeed a crucial role in forging Becket's arsenal. With his letter collection, Herbert tried to establish for posterity that God and his Word were on their side.

---

[90] *HB,* no. 1 (*PL,* 190.1420): 'Cum ... apud Sanctum Dionysium essem et praefatum magistrum Willelmum Londoniensem non quidem procaciter, sed sedulo tamen et instanter super jam saepe dicto nomine Salomae convenirem, inter modestas verborum pugnas quidam alius frater magister Willelmus nomine, quondam officio medicus, nunc vero ut speratur sicut habitum monachi et animum gerens, supervenit, qui ut altercationis causam advertit, audientia postulata, aiebat se inter Syros aliquanto tempore conversatum ...'.

[91] On 'epistolary gifts' in the context of the Becket conflict, see Barrau, *Bible, lettres et politique,* pp. 234–57.

[92] This agrees with Michael Staunton's important assessment of Herbert's *Vita* and its long theological 'digressions': 'Such passsages ... have usually been passed over by modern writers. Yet they encapsulate almost everything of Herbert's interpretation of Thomas's life and deeds', in *Thomas Becket and His Biographers* (Woodbridge, 2006), pp. 66–7.

CHAPTER SIX

Time, Change and History in Herbert of Bosham's *Historia*

Michael Staunton

H ERBERT of Bosham's account of Thomas Becket's life is usually called the *Vita Sancti Thomae*, and discussed in terms of the hagiography of the saint, but there are reasons we should think of it more in terms of history. Herbert's own preferred term for his work was the *Historia*, and he makes regular reference to it as such, in the work itself and elsewhere.[1] He justifies his approach to those who might consider it too theological and insufficiently 'historical', and denies that he is going beyond the 'law of history', insisting that his work is quite in conformity with it.[2] And in the last lines of the book Herbert addresses Thomas and calls himself 'your historian' (*historiographus tuus*).[3] Of course, just because Herbert calls it so does not make it a history: he also calls it 'this little history book' (*libellus historicus hic*),[4] and this work of around 80,000 words in length is far from a *libellus*. But the fact that Herbert so regularly uses the term *historia* with reference to his work suggests that we should consider it in terms of history, and see what a specifically historical perspective on it can reveal.

To consider Herbert's work as history does not mean that it cannot also be considered as hagiography. The distinction was not as rigid in the twelfth century as modern conventions might imply: histories could include hagiography, and

---

[1] E.g. *MTB*, iii, 155, 156, 248, 334, 338, 406, 408, 423, 467.

[2] *MTB*, iii, 247–8: 'In his, inquam, pontifices exsequendis operibus forte nimis morosus videor, et in ipsorum commendatione operum taediosus inculcator verborum, et potius theologicae aedificationi quam gestorum viri historicae explanationi insistere, et ita nimis theologum, historicum vero parum, sapere ... Et ob idem forte historiae legem excedens plus theologum sapio; nec enim absque theologia, absque Dei sermone, Dei operum virtus declarari potest aut debet.' *MTB*, iii, 259: 'O si mihi nunc liceret, et coeptae historiae lex sic permitteret, virum istum pro virtutum suarum meritis condignis efferre praeconiis! Certe totam hanc martyris historiam quasi caelestis firmamenti stella matutina illustraret.' *MTB*, iii, 533: 'Nec tamen, si quis bene historiarum inspexerit schemata, hoc contra historiae legem, immo verius secundum legem.' See R. Ray, 'Bede's *Vera Lex Historiae*', *Speculum* 55 (1980), 1–21. In the *Liber Melorum* he refers to the 'law of music' ('musicae artis lex'): *PL*, 190.1300.

[3] *MTB*, iii, 531.

[4] *MTB*, iii, 341, 396, 486, 487, 512.

saints' Lives could have features such as documentary evidence that we tend to associate with contemporary historical writing.[5] Herbert offers us a narrative of a man celebrated by its author and by the universal church as a saint, but there are indications from the start that we are about to see something different to the other Lives of St Thomas. Though he includes a number of prophetic visions, he excludes miracles. Herbert frequently proposes to pontiffs that they follow Thomas's example, describing him as an 'exemplary man' (*vir exemplaris*), but he determines to present Thomas as an exemplar to be imitated in works, rather than marvelled at in the signs 'given for unbelievers' (*propter infideles data*).[6] And although he shows some interest in pilgrimage to Thomas's tomb, prophesies fulfilled, visions of the saint, parallels with Christ, and the 'miraculous' penance of the murderers and the king, he discusses these in a separate work, the *Liber melorum*.[7]

Herbert wrote the *Historia* between around 1184 and 1186, at a time when the writing of history, and especially contemporary history, was beginning to experience an explosion of activity in England. He should be grouped among those who wrote history in the 1180s and 1190s – Roger of Howden, Ralph of Diceto, Gerald of Wales, Ralph of Coggeshall, Walter Map, Gervase of Canterbury, Richard of Devizes and William of Newburgh – as much as with the biographers of Thomas Becket of the 1170s. It is immediately possible to identify parallels between Herbert's work and theirs. Despite the long-windedness and tendency to digression, Herbert is very concerned with the order and structure of his history. His careful division of the *Historia* into books and chapters, so as to make it easier for readers to find what they are looking for, echoes the similar practice of Ralph of Diceto.[8] Herbert resembles William of Newburgh in that he was a biblical commentator before he was a historian, and a

[5] See J. O'Reilly, 'The Double Martyrdom of Thomas Becket: Hagiography or History?', *Studies in Medieval and Renaissance History* 7 (1985), 185–247; F. Lifshitz, 'Beyond Positivism and Genre: "Hagiographical" Texts as Historical Narrative', *Viator* 25 (1994), 95–114.

[6] *MTB*, iii, 156; see also 513–14. In describing Thomas's behaviour as archbishop, especially in his 'day in the life' section, Herbert often addresses pontiffs to say that they should follow Thomas's example: e.g. *MTB*, iii, 186, 198, 200, 204, 208, 210, 219, 225, 238, 241. He refers to the edificatory value of reading about Thomas's struggle: 311, 323, 379, 509, 514.

[7] *Liber Melorum*, PL, 190.1302–43.

[8] *MTB*, iii, 157–9. See *Radulfi de Diceto Decani Lundoniensis Opera Historica. The Historical works of Master Ralph de Diceto, Dean of London*, ed. W. Stubbs, 2 vols., RS (London, 1876), pp. 1–4, 33, 267–87. Herbert includes cross-references in the Arras manuscript. Especially towards the start Herbert often writes 'as the following will declare', or similar, e.g. *MTB*, iii, 247, 273, 278, 287, 315, 406, 416, 459, 467, 481. Towards the end of the *Historia* he frequently refers back to earlier passages, e.g. pp. 420, 423, 427, 429, 430, 439, 459, 488, 511, 520, 521. He also makes reference to the *Liber Melorum*, 286–7, 512, 517, to the Constitutions of Clarendon, 286, 341 and to the letter collection (not his own but the Canterbury collection), 315, 395–6, 418, 440. See also Herbert's concern in his revision of Peter Lombard's *Great Gloss* to make the text manageable by using rubrics and illustrations, and dividing the Psalms thematically: C. de Hamel, 'Manuscripts of Herbert of Bosham', in *Manuscripts at Oxford: An Exhibition in Memory of Richard William Hunt (1908–1979)*, ed. A. C. de la Mare and B. C. Barker-Benfield (Oxford, 1980), pp. 38–41, at 39; M. Doyle, *Peter Lombard and His Students* (Toronto, 2016), p. 99.

man who applied his knowledge of patristic writing and twelfth-century thought to recent history. They also share something in their scepticism about miracles and willingness to challenge orthodoxies.[9] In his education, his participation in public life and in temperament he shared more with Gerald of Wales, an enthusiast for Thomas Becket and a very self-reflective writer who was equally willing to take established literary forms and bend them to his own purposes to create something strikingly original.[10] Herbert knew Gervase of Canterbury, and the latter's *Chronicle* often echoes the language found in Herbert's *Historia*.[11] Gervase famously distinguished the chronicler, who adopts a direct and straightforward course, from the historian, who 'employs rhetorical flourishes and long-winded words', sits 'among the lofty speakers who sow grandiose words' and weighs down his work with bombastic verbiage.[12] He might as well be talking about the author of the *Historia*.

If we are to look at Herbert's work as history, we must pay attention to certain notable features that have not, perhaps, received as much attention as they might have. Here I would like to focus on time and change – themes central to Herbert's work but not always appreciated in discussions of medieval historical (or indeed hagiographical) writing. In his work we can see Herbert at every turn addressing the passing of time and the quality of change – in Thomas, in the cause of the church, in public opinion, in Thomas's persecutors and in Herbert himself. By tracing these themes through his work we can gain a deeper sense of his approach to Thomas Becket and to his task as a historian, and perhaps give some insight into twelfth-century perceptions of time and change.

'A twisted and roundabout road'

Hagiographers tend to exalt their subjects in hyperbolic terms; Becket's biographers go further than most, and Herbert further again. But when Herbert praises

---

[9] Though they differ in their view of Becket: see William of Newburgh, *Historia Rerum Anglicarum*, in *Chronicles of the Reigns of Stephen, Henry II and Richard I*, 4 vols., ed. R. Howlett, RS (London, 1884–9), i, pp. 142–3, 161. Herbert, like William, has a habit of digressing and then writing, 'let us return to the order of the history', or similar: e.g. *MTB*, iii, 192, 238, 244, 288, 311, 334, 357, 375, 379, 396, 397, 406, 408, 417, 426, 481, 513.

[10] See *De rebus a se gestis*, in *Giraldi Cambrensis Opera*, ed. J. S. Brewer, J. F. Dimock and G. F. Warner, 8 vols. RS (London, 1861–91), pp. 49–50, 53; *Vita S. Remigii*, in ibid, vii, 43–56, 60–2, 68–70.

[11] See *The Historical Works of Gervase of Canterbury*, ed. W. Stubbs, 2 vols., RS (London, 1879–80), i, pp. 353–4, 394, 471–2; M. Staunton, 'Thomas Becket in the Chronicles', in *The Cult of St Thomas Becket in the Plantagenet World, c. 1170–c. 1220*, ed. P. Webster and M.-P. Gelin (Woodbridge, 2016), pp. 95–112, at 104–9.

[12] Gervase, i, pp. 87–8: 'Forma tractandi varia, quia historicus diffuse et eleganter incedit, cronicus vero simpliciter graditur et breviter. *Proicit* historicus *ampullas et sesquipedalia verba*; cronicus vero *silvestrem musam tenui meditator avena*. Sedet historicus *inter magniloquos et grandia verba serentes*, at cronicus sub pauperis Amiclae pausat tugurio ne sit pugna pro paupere tecto.' Translated by J. Lake, *Prologues to Ancient and Medieval History: A Reader* (Toronto, 2013), p. 266. See Horace, *Ars Poetica*, 97; Vergil, *Eclogues*, 1.2; Lucan, *Bellum Civile*, 5.515–559.

Thomas he generally chooses his words carefully, and does so in a way that expresses particular ideas that often run throughout his work and are underpinned by Christian tradition. So it is when he insists that whatever changes Thomas underwent during his life, he was always and everywhere great in whatever role he adopted: 'always great: great in the court, great in the church, great when a citizen in England, great when an exile in France, but incomparably great and greater especially today' – that is, in death.[13] Again, he says that in every one of his positions he was proved great, 'always and everywhere great: great in the palace, great in the priesthood, great in the court, great in the church, great in pilgrimage, great in return from pilgrimage, but greatest in the consummation of pilgrimage'.[14] This expresses an idea central to Herbert's work: that Thomas's life combined a large variety of roles, but they were united by a certain quality of greatness. It sees Thomas's life as a pilgrimage that took many paths, all of which led towards the full revelation of his greatness. Each of Thomas's biographers had to address the apparent contradictions in Thomas's life, and they do so in various ways: by presenting his move from the court to the church as a kind of conversion, his conflict with the king and his exile as a trial through which he was perfected, his death as a consummation of and full revelation of his sanctity.[15] Herbert does this too, but in an especially developed way.

One approach that Herbert takes is to present Thomas as adopting certain qualities as he went on – perfecting himself by realising aspects of himself that had been hidden earlier. On the surface, Herbert is just reiterating a common hagiographical convention. Saints are often represented in childhood and youth as growing from strength to strength, and hagiographers sometimes echo the terms used in Luke's gospel of Jesus, who 'advanced in wisdom, and age, and grace with God and men'.[16] But Herbert recognised that Thomas did not fit this picture. As he explicitly states, Thomas advanced in favour with men, but not so much with God until later. In a long discussion at the start of Book II, Herbert points to two graces, *benignitas* and *bonitas*. *Benignitas*, he says, is a civil, urbane, benign, sweet, social and delightful grace, in which man pleases the world more, but God less. *Bonitas* is a heavenly rather than worldly grace, more pleasing to God and less pleasing to man. It is best to be pleasing to both God and men, and combine both *bonitas* and *benegnitas*, as did Joseph, a citizen of Jerusalem who could administer in Egypt the

---

[13] *MTB*, iii, 417: 'semper magnus; magnus in aula, magnus in ecclesia, magnus quando civis in Anglia, magnus quando exsul in Francia, sed incomparabiliter magnus et majore maximus hodie'.

[14] *MTB*, iii, 471: 'semper et ubique magnus; magnus in palatio, magnus in sacerdotio, magnus in aula, magnus in ecclesia, magnus in peregrinatione, magnus in peregrinationis reversione, maximus vero in peregrinationis consummatione'.

[15] See M. Staunton, *Thomas Becket and his Biographers* (Woodbridge, 2006), pp. 75–96.

[16] Luke 2:52. See, for example, Bernard, *Vita S. Malachiae*, in *Sancti Bernardi Opera Omnia*, ed. J. Leclercq, C. H. Talbot and H. M. Rochais, 8 vols (Rome, 1957–77), iii, p. 311: 'Et Malachiae quidem pueritia sic erat. Porro adolescentiam simili transivit simplicitate et puritate: nisi quod crescente aetate, crescebat simul illi sapientia et gratia apud Deum et homines. Hinc iam, id est ab ineunte adolescentia eius, coepit manifestius apparere quid esset in homine, et gratia Dei in illo vacua non videri'.

things of the Egyptians, or Daniel, who carried out the business of the Babylonians in Babylon, and Paul, who was made all things to all men.[17] *Benignitas* is one of the courtly attributes often assigned to bishops in episcopal *vitae*, and increasingly in Herbert's time to secular lords, and he takes much interest in such courtly ideals.[18] But he makes clear the source of the present discussion when he notes that St Paul places *benignitas* immediately after *bonitas* in his list of the twelve fruits of the Spirit.[19] In the first years of his youth, Thomas was rich in *benignitas* but lacked *bonitas*, but later on God added *bonitas* to the former grace, thus making him advance in favour not only before men but before God. Herbert adds that God is accustomed to do this, to supplement *benignitas* with *bonitas*, as and when He wishes, 'and those who come last are made equal to those who came before them'.[20]

Similarly, Herbert acknowledges that in the young Thomas vices coexisted with virtues, but the former were prevented from overcoming the latter because Thomas remained chaste.[21] It was as if he were dozing, between sleeping and waking: here the hand of virtues withdrew him from sleep, there the hand of vices turned him to slumber. In this he was like King David, who first slept in the sin of adultery but then, drawn by the Lord through certain graces, was fully roused. Citing the words of the bride to the Bridegroom in the Song of Songs, 'Draw me: we will run after thee to the odour of thy ointments', Herbert writes that Thomas was first drawn through chastity and other gifts of grace, and later ran in the odour of virtue, until finally he snatched the prize, the Lord of hosts, the King of glory himself.[22]

The sense of latent virtues being revealed over time is especially strong in Herbert's account of Thomas's transformation on becoming archbishop. Once elected, Thomas, 'like a man awakening from a deep sleep, considered in his heart what he had been for a long time, and how he ought to be from now on'. For a long time in court he had been like a man suffering from lethargy, but now he returned to himself and meditated in his heart. 'And out of this meditation his heart grew warm, and soon began to kindle to a flame. In this way the new man, thought to have been extinct, was nourished and strengthened, and little by little began to grow'.[23] A fuller revelation came with Thomas's consecration. Leaving the court in

---

[17] *MTB*, iii, 163–6; see also 401–2.

[18] See C. S. Jaeger, *The Envy of Angels. Cathedral Schools and Social Ideals in Medieval Europe* (Philadelphia, 1994), pp. 297–309.

[19] Gal. 5:22–3: 'Fructus autem Spiritus est caritas, gaudium, pax, patientia, benignitas, bonitas, longanimitas, mansuetudo, fides, modestia, continentia, castitas.'

[20] *MTB*, iii, 165: 'et qui novissimi veniunt his qui praevenerunt pares fiunt'. See Matt. 19:30, Mark 10:31; Luke 13:30.

[21] On Thomas's chastity, see H. Vollrath, 'Was Thomas Becket Chaste? Understanding Episodes in the Becket Lives', *Anglo-Norman Studies* 27 (2004), 198–209.

[22] *MTB*, iii, 171–2: 'Et ita pudicus iuvenis, Joseph alter, Thomas noster, primo per pudicitiam et alia gratiarum dona tractus, cucurrit postea in odore virtutum, donec, sicut nunc cernimus, non jam in odore virtutum curreret, sed ipsum Dominum virtutum, ipsum Regem gloriae, comprehenderet'; see Song 1:3; Ps. G 131:4; Ps. 24:8.

[23] *MTB*, iii, 185: 'mox quasi homo de gravi somno evigilans, quis jam diu fuisset, et qualis deinceps futurus esse debuisset, cum corde suo meditabatur. In aula aliquandiu quasi

body and heart, he put off his lavish clothes as the garment of the old man, and put on the hair shirt, the new habit of the new man, and followed the standard of the new King. He remained Thomas, while becoming a new Thomas: 'O Thomas and Thomas, now not Thomas and yet truly Thomas! Now not the silken, the purple-clad Thomas, but another Thomas.'[24]

Here, then, we can see Herbert explaining Thomas's controversial early life and characterising it in terms of progression. Indeed this growth in virtue and the revelation of his qualities continues beyond Thomas's elevation to the archbishopric as Herbert recounts the ongoing perfection of his conversion. Thomas wore the hair shirt every day as the soldier of Christ, and his *orarium*, the symbol of office, as a reminder of the duties he had undertaken.[25] He now began (with Herbert's guidance) to study the scriptures zealously, so as to banish the old ignorance he had contracted in the secular world, 'and the new image of a pontiff might be reformed in the new pontiff' (*et nova imago pontificis in novo pontifice reformetur*).[26] In his conflict with the king and his exile, Thomas's conversion became further apparent. Of his trial at Northampton in October 1164, Herbert remarks, 'What a spectacle to see Thomas, once distinguished in the court for the manifold form of his traveling clothes, now wearing a hair shirt and cross!'[27] Describing the hardships of Thomas's flight to France, Herbert dwells upon what it says about his changed circumstance and the building up of virtue. What a sight, he writes, to see Thomas, once on chariots and horses, now astride a packhorse, with only a halter around its neck for a bridle and rags for a saddle! 'What a change of circumstances, Thomas!', he exclaims. 'As you change, the things belonging to you also change, as your old things pass away and all become new. Truly God is marvellous in his saints, Who leads them down a wonderful road, from tribulation gladdening, from pressure expanding, from temptation proving, by destroying building, by persecuting healing, by killing giving life.'[28]

These examples might suggest that Herbert presents Thomas's life as a straight path to sanctity, gradually building from the limitations of his early years as virtue is added to virtue. In fact it is much more nuanced than that, as can be seen most fully in his reported speech to Thomas after the Council of Clarendon in January

---

lethargicus sui, ut videbatur, passus oblivionem, sed nunc rediens ad cor cum corde suo meditabatur. Et ex meditatione hac concalcuit cor, et sensim coepit ignis exardescere, quo novus, qui exstinctus putabatur, homo fotus et coalitus coepit paullatim coalescere, sed necdum erigere caput.' See Ps. 76:7; Ps. 38:4.

[24] *MTB*, iii, 192–4 (194): 'O Thomas et Thomas, jam non Thomas et tamen vere Thomas! jam non holosericatus, non purpuratus Thomas, sed alter Thomas.'

[25] *MTB*, iii, 194–8, 200–1, 318.

[26] *MTB*, iii, 204–5.

[27] *MTB*, iii, 306: 'O spectaculum, cernere Thomam, olim quidem in aula tam multiplici praeclarum peregrinarum vestium schemate, nunc vero in cilicio et in cruce!'

[28] *MTB*, iii, 325: 'O quam magna super te, Thoma, rerum mutatio! … Te revera transeunte, transierunt et tua; vetera enim tua transierunt et facta sunt omnia nova. Vere mirabilis Deus in sanctis suis, deducens eos in via mirabilia, de tribulatione laetificans, de pressura dilatans, de tentatione probans, destruendo aedificans, percutiendo sanans, occidendo vivificans.'

1164, when Thomas partially capitulated to the king's demands that he accept the royal customs. On the road back from the conference, Herbert noticed that the archbishop was unusually silent, and asked him what was wrong. He confessed that in accepting the king's customs he had let down the church, and he blamed the fact that he had come to the church not from the company of the Saviour but from the retinue of Caesar. But in response, Herbert reminded Thomas of the words of St Paul, that 'to them that love God, all things work together unto good, to such as, according to his purpose, are called to be saints',[29] and explains:

> So indeed that if they stray and deviate along a twisted and roundabout road and life, and wander in trackless wastes, this same trackless route may be to them a certain shortcut to the path of health, to the true fatherland, because they stray in this way with God, their leader and guide, wonderfully directing them. So also God, wonderful in his saints, leads them down a marvellous path, so marvellous that for them that digression may be a road to safety, a road home.[30]

Be confident, he continues, that if you fell, with God's support you will rise up stronger, more cautious and more humble. St Peter first denied Jesus, but did not shrink from righteousness when he was later brought before kings and rulers, and being strengthened by his earlier failures he became leader of the apostles, though first an apostate. St Paul was once a persecutor of the church but became the teacher of the gentiles. He concludes, 'And you too were once, as it seemed and was said, Saul; but now if you wish to be Paul, having removed the scales from your eyes, Jesus will show you by his work how much you ought to suffer for his name.'[31]

Thomas's path is a tortured one, but every step and every apparent deviation takes him to his glorious goal. Nor is this just a matter of personal spiritual development. It also means that, because God leads Thomas down many different roads, many different responses are demanded of him, something that is especially relevant to his dispute with the king.

'A time for all things'

Before Herbert describes the falling-out between king and archbishop, he provides two illustrations of their cooperation: the translation of the body of St Edward the

---

[29] Rom. 8:28: 'diligentibus Deum omnia cooperantur in bonum, iis qui secundum propositum vocati sunt sancti'.

[30] *MTB*, iii, 290: 'adeo etiam quod si indistorta et amfractuosa via et vita hac deviant et exorbitant, et currant in invio et non in via, hoc ipsum invium ipsis sit tanquam quoddam compendium ad salutis viam, ad veram patriam, eo ipso quod sic deviant, duce suo, rectore suo, Deo ipsos mirabiliter dirigente; unde et mirabilis Deus in sanctis suis deducens eos in via mirabilia, adeo mirabilia ut ipsum invium via fiat eis ad salutem, via ad patriam'. See Ps. 106:40; Ps. 67:36.

[31] *MTB*, iii, 292: 'Fuisti quidem et tu, ut videbatur tunc et dicebatur sic, aliquando Saulus; quod si nunc Paulus esse desideras, squamis oculorum tuorum abstersis palam ipso opera ostendet tibi Jesus tuus quanta te oporteat pati pro nomine ejus.'

Confessor in October 1163 and the dedication of Reading abbey in April 1164. In these, he says, one could see the hearts and minds of king and archbishop as one, kingship and priesthood converging in the greatest peace and tranquillity. But alas, nothing in life lasts forever, nothing stays the same, 'For everything there is a season, and a time for every matter under heaven: a time to weep, and a time to laugh, a time of love and a time of hate, a time of war and a time of peace: for everything there is a season.' Great was the harmony between king and archbishop, but brief the duration.[32] Times change, friendships cool, the church rejoices in peace and undergoes danger. Not only, then, did Thomas change over time, but he also faced changing circumstances, and although the cause of the church remained fundamentally the same, that cause demanded different responses at different times. Thomas has often been accused, then and now, of being rigid, obstinate and insensitive to the people that surrounded him and the demands of the time.[33] But in Herbert's view, he was in fact remarkably sensitive to people and to the time. Just as he quite rightly acted differently according to the different demands placed on him as archbishop, so he correctly adapted his actions to the changing circumstances that the church faced, even if he remained the righteous defender of the church throughout.

According to Herbert, this trait was present even before Thomas became archbishop. He acknowledges that in entering the court the chancellor put off the priest for a time, but he praises his discretion (*discretio*) in doing so, dissimulating his intentions and concealing his deeds. This idea of concealment is common among Thomas's biographers,[34] but Herbert emphasises a particular aspect of it: its temporary nature, and how the prudent man adapts to circumstances. Thomas was like St Paul, 'that person of many faces' (*illa multarum facierum persona*), who, acting against charity for the sake of charity, chose to be cursed by Christ for his brethren, against the law for the sake of the law had himself purified and tonsured in the temple, and against piety for the sake of piety had Timothy circumcised.[35] David pretended to be mad to escape violence, and Judith acted as a harlot to save Israel.[36] In the same way Thomas put off the priest for a time, as if he were calling out to his fellow courtiers the words of Paul, 'I am become foolish; you have compelled me' (*Factus sum insipiens, vos me coegistis*).[37]

The need to play various roles and present many faces according to the demands of the time becomes ever more pressing when Thomas becomes archbishop. In one of the most remarkable sections of the *Historia*, Herbert's long account of a day in the life of the new archbishop, we can see Thomas in the space of a day or even

---

[32] *MTB*, iii, 261: 'Omnia tempus habent, et suis spatiis transeunt universa sub caelo: tempus flendi et tempus ridendi; tempus dilectionis et tempus odii; tempus belli et tempus pacis: omnia tempus habent.' See Eccles. 3:1–8.

[33] See, for example, Gilbert Foliot's denunciation of Thomas, *Multiplicem nobis*: *CTB*, i, 498–537 no. 109, esp. 526–35.

[34] See Staunton, *Thomas Becket and His Biographers*, pp. 78–81.

[35] See Rom. 9:3; Acts 18:18; 16:3.

[36] See 1 Sam. 21:12–15; Judith 9–10.

[37] *MTB*, iii, 173–4; see 2 Cor. 12:11.

an hour adapting to particular circumstances and carrying out his quite different duties. Herbert describes the archbishop's secret asceticism, his prayer and Bible study and his judgment of cases, before coming to how he behaved at dinner.[38] He sketches in loving detail the opulent setting, the distinguished guests, the swarms of servants and the many dishes, before he pauses to address the possible objection that this description of the archbishop's table seems to be more that of Augustus than that of Christ, or Christ's anointed.

> But whoever you are who thinks this way, stop here, go no further, do not judge, but see and marvel at and imitate if you can, the animal of many eyes and the person of many faces. See the disciple according to the form of the apostle made all things to all men: rejoicing with the rejoicing, weeping with the weeping, rendering the things of the world to the world and the things of God to God; now with the holy, holy, now with the corrupt, corrupt, now with the pagan, a pagan, now with the Jew, a Jew, now with the servants, a servant, now with the liberal, liberal, now with the happy, happy, now with the infirm, infirm. For according to the word of the wise man established as a watchtower of the world, 'Everything has a time; a time of crying and of laughing, of weeping and dancing, a time of embracing and refraining from embracing. All have a time'. Which also especially belongs to a pontiff, that he submit to the time, concede to the time, and conform himself to the time. Otherwise he will not be the animal of many eyes or the person of many faces; he will not have favour before the Lord and among men.[39]

In Herbert's view, a prelate cannot make himself free for God alone, nor ought he to forsake the world entirely. Rather, he must please God and the world, as Paul told us to please men in all things, and Jesus advanced in wisdom and grace with God and men.[40] Thomas, the new pontiff, beloved of God and men, belonged entirely to God and entirely to the world, never living for himself.[41] There is no contradiction between Thomas's magnificence, circumspection and courtliness at the table and

---

[38] *MTB*, iii, 226–38.

[39] *MTB*, iii, 230: 'Sed quisquis es qui sic cogitas, sta hic; ne procedas, ne judices, sed vide et admirare et imitare, si potes, multorum oculorum animal et multarum facierum personam. Vide discipulum ad magistri formam omnibus omnia factum: gaudentem cum gaudentibus, flentem cum flentibus, reddentem quae sunt saeculi saeculo et quae sunt Dei Deo; modo cum sancto sanctum, modo cum perverso perversum, modo cum ethnico ethnicum, modo cum Judaeo Judaeum, modo cum servis servum, modo cum liberis liberum, modo cum jocundis jocundum, modo cum infirmis infirmum. Nam juxta illud sapientis et quasi in mundi specula constituti verbum, "Omnia tempus habent; tempus flendi et tempus ridendi, tempus plangendi et tempus saltandi, tempus amplexandi et tempus continendi ab amplexibus. Omnia", inquit, "tempus habent"; quod et praesertim pontificis est, ut tempori pareat, tempori indulgeat, et conformet se tempori. Alioquin non erit multorum oculorum animal nec multarum facierum persona. Alioquin non habebit gratiam apud Dominum et apud homines.' See 1 Cor. 9:19–22; Eccles. 3:4–5; Luke 2:52.

[40] See 1 Cor. 10:33; Luke 2:52.

[41] *MTB*, iii, 230–1.

his service to God: 'In fact in both tables he was boundlessly great: great at the table of God, great at the table of the world. At the altar the most devoted priest, at the dining-table a most circumspect paterfamilias, and, if we add a third table which we mentioned above, a most equitable judge at the tribunal'.[42]

This verdict might apply to any archbishop or bishop. Indeed Herbert's description of Thomas echoes earlier Lives of bishops that present the courtly image of the prelate alongside that of the prayerful bishop, acknowledging the multifaceted nature of the role. But Herbert's representation of Thomas is different to that of most prelates, in that his archiepiscopate was dominated by conflict, and action on behalf of the church. But here again running through Herbert's work we see Thomas's conduct in his dispute with the king characterised as an accommodation to different times. When he became archbishop, writes Herbert, he put on the armour of God, but put aside the breastplate of justice for a time, to be taken up in its own time, for all things have a time, a time of love and a time of hate, a time of war and a time of peace.[43] When he came to trial at Northampton he put on the face of the man and the face of the lion – the evangelical animals foreshadowed by Ezekiel's vision.[44] Early in 1163, when Thomas first began to feel the pressure of the king's demands, he twice attempted to flee from England, but both times he was repulsed, as if God was resisting in the elements, 'For as all things have a time, so also a time of advancing and a time of fleeing, but this was not the time'.[45] But after the trial at Northampton, Thomas and Herbert listened to the reading, 'If you are persecuted in one town flee to the next', and the archbishop later explained that to have resisted the anger of the king at that time would have brought no benefit to the church.[46]

Nowhere is the idea of different times demanding different responses expressed more fully than in Herbert's long and unique report of a debate between Thomas and some cardinals and learned men at the papal court at Sens in November 1164. These men, writes Herbert, sympathetic to Thomas's cause, rebuked him harshly but benignly because in these days of evil, a time of schism and destruction of the church, he had raised himself up against his prince, against such a great power. They said that he should rather prepare for the time and be restrained, for it was then the hour and the power of darkness, when Peter was ordered not to unsheath his sword, but to replace it. They pointed to two readings that Thomas should bear in mind: 'Redeeming the time, because the days are evil', and 'Therefore the prudent shall keep silence at that time, for it is an evil time'.[47] Sometimes, they argue, even

---

[42] *MTB*, iii, 236: 'In utraque revera mensa magnus et immensus; magnus in mensa Dei, magnus in mensa saeculi. In altari sacerdos devotissimus, in triclinio paterfamilias providissimus, et, si adhuc adjiciamus tertium quod supra posuimus medium, judex in tribunali aequissimus.'

[43] *MTB*, iii, 198.

[44] Ezek. 1:10; Rev. 4:14.

[45] *MTB*, iii, 293: 'Sicut enim omnia tempus habent, sic et tempus occurrendi et tempus fugiendi, fugae vero hujus necdum tempus.'

[46] *MTB*, iii, 312, 355–6; see 319–20. Matt. 10:23: 'Si vos persecuti fuerint in una civitate, fugite in aliam.'

[47] Eph. 5:16: 'redimentes tempus, quoniam dies mali sunt'; Amos 5:13: 'Ideo prudens in

strong columns of the church need to apply the hand of discretion to build stronger support for the church, bending for a time in the face of the storm, rather than being broken in futile resistance. St Paul commanded the abolition of the old law, but gave way to the time, purifying himself according to the law, entering the temple and offering sacrifice, and even circumcising Timothy, and later submitted to worldly judgment, thus recommending that 'when the time demands it, one ought to give way to the time, and redeem the time according to the time'.[48]

Thomas's long reply begins with an acknowledgement of the cardinals' central point: one ought to give way according to the time, and much ought to be borne according to the time. And he accepts that this is the hour and the power of darkness, a time of schism when the sword of Peter ought not to be drawn but sheathed, when the only hope is to cry out to the Lord, and the prudent man will be silent, for the days are evil. But, he adds, there is another time, a time of 'cloudiness' (*quasi nubilum*), when the sword of St Peter ought to be alternately suspended and resumed. He does not, he insists, seek to wield the sword now against his king, for first there comes a time of restraint, a time of mercy, and only later a time of justice. But he insists that there is nothing in the apostolic decrees that categorically rules out exercising the sword of Peter against princes, or against those who have many allies, in evil days or time of schism. St Paul drew the evangelical sword against those who disfigured the face of the church with their crimes, saying, 'If any man that is named a brother, be a fornicator, or covetous, or a server of idols, or a railer, or a drunkard, or an extortioner: with such a one, not so much as to eat'.[49] If Paul said this when the church was still tender and new, how much more should we dare to draw the sword confidently now, when the church has been made an everlasting glory?[50]

Thomas's case, then, is that there is a time to rest and retreat, and also a time to advance and take action, and both may be appropriate to a leader of the church. But in responding to the cardinals he also, as Herbert presents it, addresses their charge that he ought to 'redeem the time, for the days are evil'. He is astonished, he says, that they should use this verse against him, since he has most certainly redeemed the time. When Paul used this term, he did not teach that time ought to be redeemed at the expense of ecclesiastical liberty. Rather, he meant that in exchange for gaining time – that is, being free for divine things – one gives up temporal things. Thomas has given up temporal things in exchange for time, abandoning the riches and honours of the church of Canterbury and the favour of the king for the sake of his own liberty and peace and that of the clergy entrusted to him.[51]

During the exile we can see Thomas, with Herbert at his side, working out the principles that he argued before the cardinals at Sens. On the one hand, we can

---

    tempore illo tacebit, quia tempus malum est.'
[48] *MTB*, iii, 343–4 (344): 'cum tempus sic exigit, cedendum tempori, et tempus redimendum pro tempore'. See Acts 25:9–12.
[49] 1 Cor. 5:11: 'si is qui frater nominatur, est fornicator, aut avarus, aut idolis serviens, aut maledicus, aut ebriosus, aut rapax, cum ejusmodi nec cibum sumere'.
[50] See Isa. 60:15.
[51] *MTB*, iii, 354.

see him oscillating between retreat and advance, withdrawing when prudent, then wielding the sword in defence of the church. At the same time, Thomas can be observed redeeming the time: turning towards divine things, and perfecting his pilgrimage. And as the pilgrimage progresses, the two become intertwined.

Contemplation and action; retreat and advance

Thomas and Herbert spent the first part of their exile, from late 1164 to late 1166, at the Cistercian monastery of Pontigny. Herbert presents this as a time of rest when, after all the troubles he had endured, as if after a time of dense cloud, the archbishop began to turn himself with all his mind to the serenity and tranquillity of divine light, giving himself entirely to reading, prayer and meditation. Thomas told him that this was the time he had always longed for, even when he had been chancellor. That monastery, writes Herbert, was like a training school for combat, a school of virtue in which they were educated together.[52] In solitude between the stones and the monks they hid themselves away, remote from the world, and turned themselves entirely to spiritual things. Thomas with a wonderful ardour clung to holy scripture, to the apostolic ordinances and to theology, and although Herbert began as his teacher, soon his pupil had a greater grasp than any of them of the knotty meanings of scriptures.[53]

During the exile we see Thomas responding appropriately to changing circumstances, but we also see him changing. Thomas endured many hardships through exile, and these are presented by Herbert, who shared in many of them, as a beneficial process through which Thomas is proven. Through these trials he is perfected and prepared for martyrdom. This is expressed especially well in the address of his learned men, the *eruditi*, to Thomas when they hear the news that, following his flight, the king has expelled his kindred from England. Here they console the archbishop, reminding him that they share a common cause, punishment and battle and with God's favour they hope to share a common victory and crown. This recent punishment, they insist, should be seen as a welcome and medicinal one, like a pungent lotion applied by the celestial Doctor on their sins. Turning specifically to Thomas, they say,

> See the prosperity of this world, of this life, that flows like the dregs through the streets, when the oil has been pressed in the winepress and later stored in the cellar. And you, lord – not wishing offence to you, we speak the words of God – for a certain time were the dregs flowing through the streets, all things succeeding without any obstacle to you according to wish and desire. But it seems now that He who turns water into wine now wishes to turn the dregs into oil. If therefore you wish to be oil, you will have to endure the pressure of the wine-press, until you flow from the press into the wine-store.[54]

[52] *MTB*, iii, 358.

[53] *MTB*, iii, 379.

[54] *MTB*, iii, 363–4: 'Ecce saeculi hujus, ecce vitae hujus, prosperitas, quae quasi amurca

Thomas in reply agrees that for a long time he flowed as dregs through the wide and spacious paths of life, following his desires unchecked through the byways of the secular world, wandering off the track. But now, he says, he desires, if the Lord should deign to allow it, to be turned into oil by the pressure of the winepress.[55] Herbert writes that every day, when the archbishop saw the persecution of his kindred and supporters, he was disturbed, but like a precious spice that, the more it is shaken, the more it emits a scent; or a mustard seed when crushed reveals its quality more strongly; or a silver trumpet which the more it is beaten, the more fully it is formed. Under the pressure of the winepress he was 'never sad or disturbed',[56] but always happy, always cheerful, 'For the wise man stays the same as the sun, but the fool changes like the moon.'[57] So, in both adversity and prosperity Thomas remained the same.[58]

But in the second year of their 'pilgrimage', after this period of rest and solitude, Thomas was roused to confront the enemies of the church. Perceiving how hardened their hearts were, and how they not only failed to do penance but continued to persecute the exiles and their allies, the archbishop 'began to reflect within himself and meditate in his heart, and in this meditation a fire began to kindle, a fire not of malice but of love'. And so he who up to now had been silent, patiently bearing all, was now no longer patient, no longer slept, but 'rising and shaking himself out, as a true son of the shaken out', immediately began to confer with his men about what to do, as if he had suddenly been roused by the Lord's command, 'And you, son of man, I placed as a watchman over the house of Israel.'[59] Now Thomas addressed his fellow exiles. He has no need, he says, to remind them that there is a time for all things, a time of suffering and a time of rebelling, a time of mercy and a time of justice. As it says in the Psalm, 'When I shall take a time, I will judge justices', and St Paul, 'Serving the time'.[60] Up to now, Thomas says, we have served time and been restrained, but because up to now we have been silent will we always be silent, and do we who have slept not also awake? It is good and pleasant, he says, to sleep in the embraces of Rachel, but now the business of the bride draws us and the duty of our office urges us to the performance of necessary things. He urges his companions

---

fluit per plateas, oleo in torculari presso et postea reposito in cellaria. Et tu, domine, (ut tamen absque domini loquar offensa, Dei quippe sermones loquimur), tu quidem aliquanto tempore amurca fuisti per plateas fluens, omnibus absque omni obstaculo tibi ad nutum et votum succedentibus. Sed videtur nunc quod amurcam convertere velit in oleum qui convertit aquam in vinum. Si ergo oleum esse desideras, torcularis pressuram sustineas necesse est, donec ex torculari in apothecam defluas.'

[55] *MTB*, iii, 370–3; see Ps. 109(108):4.

[56] See Isa. 42:4: 'Non erit tristis, neque turbulentus.'

[57] Eccles. 27:12: 'Homo sanctus in sapientia manet sicut sol: nam stultus sicut luna mutatur.'

[58] *MTB*, iii, 373–4; see also 375, 427, 431–2.

[59] *MTB*, iii, 380–1: 'coepit cogitare intra se et meditari cum corde suo, et in meditatione hac ignis exardescebat, ignis certe non livoris, sed amoris ... surgens et excutiens se, tanquam verus excussorum filius ... "Et tu, fili hominis speculatorem dedi te domui Israel."'

[60] Ps. 74:3: 'Cum accepero tempus, ego justitias judicabo'; Rom. 12:11: 'Domino servientes'. Note that these are from the books he had been reading at Pontigny.

to rise up from the bed and go out to the fields, using the words of the bride in the Song of Songs, 'Come, my beloved, let us go forth into the field, let us abide in the villages, let us get up early to the vineyards.'[61]

We can see here some of Herbert's favourite images to describe the process of change. We have already seen how he uses the image of waking from sleep, and of a fire kindling. Virtue came to triumph over youthful vice in terms of waking from sleep. Upon election as archbishop, Thomas was like a man waking from a deep sleep and, returning to himself, he meditated in his heart. From this meditation a fire grew warm and kindled into a flame.[62] Upon consecration the Holy Spirit drove out the entire old man and strengthened the new archbishop in his new work. 'No longer drawn but smeared in the sacred unction' (*jam non tractus, sed sacra delibutus unctione*), he ran fast in the vigorous practice of virtues. He who had on his election meditated in his heart, was now able to take counsel from the spirit of the unction.[63] Thomas's first action against the king – his demand that he fill vacant sees – was prompted, says Herbert, by his meditation on the duty of a pontiff to correct royal misbehaviour. 'Our new archbishop, then, coming to himself in contemplation' (*archipraesul noster novus, ad se reversus, recolens*), now rebuked the king for occupying sees for so long.[64] He describes Thomas in the early days of his pontificate as shaking himself out, 'as a new son of shaking out' (*novus revera excussorum filius*).[65] Again after the setback of Clarendon, Thomas told his men that the choice was to yield disgracefully or fight bravely, and 'he immediately shook himself out as a son of shaking out' (*mox excussit se filius excussorum*).[66] The mentions of the embraces of Rachel, and the bride urging the groom to go forth to the fields, direct us to a deeper tradition of writing about action and contemplation, as developed by Augustine, Gregory the Great and Bernard of Clairvaux. There contemplation is presented as an ideal, represented by Jacob's wife Rachel, but dedication to contemplation does not diminish the value or necessity of action, as represented by Jacob's other wife, the less beautiful but more fruitful Leah. In fact, these three thinkers emphasise an alternation between contemplation and action in which one helps to stimulate the other.[67] Another element is the participation of the *eruditi*. Herbert's frequent introduction of long speeches by and to the *eruditi* serves to explain how decisions came about, and justify actions that might appear inconsistent. The *eruditi* do not just function as a chorus, but as 'companions in the battle', showing that Thomas did not act precipitously or alone. He always meditated in his heart or conferred with others, relying on the inspiration of the Holy Spirit

---

[61] Song 7:11–12: 'Veni, dilecte mi, egrediamur in agrum, commoremur in villis. Mane surgamus ad vineas.'

[62] *MTB*, iii, 170–2, 185; see Ps. 38:3.

[63] *MTB*, iii, 193–4; see Song 3:6.

[64] *MTB*, iii, 258; see Acts 12:11.

[65] *MTB*, iii, 201. See J. C. Robertson, *Becket, Archbishop of Canterbury. A Biography* (London, 1859), pp. 336–7.

[66] *MTB*, iii, 294.

[67] On the two lives, see C. Butler, *Western Mysticism* (London, 1926), pp. 277–87.

and the support of his *eruditi* as archbishop, along with his own willingness to develop in spirit and counsel.

In taking vigorous steps against the enemies of the church in 1166, Thomas again shows how action must be calibrated to the circumstances of the time. In curing sin, he tells the *eruditi*, they should follow the example of the Samaritan and first pour on oil, and later, if it is necessary, wine.[68] First, writes Herbert, he approached the king in a spirit of leniency, sending him a peaceful and gentle letter, but when he found the king's heart heartened, he wrote to him more harshly, but still leniently. And when he considered that the route of mercy and leniency had not worked, he wrote a third letter in a spirit of justice and ardour, no longer correcting the king in mercy but harshly rebuking him. Here, writes Herbert, we can see the animal of the gospels, as figured in the prophet, having before him the face of the man and the face of the lion. But despite his vigorous measures, the king remained uncorrected, and when Thomas saw this he was disturbed, and turned more intently to prayer and asceticism. He wavered between resigning his office and continuing to advance the cause of his church, and after much fluctuation of soul he finally conferred again with his *eruditi*. They entirely rejected the idea of resignation, characterising it as abandoning the race or deserting the battle. Although, they said, there are times when it is legitimate for a prelate to flee, as he had fled to France at the appropriate moment, this was not a time of fleeing but of advancing. Persuaded by their speech, Thomas took heart, and thinking nothing of flight, nothing of quiet, but only of duty and battle, he deliberated within himself and finally came to the decision to unleash censures at Vézelay against the enemies of the church.[69]

Conquering the world

Herbert describes Thomas throughout his life changing, but his transformation has consequences well beyond Thomas himself. Thomas is transformed by the struggle, as he experiences spiritual growth, and is formed by the pressure of his enemies. But at the same time, Thomas's cause changes – if not in its fundamental principles, then in its relation to the world. Its truth gradually becomes clear to the world, and in this way, culminating in the martyrdom, the world is changed by Thomas's victory over it.

In January 1169, in the aftermath of the peace conference at Montmirail, any victory for the exiles seemed far away. The peace had broken down on Thomas's insistence, to the alarm of intermediaries and supporters, that any agreement with the king must include the clause, 'Saving God's honour' (*salvo honore Dei*). But on the road back from Montmirail, Thomas justified his stance and consoled his men. "'Brothers and fellow soldiers of Christ with me", he said, "yesterday in the battle, yesterday in the fight, yesterday in the wrestling-school, we were made a spectacle to angels and men.'"[70] The world, he says, now mocks and ridicules them, but they should know that one ought not to acquiesce in the judgement of the multitude. The

---

[68] *MTB*, iii, 384.

[69] *MTB*, iii, 384–7.

[70] *MTB*, iii, 432: "'Fratres", inquiens, "et mecum Christi commilitones, heri fuimus in militia,

exiles have chosen truth and poverty for the cause of justice, and so they have few friends, but that isolation makes their cause all the more precious and pure, like a light that shines in the darkness and the darkness does not comprehend it, a garden enclosed, a fountain sealed up. Since yesterday, he insists, their cause has become purer, more just, clearer and more evident. For some time they have been advancing the cause of the church, but now as well as the cause of the church, they have taken on the cause of Christ himself, when they refused to be silent about 'God's honour'. Thomas urges his men to show themselves now as strenuous warriors. The opposition of the world is no matter, for if God is with us, who is against us?; the wisdom of the world is foolishness before God; God teases, and the world is mocked, and their ignominy will soon be turned to honour and glory.[71]

As Thomas had predicted, the world soon turned their way. Even those who had criticised his stance at the time now praised him and the justice of his cause. King Louis of France, who had snubbed the exiles after the conference, discovered that King Henry had violated the peace with the Poitevins and Bretons that he had witnessed at Montmirail, and he cried out, 'O how prudent, how discreet, how careful that archbishop of Canterbury, who with such constancy obstructed us all, so bravely resisted all, so as not to make the peace that everyone wanted and urged.'[72] Now the whole world proclaimed Thomas to be a great man, who alone stood with constancy and boldness against the many and the powerful. The whole world showed the exiles greater honour and reverence day by day, and so it was fulfilled as the archbishop had predicted, that their ignominy would be turned to glory, and as the Lord said, 'Whosoever shall glorify me, him will I glorify.'[73] Yet, adds Herbert, 'this was just a small beginning of this honour, the consummation reserved for an incomparably greater and happier consummation of the man to come'.[74]

On 18 November 1169 a further peace conference was held at Montmartre, which foundered on the king's refusal to grant the archbishop a kiss of peace. After the conference, the exiles again reflected on the lessons of the conference, and this time it was the *eruditi* who addressed Thomas. Now, they remind him, is the sixth year of

---

heri in lucta, heri in palaestra, facti spectaculum mundo et angelis et hominibus.'" See 1 Cor. 4:9.

[71] *MTB*, iii, 432–6. See John 1:5; Song 4:12; Rom. 8:31; 1 Cor. 3:19. Herbert touches on this theme earlier (183–4) when he criticises the short-sightedness of those who opposed Thomas's election as archbishop. 'O how many did suspicion deceive in this deed, and did vanity detain their minds!' (*O quam multos in facto hoc supplantavit suspicio et in vanitate detinuit sensus eorum!*), Herbert writes, an allusion to Ecclesiasticus, the preceding verse reading, 'For many things are shewn to thee above the understanding of men' (Eccles. 3:25–6). Divine judgment is transcendent, Herbert insists, whereas men judge according to worldly judgment, as Paul said in 1 Cor. 4:5, 'Judge not before the time' (*nolite ante tempus judicare*).

[72] *MTB*, iii, 438: "'O quam prudens", inquiens, "quam discretus, quam providus Cantueriensis ille archiepiscopus, qui ita omnibus nobis tam constanter obstitit, tam viriliter omnibus reluctabatur, ne faceret pacem quam volebant, quam suadebant omnes.'"

[73] *MTB*, iii, 439: "'Qui honorificaverit", inquit, "Me, honorificabo illum.'" See 1 Sam. 2:30.

[74] *MTB*, iii, 439–40: 'sed non nisi modica inchoatio haec honoris, consummatione incomparabiliter majori et feliciori futurae viri consummationi reservata'.

their pilgrimage, and during that time there have been many peace conferences, and though none achieved peace, they are consoled that throughout all they have kept their cause intact, amid so many temptations, pressures and traps. With the truth and justice of their pilgrimage as inseparable allies, their cause, as a rising light, day by day becomes more apparent to the world, as even their enemies concede. Now they turn to the reasons for the failure of the peace at Montmartre. The sole obstacle, they say, is the kiss of peace, and this should not be enough to keep Thomas away from his church, suffering as it is in the absence of a pastor. The reason for flight and the cause of his exile has been very just up to now, but it is now time to return and advance against the enemy. 'To the priestly man', they say, 'there is a time of fleeing and a time of advancing, a time of flight when the person is sought, as the Lord says, "If you are persecuted in one city, flee into another".'[75] Persuaded by their speech, Thomas determined to return to England when the time was right, to face whatever persecution he might find there.[76] When, at the end of the November 1170, the exiles were preparing to return, they were warned by a pilot that they faced certain death.[77] Herbert told Thomas that their choice was either to withdraw in disgrace or proceed bravely and act manfully. Otherwise, he says, people would say that the archbishop, who once fled at Northampton, now fled for a second time without fighting. And Herbert looks forward to 'the glorious consummation of our exile' (*gloriosa exsilii nostri consummatio*). Now for six years the sinners have persecuted Thomas, he says, and all this time they have been building an imperishable crown for him. There is no need for a file now, since the crown has already been built, nor a furnace, since the gold has already been proved in the heat, and the bones of the old man dried up like firewood. Being already proven, what is there to fear in advancing, or what need is there to delay?[78]

In Herbert's account of the murder, we see the fulfilment, the 'consummation', of many of the patterns already described. In his consecration as archbishop he had been smeared in the holy oil, and a fire had kindled in his heart, and now again when he entered his church on his first return from exile, it appeared as though with his heart aflame, his face was also on fire, exhilarated in oil, a presaging of the martyrdom to come.[79] On Christmas Day Thomas uttered sanctions against enemies of the church, and, as he had at Northampton, he again displayed the prophetic animal who had the face of the man and the face of the lion.[80] When on 29 December he entered the cathedral, pursued by the knights, many of his men abandoned him and he was left alone, treading the winepress alone.[81] His stance towards the

---

[75] *MTB*, iii, 451–6 (454): 'Unde et viro sacerdotali sicut tempus fugiendi ita et tempus est occurrendi, fugae tempus cum persona quaeritur, juxta quod Dominus, "Si vos", inquit, "persecuti fuerint in una civitate, fugite in aliam".' See Matt. 10:23.

[76] *MTB*, iii, 456–7.

[77] *MTB*, iii, 472–3.

[78] *MTB*, iii, 473–6.

[79] *MTB*, iii, 479.

[80] *MTB*, iii, 485.

[81] *MTB*, iii, 491; see also 523.

knights – physically advancing towards them in the church and rebuking them – is presented in the same way as his earlier exertions on behalf of the church: he is Samson intrepid in attack, Paul rebuking with all authority, Christ ejecting them from the temple.[82] This constancy is a rejection of his earlier flight: 'He who with the boy Jesus once fled, with the same as an adult now advances, now marches out, now reveals himself.'[83] Using the reading, 'My bone is not hidden which I made in hiding', Herbert describes how Thomas's 'bone', his inward strength of the soul, once hidden, is now revealed.[84] A sacrificial victim, he is immolated in the temple before the altar, and this holocaust gives out a 'lifegiving odour of marvellous smoothness before God and the world'.[85] In his final moments the knights hammer on his head, forging with the steel of their swords an imperishable crown.[86]

This outcome was known in advance to Thomas, who, as Herbert points out, had the gift of prophecy. Thomas's dream of receiving the talents foreshadowed his archiepiscopate.[87] When he was at Pontigny he had a vision of his murder and told it to the abbot.[88] His dream of Henry II being attacked by a flock of birds foreshadowed the rebellion of the king's sons.[89] Certain things about the significance of present events and about the future might have been observed by others who had eyes to see: Thomas left his trial at Northampton carrying his cross, surrounded by crowds seeking his blessing, 'as if a presaging of what was to come' (*quasi futurorum praesagium*).[90] Thomas began his flight on a Tuesday, set out across the sea on a Tuesday, departed from the sea on a Tuesday, in his return to England landed on a Tuesday, all foreshadowing his falling to the sword on a Tuesday.[91] But for most mortals, truth is only revealed by time, and by the 'outcome' of events, as Herbert puts it.[92]

Thomas's murder revealed in full those things that had first been hidden in him, and had gradually emerged over the years as he had advanced towards martyrdom. It also revealed with great clarity to all the truth about Thomas and his cause. Herbert, along with many other biographers, describes how the knights followed up their murder of the archbishop by plundering the palace. He gives the standard comparison to the division of Christ's clothes, but adds a new element, that the knights found two hair shirts belonging to the archbishop, which they threw away.

---

[82] *MTB*, iii, 492–4.

[83] *MTB*, iii, 495: 'qui cum puero Jesu aliquando fugit, cum eodem adulto modo occurrit, modo exit, modo se exserit'.

[84] *MTB*, iii, 493–5, 506. See Ps. 138:15: 'Non est occultatum os meum a te, quod fecisti in occulto'; also, Augustine, *Ennarrationes super Psalmos*, *CCSL* 40.2004.

[85] *MTB*, iii, 501: 'vivificum coram Deo et mundo mirae suavitatis odorem'.

[86] *MTB*, iii, 505.

[87] *MTB*, iii, 185–6; see above, p. 4.

[88] *MTB*, iii, 406.

[89] *Liber Melorum*, *PL*, 190.1320–1.

[90] *MTB*, iii, 310.

[91] *MTB*, iii, 326.

[92] E.g. *MTB*, iii, 311, 312, 479, 504.

Nevertheless, at the sight of such evident religion, many of that cohort, but secretly on account of fear, said to themselves the words of the centurion of the gospel, 'Truly this man was just!' (*Vere homo iste justus erat!*).[93] Likewise, when the monks, many of whom had been distinctly cool towards their archbishop during his life, discovered the hair shirt he was wearing, they were astonished and contrite. As if witnessing an earthquake, they called out with the centurion of the gospel, 'Truly this was the son of God!' (*Vere filius Dei erat iste!*).[94]

While Herbert disdains to describe the miracles at Thomas's tomb, in the *Liber melorum* he devotes much attention to what to him were the most remarkable of Thomas's miracles: the genuine penance of the knights and the king.[95] Here he dwells on the miraculous change wrought, and he does so in terms that recall his discussion of the changes within Thomas. The strenuous knights, proven in military arts and robust in age, died within three years of their outrage, in true penance. This, he says, is proof that even those who set out upon the worst path can by a devious route come to salvation, and those who fall furthest may later rise up taller.[96] In discussing the king's penance, Herbert writes of Henry as being triumphed over by the martyr, and in being conquered, he himself conquered the rebels in 1174. But Herbert also describes this as a conversion, a change akin to that of Saul to Paul, a transformation of the hand of God.[97] In martyrdom there occurred the ultimate victory of Thomas and his cause. Writing after the murder to the pope, Herbert reports that Thomas had appeared in a vision to a Pontigny monk, displaying his wounds and saying, 'Tell my brothers that I have conquered the world' (*Dic fratribus meis quod ego vici mundum*).[98] This victory transformed the lives of those who had encountered Thomas when he lived: the monks of Canterbury, the murderers, the king and, not least, his disciple.

Herbert's changing relationship with Thomas

Herbert's *Historia* relies on his relationship with Thomas. He is the disciple who witnessed and wrote these things.[99] He witnessed Thomas's life and struggle, and he received information from him and others that he includes in his work. His information is naturally weighted towards Thomas's adult life, and when he includes things he did not witness directly, he generally states where his information comes from.[100] But difficulties present themselves as time goes on and Herbert's subject changes. This is why he hesitates as he approaches Thomas's transformation on

---

[93] *MTB*, iii, 513.

[94] *MTB*, iii, 521–2; Matt. 27:54.

[95] *Liber Melorum, PL*, 190.1303–22.

[96] *Liber Melorum, PL*, 190.1304.

[97] *Liber Melorum, PL*, 190.1316–18, 1322.

[98] *HB*, no. 34, *PL*, 190.1467.

[99] John 21:24. See *MTB*, iii, 162, 186, 189, 204–5, 211, 272, 289, 290, etc.

[100] He says that he passes over the details of his subject's boyhood and youth, except that he has heard from those who know that he spent them in simplicity and purity, and he will

becoming archbishop. A worldly man like himself can easily represent worldly things, but how can he describe heavenly things? How can such a 'foul painter' (*foedus pictor*) as he depict the image of the celestial man, and how can an old man such as he portray the new man? Whereas Moses was led apart from the people to the summit of the mountains, to contemplate the exemplar, Herbert dwells in the valley of tears, in the midst of his people. It is within those limitations, aided by what he has seen when he followed Thomas through the valley of tears, that he will describe what he saw so that people of the future may have an image of the celestial and pontifical form to be imitated.[101] Herbert's reference to his own flaws signals that this is not merely an echo of the well-established tenet that different kinds of material require different voices. It also acknowledges that his own relationship to the subject is crucial, something that becomes more pronounced when he approaches Thomas's murder.

Herbert, of course, was not present at Canterbury cathedral when Thomas was murdered. When he describes his departure from Thomas on 27 December 1170, the feast of St John the Evangelist, he notes that up to now he has reported faithfully what he himself saw and heard, but now he writes more hesitatingly, since he depends on the witness of others.[102] He laments that because he did not taste of this feast, he cannot fully 'belch it forth' (*eructare*).[103] On the other hand, Herbert had an advantage over other writers in that he lived on long after Thomas's murder. He believes that he has, by a hidden dispensation of God, been specially preserved to write, when almost all the other companions of the struggle have died. This means that he is able to write not just about Thomas's life and battle, but about his posthumous glory.[104] But even if he is able to draw on the witness of others and look back on it from the perspective of Thomas's triumph in death, the material presents extraordinary difficulties. As he approaches the murder Herbert writes, 'But since now the material begins to grow great, from now on also the pen/style must be changed.'[105] The glory of Thomas's consummation should be written with rosy threads melting in gold, and spoken of not with the tongues of men but of angels.

But here there is another difficulty beyond the magnitude of the material. Thomas has passed over to another place, while Herbert remains wandering in pilgrimage, and Herbert signals this profound change when he repeatedly interrupts his account of Thomas's murder. As the soul has various feelings, he writes, so voices vary in their expression: love has a sweet tone, fear a measured one, joy a

---

insert a vision that he had as a child of which Thomas personally informed him: *MTB*, iii, 162.

[101] *MTB*, iii, 189–92; see Exod. 25:40. This is a method developed further in the *Liber Melorum*, where he discusses how the sound of the lyre must change according to the material.

[102] *MTB*, iii, 486–7.

[103] *MTB*, iii, 494–5. See Ps. 44:2: 'Eructavit cor meum verbum bonum.'

[104] *MTB*, iii, 192, 495–7, 503–4; see *Liber Melorum*, PL 190.1317.

[105] *MTB*, iii, 489: 'Verum quia jam materia grandescere incipit, deinceps immutandus foret et stylus.'

happy voice but compassion one filled with sighs.[106] Now his is a voice of mourning: 'In writing this I mourn alone, and in mourning I write alone.'[107] It is in two respects that he writes alone. First, he is the only witness to the battle to have survived: 'They have passed away, while I am yet in danger, abandoned in the midst of fires and waves. Hence this work and labour of writing what I saw and heard of such a great man, my lord and pupil, has been reserved uniquely to me, who is still living.'[108] But Herbert is also alone because he is bereft of his master, who has transferred to another world, and this has a deep effect on the nature of his literary response. This, he says, is why he hesitates to describe the murder and finish his narrative:

> For while describing him still in combat, the pleasing favour of the pen makes a likeness for me of the person of the combatant as if I am seeing him with my own eyes, and he is to an extent still with me. But when now triumphant he mounts his fiery chariot, the disciple is abandoned naked without the master's cloak, and does not know where to look for the master, for he does not know where he is coming from or where he is going.[109]

When Thomas triumphs he will, like Elijah, fly to the homeland, far away from those like Herbert who are still making pilgrimage, to the place where the eye does not see, nor the ears hear, nor does it rise in the heart of men.[110]

Herbert returns to the theme when he describes how Thomas protected his men from the knights, the men who followed him faithfully through his trials and exile. Again he reflects that his brothers have now been taken away from the world, while he continues on his pilgrimage imperilled in the midst of fires and waves, and laments that he is unable to 'belch forth the memory of the abundance of thy sweetness' (*tantae suavitatis abundantiam eructare*),[111] for he did not taste it. Pausing again, he says that he comes reluctantly to the end, lamenting and groaning:

> It is more pleasant and profitable for me to see him fighting than to tell about him reigning. For Thomas's battle, even if it is not of the world, is nevertheless yet in the world, and it is with me, and I see it; but the kingdom of the conquering Thomas is not of the world, nor is it in the world, it is not with me, and I do not see it.[112]

---

[106] *MTB*, iii, 496. See Bernard, *Sermones super Cantica Canticorum, Opera*, ii, p. 190.

[107] *MTB*, iii, 496: 'inter scribendum haec solus doleo, et inter dolendum solus scribo'.

[108] *MTB*, iii, 497: 'Ipsi quidem transierunt, me periclitante adhuc et in mediis ignibus et fluctibus derelicto. Unde singulariter mihi, qui adhuc superstes, scribendi de tanto viro, domino meo et alumno, quae vidi vel audivi reservatum opus et opera haec.'

[109] *MTB*, iii, 497: 'Nam dum adhuc certantem describo, styli gratum beneficium quasi oculo ad oculum certantis mihi personam effigiat, et est modicum mecum adhuc. Verum cum jam triumphans ignitum currum suum conscenderit, discipulus absque magistri pallio nudus derelictus, si magistrum quaerat, nescit ubi; nescit quippe quo veniat aut quo vadat.' See John 3:4.

[110] *MTB*, iii, 497; see 2 Kings 2:3–9; Isaiah 64:4; 1 Cor. 2:9.

[111] See Bernard, *Sermones super Cantica Canticorum, Opera*, ii, p. 263.

[112] *MTB*, iii, 503: 'Jocundius quippe mihi et fructuosius cernere Thomam certantem magis

Now, even unwilling, crying out, with his eyes looking up, following his father ascending, Herbert must be snatched away.[113] With Thomas reigning in triumph, Herbert's faculties of expression are of no avail, he is rendered mute. Nothing from now on can be said of his realm, 'which eye hath not seen, nor ear heard, neither hath it entered into the heart of man', to which word or pen is not sufficient. That material of eternity and unfailing clarity muffles a worldly tongue, overwhelms the pen, even absorbs the properties of speech.[114] All that is left to Herbert to call on is divine inspiration: 'May the Lord open my lips so that my mouth worthily declare to his glory the praise of his new martyr.'[115]

According to the account in 2 Kings 2, just before his departure, Elijah asked Elisha what he could do for him before he was taken from him. 'Let me inherit a double portion of your spirit,' said Elisha, to which Elijah replied, 'You have asked a difficult thing, yet if you see me when I am taken from you, it will be yours – otherwise it will not.'[116] Then suddenly a chariot of fire and horses of fire appeared and separated them, and Elijah was carried up to heaven in a whirlwind. Elisha cried out, and rent his garment, but he was able to pick up the cloak that had fallen from Elijah as he went up to heaven.[117] Herbert, right at the end of his book, after the catalogue of *eruditi*, offers a prayer to St Thomas, the glorious martyr who first fought on the battlefield but now sits on the throne as a glorious victor. He calls on him to watch over those who were his comrades in the battle, and in particular 'me your disciple, now – such as he is – your historian, wandering off the path and out of the way seeking you'. And he asks that saint deign to impart to him a little from his 'double spirit'. Reminding Thomas how he used to minister to him in the 'chains of the gospel' he asks that perhaps he throw down to him as he ascends, 'something from the threads of your prophetic yarn, lest I perish naked in the cold of this desert'.[118] And he assures himself

---

quam referre regnantem; Thomae quippe certamen, etsi non sit de mundo, tamen adhuc in mundo est, et mecum est, et illud video, verum Thomae vincentis regnum, sicut nec de mundo est, nec in mundo est, nec mecum est, nec illud video.'

[113] *MTB*, iii, 503–4.

[114] *MTB*, iii, 504: 'Post certantis triumphum ipso jam in gloria deinceps mutus, nihil ex tunc locuturus de regno suo, quod nec oculus vidit, nec auris audivit, nec in cor hominis ascendit; unde nec verbo nec stylo subjacet. Illa quippe aeternitatis et indeficientis claritatis materia omnem temporalis et moribundae linguae obtundit sonum, obducit stylum, dictionum etiam proprietates absorbet, utpote sicut inaudita et invisa, sic et inexcogitata materia.' See 1. Cor 2:9. See also *MTB*, iii, 507.

[115] *MTB*, iii, 505: 'Dominus labia mea aperiat ut ad gloriam suam gloriosi neomartyris sui laudem os meum digne annuntiet.' See Ps. 50:17

[116] 2 Kings 2:9–10: 'Dixitque Eliseus: Obsecro ut fiat in me duplex spiritus tuus. Qui respondit: Rem difficilem postulasti: attamen si videris me quando tollar a te, erit tibi quod petisti: si autem non videris, non erit.'

[117] 2 Kings 2:11–14.

[118] *MTB*, iii, 531–2: 'Et mihi discipulo tuo, tali quali nunc historiographo tuo, per avia et invia deserti erranti et te quaerenti, de tuo duplici spiritu vel modicum quid impertiri digneris. Non quod ego, peccator homunculus, Helysei prophetae tam eximii mihi usurpem quid, sed quia Helyas es tu, quod mundo et spiritus et virtus et (ne quid deesset) etiam ipse habitus indicavit. Mihi ergo puero tuo, qui tibi in vinculis evangelii

that even amidst the flames of his fiery chariot, even within the great abyss of eternal joy, Thomas will remain mindful of his sons yet endangered in pilgrimage.[119] Herbert knew that his master was now in a place beyond time and beyond history that his disciple and historian could not access. But he also believed that Thomas could condescend to his companions in the battle after the battle, and that he, Herbert, had indeed seen this new Elijah after he had been taken away from him.[120]

---

ministrare consueveram, vel de filis prophetici subtegminis tui, ne inter deserti hujus frigora nudus peream, tu ascendens huc projice.' See Philemon 13; Gen. 14:23.

[119] *MTB*, iii, 532.

[120] In the preface to his edition of the *Great Gloss*, Herbert writes that Thomas appeared to him and commended to him the verse of the Psalm (118:134), 'Redeem me from the calumnies of men, so that I keep your mandates' (*Redime me a calumniis hominum ut custodiam mandata tua*): Glunz, *History*, p. 348. In the *Historia* he says that Thomas appeared to him and told him that had he been present at the martyrdom he would have been baptised in the martyr's blood: *MTB*, iii, 502. It is not clear if these are two different visions or one.

CHAPTER SEVEN

John Allen Giles and Herbert of Bosham: The Criminous Clerk as Editor

Nicholas Vincent

W HAT we know of Herbert of Bosham we owe to two chief causes. The first and fundamental is the role that the self-dramatising Herbert played in the even greater drama of Thomas Becket. From this in turn springs the second cause for our knowledge of Herbert: the Victorian fascination with Becket. It was as a minor satellite of Becket's stardom that Herbert attracted an editor, John Allen Giles. In turn, it was Giles' edition of Herbert's works, published in 1845–46, that first brought Herbert to wider attention. Even now, it is Giles' edition as pirated by the Abbé Migne for volume 190 of his *Patrologia Latina* (1854) that still serves as the principal port of entry for modern scholars interested in Herbert's career. Even today, it is Giles' edition with its many failings and omissions that continues to determine Herbert's reputation in our post-Victorian age. In what follows, I hope to subject both Giles and his edition to a degree of scrutiny. To understand Giles and his work, nonetheless, we must begin not with Giles himself but with the wider Victorian reception of Thomas Becket.

Becket mattered to the Victorians in ways that have only recently begun to be appreciated.[1] As a bone of contention, left over from the great ossuary that Henry VIII and the Protestant Reformers had made of such remains, Becket could not be ignored by any historian of the Catholic Middle Ages.[2] To a majority of writers, from the 1530s through to the 1790s, he remained nonetheless a divisive and for the most part indigestible medieval relic. To declare oneself in favour of St Thomas was to side unequivocally with a Catholic or crypto-Catholic cause, with a love for saints, relics and ritual. Such was the case, for example, with the Jesuit scholar Thomas Stapleton, author of the *Tres Thomae* published in 1588 as parallel lives of St Thomas the Apostle, St Thomas Becket and St Thomas More.[3] To declare oneself

---

[1] See here N. Vincent, 'Thomas Becket', in *Making and Remaking Saints in Nineteenth-Century Britain*, ed. G. Atkins (Manchester, 2016), pp. 92–111.

[2] For his reception by the reformers, see H. L. Parish, *Monks, Miracles and Magic: Reformation Representations of the Medieval Church* (London, 2005), esp. pp. 92–105; A. F. Marotti, *Religious Ideology and Cultural Fantasy: Catholic and Anti-Catholic Discourses in Early Modern England* (Notre Dame, 2005), pp. 16, 213–14 n.28.

[3] T. Stapleton, *Tres Thomae seu res gestae S. Thomae apostoli, S. Thomae archiepiscopi*

against Thomas, by contrast, was to stand proudly for Reformation, King, country and the established Protestant church. Those in the first camp were inclined to refer to 'St' or 'the Blessed' Thomas. Those in the second, to 'Becket'. In either case, Thomas himself remained combustible stuff.

Change here came in the late eighteenth century, not least as a result of the fading away of terminal-phase anti-Popery in the aftermath of the Gordon riots of 1780. It can be traced in visual as well as literary terms. From the 1790s, images in the popular histories tend to show Becket no longer as an epicene conspirator under the red thumb of Rome, but, as in John Opie's 'Murder of Thomas a Becket' (*c.* 1795, now in the Canterbury City Art Gallery), as a Lear-like victim of tyranny, struck down by brute intimidators on the flagstones of Canterbury cathedral. In the histories themselves, we witness a shift from the Protestant certainties of Lord Lyttelton (who in 1767 had characterised Becket as 'guilty of a wilful and premeditated perjury ... in the highest degree ungrateful to a very kind master') to the far more sympathetic portrayal by Catholic writers such as Joseph Berington or John Lingard, presenting Becket as a friend of the poor, a defender of liberty and a saint martyred for his conscientious defence of the church.[4] Save in the most Catholic of retellings, Becket himself was always a figure of light and shadow, his good qualities matched and on occasion overwhelmed by the bad. Even so, from 1800 or so, the heroic version of his story tended to predominate.

Into this already contested field there entered, in the 1830s, the person of Richard Hurrell Froude (1803–36). As a defender of ecclesiastical privilege, penance, self-mortification and the cult of friendship, Froude's attraction to Becket was intense. Beginning in 1832, and continuing thereafter until the end of his brief life, Froude embarked upon a translation of those of Becket's letters that had found their way into the 'Quadripartitus' collection of letters and lives, first published in Brussels in 1682.[5] He also sought out manuscripts in the Bodleian Library at Oxford and further afield. It was in part in pursuit of such materials, in part to alleviate the symptoms of the tuberculosis that was soon to kill him, that Froude embarked for Rome in 1833. With him travelled his closest friend from the Oriel Senior Common Room, John Henry Newman. In Rome, not only did Froude and Newman seek out churches dedicated to San Tommaso, but they arranged Newman's first meeting with the keeper of Arabic manuscripts in the Vatican library, Nicholas Wiseman,

---

Cantuariensis et martyris, Thomae Mori Angliae quondam cancellarii (Douai, 1588), 2nd edn (Cologne, 1612).

[4] Vincent, 'St Thomas of Canterbury', citing George, Lord Lyttelton, *The History of the Life of King Henry the Second and of the Age in which he Lived*, 3rd ed., 6 vols. (London, 1769), iv, 361–3, and for what is otherwise the best of the modern accounts of this transformation, see C. A. Simmons, *Reversing the Conquest: History and Myth in Nineteenth-Century British Literature* (New Brunswick, 1990), esp. ch. 4, pp. 113–39.

[5] *Epistolae et vita divi Thomae martyris et archiepiscopi Cantuariensis*, ed. Christian Lupus, 2 vols. (Brussels, 1682), and for Froude's translations, published anonymously, 'Thomas a Becket', *The British Magazine and Monthly Register of Religious and Ecclesiastical Information* 2 (1832), 233–43 (starting November 1832), 453–9; 3 (1833), 31–8, 140–57, 399–411, 525–34; 4 (1833), 255–60, 376–82, 607–11; 5 (1834), 11–15, 655–8.

hoping thereby to obtain access to manuscripts of Becket's letters.[6] The rest, as the saying goes, is history.

Although Newman never fully succumbed to the allure of Becket, the *Remains* of Froude that he and John Keble published after Froude's death in 1836 included an entire volume dedicated to Froude's St Thomas. In it were many translations, some of them from Vatican manuscripts, that Newman had retrieved (and almost certainly improved) from Froude's unpublished papers.[7] Becket was thereby enshrined amongst the foundational patrons of the Oxford Movement and, in due course, of the movement's drift towards Rome. In John Henry Newman's novel *Loss and Gain* (1848), for example, and in the real-life experience of Newman's most fervent disciple, Frederick Faber, plunging to Rome in February 1846, a devotion to Becket and his physical remains played a significant role in conversion to Catholic truth.[8] Henry Manning, archdeacon of Chichester, attempting in the 1840s to bolster his childhood Protestantism, found himself reading the Constitutions of Clarendon as a medicinal exercise.[9] Far from purging him of his Catholicism, the Constitutions helped to drive him into the welcoming arms of Rome. Manning had by this time twice visited the English College in Rome, first in December 1838 (his first encounter with Wiseman, made in company with Gladstone), and again in December 1848. Both visits were deliberately timed to coincide with the feast of the martyrdom of St Thomas (29 December), the College's patron saint.[10]

I have told various of these, and other such stories, elsewhere.[11] They will in due course form parts of a book on the Victorian Becket cult. For present purposes, they sound various themes that will loom large hereafter. The first is the degree to which the letters and lives of Becket had, by the 1830s, become the focus of intense polemic within English ecclesiastical circles. Polemic, of course, was an integral feature of Becket's story from the outset, and as is often the case, polemic itself was closely related to war. Becket was a product of the England of King Stephen, just as Froude and Newman were children of the Napoleonic convulsions. In both cases,

---

[6] Vincent, 'St Thomas of Canterbury'.

[7] *Remains of the Late Reverend Richard Hurrell Froude, M.A.*, 4 vols. (London and Derby 1838–9), iv (2 part ii, 1839), including a note at p. 196, 'These letters are not among those published by Christianus Lupus. There are, however, more than 100 in the Vatican MS. which have not been published.'

[8] J. H. Newman, *Loss and Gain: The Story of a Convert*, ed. A. G. Hill (Oxford, 1986), p. 201; J. E. Bowden, *The Life and Letters of Frederick William Faber, D.D.* (London, 1869), pp. 270–3. For a sermon on Becket preached by Faber in the church of St Thomas Fulham on Becket's feast day (29 December) 1848, see F. W. Faber, *Notes on Doctrinal and Spiritual Subjects*, 2 vols (London, 1866), i, 355–80.

[9] D. Newsome, *The Parting of Friends: The Wilberforces and Henry Manning*, 2nd edn (Leominster, 1993), p. 329. Manning subsequently cited the Constitutions (in this telling a bad thing), as part of his defence of the decisions of the Vatican Council of 1870: E. S. Purcell, *Life of Cardinal Manning Archbishop of Westminster*, 2 vols (London 1896), ii, p. 481.

[10] Vincent, 'Thomas Becket', p. 103, citing W. Ward, *The Life and Times of Cardinal Wiseman*, 2 vols. (London 1897), i, pp. 271–2; Purcell, *Life of Manning*, i, pp. 155–6, 367; *The Gladstone Diaries*, ed. M. R. D. Foot and H. C. G. Matthew, 14 vols (Oxford, 1968–94), ii, p. 542.

[11] Vincent, 'St Thomas of Canterbury', pp. 92–111.

there was a tendency to invest lives and letters (be they of Becket or of Froude) with topicality and a wartime sense of struggle between good and evil, of utter black versus absolute white.[12] This tendency was perhaps exaggerated in the case of clergymen such as Froude and Newman, disbarred from any more conventional military vocation and therefore all the keener to prove the manliness and militancy of their clerical profession.

The second theme resides in the way that the Becket lives and letters, strung together into a coherent narrative, mirrored the attempts made by modernists and 'Germanisers', from the 1830s onwards, to establish the historical credentials of the life of Christ. This itself was now told through a combination of lives (the Gospels) and letters (St Paul), with the teller no longer as mere reporter but as an active critic of the sources.[13] The third theme, and one prominent in Giles' edition of Herbert of Bosham, is the extent to which the search for new Becket 'materials' had already led, by the 1830s, to a combing of Continental libraries, and in due course to a dawning awareness that a great deal of evidence for English history was to be found not in England but in manuscript collections on the 'wrong' side of the English Channel.[14]

So we come to John Allen Giles and his edition of Herbert of Bosham.[15] Herbert was unknown to Froude or Froude's followers. John Allen Giles was his prophet. Superficially, Giles and Froude had much in common. Both were West Country men, Froude from Devon, Giles (1808–84) from the Somerset levels. Both emerged from those fringes of the lower upper class from which so much Victorian achievement derived, though in Giles' case rather further towards the lower than the upper edge of that fringe. Both completed their educations in the Oxford of the 1820s. Froude's Oriel fellowship preceded Giles' at Corpus Christi by only a few years. Thomas Mosley, fellow or Oriel and in later life controversial chronicler of the Froude–Newman circle, was Giles' friend from their schooldays together at

---

[12] In general, for this sense of 'The Persistent Enemy', see P. Fussell, *The Great War and Modern Memory* (Oxford, 1975), pp. 105–13.

[13] For 'Germanisers', T. Hughes, *Tom Brown at Oxford* (Cambridge and London, 1861), ch. 26. So far as I am aware, although implied in earlier efforts such as those of Froude and Newman, a parallel between the Becket lives and the synoptic Gospels was first openly acknowledged by Edward Augustus Freeman in 1860, in an essay on 'St Thomas of Canterbury', reprinted in Freeman, *Historical Essays* (London, 1871), pp. 79–113, at 91–2. It finds its fullest expression in the work of E. A. Abbott, *St Thomas of Canterbury: His Death and Miracles*, 2 vols (London, 1898).

[14] For a wider picture here, see the introduction to N. Vincent, *Norman Charters from English Sources: Antiquaries, Archives and the Rediscovery of the Anglo-Norman Past*, Pipe Roll Society n.s. 59 (2013).

[15] For what follows, I depend upon the brief but thorough account by J. Blair, 'Giles, John Allen (1808–1884)', *ODNB*, and in particular upon the six volumes of Giles' Diary (Oxford, Bodleian Library mss. Eng. b.2097–2102). The publication of these as *The Diary and Memoirs of John Allen Giles*, ed. D. Bromwich, Somerset Record Society, 86 (2000) must be accounted a triumph, not least since it involved persuading a local record society to publish so vast a text of which only a small portion touches upon the history of any particular county. The originals nonetheless should still be consulted for their wealth of images, photographs and other miscellaneous materials not reproduced in the edition.

Charterhouse.[16] In 1829, Giles played a thrilling part in the Oxford parliamentary election in which the high church party, to which both Froude and Giles belonged, unseated Sir Robert Peel, himself branded a traitor to the Tory cause for his support of Catholic emancipation. Giles it was who paid for the bells of the University church to ring out in victory.[17] It should be remembered here that, in the 1820s, although Thomas Becket was consciously invoked by the emancipationists as a role model, the Anglican high church party was as bitter in its hostility to Rome as ever it was in its reaction against Wesley and the nonconformists.[18] Many of the protagonists here, including Giles, were inclined to controversy. This was, after all the period of slack following the great storm that had ended at Waterloo. In the 1830s, as a century later, the degree of ideological polarisation and the sheer venom of intellectual debates can be read as one consequence of a generation spared war's physical dangers, yet born and habituated to the rhetoric of war.[19]

For what we know of Giles we depend very heavily upon his *Diary*: a compilation of the late 1870s, re-editing his earlier journals into a consistent narrative, and in doing so adopting very much the combination of life and letters that was central to nineteenth-century biographical writing. The *Diary* is a remarkable record, albeit sprung from a genre in which truth tends to be not just varnished but primed, stretched, tastefully reframed and displayed in the best of all possible lights. In his youth, Giles had been no stranger to the chimes at midnight. Later, a degree of Pooterishness contributes to the autobiography of one whom John Blair describes as 'warm-hearted, considerate, convivial, but lacking practical sense and dignity of manner': in short, the very picture of a don *manqué*.[20] Across the *Diary* as a whole, two themes predominate. The first is an almost complete absence of anything that might be considered a priestly vocation; Giles does not so much as mention his ordination, either as deacon or priest, and the best that he can offer in terms of theological reasoning is an insistence that all be permitted to worship as and how they see fit, in perfect liberty.[21] The second theme is good humour maintained in the face of adversity.

[16] Giles, *Diary*, pp. 142–3 (June 1836).

[17] Ibid., pp. 81–2, recording the composition of *A Reply [by J. A. Giles] to An Expostulatory Letter Addressed to the Members of the University of Oxford who Voted for the Anti-Catholic Petition, by Pertinax Peerwell* (Oxford, 1829), and for the wider pamphlet war fought out on this occasion, see 'Oxford Election Pamphlets', in *The Crypt or Receptacle for Things Past* ns 1 part 2 (Winchester, September–December 1829), p. 221.

[18] For Becket as role model, especially in the rhetoric surrounding Daniel O'Connell 'Ireland's Liberator', see Vincent, 'St Thomas of Canterbury', pp. 100–1.

[19] For Giles' memory of the war before 1815, and especially of the invasion scares, see Giles, *Diary*, pp. 14–15, 348–9.

[20] Blair, 'John Allen Giles', also reporting the description of Giles (from Oxford, Magdalen College ms.800 i) as 'a very short, wiry little man, with iron-grey hair' (and cf. Giles, *Diary*, p. x, for a similar description by Giles' son). A portrait of him in his head-magisterial pomp, by J. D. Miller (before 1840), still hangs in the City of London School. A later photograph and portrait are reproduced in Giles, *Diary*, as frontispiece, and in T. Hinde, *Carpenter's Children: The Story of the City of London School* (London, 1995), p. 26.

[21] Giles, *Diary*, pp. 200, 229, 317.

Giles' optimism here was hard won. Aged six, he plunged his leg into a kettle of boiling water and was scarred for life.[22] Aged thirteen, he witnessed his youngest brother drown in a skating accident.[23] Some years later, his daughter, left to play with a ball of phosphorus in front of a lighted fire (not an experiment that most fathers would encourage) very nearly died. Giles was in his library when he heard the screams.[24] Giles, as we shall see, spent a lot of time in libraries. Newly elected a fellow of Corpus, he made his first extended continental tour, arriving in Paris in July 1830, just in time to experience the outbreak of a second French Revolution.[25] Returning to Bridgewater, he witnessed the suicide of his innkeeper's wife.[26] Consulting the parish registers of his native village of Mark in expectation of finding wealth and status, he discovered instead that his father, always considered an eldest son, had in fact been predeceased by an elder brother, the unforgettably named John Giblett Giles.[27]

Throughout his life, accidents multiplied to such an extent that one wonders whether contemporaries can ever have been entirely at their ease when Giles came to call. At Berne, in 1869, he witnessed a drunken Englishman fall to his death in the bear pit, 'crushed to death in a moment by the gigantic bear'.[28] Money invested by Giles in plate (stolen by absconding tenants together with a silver teapot in which Giles had placed an irreplaceable title deed, granting him the copyright to Lemprière's *Classical Dictionary*), in Bohn's publishing ventures (culminating in bankruptcy in 1844), or in a scheme to build a crammer's ('Alexandra College') in Ealing (crashing in 1865 with a loss of £3000), ran through his fingers.[29] At Bruges, in 1845, his poor command of French led to an accusation that he had mutilated books.[30] In Surrey, one of his servants was arrested for highway robbery, and another man hanged himself in front of Giles' house.[31] Bad luck was perhaps infectious, communicated merely by contact with Giles. The archbishop of Paris, Georges Darboy, who in the 1840s had made a (heavily criticised) French translation of Giles' *Life of Becket*, and whom Giles visited in September 1869, was shot dead just over a year later by the Paris communards, himself now a martyr to secular intimidation in much the same way as Becket, almost exactly seven hundred years before.[32]

Even on his first foreign tour, in 1830, Giles had experienced misfortunes. At Boulogne, for a wager, he drank two bottles of champagne and spent the night in the local lock-up. A week later, he persuaded his travelling companion to sell

---

[22] Ibid., pp. 19–20.

[23] Ibid., p. 25, and cf. 390.

[24] Ibid., pp. 19–20.

[25] Ibid., p. 100.

[26] Ibid., p. 116.

[27] Ibid., p. 4, and cf. 92, 364.

[28] Ibid., p. 384.

[29] Ibid., pp. 198, 201–2, 204–6, 209, 216, 239, 365–9.

[30] Ibid., p. 243.

[31] Ibid., p. 217.

[32] Ibid., pp. 253, 385, 398, 444.

him a valuable gold watch.[33] Outside Geneva, this was spotted by smugglers who waylaid Giles and attempted to murder him.[34] The watch featured in the story of Giles' edition of Herbert of Bosham, since it was to redeem his watch, pawned for 100 francs in Paris in December 1843, that he crossed again to France in April 1844. Thus began a tour of northern French libraries in which he first encountered the more important of the Herbert manuscripts at Arras.[35] The watch was with him still, in 1877, when he composed his recollections.[36] Watches and clocks, indeed, will play a surprisingly sinister role in the story that follows. Once again, there was perhaps a family curse. A cousin of Giles' wife was very nearly decapitated in the 1840s by sticking his head precipitously out of one of the openings in the dial of the great clock of St Paul's cathedral.[37]

Meanwhile, committed to a career in the law, and with no discernible religious bent, Giles was persuaded by his father to enter the church. He was then, in effect, disinherited as a result of his father's financial mismanagement. His career as founding headmaster of the City of London School from 1837, where it was hoped he might follow in the footsteps of Thomas Arnold, proved disastrous. Rather than Arnold's discipline of cold baths and the birch, Giles' school became a place of indiscipline and paranoia.[38] In 1840 he was ejected. After a period living in Surrey and then in north Oxford as an independent crammer and man of letters, he was offered, in January 1846, the curacy of one of the three portions of the immensely rich living of Bampton in Oxfordshire: a parish of more than 11,000 acres, with a tithe income approaching £1000. Giles was offered £150 and free accommodation, to serve as curate to the vicar of the first portion.[39]

Giles' principal misfortune was perhaps twofold: a refusal ever to decline an argument, combined with a pathological addiction to seeing his words in print. This infirmity obliged him, across the course of a long career, to publish nearly 180 books. The compulsion came upon him early. His first publication was a stirring address against Peel, as prospective MP for Oxford in 1829. It was followed a year later, and only a few months after Giles himself had obtained his BA, with an edition of Greek fragments, grandiloquently entitled *Scriptores Graeci Minores* 'Volume 1'. In this he claimed to have laid before the public 'the whole remains (including fragments) of Sappho, Alcaeus, Anyta, Corinna, Archilocus, Erinna, Hedlye, Melinno, Mimnermus, Musaeus, Myro, Nossis, Praxilla, Pythagoras, Simmias,

---

[33] Ibid., p. 98.

[34] Ibid., p. 105.

[35] Ibid., pp. 233, 236, 239.

[36] Ibid., p. 98.

[37] Ibid., p. 285.

[38] Hinde, *Carpenter's Children*, pp. 25–32.

[39] Giles, *Diary*, p. 252, noting the arrangements with Mr Kerby, senior vicar of Bampton. For the parish, see *A History of the County of Oxford: Volume 13, Bampton Hundred (Part One)*, ed. C. R. J. Currie, Victoria County History (Oxford, 1996), pp. 6ff., esp. 6, 49–50, 52–3.

Simonides, Solon, Sophron, Tyrtaeus, Stesichorus, Theosebia, Alcman, Telesilla, Phocylides and', he adds somewhat superfluously, 'a few others'.[40]

The rate of his publications did not really gather pace until the period between his sacking from London and his removal to Bampton in January 1846. It was during these years, living in lodgings in Oxford, that he executed his two-volume edition of Herbert of Bosham, itself only a portion of the eight volumes that he dedicated to the lives and letters of St Thomas in the two years 1845–46. In 1843–44 he had already published a 'complete' edition of the works of the Venerable Bede in twelve volumes, the works of St Boniface in two volumes, Lanfranc in a further two, and single volumes dedicated to St Aldhelm and the letters of Arnulf of Lisieux. In 1847–48, he went on to publish a further four volumes of Peter of Blois, and five volumes of John of Salisbury: thirty-five volumes in only four years, entitled collectively the Patres Ecclesiae Anglicanae. Over this same four-year period, and under a separate imprint, the 'Caxton Society', he also published the works of Geoffrey of Monmouth, the Peterborough Chronicle, the chroniclers of William the Conqueror, the letters of Herbert Losinga, the letters of Alan of Tewkesbury and the chronicle of Geoffrey le Baker, a further six volumes. This in addition to many other volumes of translations from religious and classical texts, and elementary school books ('First Lessons' in Roman, English and French history and so forth), eventually to grow into the twenty or more volumes of 'Dr Giles's Juvenile Library'.[41] Over more or less the same period, from 1844 to 1849, the Abbé Migne, with far superior resources and merely plagiarising the editions of his predecessors, managed only the first seventy-three volumes of the *Patrologia Latina*, a rate of production that seems snail-like in comparison to that achieved by Giles.[42] Migne's subscription to Giles' Patres Ecclesiae Anglicanae was first paid in 1843, sandwiched between rather less ominous payments from the Reverend John Keble and various Cambridge colleges.[43] In Paris, in October 1843, Giles visited Migne's 'splendid office' outside the Barrière d'Enfer. There he naively accepted a promise from Migne to 'take a copy of all the Patres that I should undertake to publish'.[44]

Two themes stand out here: the need, keenly felt by the 1840s, for accessible modern editions of medieval letters and chronicles neglected since the decline of seventeenth-century antiquarianism, and the imperative to search out new manuscripts of these sources, if necessary overseas. To this, we should add Giles' own particular addiction both to polemic and to an industrialised rate of production. Giles edited texts in much the same way that Mr Gladstone read books: by the cartload. In doing so, he

---

[40] *Scriptores Graeci minores*, 2 vols. (Oxford, 1831; 2nd edn 1839), and cf. Giles, *Diary*, p. 90 (Giles to the book's future dedicatee, Thomas Gaisford, Regius Professor of Greek and from 1831 Dean of Christ Church Oxford).

[41] See here the list of Giles' publications in Giles, *Diary*, pp. xii–xviii.

[42] For Migne's vast enterprise, see R. H. Bloch, *God's Plagiarist* (Chicago, 1994), esp. pp. 58–75.

[43] Giles, *Diary*, pp. 221–2.

[44] Ibid., pp. 229–30, 233, expressing some surprise that Migne was both clergyman and publisher.

cut almost as many corners as the Abbé Migne. Even today, one of the Bodleian Library's two copies of Pierre de Goussainville's 1667 edition of Peter of Blois carries an inscription by Giles reporting that he had donated this book in exchange for an older decayed copy that he had been allowed to mark up and send to his printer as the basis for his own edition of Peter.[45] By such means, books can be produced surprisingly quickly. To an editor of such industry, mechanisation was irresistible. Just as the motor car proved mesmeric to Mr Toad, so the printing press came to fascinate Giles. The comparison here is apt, since for Giles, as for the terrible Mr Toad, mechanisation was to spell not only ruin but incarceration in Oxford gaol.

As early as the 1840s, Giles' productivity came at a price, both financial and personal. He commanded an income from his translations and other popular works. From January 1846, he had his annual £150 and his house at Bampton, although even here his expenses on publication were such that, by 1853, he was once again advertising for pupils to board with him at Bampton for £100 a year 'according to age and requirements'.[46] The problem was that his scholarly editions simply failed to pay. Hence his yearning for a Maecenas capable of deferring the cost. Money was always a problem, and its short supply perhaps contributed to the nervous breakdown of Giles' wife, first apparent on their return from Paris in 1841.[47] It was in these circumstances that in in 1844, unsuccessfully, Giles approached the government of Sir Robert Peel offering his services as a searcher-out and transcriber of manuscripts in Continental libraries.[48] On the Continent not only were there archival resources awaiting discovery, but the costs of living for any middle-class Englishman were far lower than they would have been at home.[49] For his work on Becket, as early as March 1844 we find Giles approaching John Henry Newman, who granted him permission to take away any waste sheets of Froude's *Remains* (published in 1838–39) that might be lying around.[50] A year later, he was once again in correspondence

---

[45] As pointed out to me by Richard Sharpe.

[46] Oxford, Bodleian Library ms. Phillipps-Robinson c.522 fols. 10r–13r (prospectus, and letter from Giles to Sir Thomas Phillipps, 6 August 1853).

[47] Giles, *Diary*, pp. 198–200, 226.

[48] Ibid., pp. 240, 242, and for his letters to Peel, 4 December 1844, BL ms. Additional 40555 fols. 52–53, following a plea (fols. 11–12, 29 November 1844) to William Buckland, then canon of Christ Church, shortly to replace Samuel Wilberforce as Dean of Westminster, asked by Giles to further his cause with Peel. Giles suggested a payment of £100 for his first three or four months in the libraries of Belgium and Holland. Buckland took the trouble both of consulting James Norris, President of Corpus, Giles' old college (fols. 13–14), and of writing to Peel, who informed Buckland on 8 December of his intention to reject the proposal (fols. 15–16, and cf. the draft to Giles, fol. 54), largely on the basis of an assessment by the Revd Josiah Forshall, Secretary of the British Museum (fols. 92–98), in no way disparaging of Giles ('spoken of with respect and as a person of much more than ordinary abilities'), but demanding a scheme undertaken on far more 'definite and well matured' principles, and drawing attention to the vast extent of the manuscript holdings even of the two countries that Giles had named.

[49] Economy appears amongst the motives for his visits to France and Germany in 1841–42: Giles, *Diary*, pp. 198, 214.

[50] *The Letters and Diaries of John Henry Newman*, ed. C. S. Dessain and others

with Newman, who asked Mark Pattison to offer 'any Belgian introductions' he might have, presumably to assist Giles with his work in Flanders and northern France.[51] The progress of his edition of Herbert of Bosham, as of the other sources for St Thomas, can be traced from Giles' *Diary*, beginning at Saint-Omer and Arras in April 1843.[52] He revisited Arras in April 1844, and it was on this occasion that he made his 'discovery' of the manuscript of Herbert's Life of St Thomas. He subsequently paid an amanuensis, Louis Madelin, to transcribe this, the transcript arriving in Oxford in July 1845.[53] It is today in the British Library, bound up with Giles' own copy from the Cambridge manuscript of Herbert's Letters.[54]

At Arras, Giles could not fail to notice that the manuscript of Herbert was sadly mutilated. As yet, he seems not to have known that various of the mutilated leaves had been sold, as long ago as 1828, to Sir Thomas Phillipps. Giles was nonetheless aware of Phillipps as a famed collector of manuscripts, perhaps also as a potential source of patronage. As early as November 1844, he had written to Phillipps asking after a manuscript of Peter of Blois.[55] From this point onwards, Phillipps' correspondence takes up the tale.[56] Although immediately invited to Middle Hill, Giles was suffering a severe attack of rheumatism and was unable to accept. At the same time, he did his best to interest Phillipps in his ongoing edition of medieval authors. Claiming that not even the Bodleian could rival the Phillipps collection, Giles also suggested installing his family in a farmhouse near Middle Hill in order that he might spend several months with Phillipps' books.[57] After this perhaps rather too enthusiastic introduction, nearly two years passed without further communication.

(Birmingham and Oxford 1961–), x (1843–45), p. 152 (4 March 1844), cf. ibid., viii (1841–42), p. 501, where Newman acknowledges receipt of the prospectus for Giles' Patres Ecclesiae Anglicanae, as early as April 1842, and cf. Giles, *Diary*, p. 218.

[51] *Letters and Diaries of Newman*, x, p. 571 (24 February 1845), and cf. Giles, *Diary*, pp. 243–4, also noting letters of introduction from the archbishop of Canterbury, William Howley.

[52] Giles, *Diary*, p. 237.

[53] Ibid., pp. 245, 247. From Bruges, on 1 April 1845, he wrote to Sir Frederic Madden at the British Museum, drawing his attention to the cartulary of the Abbey Dunes in the library of the Grootseminarie and its various charters of Richard I, John and Henry III: BL ms. Egerton 2844 fols. 37–38, suggesting that Giles procure a transcript of the entire manuscript, which would cost much less made in Belgium than it would in England.

[54] BL ms. Additional 20702, acquired by the library in 1855, presumably as a result of Giles' disgrace. Here copying the materials, principally the 'Liber Melorum' from the Arras manuscript, with interleaved attempts by Giles to make good the missing or mutilated sections from the incomplete copy of the 'Liber' in Oxford, Corpus Christi College ms.146.

[55] Oxford, Bodleian Library ms. Phillipps-Robinson d.131 fols. 5r–6r (Giles to Phillipps, 1 November 1844); ibid. e.378 fols. 5v–6r (Phillipps to Giles, 7 November 1844).

[56] For Phillipps more generally, the essential authority remains A. N. L. Munby, *Phillipps Studies*, 5 vols (Cambridge 1951–60), but with Giles afforded only the briefest of notices, ibid., iv ('The Formation of the Phillipps Library from 1841 to 1872'), p. 111.

[57] Oxford, Bodleian Library ms. Phillipps-Robinson d.131 fols. 7r–8r (Giles to Phillipps, 11 November 1844).

In March 1846, however, and inconveniently just as Giles' edition of Herbert of Bosham was passing through the press, Giles learned from Parker, the Oxford bookseller and publisher of his 'Patres', that Phillipps claimed to possess not only manuscripts that might make up gaps in the existing corpus of Herbert's works, but another life of Becket, perhaps Benedict of Peterborough's (a version still untraced, that in due course Phillipps entirely denied possessing).[58] Phillipps replied that he did indeed own an alternative manuscript of Herbert's 'varying in some degree from the copy at Arras', together with leaves that had been nefariously cut out 'by that rascal Caron, the librarian at Arras, who did it to spite the mayor and corporation … because they would not grant him some request which he made'.[59] Phillipps recalled buying these leaves at Amiens together with several pounds' weight of materials excised from other Arras manuscripts:

> I offered to restore them to the mayor and the library if they would merely repay me the money I gave for them. They refused!!! and in disgust I kept them, but the greatest part being theological, I left them on the continent and sent them to an inn, but whether they ever reached their destination I never heard. The leaves of Herbert being English history I brought home.[60]

Let us note here the assumption amongst Englishmen, not unknown even today, that Continental libraries and European history more generally are chiefly of interest for what they tell us of 'English' history. Giles meanwhile had sent Phillipps the two volumes of his edition of Herbert, begging for further details of what else there might be at Middle Hill.[61] By June 1846, a visit was arranged.[62] This visit, prolonged for nearly a fortnight, proved significant to both men. Giles was allowed to consult several manuscripts, although apparently not yet the Arras leaves, still untraceable amidst the chaos at Middle Hill.[63] More to the point, he began to see his way to a rather grander scheme.

Both Giles and Phillipps were obsessive, one as an editor, the other as a collector of manuscripts. Both dreamed of publishing books faster and in greater quantity

---

[58] Ibid. c.494 fols. 104r–105r (Giles to Phillipps, 13 March 1846). The mystery 'life' was probably one or others of those attached to Phillipps' two copies of the 'Miracula' by Benedict, today Brussels, Bibliothèque royale ms. IV.600, and London, British Library ms. Egerton 2818 (formerly Phillipps ms. 10227, Miracles with the 'Life' by John of Salisbury). For the Brussels ms., see below n.138.

[59] Oxford, Bodleian Library ms. Phillipps-Robinson e.379 fols. 44v–46r (Phillipps to Giles, 22 March 1846), also referring to a manuscript of Guernes de Pont-Saint-Maixence.

[60] Ibid. fols. 47r–48v (Phillipps to Giles, 26 March 1846), an account to some extent confirmed by Phillipps' correspondence from 1829: ibid. c.425. And for the wider story here, see the articles below by Sabina Flanagan (pp. 156–67) and Christopher de Hamel (pp. 168–83), and Vincent, *Norman Charters*, pp. 40–1.

[61] Oxford, Bodleian Library ms. Phillipps-Robinson c.494 fols. 106r–107r (Giles to Phillipps, 23 March 1846).

[62] Ibid. fols. 110r–114r (Giles to Phillipps, 2 and 7 June 1846).

[63] For their non-discovery, ibid. e.379 fols. 81v–82r (Phillips to Giles, 4 June 1846). For what was seen, there is a list of manuscripts 'Dr Giles to examine': ibid. c.672 fol. 53r (June 1846, including 'Benedict of Peterborough').

than any commercial printer could achieve. Giles had long been interested in the mechanical reproduction of the written word. As headmaster of the City of London School, in 1838, he had invested in a 'curious machine' allowing him to write two letters with a single stroke of the pen.[64] Even earlier, he had admired the 'immense numbers' of books printed and bound by the press belonging to the family of his Oxford friend, Thomas Mosley.[65] As curate of Bampton, he had access to an untapped stream of labour amongst the children of his parish, many of them trained to reading and writing in the village's national school, established in 1812, teaching upwards of 150 girls and boys.[66] What if such production could be mechanised? Having observed Phillipps' printing press at Middle Hill, Giles was now determined to acquire something similar for himself at Bampton. As he put it in writing to Phillipps: 'I effectively caught the printing mania at Middle Hill.'[67]

By August 1846, fired up by his encounter with Phillipps' press, he had ordered a set of type and an Albion printing machine.[68] There followed all manner of travails, as Giles came to realise that his enterprise required official licence, not obtained until July 1849. Not only this, but his printer's assistant was afflicted with St Vitus' dance.[69] In Giles' universe, nothing ever ran entirely straight. From 1847, he nonetheless began to train up girls from the local national school to compose type: twenty-four such girls over the next seven years. This was done so successfully that even the great Dr Pusey enquired whether the experiment might be repeated by the Sisters of Mercy, Pusey's Anglican nunnery in Plymouth.[70] At the suggestion of a Mr Black, an Oxford bookseller, Giles selected his girls according to the smallness of their fingers, 'better suited for picking up and setting the type'.[71] In due course he invited an old acquaintance from his Continental travels, Major Anstruther, an exile from the revolutions of 1848, to share his house in Bampton, there to co-operate in the edition of medieval texts. It was the fact that Anstruther edited the letters of Herbert of Losinga, in succession to Giles' edition of the life and letters of Herbert of Bosham, that persuaded Giles to have his own son, born in 1845, christened Herbert Allen Giles. Herbert Giles was to enjoy a career rather less turbulent than that of his father, dying in 1935 as Professor Emeritus of Chinese at Cambridge University.[72]

---

[64] Giles, *Diary*, pp. 169–70.

[65] Ibid., p. 143.

[66] For the schools, *VCH Oxfordshire*, xiii, 58–60.

[67] Oxford, Bodleian Library ms. Phillipps-Robinson c.494 fols. 121r–122r (Giles to Phillipps, 21 October 1846).

[68] Ibid. c.494 fols. 119r–120r (Giles to Phillipps, 1 August 1846).

[69] Giles, *Diary*, pp. 261, 267–8. Giles' press is briefly noticed, with admiration for the quality of its productions, by H. R. Plomer, 'Some Private Presses of the Nineteenth Century', *The Library* ns 1 (1900), 407–28, esp. 421–2.

[70] Giles, *Diary*, pp. 268, 281, 290. In this context, it is worth noting a definition, reported in Giles' *Diary*, p. 43, that 'Puseyism/Pussyism' might best be defined as 'a mixture of *cat*echism and *dog*matism'.

[71] Ibid., p. 302.

[72] Ibid., pp. ix, 264. Herbert Giles left an intellectual autobiography, now Cambridge

Meanwhile, on 27 June 1846, the very day after his return to Bampton, Giles wrote to Phillipps promising holograph specimens from the first of his child amanuenses, the twelve-year-old Edward Carter, 'a pertinacious, dogged little fellow that will master whatever he undertakes'.[73] By August, and despite objections from the village schoolmaster, he was informing Phillipps that the boy, son of a respectable local stonemason, would be delivered to Middle Hill by his father as soon as his mother had his clothes ready: 'I think you will find him of much use, *where there are so many manuscripts*'. The intention at this stage was that Giles and Phillipps should embark on editions of a Latin chronicle of the reign of Edward IV, and the customal of the shrine of St Thomas at Canterbury, possibly also of the mysterious and apparently still untraced life of St Thomas by Benedict of Peterborough.[74] Giles then set out for Paris, reporting minor discoveries but, on his return in October 1846, reverting to the scheme to have Edward Carter installed at Middle Hill 'before the winter becomes more severe'. Middle Hill, lying high up on the Cotswold escarpment, remains a mightily cold place in winter. Despite this, Giles advised Phillipps against paying Carter any wages, advice that, given Phillipps' attitude to money, was surely superfluous.[75]

Worthy of Peter Grimes, this scheme came to nothing, no doubt much to the relief of young Carter. Phillipps suffered what he described as 'a long attack of cholera' (itself hardly a reassuring advertisement of the amenities of Middle Hill).[76] More to the point, he had been impressed by the legibility but not as yet by the speed or the firmness of Carter's script and wished the boy to obtain proper initiation in medieval writing: 'You no doubt have one or two manuscripts on vellum, one of which he can copy from until I am ready to receive him'.[77] Rather as if he were judging root vegetables, Phillipps suspected that Carter might 'improve with his stronger growth'.[78] As for Giles' Bampton printing press, Phillipps responded with modified rapture:

> I am delighted to see you have a press of your own. Every gentleman who proposes to print something annually thro(ugh) life ought to get one of his own immediately. I like your type, but I do not approve of your great space between the lines. One lead is enough. Do you not see that you are wasting your paper by so much not being printed upon, and that in fact it is making

University Library ms. 8964/1, but it begins only in the 1860s, with his introduction to eastern languages, lacking anything on childhood.

[73] Oxford, Bodleian Library ms. Phillipps-Robinson c.494 fols. 115r–116v (Giles to Phillipps, 27 June 1846).

[74] Ibid. fols. 117r–120r (Giles to Phillips, 15 July and 1 August 1846), referring to the 'officium feretrariorum s(ancti) Thomae' and the 'Vie de S. Thomas par Benoit'.

[75] Ibid. fols. 121r–122r (Giles to Phillipps, 21 October 1846): 'You will perhaps see the propriety of paying him (Carter) nothing at first.'

[76] Ibid. e.380 fol. 83v (Phillipps to Giles, 19 August 1846).

[77] Ibid. fols. 74r–v, 107v–108r (Phillipps to Giles, 10 July and 26 October 1846).

[78] Ibid. fol. 74r–v (Phillipps to Giles, 10 July 1846), also in Giles, *Diary*, p. 256.

people pay for blank paper so many as buy your book? I wish you had a living near me.[79]

The pursuit of a church living was to occupy Giles, on and off, for much of the next eight years. In part this was due to Phillipps, who kept this *ignis fatuus* always glowing, always for one reason or another plucked from Giles' grasp.[80] As for the Bampton press, although financially unsuccessful, this was kept at work in ways that Phillipps had not anticipated. Phillipps wished for editions of his own manuscripts, above all for his cartularies, considered his *sancta sanctorum*. Giles had other priorities. Whilst prepared to seek occasional subventions from Phillipps, asking at first £20, later £10, to supply a transcript of the earliest Bampton parish register, he held off until 1854 from any promises involving Phillipps' other manuscripts.[81]

His new-found interest in cartularies came after what was, in fact, only his second meeting with Phillipps, face to face, in April 1854. Giles was still anxious to inspect the leaves, looted from the Arras manuscript of Herbert of Bosham, that Phillipps was still unable to locate.[82] Above all, he needed a patron. Phillipps secured offers from Giles to print cartularies and also fifty copies of Bigland's *History of Gloucestershire*, which had earlier been rejected as a joint venture, being too large for Giles' press when set up in four columns of type. In May 1854, Phillipps visited Bampton. He found Giles away from home, but was most impressed by Giles' 'Press Gang' (the words are underlined by Phillipps): the girls operating the Bampton printing machine.[83] By this time, however, a greater nemesis had begun to unfold. It came from two directions more or less simultaneously. To begin with, Giles experienced a catastrophic falling out with his bishop, Samuel Wilberforce. They had first met in convivial circumstances, in 1849, when the conversation turned to 'Rousseau's Dream', the tune chimed by the clock of Bampton church. This, apparently, was known to monoglot locals not as 'Rousseau's' but as 'The Horse's Dream'.[84] This exchange too, as we shall see, was to suffer a haunting aftermath.

---

[79] Oxford, Bodleian Library ms. Phillipps-Robinson e.380 fols. 107v–108r (Phillipps to Giles, 26 October 1846).

[80] Hopes first pinned on the living at Buckland in Gloucestershire, thereafter transferred to Broadway and then to nearby Willersley, both in Worcestershire: ibid. d.147 fols. 135r–138r (January-February ?1847); c.503 fols. 7r–8r (Giles to Phillipps, 10 January 1847), 15–18r (Phillipps to Giles and Giles to Phillipps, 16 and 18 October 1849); e.384 fol. 25r (Phillipps to Giles, 20 June 1849); Giles, *Diary*, pp. 263, 265.

[81] Oxford, Bodleian Library ms. Phillipps-Robinson e.385 fols. 28v–29r (Phillipps to Giles, 28 October 1849); c.503 fols. 19r–25r (Giles to Phillipps, 28 and 31 October, 27 November and 13 December 1849). For the cartularies, ibid., d.160 fols. 22r–24r, 28r–32r (Giles to Philipps with responses, 26 and 28 April, 2 June, 2 and 12 July 1854), and cf. Giles, *Diary*, p. 297.

[82] Oxford, Bodleian Library ms. Phillipps-Robinson d.147 fols. 137r–139r (Giles to Phillipps, 12 February and 15 June ?1848); d.160 fols. 20r–21r; d.160 fol. 25r (Giles to Phillipps, 26 March 1854).

[83] Ibid. d.161 fols. 82r–83r, 91v–92r (Phillipps to Giles, 9, 14 and 31 May 1854), and for Bigland, see also ibid. c.494 fols. 110r–112r (Giles to Phillipps, 7 June 1846 and 12 May 1854).

[84] Giles, *Diary*, p. 265.

Giles was the broadest of broad churchmen. Until now, whatever scrapes he had got into had been personal rather than doctrinal. At the great King Alfred millennial celebrations at Wantage, in 1849, for example, he had fallen foul of the high church vicar of Wantage, William Butler, subsequently dean of Lincoln. Horrified by the vulgarity of the celebrations, and knowing that Giles was liberal in his interpretation of scripture, Butler declared that Giles was 'neither a Christian nor a gentleman'.[85] Giles' *History of the Ancient Britons* (1847) had been censured in *The Guardian* for dismissing the doctrine of the Trinity as a 'knotty point'.[86] In 1852, things took a more serious turn. There is no reason to suppose that Giles had read the 'Germanisers' of Tübingen. In 1830, it has been estimated, there had been only two German-speaking theologians in the whole of Oxford.[87] Like many clerical contemporaries, however, Giles was in no doubt that the Bible was the work of man rather than God. It was therefore encrusted with error and confusion.[88] Textually, and despite wails of disapproval from the Evangelicals, it required a more scientific edition than anything that could be claimed for the Authorised Version of 1611.[89] George Eliot's translation of David Strauss' *Das Leben Jesu* (1835) had been published amidst clerical uproar in 1846, to be followed in 1853 by her translation of Feuerbach's *Essence of Christianity* (1841).[90] Early in 1852, in company with a local squire, Mr Birch of Pudlicote near Charlbury, and the Reverend Thomas Wilson, author of a collection of 'discourses' on *Catholicity Spiritual and Intellectual*, Giles agreed to print a Bible supplied with commentary.[91] Giles' role was to deal 'with historical and critical questions only'.

By October, specimen pages from this work, already being described as the 'Bampton Bible', had been brought to the attention of Bishop Wilberforce.[92] The

---

[85] Ibid., p. 272.

[86] Ibid., p. 262.

[87] Newsome, *The Parting of Friends*, p. 78.

[88] Giles, *Diary*, pp. 324, 327, noting his agreement on these issues with Mark Pattison, who undoubtedly had read the Germans.

[89] O. Chadwick, *The Victorian Church*, 2 vols., 2nd ed. (London, 1972), ii, 40–4.

[90] For Strauss, see V. A. Dodd, *George Eliot: An Intellectual Life* (London, 1990), pp. 87–93; Chadwick, *Victorian Church*, i, 487–8; ii, 61–2. For German influence more generally, see M. A. Crowther, *Church Embattled: Religious Controversy in Mid-Victorian England* (Newton Abbot, 1970), esp. pp. 40ff.

[91] T. Wilson, *Catholicity Spiritual and Intellectual* (London, 1850): an attempt (p. 3) to assert 'the spirit of Christianity' wherever necessary contradicting 'the letter of systematic theology, Patristic or Mediaeval', thereby steering a middle way between the opposed forces, 'Roman or Rational'. For Birch, who later did his best to help Giles, but who emigrated to America in 1856, see Giles, *Diary*, pp. 325, 334.

[92] Eventually published in two parts as *The Holy Bible: First Division: The Pentateuch, or Five Books of Moses ... edited by the Rev. Thomas Wilson M. A., of C. C.C. Cambridge, author of 'Spiritual Catholicity', 'Travels in Syria, Palestine etc'* (London, John Chapman, 1853, with a fine set surviving as Cambridge University Library printed books 1897.12.43), the title here referring to Wilson's *Nozrāni in Egypt and Syria* (London, 1846), a series of lectures intended to raise funds for the restoration of Wilson's church of St Peter Mancroft in Norwich. Wilson, in his introduction to part 1 of *The Holy Bible* (1853), pp. iii–vi, sets out both the circumstances in which Giles was obliged to withdraw his name from

nomenclature here was not insignificant, threatening as it did to couple Giles' thoroughly unorthodox Bible criticism with the name of the most prestigious series of Anglican theological lectures: the 'Bampton Lectures', delivered annually in Oxford since 1780 (named after their founder, John Bampton, rather than through any association with Bampton in Oxfordshire). There followed an acrimonious exchange in which, having raised various thorny points over the dating and authorship of the Book of Joshua, Giles agreed to withdraw from the enterprise. He did so firmly proclaiming his right to return to matters of biblical history whenever it might please him, without accepting episcopal censorship.[93]

The outcome, published by Whittaker's of London in the early summer of 1854, was a book entitled *Christian Records*. Here, and in continuation of a volume published in 1853 as *Hebrew Records*, Giles set out to demonstrate that, far from being the work of Matthew, Mark, Luke and John, the Gospels and the books of Acts were 'not in existence before the year 150 of the Christian era'.[94] In this he claimed to challenge the historicity of the New Testament without in any way undermining Anglican doctrine. Bishop Wilberforce thought otherwise. In the ensuing exchange, and far from wisely, Giles complained that he was being persecuted merely for exercising his right to rational judgement:

> I have no wish to become a martyr, even though my becoming so would probably do me more worldly good than ever the church has done me. But I have hitherto adhered to the church as a progressive institution, and shall do so if I am allowed.[95]

All of this in July 1854, with Giles displaying his customary combination of flippancy, self-pity and pugnacity, perhaps not entirely by coincidence within only a few weeks of the British declaration of war in the Crimea. Having agreed to withdraw his book from sale, Giles then compounded his offence, persuading the London printer of his *Records* to publish his exchange of letters with Bishop Wilberforce.[96]

In Wilberforce's eyes this was worse than insubordination; it was positively ill mannered. As bishop of Oxford, Wilberforce was pathologically sensitive to any whiff of heterodoxy. Not only was he bishop of a diocese that would for ever be associated with the apostasy of Newman and Newman's acolytes, but he himself sprang from a family riven with confessional doubts. By virtue of their evangelical

---

association with the venture, and his own departures from 'episcopal authority' and 'Ecclesiastical interpretation', denying any 'religious obligation to believe' in miracles and emphasising the essentially 'mythical' nature of Genesis, as of much else in scripture.

[93] Giles, *Diary*, pp. 293–5.

[94] J. A. Giles, *Christian Records: An Historical Enquiry Concerning the Age, Authorship and Authenticity of the New Testament* (London, 1854), here citing p. 6, at p. 10 even threatening to redate the letters of St Paul.

[95] Giles, *Diary*, p. 299.

[96] First published as *The Lord Bishop of Oxford's Letters to the Rev. Dr Giles, for Suspending the Publication of 'Christian Records', with Dr Giles's Letters in Reply* (London, 1854), reprinted in Giles, *Diary*, pp. 299–301, the original of the 'Diary' here (Oxford, Bodleian Library ms. Eng.b.2100 pp. 485ff.) being taken from cuttings from the printed pamphlet.

father, the great abolitionist William Wilberforce, Samuel and his two brothers had been marked out from birth as special members of the Anglican communion: as close as Anglicanism permitted, outside the royal family, to a dynasty of saints. All three of the Wilberforce brothers had been enchanted by Newman and his siren songs. Samuel's youngest brother, Henry, was received as a Catholic by the Jesuits at Brussels in September 1850. The middle sibling, Robert, was likewise driven Romewards by the Gorham Case, and in 1854 was already teetering on the brink of his own, even more controversial conversion, solemnised at Paris on 31 October.[97]

There were also local but pressing reasons for caution in the Oxfordshire of 1854. In April 1853, as bishop, Samuel Wilberforce had founded his Oxford Diocesan Seminary at Cuddesdon, intended to train graduates for ordination. Cuddesdon was duly opened in June 1854. From the start, it became the focus of intense scrutiny, both from strict Protestants fearful of its Catholic tendencies as from those of broader churchmanship concerned that too much theological speculation might muddy the limpid waters of Anglicanism.[98] Giles, as the notoriously and eccentrically disorganised curate of Bampton, was already marked down in that great book of life that was Wilberforce's visitation records.[99] Indeed, Wilberforce's visitation sermon of November 1854 might almost have been composed with Giles in mind. Here we find the bishop castigating 'self-willed rashness' and urging a more professional training of the clergy. Only thus were the faithful to be steered between the Scylla and Charybdis of 'latitudinarianism on the one hand, or the poisonous blight of Roman error on the other'.[100]

All might still have been smoothed over, with Wilberforce notoriously amongst the smoothest of the smooth. Instead Giles now committed an act of suicidal recklessness. It was an act directly linked to Giles' interest in Herbert of Bosham, since it was Herbert who had first drawn Giles into the orbit of Sir Thomas Phillipps and it was from Phillipps that Giles had caught his 'mania' for the printing press. In September 1854, Jane Green, one of the girls employed for the last five years in Giles' press, asked to be married to a local shoemaker named Richard Pratt. Persuaded by the girl that gossip amongst their fellow villagers might lead to 'Rough Music', Giles agreed to marry them without banns and by special licence. On Sunday 1 October 1854, Giles used the Bampton press to run off further copies of his pamphlet against Bishop Wilberforce, now with a stinging 'additional note' drawing

---

[97] Newsome, *The Parting of Friends*, esp. pp. 354–60, 370–402.

[98] O. Chadwick, *The Founding of Cuddesdon* (Oxford, 1954), esp. pp. 14–18.

[99] *Bishop Wilberforce's Visitation Returns for the Archdeaconry of Oxford in the Year 1854*, ed. E. P. Baker, Oxfordshire Record Society, 35 (1954), pp. 10–12. Note here Giles' extremely terse return to the visitation questions compared to the far more open answer offered by the incumbents of the other two portions of Bampton. There seems to be nothing on Giles in *The Letter-Books of Samuel Wilberforce, 1843–68*, ed. R. K. Pugh and J. F. A. Mason, Oxfordshire Record Society, 47 (Leeds, 1970), and the only references to him in *The Diocese Books of Samuel Wilberforce*, ed. R. and M. Pugh, Berkshire Record Society, 13 (Reading, 1980), pp. 27, 115, are discreet to the point of deliberate *suppressio veritatis*.

[100] *A Charge to the Diocese of Oxford at his Third Visitation, November, 1854, by Samuel, Lord Bishop of Oxford* (London, 1854), esp. pp. 10–11.

attention to the recent flight to Rome by the bishop's brother, Robert.[101] Two days later, on the morning of Tuesday 3 October, Giles went to Bampton church to conduct the marriage of Jane Green, taking care to secure the key to the church the night before, without informing the parish clerk of his intentions. Arriving 'a little before 8 o'clock', and to save time waiting, he filled out the register with the names of the married couple and their witnesses. But the groom did not appear. Learning that Pratt's employer had refused him permission to leave work, Giles agreed that the marriage might take place two days later, well before work began. He himself was distracted throughout this period by the illness of his son Herbert. He was also annoyed at the waste of time that might otherwise have been devoted to his scholarly pursuits. On Thursday 4 October, 'about 7 o'clock' in the morning, he once again went to church. There he married Jane Green to Richard Pratt, with his eldest son, Arthur Giles, as witness but without waiting for the second witness whose name had already been entered in the register: his servant, the appropriately named Charlotte Lait.[102] Gold watch or not, Giles had never been a good time-keeper. The church clock at Bampton, with its musical chimes, philosophical or equine, was notoriously unreliable.[103]

By marrying Jane Green to Richard Pratt, Giles committed at least three serious offences. Despite what the bride had been told, no special licence had been obtained. Giles, contemptuous of formalities and either naively, or for want of funds, failed to purchase one. He had entered false evidence in the register, since one of the witnesses had not been present, and the ceremony itself was misdated to 3rd rather than 4th October. Far more seriously, under the terms of the 1753 Marriage Act, it was a criminal offence, punishable by up to fourteen years' transportation, for any clergyman to conduct a marriage service before 8 o'clock in the morning. The Act's intention had been to outlaw clandestine marriages and the forced abduction of heiresses. Giles claimed that in 1854 he had no idea that such a law existed.[104] Be that as it may, time had literally caught up with him.

On Saturday 7 October he received a personal complaint from Pratt's employer that Pratt had been married without permission. Giles did his best to respond. The shoemaker (like the vicar of Wantage, also named Butler) was persuaded to write to the bishop. On Monday 9 October the bishop wrote to Giles, a letter of accusatory enquiry that Giles initially tore up but then glued back together and preserved

---

[101] *The Lord Bishop of Oxford's Letters to the Rev. Dr Giles ... 2nd edition*, dated at Bampton, 1 October 1854 (copy in BL printed books 4405.k.1 no.17).

[102] Here relying heavily upon the account supplied in the late 1870s by Giles, *Diary*, pp. 302–4, 319–21. See also the account that Giles himself caused to have printed, in March 1855, of which there is a copy in Oxford, Bodleian Library ms. Phillipps-Robinson c.531 fol. 99r, noting that 'I was in a hurry to get back to my books, the hour or two before breakfast being almost my only time for private study.' The affair goes entirely unmentioned in the contemporary lives of Samuel Wilberforce or in his episcopal letter books. However, various letters preserved as Oxford, Oxfordshire Record Office CPZ1/1–105 make the extent of the bishop's involvement abundantly clear.

[103] As noted in the *VCH Oxfordshire*, xiii, 57; Giles, *Diary*, p. 307.

[104] Giles, *Diary*, pp. 303–4.

in his *Diary*.[105] By Wednesday, 11 October, when Giles went to Oxford and heard rumours that the bishop's lawyer, Mr Davenport, was determined upon prosecution, things had begun to look bleak. At some point here, Giles himself wrote the bishop a letter, subsequently used in evidence against him in court, although the text itself seems not to survive.[106] On Sunday 22 October, as he was preparing to preach in the neighbouring hamlet of Lew, Giles was arrested by the Witney constable. He was bailed on the following day, under £500 of sureties supplied by his friend, Mr Birch of Pudlicote, and an old undergraduate acquaintance, the vicar of Witney. At the same time he was warned that further charges involving a marriage conducted before 8 o'clock, two years earlier, were likely to require yet further sureties of £500. Gossip suggested that there was more to the marriage than met the eye: a clergyman, marrying off one of his indoor servants, with only his son as witness, in a ceremony conducted outside canonical hours. At this point, and advised by his brother, a lawyer, Giles determined on flight. In all likelihood, his nerve simply failed him.

Rather than appear to answer further charges on Friday 27 October, Giles set out for London. It is some indication of his disordered priorities, bordering on derangement, that as early as 31 October he was writing from London to his wife, asking that she forward him the proof sheets of whatever publications he had in hand, and also that she pack up his printing press, to be sent to London to be used by a friend. His books he asked to be sold at Sotheby's in the Strand. The whole debacle he blamed on the vicar of Wantage, William Butler, acting in league with Bishop Wilberforce.[107]

Even Giles' friends in Bampton, including the Reverend Dacres Adams, the resident vicar, were prepared to admit that the parish was now 'freed for ever from the ministrations of one who for many years was quite unfitted for his office'. Despite this, Adams insisted, Giles was guilty of no immoral conduct, merely of 'folly and ignorance which has marked his every step in this miserable transaction'. The only parties now determined on prosecution with a fervour bordering on persecution were the Witney magistrate, Leonard Pickering, who refused any offer of backstairs negotiation from the bishop's lawyers, and Frederick Newman, Giles' fellow curate at Bampton. A high churchman who insisted on preaching in a surplice, Newman

[105] Ibid., p. 304, from Oxford, Bodleian Library ms. Eng. b.2100 p. 492, where the torn fragments are preserved together with a transcript, and for this act of preservation cf. Giles, *Diary*, p. 317.

[106] It is referred to in letters from Giles' brother, William, sent to the bishop from Taunton on 24 October, Oxford, Oxfordshire Record Office CPZ1/18: 'I found waiting for your lordship the accompanying letter, which had been sent off by my brother before my arrival, and which I now transmit to you ... I am aware, and am not surprised at the facts, that there many of the parishioners who from proper motives have desired my brother's removal from his office, but I am quite sure that that being attained, there will be no wish to bring on him consequences so disproportionate to the case and so utterly inappropriate to that which is the root of the evil – his disaffection to the church.' Cf. ibid., no. 102, where on 7 March 1855 Davenport writes to the bishop over 'the delicate matter of producing in court the letters written by Dr Giles to your lordship', seeking to exonerate himself and instead blaming Giles' counsel for the circumstances in which these letters were cited in evidence against their client.

[107] Giles, *Diary*, pp. 305–6.

was determined to give evidence against Giles, should there be even the remotest chance of an acquittal.[108]

In theory Giles was now a fugitive from justice, having forfeited the £500 raised as surety for his bail. In practice, sounder sense prevailed.[109] The bishop, anxious to avoid a scandal, made it known, even before the end of October, that he had no desire to pursue the full rigour of the law.[110] Consultation with an eminent solicitor, Gabriel Goldney (later 1st Baronet), persuaded Giles to appear before the magistrates at Witney on 5 December. By Christmas, Richard and Jane Pratt, the chief prosecution witnesses, whether legally married or not, had emigrated to Australia, speeded on their way with £50 supplied by a friend of Giles.[111] A suggestion was made by Davenport to the Witney magistrates that the bishop might prefer the prosecution to be dropped, if only Giles would retire to live as a tutor near London.[112] Doubt was cast upon the supposed timing of events, not least because of the notorious inaccuracy of the Bampton church clock. Even so, on 5 December further charges were raised in respect to earlier marriages that Giles had conducted, and sureties totalling £3200 were demanded for bail. The whole sad saga came before the Oxford assizes in March 1855. There, in a court presided over by Lord Campbell (born 1779, Chief Justice since 1850), Giles was convicted of falsifying an entry in the register, having married Richard Pratt to Jane Green outside the canonical hours. His conviction owed a great deal to letters that he himself had written to Bishop Wilberforce, in effect confessing his guilt: letters that in circumstances of less than perfect candour, Wilbeforce allowed to be read out in court.[113] Giles was sentenced to twelve months in Oxford gaol, although with a private assurance that he would be released earlier. In fact, his release came on 3 June, after only three months, thanks to interventions by Wilberforce, themselves provoked by Giles' many friends.[114]

Here was melodrama worthy of any number of Victorian novels; the forgery of signatures and false witness (Trollope's *Orley Farm*, 1861–62, and *Last Chronicle of Barset*, 1867), scheming lawyers (Dickens, *Bleak House*, 1852–53), tampering with parish registers (Wilkie Collins, *The Woman in White*, 1859) and the nobbling of witnesses to protect a clergyman in difficulties (Trollope, *The Vicar of Bullhampton*, 1870). Even the 'Rough Music' threatened by Giles' parishioners reminds us of the

---

[108] Oxford, Oxfordshire Record Office CPZ1/33, 35, 45. For the surplice, Giles, *Diary*, p. 319. For Leonard Pickering, the Witney magistrate, who both initiated the prosecution and refused any hint that it might be set aside, ibid., pp. 305, 314.

[109] For what follows, Giles, *Diary*, pp. 306–14.

[110] Oxford, Oxfordshire Record Office CPZ1/19, 26, 32, recording negotiations between Wilberforce, Davenport and Giles' brother William. Other letters in this collection (esp. CPZ1/3, 4, 7, 9, 11) make the extent of the collusion between Wilberforce and Davenport abundantly clear.

[111] Giles, *Diary*, pp. 307, 314–15, 324–5, and for Giles' subsequent low opinion of the advice and (high) fees of Goldney, see p. 320.

[112] Oxford, Oxfordshire Record Office CPZ1/33, 35.

[113] Giles, *Diary*, pp. 312–13, and cf. 485–6.

[114] Ibid., pp. 312, 325.

fictional *Mayor of Casterbridge* (Thomas Hardy, published in 1886 though set in the 1840s). Perhaps it is no coincidence that this was an era of doubt and dissolving certainties. The falsification of church records, especially those involving marriage, that most brittle and endangered of Victorian sacraments, served as metaphor for the far wider collapse of faith in scriptural certainties literal and historic. Truly, the sea of faith was no longer at the full (Matthew Arnold, *Dover Beach*, c. 1851). Giles was undone by precisely the forensic methods that he himself had employed in his *Christian Records*.[115] Perhaps fortunately for the parties concerned, Giles himself was cut from no tragic cloth. On the contrary, he accepted his fate, served out his sentence and then bounced back. Even in gaol, he continued to edit and translate, in this instance collecting evidences for the early history of the Jews that in due course became his *Heathen Records* (1856), a companion to his *Hebrew* and *Christian Records*, in due course reissued in 1877 as a two-volume set.[116] By such means did he signal his refusal, even now, to submit to episcopal discipline.

In January 1858, following his release from prison, he sent his former judge, Lord Campbell, an eight-volume set of his Becket materials. Campbell, acknowledging the gift, reciprocated by sending Giles a set of his *Lives of the Lord Chancellors*, a full ten volumes in the fourth edition of 1856–57, whose first substantial biography (ch. 3) dealt appropriately enough with Thomas Becket.[117] In due course, even the perfidy of Samuel Wilberforce faded from recollection, though from time to time the embers still glowed. They glowed most brightly after 1870, when, now as rector of Sutton in Surrey, Giles found himself once again under Wilberforce's jurisdiction as bishop of Winchester. On their one further meeting, at Sutton rectory, there was a tussle over a gooseberry tart. From this Giles claimed to have emerged the moral if not the physical victor.[118] There were also reiterated threats of prosecution from Wilberforce, in 1871, over the funeral arrangements for the infant child of a dissenting minister, and in 1873, over the clearing of human remains from Sutton churchyard.[119] Wilberforce returned a frosty refusal to Giles' offer to assist with a revised edition of the biblical Apocrypha.[120] Even after his sudden death in 1873, the bishop remained an object of loathing amongst Giles' children, especially to Herbert Giles, less so to Giles himself.[121]

As for his supposed return to Anglican conformity, in 1856, less than a year after his release, Giles was publishing notes on scripture 'for the use of little children',

---

[115] A point rather gloated over by various of his detractors: ibid., pp. 313, 322.

[116] J. A. Giles, *Heathen Records to the Jewish Scripture History; containing all the extracts from the Greek and Latin writers, in which the Jews and Christians are named* (London, 1856); J. A. Giles, *Hebrew and Christian Records: An Historical Enquiry Concerning the Age and Authorship of the Old and New Testaments*, 2 vols (London, 1877). For his routine in Oxford gaol, see Giles, *Diary*, pp. 323–4.

[117] Giles, *Diary*, pp. 313, 342, and cf. 527 for Giles' continued interest in Campbell and his works.

[118] Ibid., pp. 386–8, an encounter also noted at pp. 325, 496.

[119] Ibid., pp. 410, 441.

[120] Ibid., pp. 449–50.

[121] Ibid., pp. 454, 460, 464, 491.

remarkably vague on the Christian mysteries. His retelling of the Gospels ends, indeed, without any mention of Christ's resurrection, save for a concluding remark that, having been 'again seen alive by his disciples … He afterwards went up in to heaven and was seen no more'.[122] Giles himself, by contrast, lived for a further thirty years, seen by a wide body of friends and enemies, unluckily optimistic, impossibly argumentative to the end.[123]

In the meantime, at least two further outcomes flowed from the events of 1854–55, both of them with direct consequences for Giles' edition of Herbert of Bosham. The first concerned Giles' relations with Sir Thomas Phillipps. Here was more farce than tragedy. In the immediate aftermath of Giles' arrest, Phillipps appeared to offer support and a refuge for Mrs Giles and her family, should they care to stay in his house at Broadway.[124] Unfortunately, neither party to this arrangement fully understood the other's intentions. Giles and his wife believed that Phillipps was bent on kindness. Phillipps himself cared nothing for kindness but a great deal for Giles' printing press. He had always struggled to find a printer to operate his own press at Middle Hill. Giles, by contrast, had been followed into disgrace and exile by various of the Bampton girls. As soon as Phillipps learned that Giles' press was in London rather than ready to be moved from Bampton, he withdrew his offer. Not only this, but having agreed to purchase various manuscripts from Giles, including one described as an unknown work by Peter of Blois, he now turned from friend into accuser, demanding 'a better explanation than you have yet given' to justify Giles' false entries in the marriage register, and confessing himself:

> Vexed to find that you have not secured to me a printer *as you promised*. If you had found that could not go on with your own press, the least you could have done would have been to transfer your printers to me, *after your promise.*[125]

The italics here show quite clearly what Phillipps' intentions had been. Giles replied with a full account of the Pratt fiasco, and also with an undertaking to do what he could to persuade various of the Bampton girls to remove themselves to Broadway, even though Phillipps' press was a wooden one that the girls would lack the strength

---

[122] J. A. Giles, *First Lessons in Bible and Gospel History for the Use of Beginners* (London, 1856), intended according to its preface 'for the use of little children to give them a short general view of the Jewish and Christian sacred History', noting the resurrection at pp. 77–8.

[123] For some indication of the lingering whiff of scandal, see Newman, *Diaries*, 21 (1864–65), p. 360, where Newman reports what he feared might be efforts by Giles to reprint Tract XC.

[124] Oxford, Bodleian Library ms. Phillipps-Robinson d.160 fols. 10r, 12r–17r, 33r–38r (Giles to Phillipps, 8 November 1854; Phillips to Giles, 9 November, 1854; Mrs Giles to Phillipps, 9, 11 and 29 November 1854).

[125] Ibid. fol. 17v, 41r–42r (Phillipps to Giles, 10 and 20 December 1854). The manuscripts perhaps included the scrap-book of fragments once belonging to Giles, today BL ms. Egerton 3323, formerly Phillipps ms. 21162, parts of it (especially fol. 17) with Arras connections, perhaps recovered from amongst the detritus that both Phillipps and Giles saw in Arras itself.

to operate.[126] Even from prison, he continued to write to Phillipps, not least to ask whether he had as yet found the missing Arras leaves of Herbert of Bosham.[127] Phillipps' reply was phrased in the frosty third person:

> Sir T(homas) P(hillipps) is very sorry for Dr Giles's misfortunes but regrets that Dr Giles's neglect of his promise to Sir TP prevents his acceding to Dr G's request, as it implies a neglect of those who wished to be his friends.[128]

So, despite further overtures from Giles, their relations ended.[129] Giles was never to see the elusive Arras leaves.

Meanwhile, this carries us to the second outcome of Giles' disgrace: his determination to retain control over the Becket materials and to prevent their being republished by any other authority without his permission. He had reasonable cause for grievance here. In 1854, at more or less the same time as his struggles with Bishop Wilberforce, he learned that the Abbé Migne, long a subscriber to his editions of Becket, intended to use them as part of volume 190 of the 'Patrologia'. Giles, naively as ever, seems to have hoped to collaborate with Migne, not least in improving his earlier editions using manuscripts more recently discovered.[130] Migne, of course, acknowledged no such thing as a collaborator. He merely informed Giles that the 'Patrologia' was finished, and that the relevant volume (of which he claimed, mendaciously, that Giles' work formed only a small part) was already in print.[131] Thus were Giles' endeavours pirated, without any profit to their author.

The scars here were still apparent, a decade later, when the officially sponsored Rolls Series first contemplated a new edition of Becket materials, to be edited by James Craigie Robertson. Giles already had grievances both against the Rolls Series and Robertson. As we have seen, in the 1840s Giles had appealed to the government of Sir Robert Peel for funds with which to complete a proper listing of Continental manuscripts relating to the history of medieval England. From 1862 onwards, precisely such a list was produced for the Rolls Series by Thomas Duffus Hardy. Far from offering proper acknowledgement to Giles, Hardy passed over the majority of Giles' work in silence, creating the impression that little or no serious work had been completed in Giles' field between the demise of Henry Petrie, Hardy's own mentor, and the emergence of the Rolls Series. The thirty-seven volumes of Giles' 'Patres' were dismissed in a single entry in Hardy's index. All the more galling, Hardy's

---

[126] Oxford, Bodleian Library ms. Phillipps-Robinson d.160 fols. 43r–44r (Giles to Phillipps, 21 December 1854).

[127] Ibid. c.531 fols. 95r–6r (Giles to Phillipps, from Oxford Castle, 10 April 1855): 'Can you find the missing leaves of Herbert of Bosham's Life of Beckett, that they may be copied into the French edition by Monsieur Migne of Paris?'

[128] Ibid. c.542 fol. 76r (Phillipps to Giles, 18 April 1855).

[129] Ibid. b.158 fols. 12r–13r (Giles to Phillipps, 14 May 1859).

[130] Above n.126 (Giles to Phillipps, 10 April 1855).

[131] Giles, *Diary*, p. 326.

Catalogue was itself a work shot through with error and confusion.[132] Robertson, meanwhile, had compounded the offence. In 1859 he had published a life of Becket necessarily heavily dependent upon Giles' editions of the lives and letters. Far from acknowledging Giles' hard work, however, Robertson had devoted several pages of his book to a denunciation of his predecessor.[133]

Giles, so Robertson wrote, had entirely failed to clear up the chronological sequence of the Becket letters. On the contrary, by arranging his edition by author rather than date, and thereafter by the status of addressees, from clergy via kings to mere laymen, he had 'done all that was in his power to prevent the possibility of reading [the Becket correspondence] with ease or pleasure, and even to throw impediments in the way of understanding it'. Where Froude had corrected various mistakes in dating, Giles had piled error upon error. So much so that:

> It really seems as if this editor were animated by a malignant desire to worry and baffle his readers – at once to multiply their toil and to mar the results of it.

Not only was Giles' edition disordered but it lacked any index. Adapting a remark made by Thomas Carlyle in his edition of the letters of Oliver Cromwell, Robertson accused Giles of belonging to the class of editors who edit 'as you edit waggon-loads of rubbish, by turning the waggon-upside-down'. In illustration, he then set about listing various of the more egregious slips in Giles' Latin. His hatchet work here was all the more vicious both for its reference to Lord Campbell as a previous biographer of Becket (a reference that in 1859 could not but be received by Giles and those who knew his circumstances as an allusion to the trial of 1855) and for its willingness to cite Migne's 'Patrologia' as a source of correction, here employing a notoriously pirated reprint as a stick with which to beat Giles, in reality the victim of Migne's piracy.[134]

Certain of Robertson's cuts went deep. What, for example, was one to make of an editor who, as Giles had done, had allowed his own private thoughts to slip from the margins to the text of his edition. Here, for example, in a letter from St Thomas to the cardinal Hyacinthus, we find the (English) thoughts of Giles or his amanuensis, pining for their lunch, suddenly intruded within a passage of over-flowery (Latin prose): 'Sed vobis ut vobis voraciter ðuſſ'. Migne and more recently Anne Duggan

---

[132] T. D. Hardy, *Descriptive Catalogue of Materials Relating to the History of Great Britain and Ireland*, 2 vols. in 3 parts, RS, 26 (London, 1862–65), esp. i part 1, pp. xlvi–liii; i part 2, p. 858; Giles, *Diary*, p. 547.

[133] J. C. Robertson, *Becket, Archbishop of Canterbury* (London, 1859), pp. 168ff., and for Robertson, son of a Scots Presbyterian father, from 1846 vicar of Bekesbourne near Canterbury, and from 1859 canon of Canterbury Cathedral, see N. Vincent, 'William of Canterbury and Benedict of Peterborough: The Manuscripts, Date and Context of the Becket Miracle Collections', in *Hagiographie, idéologie et politique au Moyen Âge en Occident*, ed. E. Bozóky (Turnhout, 2012), 347–87, at pp. 352–4.

[134] Robertson, *Becket, Archbishop of Canterbury*, pp. 169–72, duly indexed in Robertson's book under 'Giles', also noting the much kinder if still condescending comments at pp. 4–5.

have correctly construed this as 'Sed nos, ut vobis veraciter dicimus'.[135] Robertson, apparently unable to comprehend the full horror of Giles' mistake, initially offered the far lamer 'Sed nos, ut vobis veraciter dico'.[136] Between 'dicimus', 'dico' and 'dull' stretch scholarly chasms that Giles, and for that matter Robertson, never found easy to leap.

There is no doubt that Giles was an impulsive and impatient editor. At the same time, there is equally no doubt that Robertson's attack, backed up in due course by further sallies from Edward Augustus Freeman, was intended to wound with intent. Robertson and his friends were determined that it should be Robertson rather than Giles who served as editor of the Rolls Series edition of Becket Materials: an undertaking whose editor could expect a far more handsome financial return than anything Giles had achieved from his eight volumes of Lives and Letters.[137] Here too, however, there were consequences for the modern reception of Becket that deserve more general acknowledgement. Precisely because he was determined to signal his departure from Giles and his methods, Robertson decided to begin his Rolls Series edition with a text that Giles himself had not published. Hence the decision that volume one of the Becket Materials should be devoted to the miracle stories collected by William of Canterbury. These were supplied to Robertson from a manuscript at Winchester College, unknown to Giles, and only discovered in 1854, Giles' *annus horribilis*, by the local antiquary (and eccentric), Francis Baigent. In proceeding thus Robertson himself fell into error, pushing ahead with an edition of William of Canterbury that would have been much better had he waited for the discovery of earlier manuscripts, in due course reported from Montpellier and more recently from Evreux.[138]

Not only this, but in his determination to signal his break from Giles and his methods, Robertson 'improved' Giles' edition of Herbert of Bosham by abridgements that today render the Rolls Series edition in many ways less useful even than that by Giles. Giles had attempted, for example, to publish Herbert's 'Liber Melorum' complete and unabridged from the manuscript at Arras. The missing passages here were subsequently the subject of extended correspondence between Giles and Sir Thomas Phillipps. Although unable to locate the most significant witness (the leaves

---

[135] J. A. Giles, *Epistolae Sancti Thomae Cantuariensis*, i (in Giles, *The Works of Thomas Becket*, iii) (Oxford, 1845), p. 131 no. 51; *PL*, 190.513; *CTB*, i, 652 no. 141.

[136] Robertson, *Becket, Archbishop of Canterbury*, p. 172 n., subsequently brought into conformity with Migne, in Robertson's edition of *MTB*, vi, 215 no. 315.

[137] As is apparent from a letter from J. R. Green to Freeman, of April or May 1864: *Letters of John Richard Green*, ed. L. Stephen (London, 1901), pp. 144–5, noting in particular fears that the Treasury might oppose any proposal that smacked of 'reprinting things printed', but, as antidote, remarking that 'Robertson has (or rather an obscure friend of his has) disinterred "William of Canterbury's Life of Thomas" at Winchester'. For the financial profits that accrued to Rolls Series editors, including something approaching £6600 paid to Stubbs and £6400 to Luard, see M. D. Knowles, 'Great Historical Enterprises IV: The Rolls Series', *Transactions of the Royal Historical Society*, 5th ser. 11 (1961), 157–8, reprinted in M. D. Knowles, *Great Historical Enterprises* (London 1963), p. 131.

[138] Vincent, 'William of Canterbury and Benedict of Peterborough', esp. pp. 350–6. See Flanagan, below, pp. 156–67.

looted from Arras in 1828), Giles was at least enabled, thanks to another Phillipps manuscript, to repair some of the gaps in his edition of Herbert's 'Life' of St Thomas, collating his version (from Arras) with Phillipps' copy, today in the Bibliothèque royale at Brussels, and publishing the resulting corrections in 1851.[139] Robertson, by contrast, supplied merely selections from Giles' edition of the 'Liber Melorum', making no attempt whatsoever to repair the Arras gaps from the Phillipps leaves.[140] Likewise, Giles had done his best to supply a complete edition of Herbert's letters, as preserved in a unique manuscript at Corpus Christi College, Cambridge. His progress here can be charted from his *Diary*, recording both his initial search of Cambridge collections, conducted in January 1844, and thereafter a much later visit to Corpus, made in June 1880, when he was once again permitted to handle the manuscript of Herbert that he had first seen nearly forty years before.[141] Once again, as table 1 below shows, Robertson, in integrating these letters into the Rolls Series Becket Materials, whilst arranging them more sensibly than Giles, in chronological rather than authorial sequence, omitted a great deal that Giles had included. The consequence here is that, even today, Giles remains our chief means of access to no less than fourteen of Herbert's letters of which Giles published forty-two, Robertson a mere twenty-eight.

What are we to conclude from all this? Firstly that, as with any textual edition, it is often as important to understand the editor's circumstances as it is to know those of the text itself. Secondly, that from Froude in the 1830s, through to Giles a decade or more later, the post-Napoleonic years witnessed an admirable determination on the part of English historians to seek out materials until then sunk in Continental obscurity. So much so that, by the 1850s, virtually all of the materials for Herbert of Bosham in use today were already listed and, save for the Arras leaves, presented in print. However slapdash he may have been as an editor, Giles was an assiduous hunter down of manuscripts. It was in those areas where he himself did not venture, as for example in the edition of the Becket miracle collections, that the most serious gaps remained in knowledge of the manuscript transmission. Thirdly, it must by now be apparent that the time has come, after nearly two hundred years, to redefine and in large part re-edit the collections of Becket materials that first Giles and then Robertson bequeathed. Anne Duggan has already led the way, with her magnificent work on Becket's *Correspondence*. Even here, however, nearly a third of the Becket letters presented by Giles and Robertson remain accessible only in their nineteenth-century editions. Not only this, but the time has surely come for new editions of the lives, and especially of the Becket miracles. Such efforts must extend, before long,

---

[139] Phillipps' copy of Herbert's *Vita Sancti Thomae c.*1200 (from Aulne-sur-Sambre), once Phillipps ms. 4622, is today Brussels, Bibliothèque royale ms. IV.600, bound up with the *Miracula* of Benedict of Peterborough. For Giles' published corrections, see J. A. Giles, *Anecdota Bedae, Lanfranci et aliorum*, Caxton Society (Oxford, 1851), pp. xii–xiii, 97–113.

[140] Giles, *Herberti de Boseham … Opera*, 2 vols., as vols. 7–8 of Giles' *Works of Thomas Becket* (Oxford, 1845–46), ii (Works, vol. 8), pp. 1–184; *MTB*, iii, 535–54. For the gaps repaired from Phillipps' ms., see above n.138.

[141] Giles, *Diary*, pp. 234–5, 576, reporting that it was Dr Lamb, Master of Corpus, who had served as his host in 1844.

to Herbert's 'Life', 'Letters' and 'Liber Melorum'. The present collection of essays, if it is to serve any purpose, should surely point towards such future endeavours. If they are to prove successful, then best that they be carried out with full knowledge of the circumstances in which, thanks to excessive haste and inadequate time-keeping, John Allen Giles so notoriously yet so heroically failed.

Table 1   Herbert of Bosham's letters in the Giles and Robertson editions

Giles			MTB	Other
1	... \<di\>scretio tua serenissime	Herbert to (Henry count of Champagne)	-	(Smalley)
2	Quod tam crebris	Thomas to Pope	530	
3	Quum ego pauper	Thomas to Pope	537	
4	Etsi tibi pater sancte	Stephen bishop of Meaux to the Pope	240	
5	Quibus nunc potest	Herbert to William archbishop of Sens	653	
6	Etsi tanta cui scribitur	Herbert to the same	654	
7	Qua verborum facundia	Herbert to the same	652	
(8)	Sciatis (k)arissimi	Thomas to England's clergy	636	CTB 260
(9)	Gratias ago domino meo	Thomas to England's bishops	536	CTB 271
10	Quid nobis de vestra	Thomas to Roger of Worcester	670	
11	Quod nec tanta	Thomas to Robert of St-Omer	171	
12	Suscepi caritatis	Herbert to Nicholas of Mont-aux-Malades	271	
13	Quum ego arripiens	Herbert to prior Wibert	177	
(14)	Que pater in longinquo	Bishops of Canterbury province to Thomas	205	GFL 167
15	Expectans expectaui	Thomas to the bishops	221	
16	Vestre fraternitatis literas	Thomas to the bishops	222	
(17)	Fraternitatis vestae scriptum	Thomas to the bishops	223	(CTB 95)
18	Quum ego arriperem	Herbert to William elect Chartres	175	
19	Quod mihi vel nunc	Herbert to Gregory abbot Malmesbury	176	
20	Omne gaudium existimo	Thomas to the Pope	156	
(21)	Inter scribendum haec	Herbert to Henry bishop Bayeux	-	
22	Expectans expectaui promissi	Abbot of Soissons to Herbert	-	

23	Lectus dignationis tuae sermo	Herbert to the Abbot of Soissons	-	
24	Quod impraesentiarum aures	Henry count of Champagne to Pope	280	
25	Quia semel coepi	Matthew precentor Sens to Pope	281	
26	Qui quotidie cogor	Thomas to cardinal Raymond	251	
27	Gloria in excelsis	Thomas to Louis VII	247	
28	Ex aliorum relatione	Thomas to Waldemar of Denmark	365	
29	Literas caritatis vestrae	Herbert to William abbot Vézelay	-	
30	Qui quotidie cogor	Herbert to Bartholomew bishop of Exeter	-	
31	Carissime mihi in Cristo	Herbert to Baldwin archdeacon of Exeter	-	
32	Etsi vobis pater sancte	Bishop of Senlis to Pope	241	
(33)	Inter scribendum haec	William archbishop Sens to Pope	735	
34	Quod tantae maiestatis	Herbert to Pope	798	
35	Quoties vel membranula	Herbert to John of Salisbury	-	
36	Gloria in excelsis Deo	Herbert to Gunther	-	
37	Nos qui teneros	William archbishop Sens to abbot Vézelay	-	
38	Omnes nouimus quod omnes	Herbert to John bishop of Poitiers	770	
39	Id in primis scribo	Herbert to cardinals	769	
40	Ego Herbertus sanctitatae	Herbert to the Pope	779	
41	Deuotionis tuae literas	Pope to Herbert	778	
42	Cognito quod horum	Herbert to Hugh bishop of Durham	-	
(43)	Ne in dubium	Cardinals to Henry II	772	
43a	.... (n)obis velitis quam citius	?William bishop of Ely to Herbert	-	
44	Celsitudinis vestrae qua debuit	?Herbert to William bishop of Ely	-	
45	Gratissima vestrae consolationis	William bishop of Ely to Herbert	-	
46	Magnam michi	Arnulf of Lisieux to Thomas	(162)	(CTB 45) (Arn 42)

CHAPTER EIGHT

The Missing Leaves of Arras MS 649: A Tale of Lost and Found

Sabina Flanagan

I

A LTHOUGH Arras MS 649 contains the fullest version of Herbert of Bosham's *Vita S. Thomae*, several abbreviated or otherwise incomplete versions being extant, it was not a particular interest in the archbishop's life and death which sent me to the text.[1] Rather, I was in search of Herbert's own autobiographical interpolations, especially the one where he discusses doubts about the timing of the Incarnation.[2] It was in the course of this enquiry that I became aware of the tangled tale of the missing leaves of Arras 649.

The fact that MS 649 had been mutilated is well known to scholars in the field, but the actual history of the excised leaves and such basic questions as their number and whereabouts at different times are the subject of conflicting accounts. Indeed there is a good deal of what might be thought of as mythology surrounding the story. The aim of this paper is to correct some widespread misapprehensions and to point up some bibliographical lessons along the way.

The preferred edition of Herbert's text of the *Vita S. Thomae* and its appendage the *Liber Melorum* is still that of James Craigie Robertson in volume three of *Materials for the History of Thomas Becket, Archbishop of Canterbury*.[3] His edition supersedes that of John Allen Giles, published in *Herberti de Boseham opera quae extant omnia*, which text formed part of his ambitious series, the Patres Ecclesiae Anglicanae. It was the Giles edition that J.-P. Migne later appropriated, for the even less reliable version printed in volume 190 of the *Patrologia Latina*.[4]

[1] Arras, Médiathèque municipale, MS 649 [formerly 375]; Oxford, Corpus Christi College, MS 146 (short version, incomplete); Brussels, Bibliothèque Royale, MS IV 600 [formerly Phillipps 5622] (short version); Charleville-Mézières, Bibliothèque municipale, MS 222 (short version).

[2] *Vita, MTB*, iii, 13. For an account of these doubts and the miraculous dream by which they were purportedly overcome, see S. Flanagan, *Doubt in an Age of Faith: Uncertainty in the Long Twelfth Century*, Disputatio 17 (Turnhout, 2008), pp. 81–5.

[3] *Materials for the History of Thomas Becket, Archbishop of Canterbury*, ed. J. C. Robertson, 7 vols., RS 67 (London, 1875–85).

[4] *Herberti de Boseham opera quae extant omnia*, ed. J. A. Giles, 2 vols., Patres Ecclesiae

However, when I had ordered up Volume III of the *Materials* from the University of Adelaide Library I was disconcerted to find a line of asterisks at a crucial juncture of the text.[5] They occur at the transition from Herbert's account of Thomas's decidedly brisk manner in getting through the mass to his own doubts about the Incarnation. It was at this point that I consulted Robertson's Introduction to the *Materials* in Volume I for an explanation of what had happened, and so began my search for the missing leaves of the Arras manuscript.

In his *Introduction* Robertson asserts that the Arras manuscript is:

> greatly superior to the Oxford manuscript [i.e. Corpus Christi College MS 146, which he also used] in appearance, and contains the books which are wanting in it [i.e. the first three books of *Vita*], but [Arras] has throughout undergone mutilation by cutting out of leaves here and there and unfortunately the leaves which are missing are not always those which we could best have spared.[6]

It may come as a surprise to learn that an editor would think that any of the leaves were dispensable, but at the time there was more interest in the historical aspects of the text and less value given to what were thought of as Herbert's frequent and often lengthy theological digressions.

For his information about the missing leaves Robertson was himself indebted to the edition of the *Vita S. Thomae* produced some thirty years earlier by John Allen Giles. In the *Oxford Dictionary of National Biography* Giles is described as 'translator and literary editor', but there was more to this Anglican clergyman and fellow of Corpus Christi College, Oxford, than this brief description might suggest.[7] He was for a time imprisoned in Oxford Castle for performing a marriage out of hours and then perjuring himself about it. He is said to have published around 180 works. These ranged from such scholarly, though by no means flawless, editions in the Patres Ecclesiae Anglicanae series, which includes the Herbert texts, to potboilers such as Dr Giles Juvenile Library on everything from Scottish history to optics, 'adapted to the capacity of children between the ages of six and twelve' and a series of cribs for their older brothers (and just possibly sisters) to Latin and Greek authors.[8]

While Giles would have been the first to admit that he was not a meticulous scholar and that he was often forced to write for money, his memoirs show him as a fascinating and rather attractive character with many enthusiasms and a wide range of accomplishments. Although it might not have been unusual for a Victorian clergyman to compose Latin epitaphs for various family pets or to draw up

---

Anglicanae 136–7 (Oxford, 1845–46); *Patrologia Latina*, ed. J.-P. Migne, vol. 190 (Paris, 1854).

[5] *MTB*, iii, 212.

[6] *MTB*, i, xxi.

[7] J. Blair, 'Giles, John Allen (1808–1884)', *ODNB*. See N. Vincent's article above, pp. 127–55.

[8] See the list in *Diary and Memoirs of John Allen Giles*, ed. D. Bromwich, Somerset Record Society, 86 (Taunton, 2000), pp. xii–xviii. Giles compiled this work in 1878 from the diaries and letters he had kept throughout his life.

architectural plans for renovating his house, the scheme for training girls from the National School to be compositors for his own printing press was certainly original.[9]

Giles made an expedition to look for manuscripts for his Patres Anglicanae in the early 1840s, which took him to Belgium and France. While he was in Arras he found in the municipal library the manuscript now known as Arras 649 containing the *Vita S. Thomae* and the *Liber Melorum*. In the account given in his *Memoirs* for 9 April 1845 he writes:

> At Arras my labours met with a rich reward in the discovery of Herbert de Bosham's contemporary life of Thomas à Becket, preserved in a MS. of early date, and having one defect only, but that was of a serious nature. The librarian told me that his predecessor had cut out every 10th leaf and sold it for a trifle as parchment or vellum, to a tailor to make measures. However, I sent for a copyist and directed him to copy all that remained, line for line, and page for page. He began his task whilst I was there.[10]

There are several versions of how the leaves were removed, given at different times by different people and, indeed, different stories given at different times by the same person. Here is what Giles wrote about the loss of the leaves in the introduction to his 1846 edition of Herbert's works: 'a mercenary librarian had mutilated the book about forty years ago, by tearing out nearly a quarter of the volume for the sake of the parchment'.[11] In the Latin dedication (to James Norris, the president of his alma mater, Corpus Christi College, Oxford) he goes even further – condemning the *ignominiosus bibliothecarius* who with 'sacrilegious hand' excised 'every tenth leaf' *decimum quodque folium*.[12] From this account it would appear that the Arras manuscript must have suffered the depredations of the librarian around 1806 and that every tenth leaf, or a quarter of the whole, had been removed.[13]

We might note in passing the chequered career of the Library of Arras, an institution badly situated from a geopolitical point of view, apart from being prone to depredations from within. The municipal library was formed after the French Revolution, chiefly from the confiscated books and manuscripts of the Benedictine monastery of St Vedast (Vaast) and the cathedral chapter of Arras. In 1915 the library and most of its contents were destroyed by fire, with the exception of the manuscripts which had been removed for safekeeping. In the Second World War

---

[9] See ibid., pp. 370, 222; 584–5; 268. He was also much involved in the doings of both his immediate and extended family. The account of the death of his infant sons within a couple of weeks of each other from measles is affecting without being mawkish (pp. 157–9). While he was working on the Bosham editions in the 1840s a fourth son was born and christened Herbert. This auspicious name did not produce a clergyman or a medieval historian – rather, Herbert Allen Giles, after a distinguished career in the consular service in China, was to become Cambridge's second Professor of Chinese.

[10] *Diary and Memoirs*, ed. Bromwich, p. 245.

[11] *Herberti de Boseham*, ed. Giles, i, xii.

[12] *Epistola Dedicatoria*, ibid., pp. vi–vii.

[13] There seems to be some arithmetical confusion here, since every tenth leaf could never represent a quarter of the total. I shall return to this question.

the rebuilt and restocked library again suffered, first from occupation by British troops and then by the postal division of the German army, but principally in the general bombardment. Once again the manuscripts had been sent away, and so have more or less survived.

But now, another character in the story must be introduced. A man goes into a tailor's shop in Arras (or, in another version, Amiens, some 60 km distant, or, according to yet another version, into a book binder's) and observes the tailor about to cut out a pattern from some old vellum, of which he has an ample stock. Now the man, being something of a collector, knows that old vellum usually comes from old manuscripts. The collector offers the tailor a trifling sum of money and goes off with 'several pounds weight' of *disjecta membra*. It does not take the purchaser long to recognise (since he has earlier made a catalogue of the library of Arras) that this must be the origin of the leaves. The collector then offers to restore them to the mayor and the library in exchange for what he paid for them. He continues in a letter to Giles:

> 'They refused!!!! & in disgust I kept them.' But here's the rub: he goes on to say: 'the greater part being Theological, I left on the Continent & sent them to an Inn but whether they ever reached their destination I never heard. The leaves of Herbert being English History I brought home.'[14]

The collector was, of course, Sir Thomas Phillipps, who managed to buy up huge quantities of medieval manuscripts when they were coming onto the Continental market in the first decades of the nineteenth century.

The information about his finding the leaves comes in Phillipps' letter to J. A. Giles dated 26 March 1846. Giles had earlier sent a copy of his work on Herbert to Phillipps without suspecting that the latter had in his possession some of the missing Arras leaves. Giles apparently then expressed keen interest in seeing them. But in a letter written several months later Phillipps says he is still looking for the leaves among his very large and chaotically disordered collection. At the same time he informed Giles that he also possessed another version of Herbert of Bosham's *Vita S. Thomae*, 'a fine MS, & I think of the 12th century. It came from the Abbey of Alna [Aulne].'[15]

Around this time Giles was invited to visit Phillipps at his home in Middle Hill, a visit he later described in his *Diary and Memoirs*: 'On arriving at the mansion I had some difficulty in finding the door, as it seemed to be a window, and was partly blocked up by books, of which nearly every room in the house was full …' Giles stayed for a week in this eccentric household, and reports: 'we lived entirely in the breakfast room: the dining and drawing rooms were full of books and the floors were wholly covered'. They looked together at Phillipps' copy of Herbert of Bosham, which turned out to be an abbreviated text of the *Vita*. Phillipps also enlarged on the story of his discovery of the missing leaves (which, unfortunately, were still missing somewhere in his house).[16]

---

[14] *Diary and Memoirs*, ed. Bromwich, p. 254.

[15] Ibid., p. 255. Letter dated 4 June 1846.

[16] Ibid., p. 256.

According to the story Phillipps told on that occasion, 'he was at Arras when that dishonest librarian cut the leaves out that he might sell them for the value of the vellum and the very next day he went into the tailor's shop where he saw the tailor preparing to cut them up ...' – and from here the story follows more or less as before. Giles notes that this does not tally as to dates or place or motive with what he had been told in the earlier letter, and subsequent history bears him out.

We now know that Phillipps never did manage to locate the leaves at Middle Hill, but in a 1920 article in the *English Historical Review* Theodore Craib gave some idea of their content and a more likely date for when Phillipps first happened upon them. He pointed out that in the Public Record Office there are two letters, one dated 'Rouen 7 December 1828' and another 'Jan 1829', written by Phillipps to Henry Petrie, Keeper of the Records in the Tower, giving an account of his discovery.[17] Phillipps included 'a transcript of considerable portions of the leaves recovered', which Craib reproduced at length. This document goes some way to filling in some of the gaps in the Arras manuscript, but unfortunately not all the gaps, and particularly not the one that I was most interested in.

Several questions are raised by the account so far. First, how many leaves did Phillipps retain of those he got from the tailor (or the bookbinder) and how many were sent off to the inn (whatever that might mean) and subsequently lost? Further, how much of those he retained (that is, the more narrowly historical leaves) did he transcribe for Petrie? These questions remained unanswered, and indeed unanswerable, for close on sixty years. Although what I have recounted so far can be reconstructed by any interested person from the public record, this has not always been the case. Happenstance has played a part in the story at several points. Apart from Phillipps happening on the leaves, it was only by chance that Giles happened to find out about them (after he sent a copy of his work to Phillipps). The same lucky chance led to his learning of the existence of the manuscript from Aulne which was also later used by Robertson. This manuscript, Phillipps MS 4662, also sank from view within the Phillipps library after Giles and Robertson had seen it, only resurfacing again in 1969 when sold to the Bibliothèque Royale in Brussels, where it joined other manuscripts from Aulne as MS IV 600.

Chance also played a part in my investigation of the history of the leaves, since their post-1920 traces in the public domain are few and enigmatic. An image of one leaf appeared in a 1980 exhibition catalogue from the Bodleian Library, with the ascription 'Lent from a private collection'. However, since the publication is simply entitled *Manuscripts at Oxford: an exhibition in memory of Richard William Hunt ...* you would need to be a clairvoyant to divine its presence in the exhibition.[18]

---

[17] T. Craib, 'The Arras MS. of Herbert of Bosham', *EHR* 35 (1920), 218–24. The documents to which he refers are among the Petrie Papers: PRO 30/17/4 part 2. The letter dated 7 December 1828 unfortunately does not describe the finding of the leaves – consisting almost entirely of transcripts (some headed 'Henry of Boseham') – while the other pages of transcription bearing the date 1829 show no traces of having been sent through the post and were probably sent by the diplomatic bag from Paris as Phillipps proposed to do in the earlier letter.

[18] *Manuscripts at Oxford: an exhibition in memory of Richard William Hunt (1908–1979)*

It was also by a happy chance that at the Leeds Conference in 2007 I met a group of people interested in Herbert at a session convened by Michael Staunton, who has written the most recent book on Becket's biographers.[19] But in his book Michael gave little away, merely indicating in a footnote that the Herbert of Bosham text was mutilated, saying nothing specifically about the missing leaves. However, since he had mentioned the Arras manuscript I later e-mailed him to ask whether he agreed with my calculations about the missing leaves, that is, that there were considerably more missing from the place I was interested in than a single leaf. I also asked whether he had any more information about them. After confirming my suspicions as to the extent of the gaps in the text, he gave the name of someone who might be able to help me further. In fact, it turns out that within the last thirty years the Phillipps leaves had been in the possession of a person already known to me and many another medievalist. I refer of course to Dr Christopher de Hamel, whose long-standing connection with the Bosham manuscripts is the subject of chapter 9.

When I wrote to Christopher he told me that he had photocopies of the leaves in question and that he would send me copies when he had located them. Six months passed and they were not forthcoming. In an eerie repetition of the original case it seemed as if the photocopies of the missing leaves were also missing. When going through the final edit of my book which included the Herbert material I e-mailed Christopher once more to see if he had found them. The answer came as follows:

> Here's an odd thing. At this very moment, I am at Sotheby's. I have just opened up someone else's computer, as I need to tell a library in Australia that they have just successfully bought a manuscript this morning. Half an hour ago, looking nostalgically along the shelves of the office where I used to work, I found my Herbert of Bosham box. In it are photocopies of the leaves which were once mine.[20]

Soon afterwards I had eleven photocopied sheets of the missing leaves in my hands (one side of one of the leaves was still unaccounted for). I had hardly expected that they would supply the missing material in which I was interested, but it did prove that 'every tenth leaf' was not an accurate way of describing the excision, since at least four leaves must have been removed from this particular point in the text. Moreover, there remained a gap in the text that could not be filled in by the leaves themselves, by the extant abbreviated manuscripts or by Craib's transcription.

In addition to the six places from where the Phillipps leaves are taken, Robertson identified eight other places where leaves are missing, sometimes a single leaf and sometimes as many as four together. It is difficult to calculate the exact number of

---

Keeper of Western manuscripts at the Bodleian Library Oxford, 1945–1975, on the themes selected and described by some of his friends, ed. A. C. De la Mare and B. C. Barker-Benfield, Exhibition catalogue, Bodleian Library (Oxford, 1980), pp. 38–41. The leaf (p. 41) is Phillipps' fol. 6. (Phillipps had the leaves bound in a small booklet, back to front and in reverse order so the leaf is actually the first Phillipps leaf missing from original text.)

[19] M. Staunton, *Thomas Becket and his Biographers* (Woodbridge, 2006), p. 63.

[20] E-mail dated 11 July 2008.

missing leaves because the text that has been used as a substitute is itself randomly abbreviated, and also because sometimes passages from the *Quadrilogus* are included which are not found on the Arras leaves, so a one-to-one comparison of missing leaves with printed text cannot be made. My calculation would suggest that perhaps twenty leaves are missing from the *Vita* alone. Since we know that 167 leaves of the manuscript remain, if one tenth had been excised this would be around 18 leaves; on the other hand, if a quarter had been removed it would be more like 55. I am not sure how this question can be resolved, but if we allow for a similar rate of depredation for *Liber Melorum*, the second, higher figure might be more accurate. On the other hand, since all the extracts published by Craib from Phillipps' letters to Petrie are taken from these particular leaves I think Phillipps only ever brought back the six that we now know of.

Giles seemed to think that only five leaves were missing from the *Vita S. Thomae* (and in his edition actually left gaps which could be filled in if and when the leaves were rediscovered), but he did not commit himself as to gaps in the *Liber Melorum* (nor does Robertson, who prints only brief extracts in the *Materials*). Indeed, I think that Giles hardly used his transcription of the Arras MS for his edition, preferring the version he found in Corpus Christi College, Oxford, even though it was incomplete. Indeed nobody seemed to worry about the fact that the *Liber Melorum* was a shortened version, believing the original to be practically unreadable anyway.

Giles himself further confuses the matter by raising the spectre of a *Vita S. Thomae* and *Liber Melorum* at Corpus Christi College, Cambridge. In an entry for 1846 in the *Memoirs* he appears to make this claim when he writes: 'Received a letter from Dr Lamb Master of Corpus Christi College. In their library are contained several beautiful and valuable MSS. from one of which I copied the *Liber Melorum* and published it among the works of Herbert de Bosham its author.'[21] However, I believe that he must have been thinking of CCCC MS 123, which in fact he had used for the *Letters*. So it seems that if there were more leaves from the Arras manuscript at the binder's, quite a few leaves were either not recognised by Phillipps as being from the Arras manuscript, or they were consciously rejected by him as being too 'Theological' and left at the inn.

Several themes are worth pondering at this point. One concerns the divergent fates of manuscripts held in public or private hands. The Benedictines of St Vedast managed to keep the Arras manuscript safe for around 500 years, but it was inaccessible to scholars until they opened the library to savants in 1784. La Bibliothèque municipale of Arras has managed to preserve the manuscript (apart from the regrettable excisions) to this day. Presumably if I were to visit the library, or médiathèque as it is now called, I would be able to see it.[22]

---

[21] *Diary and Memoirs*, ed. Bromwich, p. 252. Dr Lamb was Master of Corpus Christi College Cambridge. See the entry for 8 June 1880, p. 576: 'Went to Cambridge … a fellow of Corpus … showed me the library of his college. I there again handled the MS. containing the Letters &c. of Herbert de Boseham, which I copied when I was the guest of Dr Lamb master of the college so many years ago.'

[22] I should add, however, that the Library failed to reply to my e-mail request for information about the manuscript in 2013.

The description of the manuscript in the printed catalogue of 1860 for MS 375, as it then was, does not refer to the missing leaves, although in the preface M. Caron, the librarian, writes (perhaps somewhat disingenuously): 'Nous devons dire, en terminant, que la plupart des manuscrits ont tellement souffert et du temps et des hommes, qu'il nous a été impossible de constater d'une manière certaine s'ils sont, ou non, complets.'[23] An interesting question arises here. In the heading to his letter to the mayor in 1829 Phillipps names the villainous librarian himself as Caron.[24] Presumably this is not the same person who made the catalogue in 1860. Could he have been some relative of the disgraced librarian? If so, the final lines of the preface have even more significance.[25] The present Combined Catalogue of French libraries (CCFr) entry for Arras BM/M 649 is also rather cagey about the missing leaves, stating simply that the manuscript has 167 leaves remaining (*subsistants*).[26] Perhaps I was undiplomatic in stating that my interest was in the missing leaves, rather than simply in the manuscript itself.

Be that as it may, Phillipps saved the leaves (or some of them), but they were inaccessible to scholars because they were lost in his library. More recent collectors have also ensured their continuing survival, but they were not generally accessible because not generally known about. The moral here is that while manuscripts and their parts can be subject to loss in the sense of being destroyed, they can also be lost to scholarship if there is no public and reliable way of locating them.

II

This brings me to my second theme. I had been working exclusively with volume III of Robertson's *Materials*, but in order to unravel the mystery of the missing leaves I thought I should look at the entire seven volumes in the series. When I managed to assemble the set (some were on the open shelves of the Barr Smith Library of the University of Adelaide and some in storage) I found that several of the volumes could be identified as Robertson's own copies. Moreover, there were letters tipped in to the front of volume I and volume IV and, more importantly, volume II had a collation of his base text of the *Miracles* with the Montpellier manuscript.[27]

Just when these books entered the University of Adelaide Barr Smith Library's collection is not clear – the acquisition record being patchy at best before the turn of the twentieth century – though the particular style of stamping in gold with the

---

[23] Z.-F.-C. Caron, *Catalogue des manuscrits de la bibliothèque de la ville d'Arras* (Arras, 1860). Some of the entries note that the manuscript is 'mutilé, incomplet', though not all. On p. 161 the entry for MS 360, *Magister Sententiarum*, notes that it comprises '70 feuillets' – ignoring the fact that at the time it was known to be missing a further 89.

[24] See A. Munby, *Phillipps Studies* III (Cambridge, 1954), pp. 38–40.

[25] I think this unlikely, especially since Caron seems to have been quite a common name in the area.

[26] See http://ccfr.bnf.fr/portailccfr/servlet/ViewManager?menu=public_menu_view&record=eadcgm:EADC:D04010877&setCache=all_simple.PUBLIC_CATALOGUE_SIMPLE_MULTI&fromList=true (accessed 5 February 2018).

[27] Bibliothèque interuniversitaire de Montpellier, Section medicine, MS H2.

words BARR SMITH LIBRARY puts their acquisition before about 1916, when this initial bequest was exhausted.[28] That they were a gift from Robertson himself is unlikely, since the seventh volume bears a plate recording that it was presented to Mrs Robertson by the Master of the Rolls after the canon's death.

The Library Committee at the University of Adelaide (founded 1874) was on the look-out for a set of the Rolls Series as early as 1898. They appear somewhat strangely on a 'list of books obtained by Professor Lamb' for that year. This is strange, because Professor Horace Lamb was not only the inaugural Professor of Physics at Adelaide but had moved to Manchester in the 1880s. But for some time after his return to England he apparently acted as unofficial agent for the Library, which was keen to buy second-hand copies of more expensive works.[29] So I presume that Robertson's books came onto the second-hand market after Mrs Robertson's death in 1897 and were used by a bookseller to make up a composite set of the Rolls Series. There are several other volumes in the set which bear plates reading 'transmitted to James Craigie Robertson by the Master of the Rolls' (the Histories of Matthew Paris and Gervase of Canterbury), but there is also a volume sent by the Master of the Rolls to 'the Rev. C. Babington' in 1865.[30] Many of the volumes have no ascription or marks of ownership.

I communicated these facts to some interested members of the Bosham group, and also to the Barr Smith Library. My information was noted in the online catalogue and Robertson's *Materials* were promptly removed to Special Collections. Theoretically, someone hunting through antipodean holdings of the Rolls Series would then have been able to access this information online in the revised entry for *Materials* in the Barr Smith Library catalogue.

That, at least, is how things stood *c.* 2008 after I had first alerted the Library to my find, but it seems now that this information, briefly available, may itself have gone the way of the lost leaves (though here it has become lost in a much more modern way). The Barr Smith Library has adopted a new internet-type of search engine which combines its real and virtual holdings – like Discovery at the British National Archives or Trove at the Australian National Library. The old online catalogue is about to be retired and will no longer be available for consultation (here it differs from the old card catalogue, which maintains a kind of afterlife in a distant corridor). Now, a search for James Craigie Robertson will reveal, under the entry for the *Materials*, that the books were the editor's own copies. But the information about the annotations, letters and other inclusions has disappeared.[31]

---

[28] I should like to thank Cheryl Hoskin, Rare Books Librarian, and Margaret Hosking, Subject Librarian for History, for sharing their knowledge of the early days and policies of the Barr Smith Library with me.

[29] University of Adelaide Library Archives 4/52/1 (1893–98), p. 28.

[30] This was Churchill Babington (1821–89), who edited Peacock's *Repressor* and two volumes of Higden's *Polychronicon*.

[31] A check of the catalogue in May 2018 reveals that the missing information about authorial annotations, signatures and letters has now reappeared in the entry under 'Public notes'.

Thus the vagaries of bibliographic control can lead to the disappearance and reappearance (and disappearance) of materials even when they still exist somewhere in physical form. Giles himself gave an early example of the problem when he described in the preface to his edition of the *Vita S. Thomae* how he had heard of the presence of a Bosham MS in his own college (Corpus Christi, Oxford), but was unable to locate it until the manuscripts were actually catalogued by Coxe of the Bodleian Library,[32] fortunately, in time to be used for the publication of his *Vita*. This is the copy lacking the first three books and with part of *Liber Melorum* missing at the end. When the Phillipps MS from Aulne resurfaced (after Giles' initial publication), he used it to fill in some of the gaps in the first three books, though he published the additions somewhat obscurely in his *Anecdota Bedae, Lanfranci, et aliorum*, in 1851.[33]

So, if nothing else, this brief account of my quest to fill in a gap in Herbert of Bosham's *Vita S. Thomae* might lead us to hope that more of the missing leaves could still be extant somewhere but have yet to be identified and described. In short, they are, perhaps: Not gone but sleeping.

III

That was how I ended my presentation in April 2013. Since then there have been two further notable developments. The first concerns the possible survival of more missing leaves from Arras, and particularly from MS 649. The second concerns the final whereabouts of the six leaves recovered by Phillipps.

According to Phillipps, when the Mairie of Arras failed to take up his offer to buy back the large stash of leaves he found in Amiens, he took a selection but 'left the greatest part, being Theological ... on the Continent & sent them to an Inn'.[34] In the absence of further information about the fate of the latter it seemed possible that they still existed somewhere. Yet it was also rumoured that the leaves Phillipps had bought and then abandoned were rediscovered in the nineteenth century, returned to Arras and subsequently destroyed in the bombing of the palace of St Vaast in 1915.

---

[32] From the dedication to Norris, *Herberti Opera*, ed. Giles, i, vi: 'Nam in bibiotheca fraternitatis vestrae, immo nostrae, superest adhuc codex qui aureum hoc opus, tribus tantum libris prioribus exceptis continet. De quo suspicio quidem mihi olim inciderat; sed quia codices qui in collegio nostro servantur, ex confusione tanta laborabant, ut libri qui quaerentur vix ulla diligentia inveniri possent, istum codicem nunquam videram, nec si vidissem, faciliter recognovissem, quia nullius auctoris nomen prae se fert, nec initium quidem mutilus et imperfectus habet.' ['For in the library of your, or rather, our, fraternity there is a manuscript which contains this golden work, with the exception of the first three books. I had long suspected this but since the surviving college manuscripts were in such confusion that books which were sought could scarcely be found by greatest diligence, I never saw it, and had I seen it, I could not have easily recognised it since it was prefaced by no author's name, the beginning being mutilated and imperfect.']

[33] *Anecdota Bedae, Lanfranci, et aliorum: Inedited tracts, letters, poems, &c. of Venerable Bede, Lanfranc, Tatwin and others*, ed. J.A. Giles, Caxton Society Publications (London, 1851), pp. 97–113.

[34] *Diary and Memoirs*, ed. Bromwich, p. 254.

This would appear to rule out the possibility of the continuing existence of additional leaves from MS 649 if they had been among those Phillipps originally recovered.

However, further information on the subject is to be found in a slim volume held by the Bibliothèque nationale[35] which adds yet another twist to the story of the leaves and continues the theme of serendipitous discovery. In July 1884, when Henri Loriquet, archivist for the Département du Pas-de-Calais, was conducting an inspection of the archives in the Bibliothèque de Calais, he was surprised to find 'dans un coin de rayon, deux forts paquets de parchemins, encore ficelés, déposés là depuis longtemps, contenant plusieurs centaines de feuillets dépareillés'.[36]

Having had occasion to consult the *Catalogue* from Arras compiled by Jules Quicherat in 1841 he was already acquainted with the sorry tale of the depredations practised on the manuscripts and immediately suspected that he had found some of the missing leaves.[37] He checked, as far as he could, the accounts of the theft given in Quicherat and found independent confirmation of the crimes of the first Caron in the Arras archives.[38] Here we discover that not only did Caron steal parchment but also 'prend pour son chauffage les ais de bois qui recouvrent ceux-ci, porte aux sculpteurs les marbres et les statues, paye sa pension avec les orfévreries des manuscrits et des vases du culte'.[39] Quicherat had already suggested that after failing to resell the stolen leaves to the authorities at Arras Phillipps sold or gave them to a M. Dufaitel. Loriquet writes: 'sir Phillips [*sic*] fut heureux de se débarrasser de la portion qui nous intéresse entre les mains d'un autre collectionneur, M. Dufaitel, de Calais, qui à son tour, l'ayant offerte sans succès à l'ancienne propriétaire pour la modique somme de 80 fr., se décida à la garder'.[40]

Loriquet believed that they came into the library at Calais when Dufaitel's collections were sold after his death in 1858. The library at Calais seems to have been unaware of the value of what it had received and soon forgot about them, as Loriquet explains 'car tels ils étaient ficelés lors leur arrivée, tels j'ai retrouvé ces

---

[35] H. Loriquet, *Rapport présenté à M. le Ministre de l'Instruction publique sur l'identification de fragments de manuscrits trouvés à Calais, en 1884, suivi d'un tableau des déprédations commises en 1816 sur les manuscrits de la bibliothèque d'Arras* (Arras, 1886).

[36] Ibid., p. I ['in a corner of a shelf, two stout bundles of parchment, still tied up, placed there long ago, containing many hundreds of separate leaves'].

[37] See *Catalogue général des manuscrits des bibliothèques publiques des départements publié sous les auspices du ministre de l'instruction publique. IV: Arras – Avranches –Boulogne* (Paris, 1849–85). The tale of the mismanagement of the library that he gives in his foreword – though he does not indicate the extent of individual losses in the description of the manuscripts – may have prompted the Mairie to produce its own catalogue in 1860.

[38] He gives the reference as: 'Dossier coté 34; *Bibliothèque, affaire Caron*. – Enquêtes du commissaire de police des 7, 9, 14 décembre 1816'. *Rapport*, p. 3.

[39] Loriquet, *Rapport*, pp. 3–4: 'took the wooden boards which had covered them for his fire, the marble and statues to the sculptors, paid for his lodgings with the precious embellishments of the books and religious vessels'.

[40] Ibid., p. 10: 'sir Phillips was pleased to get rid of the portion that interests us by passing them on to a fellow collector, M. Dufaitel of Calais, who in his turn, having offered them without success to the original owners for the moderate sum of 80 francs, decided to keep them'.

parchemins en 1884, blottis dans un fond de rayon, sous deux doigts de poussière, bien dissimulés derrière des monceaux d'archives inexplorées'.[41]

The rest of Loriquet's report details how he painstakingly sorted and collated the 1,370 leaves which the packages contained.[42] Eventually, with the aid of a list drawn up by the librarian Fauchison in 1826, 1830 and 1839 which lists what was missing from the various manuscripts (vital information ignored by Quicherat and the second Caron for their catalogues), Loriquet was able to assign the leaves which he had found at Calais to their original manuscripts.[43] Moreover he was able to report that 'la supplique de la ville d'Arras ont trouvé dans l'administration municipale de Calais une oreille éclairée et favorable, et, le 29 décembre dernier [i.e. 1885], la Bibliothèque d'Arras a pu rentrer en possession de la portion du vol demeurée en France'.[44]

There seems, however, to have been an unconscionable delay in reuniting the leaves with their parent manuscripts, so that thirty years later, although the manuscripts had been sent away for safekeeping, the recovered leaves had not, and perished in the burning of the library in 1915.[45] This sad circumstance led to the idea that any further missing leaves from Arras 469 had disappeared altogether. However, if we consult Loriquet's table we find for MS 375/649 that he lists 167 leaves as present in the manuscript and 43 as missing, but not one as having been rediscovered among the Calais collection. So, at least that means that they did not meet the fate of those that had been recovered.

The fact that more leaves from MS 649 were not found by Phillipps at Amiens is explicable if we consider Caron's modus operandi. Apparently he removed leaves from the same manuscript at different times over the space of a year and in differing quantities, and thus all the leaves missing from Arras 649 may not have been in the possession of the bookbinder when Phillipps was there in 1828.[46] Thus the pious hope with which I concluded my paper at the conference in 2013 need not be abandoned.

The second addition to the tale of the leaves recovered by Phillipps has an altogether more positive and assured outcome and can be briefly told. On Wednesday, 20 November 2013 they were offered at auction by Christie's and (with the encouragement of some of the friends of Herbert of Bosham) purchased by the Lambeth Palace Library. They have now found what we may hope is a permanent home in London. Their new public designation is Lambeth Palace Library MS 5048.

---

[41] Ibid., p.11: 'for I found the parchments in 1884, just as they had been tied up at the time of their arrival, huddled at the end of a shelf under two inches of dust, well hidden behind piles of untouched archives'.

[42] Ibid., pp. 11–17.

[43] Ibid., pp. 21–31.

[44] Ibid., p. III: 'the request of the town of Arras had found a willing and favourable ear in the municipality of Calais and on 29 December last [1884] the Library of Arras was able to take possession of the portion of the theft that remained in the country'.

[45] For an account see www.archivespasdecalais.fr/Activites-culturelles/ Un-document-a-l-honneur/Les-archives-en-guerre-la-Premiere-Guerre-mondiale.

[46] Loriquet, *Rapport*, p. 7.

CHAPTER NINE

Encounters with Herbert of Bosham

Christopher de Hamel

I am about to do something very unusual in this paper. Rather like the hero of this volume, Herbert of Bosham himself, who tells of Thomas Becket from the perspective of a reminiscent participant, I have been persuaded to relate a little about my own first encounters with Herbert of Bosham and his surviving manuscripts; and, if such an approach seems inappropriately personal and autobiographical in such a serious publication, let me assure you at the outset that this is a tale from which I emerge consistently badly, and in which I am shown to be incompetent as well as foolish, not merely once but multiple times.

The story goes back to my arrival in Oxford as a graduate student in 1972, and my first meeting with my appointed thesis supervisor, Richard Hunt (1908–79), then Keeper of Western Manuscripts in the Bodleian Library.[1] I had no real research topic in mind. He suggested, in his vague and diffident way, that maybe I might investigate the production of glossed books of the Bible, and he told me to look at MS Auct.E.inf.7, the huge glossed Pentateuch once owned by Thomas Becket, who brought it back to England shortly before his martyrdom in December 1170,[2] and at the very similar manuscript, adjacent to it on the Bodleian shelves, of the second volume of Herbert of Bosham's re-working of Peter Lombard's Great Gloss on the Psalms, Auct.E.inf.6. This had originally been intended for Becket himself but it was not finished by Herbert until after Becket's death.[3] I asked what I should be seeking. 'Oh, just look at them, and get to know them, and come and tell me about them', Dr Hunt said.

---

[1] For Hunt, see J. J. G. Alexander and M. T. Gibson, eds, *Medieval Learning and Literature, Essays presented to Richard William Hunt* (Oxford, 1976); A. C. de la Mare and B. C. Barker-Benfield, eds, *Manuscripts at Oxford, An Exhibition in Memory of Richard William Hunt (1908–1979), Keeper of Western Manuscripts at the Bodleian Library, Oxford, 1945–1975, An exhibition on themes selected and described by some of his friends* (Oxford, 1980); D. Vaisey, 'Hunt, Richard William (1908–1979)', *ODNB*.

[2] O. Pächt and J. J. G. Alexander, *Illuminated Manuscripts in the Bodleian Library, Oxford*, III (Oxford, 1973), no. 200; C. de Hamel, *Bibles, An Illustrated History from Papyrus to Print* (Oxford, 2011), no. 25.

[3] Pächt and Alexander, no. 201; W. Cahn, *Romanesque Manuscripts, The Twelfth Century*, 2 vols., A Survey of the Illuminated Manuscripts of France (London, 1996) ii, pp. 107–9, no. 88; for volume I of the set (Trinity College, Cambridge, MS B.5.4), but with reference to the Bodleian volume too, see *The Cambridge Illuminations, Ten Centuries of Book*

Thus it was that I came to spend many weeks in Selden End in the Bodleian, with Herbert's vast and intricate manuscript propped open in front of me. It was one of the first twelfth-century books I had ever really looked at. It introduced me to Prior Eastry's early fourteenth-century library catalogue of Christ Church, Canterbury, which listed the Pentateuch among the books once owned by Becket and, over the page, Herbert of Bosham's edition of the Great Gloss on the Psalms as the second of five volumes given or left to the cathedral priory by Herbert himself.[4] The identifying code letters on the manuscripts' first leaves, used in the twelfth century in Canterbury to distinguish one copy of a text from another, were respectively 'to', for 'thomas', and 'BOS', both abbreviated from their donors' names. The intimacy of this was very moving. Herbert of Bosham's manuscript had not attracted much attention in the 350 years it had been in Oxford. Its illumination is extensive but restless and tinselly, and was not to the taste of modern manuscript historians. The first reference to the manuscript in print appears to be J. A. Giles in 1846, who dismisses it as being without 'the slightest particle of interest' and he recommends that it 'may still be allowed to slumber in the Bodleian library, where it is found'.[5] I probably disturbed its sleep in the early 1970s more than anyone had done since the twelfth century, and I rather warmed to Herbert. His life of Becket was described even by his apologist in the *Dictionary of National Biography* in 1891 as 'rambling, long-winded ... prosy, sermonising, and turgid';[6] and an author like Herbert, who

Production in the Medieval West, ed. P. Binski and S. Panayotova (London and Turnhout, 2005), pp. 92–4, no. 26; S. Panayotova, 'Tutorial in Images for Thomas Becket', in *The Cambridge Illuminations, The Conference Papers*, ed. S. Panayotova (London, 2007), pp. 76–86; and *A Catalogue of Western Book Illumination in the Fitzwilliam Museum and the Cambridge Colleges*, III, *France*, ii, *c. 1000–c. 1250*, ed. D. Jackson, N. Morgan and S. Panayotova (London and Turnhout, 2015), pp. 103–8, no. 32.

[4] The glossed Pentateuch is no. 784 [modern numbering] among seventy-one volumes given by Becket and part ii of the Great Gloss on the Psalter is no. 855 among five volumes given by Herbert. See M. R. James, *The Ancient Libraries of Canterbury and Dover* (Cambridge, 1903), pp. 82–5; N. R. Ker, *Medieval Libraries of Great Britain, A List of Surviving Books*, 2nd ed. (London, 1964), pp. 37–8. The companion volumes of Herbert of Bosham's manuscripts of the Great Gloss on the Pauline Epistles are now Trinity College, Cambridge, MSS B.5.6–7. See Jackson, Morgan and Panayotova, *Catalogue*, pp. 109–17, nos. 33–4. These and several other books from Becket's bequest were transferred to Trinity College by Thomas Nevil, Master of Trinity 1593–1615 and dean of Canterbury from 1597. Herbert's volume was given in the Bodleian was given in 1616 by the family of Richard Colfe, prebendary of Canterbury 1581–1613. See N. Ramsay, 'The Cathedral Archives and Library', in *A History of Canterbury Cathedral*, ed. P. Collinson, N. Ramsay and M. Sparks (Oxford, 1995), pp. 341–407, at 378; C. de Hamel, 'The Dispersal of the Library of Christ Church, Canterbury, from the Fourteenth to the Sixteenth Century', in *Books and Collectors, 1200–1700, Essays Presented to Andrew Watson*, ed. J. P. Carley and C. G. C. Tite (London, 1997), pp. 263–79, at 273–4.

[5] *Herberti de Boseham, S. Thomae Cantuariensis clerici a secretis, Opera quae Extant Omnia*, ed. J. A. Giles, 2 vols. (Oxford, 1845–6), ii, p. vi. Sydney Cockerell, one of the first to comment on the illumination, described it as 'rather ungainly', *Exhibition of Illuminated Manuscripts: Burlington Fine Arts Club* (London, 1908), p. 11, no. 24.

[6] K. Norgate, 'Herbert of Bosham (*fl.* 1162–1186)', *Dictionary of National Biography*, ed. S. Lee, 26 (London, 1891), p. 169.

never entirely finished tinkering with an excessively long text, is a patron saint to any struggling doctoral candidate. My interest in Herbert of Bosham – increasingly an obsession – brought me into relationship with Beryl Smalley (1905–84), who was then working on her book *The Becket Conflict and the Schools*, published in 1973, in which chapter 3 is on Herbert of Bosham.[7] She certainly has a place in the rehabilitation of Herbert's memory. Beryl Smalley was a tiny, terrifying, bird-like woman, given to sudden silences in conversation, which you found yourself filling with inanities, revealing nothing but your own ignorance. She would invite you back for lunch in her little top-floor flat in Rawlinson Road, where you were never given enough to eat. We talked about Herbert of Bosham endlessly. Beryl Smalley was eventually, with Neil Ker, one of the two examiners of my thesis, which had a central chapter on those glossed manuscripts made for Thomas Becket and his closest friend Herbert.[8] All that seems long ago now.

In the meantime, I had joined Sotheby's, and for the first time I had a modest income. I suppose I have always had a little of the collector's instinct. In the summer of 1976 Maggs Brothers, booksellers then in Berkeley Square, issued a catalogue which included a number of manuscript fragments, most of which were English. One of these, which was illustrated in the catalogue, was a bifolium from a twelfth-century glossed Gospel of Saint John, priced at £75.[9] After agonising for days over the self-indulgence, I decided that I would celebrate my thesis by buying it, and I went round to Maggs to discover that it was already sold. Instead, they showed me the previous item in the same catalogue, a large late twelfth-century parchment leaf described as a 'Latin work on church history' at the even more expensive price of £120.[10] However, unnoticed by them, it had on one side those distinctive marginal marks which are characteristic of manuscripts once in the medieval library of Christ Church cathedral priory in Canterbury. Between the columns are clusters of four dots joined by vertical rows of further dots, sometimes found in conjunction with a symbol resembling a sideways ice-cream cone. These marks are fifteenth-century (the latest datable example I have found is 1446), and they are entirely unique to Canterbury.[11] For that reason alone, then, I agreed to buy the substitute

---

[7] Smalley, *Becket Conflict*, p. 59–86. For Miss Smalley herself, see H. Leyser and D. C. Klepper, 'Beryl Smalley (1905–1984), The Medieval Bible in the Modern Academy', in *Women Medievalists and the Academy*, ed. J. Chance (Madison, 2005), pp. 657–69, and G. H. Martin, 'Beryl Smalley (1905–1984)', *ODNB*.

[8] The thesis was published as *Glossed Books of the Bible and the Origins of the Paris Booktrade* (Cambridge and Dover, N. H., 1984), with chapter 4 on the manuscripts of Becket and Herbert of Bosham, pp. 38–54.

[9] Maggs, *Ancient, Medieval and Modern*, 14 (catalogue 973), June 1976, no. 158.

[10] No. 157. Clifford Maggs told me that many of the English leaves in that catalogue had been from a group bought at auction some fifteen or twenty years earlier, and I wonder whether they were from Sotheby's, 15 June 1959, lot 130, a collection of whole or partial leaves 'formed to illustrate the development of handwriting'. Many years later I finally acquired another bifolium from that glossed Saint John, lost in 1976, but at almost ten times the price.

[11] N. R. Ker, 'Membra Disiecta', *British Museum Quarterly* 14 (1940), 79–86, at 85; the latest

leaf as my consolation for losing the glossed Saint John, even though it was not my first choice and was almost twice the price. It is a handsome enough specimen of book production, 373 mm by 255 mm, written in two columns of 33 lines, written-space 270 mm by 179 mm, with two small decorated initials (Figs. 9.1, 9.2). Its text concerns theophany, an inward spiritual experience which the author describes but admits that, to his regret, he himself has never actually experienced, living, as he does, not in the higher spheres of angels, but in a humble mud hut, 'infelix ego, luteam domum inhabitans'. It pleased me to own such a modest confession from a theologian, especially as it had once been in the cloister of Canterbury Cathedral priory, and I propped it up behind my desk and did no more.

Some eighteen months later, sitting in the theology section of the Lower Reading Room of the Bodleian, I had what is probably the nearest I have ever come to an experience of theophany. I was flipping idly through the *Patrologia* reprint of Giles' edition of Herbert of Bosham when, in a heart-stopping moment of incredulity, I realised that I was reading the very text of my manuscript leaf, which is from part of Book III of his *Liber melorum*.[12] This text, as all readers of this volume will know, forms the text found at the end of Herbert of Bosham's life of Thomas Becket.

The fact that the manuscript must have been at Christ Church, Canterbury, led, in turn, to a small discovery, or at least to a realisation which had not then been made before. The five volumes which Herbert gave or bequeathed to Christ Church were listed in the Eastry catalogue as the pairs of manuscripts of the Great Gloss on the Psalms and Epistles, together with an enigmatic fifth item, no. 858, listed simply as 'Thomus'. Those who had commented on this entry, including Rosy Schilling and Beryl Smalley, supposed that a '*tomus*' simply meant an unspecified and unidentified 'volume', and it had been suggested that this might even have been the stylistically related manuscript of Gratian, now in the J. Paul Getty Museum.[13] In reality, 'Thomus' simply means 'Thomas'. The only other '*Thomus*' in Eastry's catalogue is no. 979 there, a '*Thomus*' containing two further works on Becket, which is quite possibly identifiable with Corpus Christi College, Oxford, MS 146, a late thirteenth-century manuscript of Herbert of Bosham's biography of Becket with a Canterbury

---

examples I have seen are in the *Summa* of Alexander of Hales copied for Christ Church between 1446 and 1449 (Trinity College, Cambridge, MS B.16.1).

[12] *PL*, 190.1368, line 24, to 1370, line 14, reprinting Giles, *Herberti de Boseham*, pp. 125–8. The *Liber melorum*, or 'Book of melodies', has never been fully studied but was the subject of a Harvard PhD dissertation by Jessica Weiss, 'Herbert of Bosham's *Liber Melorum*: Literature and Sacred Sciences in the Twelfth Century' (2003).

[13] James, *Ancient Libraries*, p. 85. R. Schilling, 'The *Decretum Gratiani* formerly in the Dyson Perrins Collection', *Journal of the British Archaeological Association* 3rd ser., 26 (1963), 27–39, cited in Smalley, *Becket Conflict*, p. 83, n.93. The Gratian manuscript, which has no imaginable association with the library at Canterbury, is now Los Angeles, J. Paul Getty Museum, MS XIV.2. See A. von Euw and J. M. Plotzek, *Die Handschriften der Sammlung Ludwig*, 4 (Cologne, 1985), pp. 41–8. It is still being associated with the Becket entourage on extremely dubious evidence: see L. Löfstedt, 'Traces of Saint Thomas Becket in the Getty Gratian (J. Paul Getty Museum Ms Ludwig XIV 2)', *Getty Research Journal* 7 (2015), 151–6; I am grateful to Elizabeth Morrison for a copy.

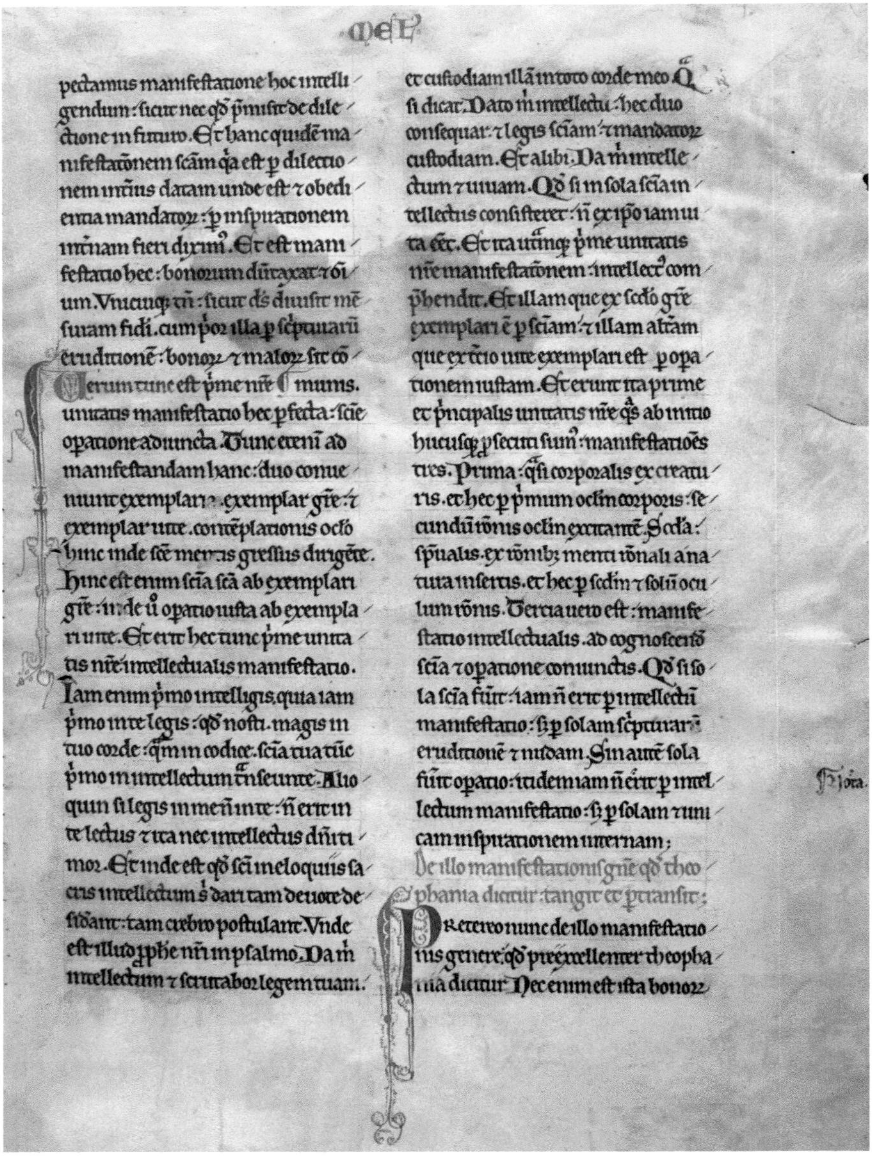

pectamus manifestatione hoc intelli
gendum: sicut nec qd pmisit de dile
ctione in finitum. Et hanc quidem ma
nifestationem scam qa est p dilectio
nem intus datam unde est r obedi
entia mandator: p inspirationem
internam fieri diximi. Et est mani
festatio hec: bonorum duntaxat rei
um. Vnicunq tn: sicut ds diuisit me
suram fidi. cum por illa p scptuari
erudicione: bonor r malor sic co
Uerum tunc est pme nre munis.
unitatis manifestatio hec pfecta: scie
operatione adiuncta. Tunc etени ad
manifestandam hanc: duo conue
niunt exemplari exemplar gre r
exemplar uite. cotemplationis octo
hinc inde sce menus gressus dirigete.
Hinc est enim scia sca ab exemplari
gre: unde u operatio iusta ab exempla
ri uite. Et erit hec tunc pme unita
tis nre intellectualis manifestatio.
Iam enim pmo intelligis. quia iam
pmo inre legis: qd nosti. magis in
tuo corde: qm in codice. scia tua tuc
pmo in intellectum inseunt. Alio
quin si legis in mente inte: si erit in
te lectus r ita nec intellectus disiti
mor. Et inde est qd scī in eloquiis sa
cris intellectum s dari tam deuote de
sidant: tam crebro postulant. Vnde
est illud phe nrm in psalmo. Da m
intellectum r scrutabor legem tuam.

et custodiam illam in toto corde meo Q̄
si dicat. Dato in intellectu hec duo
consequar: r legis sciam r mandator
custodiam. Et alibi. Da m intelle
ctum r uiuam. Qd si in sola scia in
tellectus consisteret: ii ex ipo iam ui
ta eet. Et ita utinq pme unitatis
nre manifestatonem intellecr com
phendit. Et illam que ex seclo gre
exemplari e p sciam: r illam atiam
que ex tcio uite exemplari est popa
tionem iustam. Et erunt ita prime
et pncipalis unitatis nre qs ab initio
hucusq p secm sum manifestatioes
tres. Prima: qsi corporalis ex creatu
ris. et hec p pmum octin corporis: se
cundu tonis octin extranee. Scda:
spualis. ex tonibz menti tonali ana
tuta insertis. et hec p sedm r solii ocu
lum tonis. Tercia uero est: manife
statio intellectualis. ad cognoscendo
scia r operatione coniunctis. Qd si so
la scia fuit: iam n erit p intellectu
manifestatio: sip solam scptuari
erudicione r nudam. Sin aute sola
fuit operatio: tradem iam ii erit p intel
lectum manifestatio: sip solam r uni
cam inspirationem internam:
De illo manifestationis gne qd theo
phania dicitur: tangit et ptransit:
Preterio nunc de illo manifestatio
nis genere: qd preexcellenter theopha
nia dicitur. Nec enim est ista bonor

Fig. 9.1 The recto of the leaf of the former Canterbury copy of the *Liber melorum*, with two decorated initials.

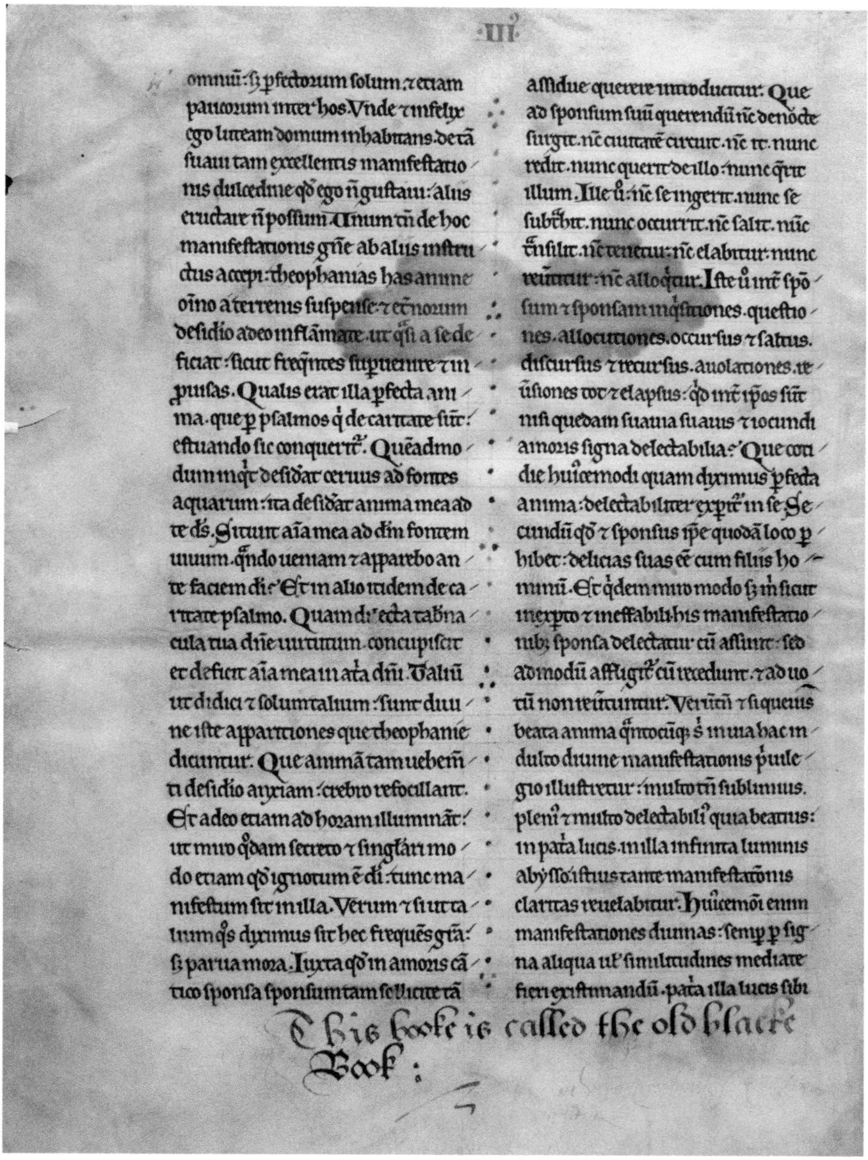

omnıũ: ſ; pfectoɽũ ſolũ. ɿ eciam
paucoɽũ ınter hos Vñde ɿ ınfelıx
ego lıtteam domũ ınhabıtans. de tã
ſuauı tam excellentıſ manıfeſtacıo
nıſ dulcedıne qɖ ego ñ guſtauı: alııſ
eructare ñ poſſım Vnũ tñ de hoc
manıfeſtacıonıſ gñe ab alııſ ınſtru
ctus accepı: theophanıas has auıue
oıno a terrenıſ ſuſpenſe. ɿ eɽnoɽũ
deſıdıo adeo ınflãmate. ut qñ a ſe de
fıcıat: ſıcut frequtes ſupuenıre ɿ ın
puıſas. Qualıſ erat ılla pfecta anı
ma. que p pſalmos q̃ de carıtate ſũt:
eſtuando ſıc conquerıt̃. Qñ admo
dũ ınq̃r deſıdat cuıuus ad fontes
aquarũ: ıta deſıdat anıma mea ad
te dſ. Sıtıuıt aıa mea ad dñm fontem
uıuũ. q̃ndo uenıam ɿ apparebo an
te facıem dıe Eſt ın alıo tudem de ca
rıtate pſalmo. Quam dı ecta tabına
cula tua dñe uırtutũ. concupıſcıt
et defıcıt aıa mea ın ata dñı. Valıũ
ut dıdıcı ɿ ſolũ talıum: ſunt dıuı
ne ıſte apparıtıones que theophanıe
dıcuntur. Que anımã tam uehem
tı deſıdıo auxıam: crebro refocıllant.
Et adeo etıam ad horam ıllumınat:
ut mıro q̃dam ſecreto ɿ ſınguları mo
do etıam qɖ ıgnotum ẽ dı: tunc ma
nıfeſtum ſtr ın ılla. Verum ɿ ſı urta
tıũ q̃s dıxımus ſıt hec frequẽs gra:
ſ; parua mora. Iuxta qɖ ın amonſ cã
tıco ſponſa ſponſum tam ſollıcıte tã

aſſıdue querere ıntroducıtur: Que
ad ſponſum ſuũ querendũ rıc de nocte
ſurgıt. nc cuırate cırcuıt. ıſe tc. nunc
redıt. nunc querıt de ıllo. nunc q̃rıt
ıllum. Ille ũ. nıe ſe ıngerıt. nunc ſe
ſubtſıt. nunc occurrıt. ıc ſalıt. nıe
cñſılıt. ıc teneuat: ıc elabıtur: nunc
reuırtıt. ıc alloqtur. Iſte ũ ınt ſpõ
ſum ɿ ſponſam ınq̃ſtıones. queſtıo
nes. allocutıones. occurſus ɿ ſaltus.
dıſcurſus ɿ recurſus. auolatıones. re
uſıones tc ɿ elapſus: qɖ ınt ıpos ſũt
nıſı quedam ſuauıa ſuauıs ɿ ıocundı
amorıs ſıgna delectabılıa: Que con
dıe huıcemodı quam dıxımus pfecta
anıma: delectabılıter exprı ın ſe Se
cundũ qɖ ɿ ſponſus ıpe quodã loco p
hıbet: delıcıas ſuas eſ cum filııs ho
mınũ. Et q̃dem mıro modo ſ; ın ſtar
ınexpto ɿ ıneffabılıbıs manıfeſtatıo
nıb; ſponſa delectatur cũ aſſunt: ſed
admodũ afflıgıt cũ recedunt. ɿ ad uo
tũ non reuırtuntur. Verum ɿ ſı quemſ
beata anıma q̃ntocũq; ſ ın uıa hac ın
dulto dıuıne manıfeſtatıonıſ pulc̃
gıo ılluſtretur: multo tñ ſublımıus.
plenıũ ɿ multo delectabılı quıa beatıus:
ın pata lucıs. ın ılla ınfinıta lumınıs
abyſſo: ıſtıus tante manıfeſtatıonıs
clarıtas reuelabıtur. Huıcemõı enım
manıfeſtatıones dıuınas: ſemp p ſıg
na alıqua ut ſımılıtudıneſ medıate
fıerı exıſtımandũ. pata ılla lucıs ſıbı

This booke is called the old blacke
Book:

Fig. 9.2 The verso of the leaf of the former Canterbury copy of the *Liber melorum*, showing the Christ Church markings between the columns and the added title of 'the old blacke Book' into which the leaf was bound.

provenance at the Reformation.[14] It is the only substantially intact English manuscript of the text. Confirmation of '*Thomus*' as the text's original medieval title comes from Corpus Christi College, Cambridge, MS 298, the unique copy of Laurence Wade's Middle English verse translation of Herbert's life of Becket, made in Christ Church in 1497.[15] Its opening heading states that it was '*translatyd in to our vulgar tonge owt off a boke callyd Thomys*', and a few lines later it names '*Master herbert Bosham, auctor off the forsayd boke off Thomys*' (folio 1v). 'Thomus', in short, is a pun, the volume on Thomas, divided as it is into seven *tomi*, seven books and seven different Thomases. There is also the wonderful arrogance of Herbert in naming his work 'the volume', on a par with the '*codex*', which meant the only necessary text of Roman law, and '*biblia*', 'the books', which can only refer to the scriptures.

With only two copies of '*Thomus*' recorded in the medieval Canterbury catalogue – one given by the author, the other late thirteenth century – there is no reasonable doubt that my purchase from Maggs, which probably dates from the later 1180s and was certainly at Canterbury, is a relic from the former, Herbert's own lost dedication copy, Eastry no. 858.[16] Like the glossed books which Herbert also gave, it was clearly a luxury manuscript, and, so far as I am competent to make that judgement, I believe it to be copied by the same scribe.

Let us go back a step. The reason why I was initially employed by Sotheby's was to help Anthony Hobson with the sale descriptions of the residue of the great manuscript collection of Sir Thomas Phillipps (1792–1872). Auctions of selections from this unmanageably vast hoard of some 60,000 manuscripts began in August

[14] James, *Ancient Libraries*, p. 95, 'Thomus, *In hoc vol. cont.* Omelia in festo Sancti Thome. Item cause exilii beati Thome'. For Corpus MS 146, see R. M. Thomson, *A Descriptive Catalogue of the Medieval Manuscripts of Corpus Christi College, Oxford, Western Manuscripts* (Cambridge, 2011), p. 74, 'presumably from Canterbury'. It lacks leaves at each end. It was bequeathed to Corpus Christi College in 1644 by Brian Twyne, grandson of John Twyne (*c.* 1505–81), the Canterbury collector and antiquary. It contains a note by J. A. Giles dated 1845 and it was used by him for his edition.

[15] M. R. James, *A Descriptive Catalogue of the Manuscripts in the Library of Corpus Christi College, Cambridge*, 2 vols. (Cambridge, 1912), ii, p. 80; W. A. Ringler, Jr, with M. Rudick and S. J. Ringler, *Bibliography and Index of English Verse in Manuscript, 1501–1558* (London and New York, 1992), p. 182, no. TM 1258. The manuscript later belonged to Thomas Cranmer, a touching association between Herbert of Bosham and the two archiepiscopal martyrs of Canterbury called Thomas.

[16] It is identified with Eastry 858 in A. G. Watson, *Medieval Libraries of Great Britain, A List of Surviving Books ... Supplement to the Second Edition* (London, 1987), p. 11, and R. Sharpe, *A Handlist of Latin Writers of Great Britain and Ireland before 1540*, Publications of the Journal of Medieval Latin, i (Turnhout, 1997), p. 177. Eastry's entry shows that the overall title *Thomus* was taken to include the *Liber melorum*. The manuscripts of the Great Gloss were dedicated to William of the White Hands (d. 1202) as archbishop of Sens 1169–76, but they were evidently retained by Herbert and never presented. Similarly, *Thomus* was dedicated to Baldwin, archbishop 1184–90, but the manuscript was listed as Herbert's property, not as that of Baldwin (as in James, *Ancient Libraries*, p. 28). Herbert was still working on the text until at least August 1186 (*MTB*, iii, xxii), and it is not apparent whether he gave the five books in his lifetime or bequeathed them to Christ Church after his death around 1194, some four years later than that of the named dedicatee.

1886 and sales continued unrelentingly for almost a hundred years. The name of Phillipps, of course, has a certain resonance in Herbert of Bosham studies because of his acquisition of the famous missing leaves from the Arras manuscript of Herbert's life of Becket, which are the subject of the article here by Sabina Flanagan.[17] Herbert of Bosham's text as published still has gaps where the manuscript in Arras had been mutilated. Giles wrote in 1846 that 'the most unlucky part of this story is that Sir Thomas Phillipps has since mislaid these leaves, and as yet is unable to discover in which part of his immense library they have been misplaced'; Robertson added in 1877 that the lost fragments had never been located by Phillipps' heirs.[18] That remained largely true until the early months of 1978, when the last boxes of a couple of dozen remaining medieval manuscripts from the Phillipps library were unloaded onto my desk in Sotheby's in Bond Street, for what was planned to be the final auction from the collection. As you will anticipate, I had another of those unforgettable moments in opening a fascicule in salmon-coloured paper boards to reveal a clutch of loosely stitched twelfth-century leaves with the contemporary title '*Thomus*' in red capitals along the upper margins. After tens of thousands of Phillipps dispersals, that cornucopia of manuscripts had at the last moment eventually disgorged the long-lost leaves from the Arras manuscript of Herbert of Bosham, and I was lucky enough to be at that time practically the only person in the world who might have recognised them. I claim no rights of discovery: they were simply placed on my desk. Before the catalogue went to press, that residue of the Phillipps library was unexpectedly sold instead *en bloc* to the New York bookseller, H. P. Kraus. The Sotheby's auction was cancelled, and I had the sad experience of seeing the Arras leaves packed up for export.[19] I did, however, keep my notes and I wrote immediately to Mr Kraus, asking whether he would ever consider selling the pieces to me personally. A friendly deal was eventually struck, the leaves were sent back to England, and I took possession of the second of the only two fragments of

---

[17] Above, pp. 156–67.

[18] Giles, *Herberti de Boseham*, p. xiv; *MTB*, iii, xxvii. The leaves had been part of the manuscript now Arras, Bibliothèque municipale, ms 375; partial transcripts made by Phillipps in 1828–29 were printed by T. Craib, 'The Arras MS of Herbert of Bosham', *EHR* 35 (1920), 218–24. For the circumstances of the mutilation by the librarian of Arras around 1816, in addition to Flanagan, see D. Bromwich, ed., *The Diary and Memoirs of John Allen Giles*, Somerset Record Society, 86 (Taunton, 2000), p. 255. Other fragments cut from manuscripts in Arras acquired by Phillipps include his MS 24510 (Kraus, catalogue 153, 1979, no. 1, now New Haven, Yale University, Beinecke Library, Takamiya MS 58); Phillipps MS 22229, cut from Arras ms 1079 (now Bloomington, Indiana University, Poole 82; C. de Hamel, *Gilding the Lily, A Hundred Medieval and Illuminated Manuscripts in the Lilly Library* [Bloomington, 2010], p. 22, no. 8, and cf. pp. 10–11, no. 2); and, although imperfectly noticed by its cataloguer, Phillipps MS 21625, cut from Arras ms 1043 (Bloomsbury Auctions, 8 July 2015, lot 29, to Pirages). The Herbert of Bosham leaves had been seen and cited by A. N. L. Munby, *The Formation of the Phillipps Library up to the Year 1840*, Phillipps Studies, 3 (Cambridge, 1954), p. 40.

[19] H. P. Kraus, *A Rare Book Saga, The Autobiography of H. P. Kraus* (London and New York, 1979), p. 228; A. R. A. Hobson, 'The Phillipps Sales', in *Out of Print & into Profit, A History of the Rare and Secondhand Book Trade in Britain in the 20th Century*, ed. G. Mandelbrote (London and Newcastle, DE, 2006), pp. 157–64, esp. p. 163.

Herbert of Bosham then known to have changed hands since the Middle Ages. That was the situation when I lent both fragments to the Bodleian exhibition in 1980, mounted in memory of my late thesis supervisor, Richard Hunt.[20]

Then again I succumbed to Herbert of Bosham's weaknesses of indolence, unfinished intentions and thwarted ambition, and other aspects of my domestic life fell apart, and in November 1990 I was obliged to sell the Arras leaves through Bernard Quaritch for a sum sufficient to provide me with a deposit on a little house in south London. Via Norway and Switzerland, the leaves of Herbert of Bosham are now safely and appropriately in the library of Lambeth Palace, within walking distance of the house bought for me by Herbert of Bosham some 800 years after his death.[21] I kept the Canterbury leaf.

However, there is still another chapter to this tale. In June 1998 I had to give a big lecture in Detroit, in Michigan. My host, evidently desperate to entertain me, took me the next morning to the only local antiquarian bookshop there, run by John K. King. They chanced to have in stock a number of manuscript leaves in a big box arranged in paper folders as a teaching set of palaeographical specimens. One late thirteenth-century leaf was marked up, as my original Herbert of Bosham leaf had been, with those distinctive marginal markings of dots and ice-cream cones which identify a provenance at Christ Church, Canterbury, and, more-or-less for that reason alone, I spent my entire lecture fee on buying the whole box. The Canterbury piece was a fragment of Thomas Aquinas, which eventually became the subject of one of my Lyell Lectures in Oxford in 2008–9.[22] I cannot say that I neglected the rest of the leaves from Detroit, in their stiff paper folders, but I did nothing much with them. Among the set, however, was (and still is) a worn leaf, ragged along one side and stained from use in a bookbinding, with a modern pencil note describing it as '13th Century' (end of the twelfth is more likely). You will guess what is coming, but I certainly did not. The leaf is from a complicated Latin discussion on the nature of Christ's divinity. There are no running-titles or obvious clues. It is not especially well written. Some years later, I chanced upon another leaf from the same unidentified manuscript in the fragment collection at Keio University in Tokyo,[23] described

[20] C. de Hamel, 'Manuscripts of Herbert of Bosham', *Manuscripts at Oxford*, pp. 38–41, nos. VIII.2 and 4. I had a secret ambition to edit the Arras leaves for a Roxburghe Club book.

[21] Quaritch sold the leaves to Martin Schøyen, of Oslo, his MS 700; he re-sold them at Sotheby's, 1 December 1998, lot 79, bought by Ernst Boehlen, of Berne, who in turn re-sold them at Christie's, 20 November 2013, lot 22, where they were bought by Lambeth Palace Library and are now MS 5048.

[22] The leaf, together with a second fragment from the same manuscript which I had bought in San Francisco in 1988, are from a copy of the *De veritate* which can be traced back through use in a binding in the archives at Merton College to Canterbury College in Oxford (James, *Ancient Libraries*, p. 167, no. 90) and earlier to Christ Church (ibid., pp. 136–7, no. 1664), to which it had been bequeathed by Robert Winchelsey, archbishop 1294–1313, himself a pupil of Aquinas. Herbert-like, I have prevaricated indolently over the Lyell Lectures and they are still unpublished, but I lent one Aquinas leaf to C. Z. Rothkopf, ed., *The Grolier Club Collects* (New York, 2002), p. 4.

[23] Keio University Library, 170X9@18/21: see C. de Hamel, 'Phillipps Fragments in Tokyo', in *The Medieval Book and a Modern Collector, Essays in Honour of Toshiyuki Takamiya*, ed. T.

in their catalogue as 'theological, German, twelfth century'. The script of the leaves is very certainly English, but I could not fault the rest.

For another few years I did absolutely nothing further. One day – and I cannot even remember why, for it is odd that I had not tried this before – I typed a couple of words from the leaf into the online search facility of the *Patrologia Latina*, a resource quite unimaginable when I started out, and up came Herbert of Bosham, *Liber melorum*, book III, a couple of pages from the end, immediately following the text of its companion leaf in Tokyo.[24] To say that I could hardly believe what I saw would be an understatement. Manuscripts of Herbert of Bosham are about ten times rarer than complete Gutenberg Bibles. Only four substantial copies of his *Thomus* survive at all, one each in Arras (mutilated), Charleville-Mézières and Brussels (abridged and defective at the end),[25] and that single manuscript in England, now at Corpus Christi, Oxford, as mentioned earlier, missing leaves at each end. In addition, three fragments – only three, ever – had come onto the market since the Reformation, all since 1976, and all three belonged to me, one delivered to my desk without my having to do as much as raise an eyebrow, and two bought by me by such careless accident that, for several years in each case, I was too lazy even to realise it had happened.

In fact, there is a fourth. To pre-empt sarcastic ribaldry of readers, let me assure you that it is not in my possession. Many years ago, Nigel Ramsay drew my attention to two halves of a leaf in a binding in the diocesan library of Derry, described in 1879 in the *Proceedings of the Royal Irish Academy*, and after persistent and fruitless inquiry in Ireland I found quite recently that the book in which the fragments are still fly-leaves has been in the British Museum (now Library) since 1891. I cannot be absolutely sure whether they are from the complete *Thomus* of Herbert or from a text which cites it. They are in a large and spacious semi-liturgical hand of the early thirteenth century, not from either of the manuscripts of the other leaves, and they look as though they were for public reading, perhaps used in the liturgy on the feast of Saint Thomas.[26]

Matsuda, R. A. Linenthal and J. Scahill (Cambridge and Tokyo, 2004), pp. 19–44, at 25–6 and pl. 3–2.

[24] *PL*, 190, col. 1397, line 23, to col. 1400, line 23; the Keio leaf preceded it, from cols. 1394–7. My leaf is 306 mm by 223mm, double column, 39 lines, written-space 246 mm by 172 mm.

[25] Charleville-Mézières, Bibliothèque municipale, ms 222, late twelfth century, from Signy Abbey, with a second prologue from Adam and Ralph, monks of Signy, addressed to Odo of Canterbury, abbot of Battle 1175–1200; see G. Raynaud in *Catalogue général des manuscrits des bibliothèques publiques des departements*, v (Paris, 1879), pp. 648–9; to judge from the images on the *Enluminures* website of the Institut de recherche et d'histoire des textes, the manuscript may well be English; Sharpe, *Handlist*, p. 178. Brussels, Bibliothèque royale, ms IV.600, *c.* 1200 (previously Phillipps MS 4622, Sotheby's, 25 November 1969, lot 449). There is also a nineteenth-century transcript of the Arras manuscript in the British Library, Add. MS 20702, made in 1845 for J. A. Giles.

[26] J. K. Ingram, 'On Two Collections of Medieval Moralized Tales', *Proceedings of the Royal Irish Academy, Polite Literature and Antiquities* 2 (1879–88), 129–44, citing the Herbert fragments on p. 136, n.5. The book is now British Library, Add. MS 33957, a fifteenth-century miscellany of religious texts on paper and parchment including *Saint Patrick's*

Herbert of Bosham, like Matthew Paris, has a significance out of proportion to the very limited medieval circulation of his books. In his editions of the Gloss as well as in his *Thomus*, Herbert had implored future scribes to copy the texts in full or not at all. However, he wrote too much, too long-windedly, too unreadably, and (as with Matthew Paris) scribes copied him – if they did – almost exclusively in abridgements and extracts. For the final part of this paper, let us look at the two fragments in my possession, and ask whether they tell us anything about the reception and later chance survival of the *Liber melorum* in England.

The box of leaves I acquired in Detroit was one of at least four similar sets assembled by the booksellers Lionel and Philip Robinson, of Pall Mall in London, who had bought the still vast residue of the Phillipps library from the collector's descendants in 1945–46. Their idea was that any loose leaves or detached gatherings found among the vast Phillipps *nachlass* could be separated and shared out for sale as palaeographical specimens, since their texts were likely to prove unidentifiable.[27] We must be grateful that the leaves from Arras were not similarly separated and dispersed, as might easily have happened. Sir Thomas Phillipps was not particularly a collector of fragments, but he did buy two very large albums of manuscript pastedowns in the Bliss sale at Sotheby's on 21 August 1858, lots 100 and 119. One of these Bliss albums, containing 327 leaves and fragments, was re-sold in the Phillipps sale at Sotheby's of 1911 and has its own subsequent fate.[28] The other, still in the collection in the late 1940s, was the principal quarry for those sets of specimens and others (including the leaf at Keio), and there is little doubt that both the two Herbert of Bosham pastedowns were from that source.

Philip Bliss (1787–1857) was a not very diligent clergyman, who went up to St John's College in Oxford in 1806, and (we all know the type) never really left university again. He drifted genially and untaxingly through various minor jobs in

---

Purgatory and the *Speculum Laicorum*, in a modern binding: H. L. D. Ward, *Catalogue of Romances in the Department of Manuscripts in the British Museum*, ii (London, 1893), pp. 465–6. Its end leaves, now numbered as folios 1 and 224, comprise the upper and lower halves of a single parchment leaf, with one line of text missing between them, comprising Herbert's *Thomus* from p. 253, line 30, in Robertson's edition, to p. 255, line 31. The full leaf would have been 278 mm. by 203 mm., double column, 27 lines (beginning 'above top line'), written-space 233 mm by 157 mm. Extracts from Herbert's *Thomus* were anthologised in the various composite *Quadrilogus* lives of Becket.

[27] One set was sold in 1947 to George A. Poole, jr (1907–90), and was acquired in 1958 by the Lilly Library, Indiana University; another was sold probably around 1950 to Estelle Doheny (1875–1958) and re-emerged at California Book Auctions, 27 January 1980, lot 192, and was afterwards Takamiya MS 45, the principal subject of my article cited in n.22 above, and has now been given to York University, in honour of Professor Linne Mooney; a third was sold by the Robinsons in 1953 to the Bodleian Library, now MS Lat. misc. a. 3. My set, which had apparently belonged to a collector in Ithaca, New York, was John K. King, *Used & Rare Books*, cat. 73, 1993, no. 639.

[28] Sotheby's 24 April 1911, lot 390, bought by E. H. Dring (1864–1928), inherited by his son E. M. Dring (1906–90), who in 1964 gave to the Bodleian Library many leaves of obvious Oxford interest and those of which there were multiple pieces from the same manuscript, now MS Lat. misc. b.18; the others were mostly dispersed by Quaritch in their catalogues *Bookhands*, I, cat. 1036 (1984), and II, cat. 1056 (1985).

the Bodleian and elsewhere, all of which were supplementary to his real occupation, which was Oxford antiquarianism and book-collecting. He lived in Oxford during the great period of the rebinding of books in the college libraries, when it was fashionable to tidy up primitive books and to remove their messy end-leaves. Sir Frederic Madden's diary for 1825 records a visit to Bliss: 'Whenever any of the Colleges send their MSS. or old books to be rebound, the fly leaves & odd scraps are always <u>torn off</u> by the bookbinder and <u>thrown away</u>! Dr Bliss therefore made a bargain with the bookbinder, that for every bundle of these old MSS. and <u>bl. letter</u> scraps the latter brought him, he (Dr B) would give the man a <u>pot of beer</u>.'[29] Former Bliss fragments emerging from the Phillipps sales include leaves extracted from use in many Oxford college bindings, including those with recognisable pressmarks or bookplates from Merton, New College, All Souls and others.

The *Liber melorum* leaf now in Tokyo was clearly a front pastedown and it preserves the offset of the chain-hasp at the top left and two successive pressmarks in its upper margin, 'E.13.8 Theol', roughly crossed out, and 'g.15.11' substituted, a form characteristic of the chained library of Magdalen College. I am indebted to Daryl Green, the Magdalen librarian, for identifying the volume, which is now e.7.13 on the shelves there, the edition by Erasmus of the works of Irenaeus, bishop of Lyon, published by Froben in Basel in 1528. The volume at Magdalen is rebound in dull half calf over purple hessian in the style of the middle of the first half of the nineteenth century, exactly the period when Bliss was gathering vellum leaves discarded by the Oxford binders' workshops. The title has an offset of the same chain-hasp at the upper right and the former pressmark g.15.11 crossed through. My leaf was upside down at the back of the same volume, and it shares its shadowy stains and splashes of yellow colour with the last page of the book. There can be no evidence of where or when the Irenaeus was first bound, but the word 'colleg' in a small sixteenth-century hand at the extreme upper outer corner of the title does suggest that the book was already in Oxford and the likelihood is that the manuscript of Herbert of Bosham was cut up as binder's waste in Oxford too when the Irenaeus was relatively new.

Herbert of Bosham's book on Becket was never common in England.[30] There was,

[29] N. R. Ker, *Fragments of Medieval Manuscripts used as Pastedowns in Oxford Bindings with a Summary of Oxford Binding, c. 1515–1620*, Oxford Bibliographical Society, 3rd ser., 4 (Oxford, 1954), p. xvi, n.3; C. K. F. Brown, 'Sir Frederic Madden at Oxford', *Oxoniensia* 35 (1970), 34–53, esp. 45; H. R. Woudhuysen, 'Scraps for Beer', *Times Literary Supplement*, 28 November 1997. For Bliss, see A. Bell, 'Bliss, Philip (1787–1857)', *ODNB*. Bliss was the source of the Aquinas leaves mentioned in n.21.

[30] John Leland recorded a copy at Tewkesbury Abbey in Gloucestershire shortly before the surrender of the house in 1540 (see *English Benedictine Libraries, The Shorter Catalogues*, ed. R. Sharpe, J. P. Carley, R. M. Thomson and A. G. Watson, Corpus of British Medieval Library Catalogues, 4 (London, 1996), p. 596, no. 1). Its likely original owner was Alan of Tewkesbury, biographer of Becket and prior of Christ Church until 1186, when he was appointed prior of Tewkesbury until his death there in 1202. It does not survive. It was probably not the source of the leaves from the Merton binding (although I suggested this in my 'Phillipps Fragments', p. 25), if only because that book is dated 1528 and Tewkesbury was not suppressed until 1540. There was also a copy at St Augustine's Abbey, Canterbury, given by Thomas of Goat Lees, perhaps in the fourteenth century: *St*

however, a copy in Oxford which was likely to have been discarded and available for re-use at the right moment. Among the books given to Merton College in 1374 by William Reed, bishop of Chichester 1369–85, was a text described in his donation document as 'vitam sancti T. Cantuar' peroptimam septem libros continentem', which must have been the *Thomus* of Herbert, for that is the only medieval life of Becket divided into seven books.[31] The books in Reed's various bequests to Oxford colleges had generally been bought by him second-hand from the estates of deceased friends and colleagues. Reed spent most of his adult life in Kent and the sources of his purchases included items acquired from the executors of Thomas Bradwardine, archbishop of Canterbury in 1349, Simon Islip, archbishop 1349–66, and, especially, Thomas Trillek, bishop of Rochester 1365–72. Any of these might easily have owned an old life of Becket copied in Canterbury. The book at Merton did not survive the Reformation, and it could well have provided parchment pages for Oxford binders. The pastedowns used for the Irenaeus at Magdalen College were very possibly among them.

The larger Canterbury leaf also survived from re-use in a binding. It was clearly once a front fly-leaf in some volume whose title is preserved in a flamboyant late sixteenth-century hand at the foot of the recto, 'This booke is called the old blacke Book'. To identify a volume by the colour of its binding was a common practice in distinguishing cartularies and archival registers, and the number of so-named 'black', or 'red', or 'white' books in early modern England is legion.

Our attention therefore focuses on what is likely to have happened to the complete manuscript of Herbert of Bosham's *Thomus* at the Reformation. We know that it was still in Christ Church cathedral priory in the 1430s or 1440s, on the evidence of those Canterbury marginal symbols. It may have been there in 1497, if Laurence Wade translated from the original '*Thomys*' itself. Perhaps it was on that occasion that Herbert's manuscript was brought out and dusted down. It was a time when the reference collection at Canterbury was being radically weeded by the monks and many apparently obsolete books were put aside.[32] The invention of printing and the early arrival of humanism in Canterbury probably both caused reassessment of the unwieldy old manuscript library. Great numbers of volumes were sent away for student use at Canterbury College in Oxford, but it is impossible

---

Augustine's Abbey, Canterbury, ed. B. Barker-Benfield, Corpus of British Medieval Library Catalogues, 13 (London, 2008), pp. 1446–7. There were presumably copies at Battle abbey (see n. 24) and at Crowland Abbey in Lincolnshire, since it was there that Elias of Evesham prepared the second text of the *Quadrilogus* in 1198–99.

[31] H. W. Garrard (ed. J. R. L. Highfield), 'An Indenture between William Rede, Bishop of Chichester, and John Bloxham and Henry Stapilton, Fellows of Merton College, Oxford, London, 22 October 1374', *Bodleian Library Record* 10 (1978), 9–19, listing the life of Saint Thomas on p. 16, with its second leaf beginning *qu' omnibus*; the author is identified by Richard Sharpe as UO49.41 in *Medieval Libraries of Great Britain*, 2, online. For the donations of Reed (or Rede), see R. M. Thomson, *A Descriptive Catalogue of the Medieval Manuscripts of Merton College, Oxford* (Woodbridge, 2009), pp. xxiv–xxxi.

[32] This is the principal theme of my article, 'The Dispersal of the Library of Christ Church', cited in n. 4 above.

to match up the *Thomus* securely with any of the various lives of Becket recorded in the successive inventories of the priory's Oxford college.[33] Other manuscripts in Canterbury, especially if of large dimensions and already defective, were liable to be set aside for re-use of their parchment in book bindings or as archival wrappers.[34] In 1508 just under 300 volumes deemed important were newly chained in the library over the prior's chapel at Christ Church, and (as first suggested by Neil Ker) this was by that date probably more or less all that remained intact on the shelves in Canterbury. The list accounts for a very large number of the books from Christ Church which still survive. It includes all four volumes of Herbert's editions of the Gloss safely conserved, but his *Thomus* is no longer there.[35]

One route for parchment fragments out of Canterbury following the Reformation evidently brought a number of discarded manuscripts to Sandwich in eastern Kent, where they were used for binding archives, including leaves of a twelfth-century Eusebius, of which other pieces remain in the cathedral library.[36] The chase leads to the Kent History and Library Centre in Maidstone, where the answer is revealed. The Herbert of Bosham leaf became the front fly-leaf in the monumental manuscript year book of Sandwich corporation for the years 1432 to 1487, which was bound in

[33] W. A. Pantin, *Canterbury College, Oxford*, 4 vols., Oxford Historical Society, n.s. 6–8, 30 (Oxford, 1947–85), i. Four lives of Becket are listed there: (a) pp. 19, 48, 59 and 76, nos. 58 and 123, second leaf beginning *tis et ad hoc*; (b) p. 42, no. 112, second leaf beginning *sic aliquid*; (c) p. 49, no. 190, second leaf beginning *beatus igitur* (consistent with the life by Edward Grim); and (d) p. 50, no. 209, second leaf beginning *fuerat*; none of these words is findable in early pages of Herbert's *Thomus*. When Leland visited Canterbury at the Reformation he noted wistfully that the entire library there seemed to have been transferred up to Oxford ('tota enim huius bibliothecae'): James, *Ancient Libraries*, p. xlvii; Pantin, *Canterbury College, Oxford*, iv, pp. 156–60. From the closure of Canterbury College, many former Christ Church manuscripts found their way into re-use as pastedowns in Oxford bindings: the Aquinas leaves were among them; another is in my *Gilding the Lilly*, pp. 58–9, no. 26.

[34] N. R. Ker, *Medieval Manuscripts in British Libraries*, ii, *Abbotsford–Keele* (Oxford, 1977), esp. pp. 312–5; R. Gameson, *The Earliest Books of Canterbury Cathedral, Manuscripts and Fragments to c. 1200* (London and Canterbury, 2008).

[35] James, *Ancient Libraries*, pp. 152–63; N. R. Ker, 'The Migration of Manuscripts from the English Medieval Libraries', *The Library*, 4th ser., 23 (1942), pp. 1–11, esp. 10–11; reprinted in his *Books, Collectors and Libraries, Studies in the Medieval Heritage*, ed. A. G. Watson (London and Ronceverte, 1985), pp. 459–70, esp. 468–9. Herbert of Bosham's Psalter volumes are nos. 56–7 (identifiable by the opening words of their second leaves), and the Pauline Epistle volumes are nos. 45–6, explicitly described as Herbert's copies.

[36] M. B. Parkes, 'Fragments of Medieval Manuscripts', in *Guide to Kent County Archives Office*, ed. F. Hull (Maidstone, 1958), pp. 227–30, reprinted in Parkes, *Scribes, Script and Readers* (London, 1991), pp. 313–17, including description of an album of fragments once owned by the Hills family of Ash-next-Sandwich. They were archival wrappers, one used for documents of '5 Edward '6' (1551–52) and another for 'Clement Banstock his fyrst accompte'. The album was given by Lady Hills to the Bodleian Library in January 1956, in memory of her son who died in Oxford the previous year. This is now Bodleian, MS Lat. misc. b.15, with photocopies of several other fragments, including the Eusebius, which then belonged to Malcolm Parkes himself (it was afterwards Bennett and Kerr, cat. 182, December 2013, item II); Gameson, *Earliest Books*, pp. 379 and 382.

the third quarter of the sixteenth century and is now Sa/AC.1 in Maidstone.[37] It fits exactly. The volume's final paper fly-leaf, folio 318v, is calligraphically inscribed in the same hand as the title on my leaf, 'The yeare booke called the Old blacke Booke', punctuated with the same two vertical dots. There is no doubt about the identification. The Old Black Book of Sandwich, as it is still called, was repaired at the front and stoutly rebound in mottled leather and marbled endpapers in the second half of the nineteenth century, when the leaf of Herbert of Bosham's *Liber melorum* must have been removed as an unrelated curiosity.[38]

Like Herbert, I have no experience of theophany. Like him, I have no knowledge of a literal afterlife. However, let me conclude with a metaphor, which might have been imaginable in a more credulous age than our own. Herbert of Bosham felt he was unjustly neglected and ignored in his lifetime. Think how much worse he must have felt, watching from his celestial cloud, to see his manuscripts going uncopied throughout the Middle Ages, or to hear J. A. Giles saying of his glossed books, on which Herbert had spent more than a decade of his life, that they should be left alone to slumber in the Bodleian Library. If even the *Dictionary of National Biography* used the word 'intolerable' of his life of Becket, Herbert in Heaven must have been suicidal with disappointment. Imagine his astonishment in 1972, peering down into our world, to see an apparently devoted student from New Zealand studying his precious manuscripts day after day. Here at last, thinks Herbert, is a possible champion, after 800 years of neglect. What does he do? He calls in a few favours with Gabriel and sends the student the only surviving fragment of his own copy of the *Thomus*; and the student fails to recognise it. He sends him the missing leaves from the manuscript in Arras; and the student does nothing and then disposes of them. He finally sends the student a portion of Bishop Reed's copy; and the student has no idea what it is. Herbert of Bosham realises he has made a terrible mistake. He despairs. He makes contact instead with Michael Staunton, and with Anne Duggan, Matthew Doyle, Laura Cleaver, Julie Barrau, Nicholas Vincent and Sabina Flanagan, and all is well again.

---

[37] Maidstone, Kent History and Library Centre, Sa/AC/1. The manuscript measures 387 mm by 275 mm. There is a pencil note on the flyleaf, 'This book was bound temp. Elizabeth'. The worn leather sides of that binding are now pasted in at each end, blind-stamped with a roll tool in a saltire within a double frame. The tool appears to be MW d (3), as classified in J. B. Oldham, *English Blind-Stamped Bindings, The Sandars Lectures, 1949* (Cambridge, 1952), pl. LI, no. 865, recorded principally in London 1540–63, but not necessarily not used elsewhere. The leather is dark brown but not especially black, and so there was presumably an earlier binding in that colour.

[38] The Old Black Book was described by H. J. Riley for the Historical Manuscripts Commission, *Fifth Report* (London, 1876), p. 568, as still being 'bound in old embossed leather'; it must have been rebound soon afterwards. In 1956 the municipal archives from the Town Hall in Sandwich were deposited in the Kent county archives.

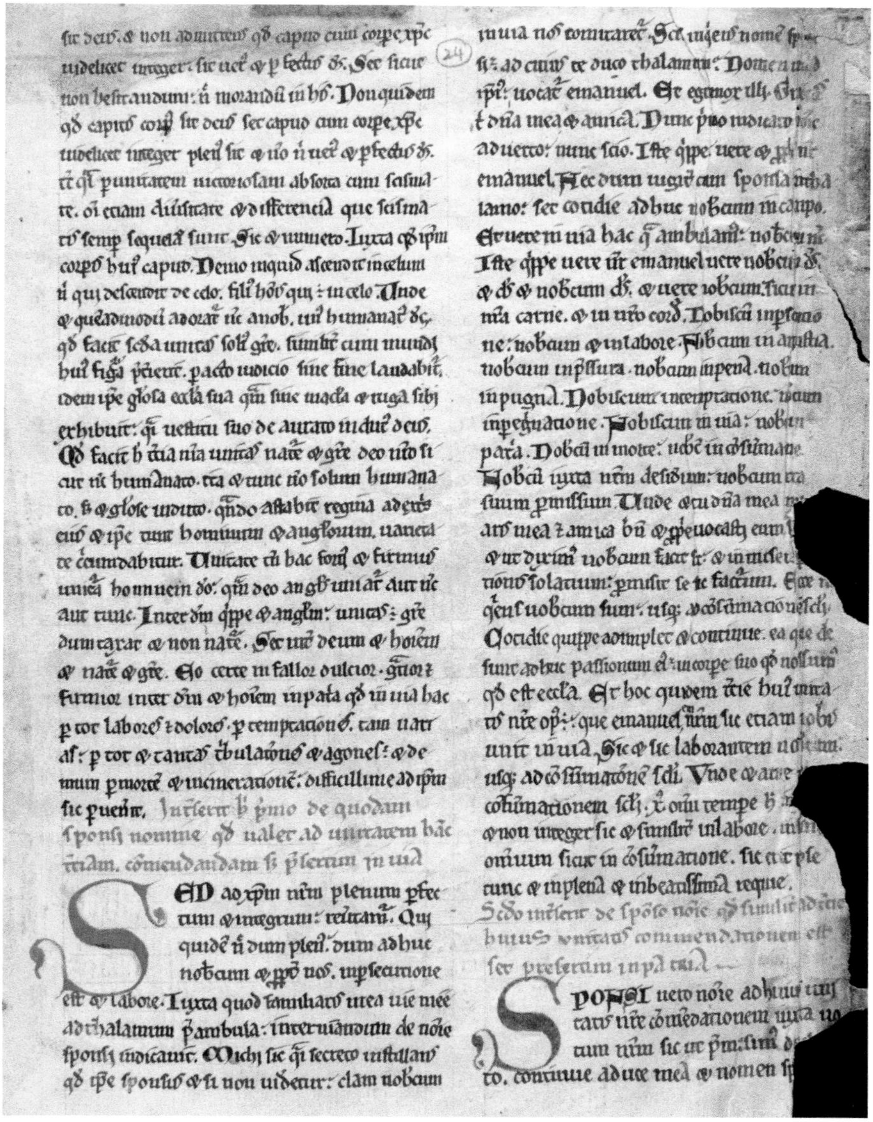

Fig. 9.3 The leaf of the *Liber melorum* once used in a binding at Magdalen College, Oxford and later owned by Philip Bliss.

Appendix:
A New Letter of Herbert of Bosham (1175 x 1178)

The document printed below survives in the mid-thirteenth-century cartulary of the abbey of Sainte-Geneviève at Paris. It confirms a settlement in which Master Herbert appears as one of eleven 'assessors' assisting the papal legate, Peter of Pavia, acting alongside a group of French and Italian dignitaries, including Herbert's fellow masters at Paris: Gerard Pucelle, Bernard of Pisa and Stephen of Tournai. The settlement was known to Beryl Smalley, but not Herbert's confirmation, which came to light only in January 2018, as the present volume was going to press.[1] Although in many ways a standard instrument, merely confirming Herbert's presence at the legate's settlement, Herbert's choice of *intitulatio*, as 'clerk of St Thomas, our glorious martyr', is remarkable, demonstrating both his customary magniloquence and his determination, after 1170, to be seen dwelling constantly in Becket's shadow.[2] Even the opening formula of the document declares this, being adapted from the first epistle of St John (1 John 1:1–3), the words of the disciple 'whom Jesus loved', witnessing to the truth of his master's teaching. Perhaps even more remarkably, Herbert, like St John the Evangelist, adopts the first person plural. This at a time when even bishops and were not always entirely confident in abandoning the first person singular.[3] Before we attribute these features to Herbert's particular vanity, however, we should note that the quotation from St John occurs in others of the letters corroborating the legatine settlement, as does the first person plural. Although it is also worth noting here that the abbot and prior of Saint-Victor, in these same circumstances, employ first person singular.[4] Herbert's seal, referred

---

[1] Smalley, *Becket Conflict*, p. 71, following the edition of Peter of Pavia's settlement in *Cartulaire général de Paris: ou, Recueil de documents relatifs à l'histoire et à la topographie de Paris*, ed. R. de Lasteyrie (Paris 1887), p. 429 no. 519. Herbert's confirmation was noticed in passing by Dietrich Lohrmann: *Papsturkunden in Frankreich: 8, Diözese Paris I*, ed. Lohrmann (Göttingen, 1989), pp. 337–8 n.

[2] For other letters in which Herbert adopts similarly elaborate self-descriptions, see *Herberti … opera*, ed. Giles, ii (1846), p. 233 no. 6, p. 262 no. 19, pp. 289–91 nos. 30–1, and cf. p. 304 no. 42 (*Herbertus miserabilis nunc et exul*), pp. 241–2 nos. 12–13 (*H(erbertus) Thome Cant' archiepiscopi miserabilis nunc et insignis exulis socius*).

[3] For examples of first person singular, as late as the 1170s, see *English Episcopal Acta VI: Norwich 1070–1214*, ed. C. Harper-Bill (Oxford, 1990), pp. lxi–lxii; *English Episcopal Acta VII: Hereford 1079–1234*, ed. J. Barrow (Oxford, 1993), pp. lxviii–lxix.

[4] Cf. the letters confirming the legatine settlement, issued by Barba Aureus dean of Notre-Dame, William abbot of Saint-Denis (Paris, Bibliothèque Sainte-Geneviève ms. 356 pp. 221–2, *Quam vidimus et audiuimus hoc testamur et testimonium nostrum verum*

to at the end of the letter, is now lost. Can we doubt that it showed one of the earliest images of Becket's martyrdom?

Nicholas Vincent

Notification by Master Herbert of Bosham of his presence at a settlement made at Saint-Martin-des-Champs Paris, according to papal authority, by Peter (of Pavia), cardinal priest of S. Crisogono, papal legate, in disputes between the abbey of Sainte-Geneviève and Thibaut and Eudes the sons of Ranier de Val, two men of Vanves (Hauts-de-Seine, cant. Clamart), over services owing to the abbey.

[June 1174 x July 1178]

B = Paris, Bibliothèque Sainte-Geneviève ms. 356 (Cartulary of Sainte-Geneviève), p. 224, headed *Item testimonium magistri Herberti de Boseham pro sententia lata contra Theobaldum et Odonem de Vanuis homines ecclesie nostre*, s.xiii med.

Date: The legate's settlement confirmed here has been several times printed, most recently and accurately in *Papsturkunden in Frankreich: 8*, ed. Lohrmann, 337–9 no. 144, confirmed by Alexander III, 10 July 1178 (ibid., pp. 339–40 no. 145), which supplies a *terminus ad quem*. It therefore dates to Peter of Pavia's first French legation (1174–78). Lohrmann, wishing to associate it with various other dealings involving the abbey's tenantry in 1178–79, assigned it to the months immediately before the pope's confirmation: ibid., p. 338, a dating accepted by S. Weiss, *Die Urkunden der päpstlichen Legaten von Leo IX bis Coelestin III (1049–1198)* (Cologne, 1995), pp. 254–9, esp. 258 no. 19. This, however, is to contradict an earlier dating of 1174–75 suggested by W. Janssen, *Die päpstlichen Legaten in Frankreich von Schisma Anaklets II. bis zum Tode Coelestins III. (1130–1198)* (Cologne, 1961), pp. 94–5, itself conjectural, but based upon a papal mandate to the legate (*Licet mandaverimus*, 29 October 1174), requiring him to intervene in the affairs of the Paris schools to the benefit of Peter Comestor (JL 12397, from the French royal chancery register, now Vatican BAV ms. Reg. Lat. 179, whence *Papsturkunden in Frankreich: 8*, ed. Lohrmann, p. 85 no. 18; G. Teske, *Die Briefsammlungen des 12. Jahrhunderts in St. Viktor/Paris* (Bonn, 1993), p. 348 no. 18). Neither Lohrmann nor Janssen's conjectures here are conclusive. Nonetheless, as pointed out to me by Anne Duggan, there is a slight tipping of the scales in favour of Janssen from the fact that Master Gerard Pucelle, named here as a party to the settlement, seems to have departed the schools in 1174, to enter the household of Richard archbishop of Canterbury. For the abbey's dealings with its tenants, including the present settlement, see C. H. M. Archibald, 'The Serfs of Sainte-Geneviève', *EHR* 25 (1910), 1–25. The legate's settlement names eleven *assessores*, giving counsel: Henry bishop of Senlis

---

est), and Michael dean of Meaux (p. 223, *Quod vidimus et audiuimus hec testamur*). The abbot of Saint-Germain-des-Prés employs first person plural but an alternative opening formula (p. 223, *Nouerit presens etas omniumque sequitura posteritas …*). The abbot and prior of Saint-Victor use first person singular (p. 103, *Ego … testificor*).

(1168–85), William abbot of Saint-Denis (1172/3–86), Hugh abbot of Saint-Germain-des-Près (1162–81), Ansold abbot of Saint-Corneille de Compiègne (1158–pre 1189), Barba Aureus dean of Notre-Dame Paris (1168–pre 1184), Michael dean of Meaux (1165–pre 1187), Master Gerard Pucelle (later bishop of Coventry, 1183–84), Master Bernard of Pisa, Master Guido treasurer of Novara, Master Stephen of Tournai (not to be confused with Stephen of Orléans, canon of Sainte-Geneviève, later abbot 1177, and bishop of Tournai 1192–1203) and Master Herbert of Bosham. The cartulary preserves letters of testimony, similar to that of Master Herbert, from Barba Aureus (Paris, Bibliothèque Sainte-Geneviève ms. 356 p. 221), William abbot of Saint-Denis (pp. 222–3), Hugh abbot of Saint-Germain (p. 223), Michael dean of Meaux (pp. 223–4), as also from Gerard archdeacon of Paris (p. 128), and the abbot and prior of Saint-Victor Paris (p. 103).

Magister Herbertus de Boseham sancti Thome gloriosi nostri martiris clericus omnibus ad quos littere iste peruenerint in domino salutem in perpetuum. Quod vidimus et audiuimus hec testamur. Inde est quod ad communem omnium noticiam volumus peruenire quod cum magister Petrus tituli sancti Crisogoni presbiter card(inalis) apostolice sedis legatus ex mandato domini pape cognosceret de causa status quod vertebatur inter ecclesiam sancte Genouese et quosdam homines de Vanuis, scilicet Theboldum et Odonem filios Rainerii de Valle, allegationibus et attestationibus utriusque partis diligenter auditis et cognitis, consilio habito cum multis religiosis et sapientibus viris, nobis quoque presentibus Parisius apud Sanctum Martinum de Campis, pronunciauit idem sancte Romane ecclesie card(inalis) et legatus predictos Theboldum et Odonem pro censu capitis iiii.ᵒʳ denarios non debere ecclesie sancte Genouese, eosdem autem esse homines predicte ecclesie cum hiis consuetudinibus. Non possunt filios suos clericos facere nisi ex concessione ecclesie, filios suos aut filias suas non possunt matrimonio coniungere cum hominibus alterius balliue vel dominatus, caducum i. mortuam manum debent, in necc(es)itatibus ecclesie dabunt conueniens auxilium de suo iuxta consuetudinem regni. Huic sententie cum proferretur presentes interfuimus et quia sic et formata et recitata a domino card(inale) eodemque legato fuerit, testimonium perhibemus. Quod ne forte alicuius astucia vel malicia, quod non credimus, impediri possit, presenti cartule commendauimus et sigillo nostro fecimus confirmari.

Master Herbert of Bosham, clerk of St Thomas our glorious martyr, sends greeting in perpetuity to all to whom these letters come. We hereby testify to what we saw and heard (cf. 1 John 1:1–3). We thus wish it to come to the common notice of all that when, by papal mandate, Master Peter, cardinal-priest of S. Crisogono, papal legate, heard the case then pending between the church of Ste-Geneviève and certain men of Vanves, namely Thibaut and Eudes the sons of Ranier de Val, having diligently heard and understood the allegations and evidences of either party, and having taken counsel with many wise and religious men, he pronounced in our presence at Paris, at St-Martin-des-Champs, that the aforesaid Thibaut and Eudes did not owe a head tax of fourpence to the church of Ste-Geneviève, even though they were men of that church bound by the following customs; namely that they could not have their sons made clerks without the church's permission, nor join their sons or daughters in marriage with people of another bailiwick or lordship; that they owed a staff in mortmain, and that that should provide appropriate aid from their own resources whenever the church was in need, according to the custom of the realm. We were present when this sentence was published and bear witness that it was duly formulated and recited by the lord cardinal and legate. So that it may not be impeded by any ruse or malice, which we refuse to credit, we have commended it to the present brief charter and had it confirmed with our seal.

Select Bibliography

Works by Herbert of Bosham

1. Revision of Peter Lombard's *Magna Glosatura*:
[Prefaces:] Glunz, H. H., *History of the Vulgate in England: From Alcuin to Roger Bacon* (Cambridge, 1933), 346–50.

2. *Historia*:
'Vita Sancti Thomae, archiepiscopi et martyris, auctore Herberto de Boseham', in *Materials for the History of Thomas Becket, Archbishop of Canterbury* [*MTB*], ed. J. C. Robertson and J. B. Sheppard, 7 vols., RS 67 (London, 1875–85), iii, 155–534. *Herberti de Boseham S. Thomae Cantuariensis clerici a secretis opera quae extant omnia*, ed. J. A. Giles, 2 vols., Patres Ecclesiae Anglicanae 136–7 (London, 1845–46), i; repr. in *Patrologiae Cursus Completus, series Latina* [*PL*], ed. J.-P. Migne, 221 vols. (Paris, 1854), 190, cols. 1073–1292. [Extracts:] Giles, J. A., 'Supplementa Herberti de Boseham', in *Anecdota Bedae, Lanfranci, et aliorum: Inedited tracts, letters, poems, &c. of Venerable Bede, Lanfranc, Tatwin and others*, Caxton Society Publications (London, 1851), 97–113. [Extracts:] Craib, T., 'The Arras MS. of Herbert of Bosham', *EHR* 35 (1920), 218–24.

3. *Liber Melorum*:
'Herberti de Boseham Liber Melorum', in *Herberti ... opera*, ii, pp. 1–184; repr. in *PL*, 190.1293–1404. [Extracts:] *MTB*, iii, 535–54.

4. *Homilia*:
'Homilia Herberti de Boseham discipuli historiographi martyris de natalitio martyris die', in *Herberti ... opera*, ii, pp. 185–200; repr. in *PL*, 190.1403–14.

5. *Epistolae*:
'Epistolae Herberti de Boseham in persona S. Thomae Cantuariensis et aliorum scriptae', in *Herberti ... opera*, ii, pp. 207–336; repr. in *PL* 190.1419–74.

6. *Psalterium cum commento*:
[Dedicatory letter:] Smalley, B., 'A Commentary on the *Hebraica* by Herbert of Bosham', *Recherches de théologie ancienne et médiévale* 18 (1951), 29–65 (30–1).

Works relating to Herbert of Bosham

Abbott, E. A., *St Thomas of Canterbury: His Death and Miracles*, 2 vols. (London, 1898).
Abulafia, A. Sapir, 'Continuity and Change in Twelfth-Century Christian–Jewish

Relations', in *European Transformations: The Long Twelfth Century*, ed. T. F. X. Noble and J. Van Engen (Notre Dame, 2012), pp. 314–37.

Barlow, F., 'Bosham, Herbert of (d. c. 1194)', *Oxford Dictionary of National Biography* (Oxford, 2004).

—*Thomas Becket* (London, 1986).

—*Thomas Becket and His Clerks* (Oxford, 1987).

Bibliotheca Hagiographica Latina, ed. Socii Bollandiani: Subsid. hagiog., 2 vols. (Brussels, 1898–1901).

Binski, P. and S. Panayotova, eds, *The Cambridge Illuminations, Ten Centuries of Book Production in the Medieval West* (London and Turnhout, 2005).

Blair, J., 'Giles, John Allen (1808–1884)', *Oxford Dictionary of National Biography* (Oxford, 2004).

Cahn, W., *Romanesque Manuscripts, The Twelfth Century*, 2 vols., A Survey of the Illuminated Manuscripts of France (London, 1996).

Craib, T., 'The Arras MS. of Herbert of Bosham', *EHR* 35 (1920), 218–24.

De Hamel, C., 'A Contemporary Miniature of Thomas Becket', in *Intellectual Life in the Middle Ages: Essays Presented to Margaret Gibson*, ed. L. M. Smith and B. Ward (London, 1992), pp. 179–84.

—*Glossed Books of the Bible and the Origins of the Paris Book Trade* (Woodbridge, 1984).

—'Manuscripts of Herbert of Bosham', in *Manuscripts at Oxford: An Exhibition in Memory of Richard William Hunt (1908–1979)*, ed. A. C. de la Mare and B. C. Barker-Benfield (Oxford, 1980), pp. 38–41.

De Lasteyrie, R., *Cartulaire générale de Paris. 1: 528–1180* (Paris, 1887).

De Lubac, H., *Medieval Exegesis. Volume 1: The Four Senses of Scripture*, tr. M. Sebanc (Grand Rapids, 1998).

De Visscher, E. 'An Ave Maria in Hebrew: The Transmission of Hebrew Learning from Jewish to Christian Scholars in Medieval England', in *Christians and Jews in Angevin England: The York Massacre of 1190, Narratives and Contexts*, ed. S. Rees Jones and S. Watson (Woodbridge, 2013), pp. 174–83.

—'"Closer to the Hebrew": Herbert of Bosham's Interpretation of Literal Exegesis', in *The Multiple Meaning of Scripture: The Role of Exegesis in Early-Christian and Medieval Culture*, ed. I. van't Spijker (Leiden, 2009), pp. 249–72.

—'Putting Theory into Practice? Hugh of Saint Victor's Influence on Herbert of Bosham's Psalterium cum commento', in *Bibel und Exegese in der Abtei Sankt Viktor zu Paris: Form und Funktion eines Grundtextes im europäischen Rahmen*, ed. R. Berndt (Münster, 2009), pp. 491–502.

—*Reading the Rabbis: Christian Hebraism in the Works of Herbert of Bosham* (Leiden, 2014).

Dodwell, C. R., *The Canterbury School of Illumination 1066–1200* (Cambridge, 1954).

Doyle, M., *Peter Lombard and His Students* (Toronto, 2016).

Duggan, A. J., ed. *The Correspondence of Thomas Becket, Archbishop of Canterbury, 1162–1170*, 2 vols. (Oxford, 2000).

—'The Lyell Version of the *Quadrilogus* Life of St Thomas of Canterbury', *Analecta*

Bollandiana 112 (1994), 105–38; repr. in Duggan, A. J., *Thomas Becket: Friends, Networks, Texts, and Cult* (Aldershot, 2007), no. XV.

— 'The Price of Loyalty: The Fate of Thomas Becket's Learned Household', in A. J., Duggan, *Thomas Becket: Friends, Networks, Texts, and Cult* (Aldershot, 2007), no. III.

— *Thomas Becket* (London, 2004).

— *Thomas Becket: A Textual History of His Letters* (Oxford, 1980).

The Early South-English Legendary, ed. C. Horstmann, Early English Text Society 87 (London, 1887).

Flanagan, S., *Doubt in an Age of Faith: Uncertainty in the Long Twelfth Century* (Turnhout, 2008).

Foreville, R., *Thomas Becket dans la tradition historique et hagiographique* (London, 1981).

Gervase of Canterbury, *The Historical Works of Gervase of Canterbury*, ed. W. Stubbs, 2 vols., RS 73 (London, 1879–80).

Giles, J. A., *The Diary and Memoirs of John Allen Giles*, ed. D. Bromwich, Somerset Record Society 86 (Taunton, 2000).

Gillingham, J., 'From "Civilitas" to Civility: Codes of Manners in Medieval and Early Modern England', *Transactions of the Royal Historical Society*, ser. 6, 12 (2002), 267–89.

Glorieux, P., 'Essai sur les "Quaestiones in epistolas Pauli"', *Recherches de théologie ancienne et médiévale* 19 (1952), 48–59.

Glunz, H. H., *History of the Vulgate in England: From Alcuin to Roger Bacon* (Cambridge, 1933).

Goodwin, D., 'Herbert of Bosham and the Horizons of Twelfth-Century Exegesis', *Traditio* 58 (2003), 133–73.

— 'Nothing in Our Histories: A Postcolonial Perspective on Twelfth-Century Christian Hebraism', *Medieval Encounters* 15 (2009), 35–65.

— 'Take Hold of the Robe of a Jew': Herbert of Bosham's Christian Hebraism* (Leiden and Boston, 2006).

Hardy, T. D., *Descriptive Catalogue of Materials Relating to the History of Great Britain and Ireland*, 2 vols. in 3 parts, RS 26 (London, 1862–65).

Hirata, Y., 'St Anselm and two clerks of Thomas Becket', in Y. Hirata, *Collected Papers on John of Salisbury and His Correspondents* (Tokyo, 1996), pp. 135–55.

Horstmann, C., ed., 'Thomas Becket, epische Legende von Laurentius Wade', *Englische Studien* 3 (1880), 411–69.

Huscroft, R., *Tales from the Long Twelfth Century. The Rise and Fall of the Angevin Empire* (New Haven, 2016).

Jackson, D., N. Morgan and S. Panayotova, eds., *A Catalogue of Western Book Illumination in the Fitzwilliam Museum and the Cambridge Colleges*, III, *France, ii, c. 1000–c. 1250* (London and Turnhout, 2015).

Jaeger, C. S., *The Envy of Angels. Cathedral Schools and Social Ideals in Medieval Europe* (Philadelphia, 1994).

James, M. R., *The Ancient Libraries of Canterbury and Dover* (Cambridge, 1903).

—*A Descriptive Catalogue of the Manuscripts in the Library of Corpus Christi College,* 2 vols. (Cambridge, 1912).

—*The Western Manuscripts in the Library of Trinity College Cambridge: A Descriptive Catalogue,* 3 vols. (Cambridge, 1900).

Jansen, S., *Wo ist Thomas Becket? Der ermordete Heilige zwischen Erinnerung und Erzählung* (Husum, 2002).

Javelet, R, 'Interprétation de l'argument ontologique par la "Speculatio": Herbert de Bosham et Saint Anselme', *Analecta Anselmiana* 4 (1975), 59–103.

Ker, N. R., *Medieval Manuscripts in British Libraries I: London* (Oxford, 1969).

Knowles, D., *Thomas Becket* (London, 1970).

Leyser, K. J., 'Frederick Barbarossa, Henry II and the Hand of St James', *EHR* 356 (1975), 481–506.

Loewe, R., 'Herbert of Bosham's Commentary on Jerome's Hebrew Psalter', *Biblica* 34 (1953), 44–77, 159–92, 275–98.

—'The Mediaeval Christian Hebraists of England: Herbert of Bosham and Earlier Scholars', *Transactions of the Jewish Historical Society of England* 17 (1953), 225–49.

Loriquet, H., *Rapport présenté à M. le Ministre de l'Instruction publique sur l'identification de fragments de manuscrits trouvés à Calais, en 1884, suivi d'un tableau des déprédations commises en 1816 sur les manuscrits de la bibliothèque d'Arras* (Arras, 1886).

Morard, M. 'Entre mode et tradition: les commentaires des Psaumes de 1160 à 1350', in *La Bibbia del XIII secolo. Storia del testo, storia dell'esegesi. Convegno della Società Internazionale per lo studio del Medioevo Latino (SISMEL), Firenze, 1–2 giugno 2001,* ed. G. Cremascoli and F. Santi (Florence, 2004), pp. 323–52.

Naydenova-Slade M., and D. Park, 'The Earliest Holy Kinship Image, the Salomite Controversy, and a Little-Known Centre of Learning in Northern England in the Twelfth Century', *Journal of the Warburg and Courtauld Institutes* 71 (2008), 95–119.

Norgate, K., 'Herbert of Bosham (fl. 1162–1186)', *Dictionary of National Biography,* ed. S. Lee, 26 (London, 1891).

Ohly, F., 'Neue Zeugen des Buchs der Natur aus dem Mittelalter', in *Iconologia Sacra: Mythos, Bildkunst und Dichtung in der Religions- und Sozialgeschichte Alteuropas. Festschrift für Karl Hauck zum 75. Geburtstag,* ed. H. Keller and N. Staubach (Berlin, 1994), pp. 546–68.

O'Reilly, J., 'The Double Martyrdom of Thomas Becket: Hagiography or History?', *Medieval and Renaissance History* 7 (1985), 185–247.

Pächt, O. and J. J. G. Alexander, *Illuminated Manuscripts in the Bodleian Library, Oxford,* III (Oxford, 1973).

Panayotova, S., 'Tutorial in Images for Thomas Becket', in *The Cambridge Illuminations, The Conference Papers,* ed. S. Panayotova (London and Turnhout, 2007).

Peyrafort-Huin, M., *La bibliothèque médiévale de l'abbaye de Pontigny (XIIe–XIXe siècles): histoire, inventaires anciens, manuscrits* (Paris, 2001).

Quadrilogus II: 'Vita S. Thomae, seu Quadrilogus', in *MTB,* iv, 266–430.

Roberts, P. B., *Thomas Becket in the Medieval Latin Preaching Tradition. An Inventory of Sermons about St Thomas Becket c. 1170–c. 1400* (Steenbrugge, 1992).

Robertson, J. C., *Becket, Archbishop of Canterbury* (London, 1859).

Robinson, P. R., *Catalogue of Dated and Datable Manuscripts c. 737–1600 in Cambridge Libraries*, 2 vols. (Cambridge, 1988).

Schmidt, P. G., *Thomas von Froidmont, Biograph des Heiligen Thomas Becket* (Wiesbaden, 1989).

Sharpe, R., *A Handlist of Latin Writers of Great Britain and Ireland before 1540* (Turnhout, 1997).

Smalley, B., *The Becket Conflict and the Schools: A Study of Intellectuals in Politics* (Oxford, 1973).

—'A Commentary on the *Hebraica* by Herbert of Bosham', *Recherches de théologie ancienne et médiévale* 18 (1951), 29–65.

—*The Study of the Bible in the Middle Ages*, 3rd edn (Oxford, 1983).

Smith, L., *Masters of the Sacred Page: Manuscripts of Theology in the Latin West to 1274* (Notre Dame, IN, 2001).

Staunton, M., *The Lives of Thomas Becket* (Manchester, 2001).

—*Thomas Becket and his Biographers* (Woodbridge, 2006).

—'Thomas Becket in the Chronicles', in *The Cult of St Thomas Becket in the Plantagenet World, c. 1170–c. 1220*, ed. P. Webster and M.-P. Gelin (Woodbridge, 2016), pp. 95–112.

Stirnemann, P., 'Compte rendu: C. de Hamel, *Glossed Books of the Bible and the Origins of the Paris Booktrade* (Cambridge, 1984)', *Bulletin Monumental* 143 (1985), 363–7.

—'En quête de Sens', in *Quand la peinture était dans les livres: Mélanges en l'honneur de François Avril*, ed. M. Hoffmann, E. König and C. Zöhl (Turnhout, 2007), pp. 303–12.

Tatton-Brown, T., 'The Medieval Library at Canterbury Cathedral', *Canterbury Cathedral Chronicle* 82 (1988), 35–42.

Thomas of Froidmont, *Thomas von Froidmont: Die Vita des heiligen Thomas Becket: Erzbischof von Canterbury*, ed. and tr. P. G. Schmidt (Stuttgart, 1991).

Turcheck, J. P., 'A Neglected Manuscript of Peter Lombard's *Liber Sententiarum* and Parisian Illumination of the Late Twelfth Century', *The Journal of the Walters Art Gallery* 44 (1986), 48–69.

Vincent, N., 'The Murderers of Thomas Becket', in *Bischofsmord im Mittelalter: Murder of Bishops*, ed. N. Fryde and D. Reitz (Göttingen, 2003), pp. 211–72.

Vollrath, H. '"Gewissensmoral" und Konfliktverständnis: Thomas Becket in der Darstellung seiner Biographen', *Historisches Jahrbuch* 109 (1989), 24–55.

Walberg, E., *La tradition hagiographique de saint Thomas Becket avant la fin du XIIe siècle* (Paris, 1929; repr. Geneva, 1975).

Weiss, J. L., 'Herbert of Bosham's *Liber Melorum*: Literature and Sacred Sciences in the Twelfth Century' (Unpublished PhD dissertation, Harvard University, 2003).

William Fitzstephen, 'Vita Sancti Thomae', in *MTB*, iii, 1–154.

Williams, J. R., 'William of the White Hands and Men of Letters', in *Haskins Anniversary Essays in Mediaeval History*, ed. C. H. Taylor and J. L. La Monte (Boston and New York, 1929), pp. 365–88.

Index